ONE POLICEMAN'S STORY

E. St. J. addressing the International Police
Academy, Washington, D.C., 1969

HM Chief Inspector of Constabulary for England and Wales 1967–1970.

[*Press Association*

One Policeman's Story

To S.I.B.
With much gratitude for his friendship and all the great help & wise advice he gave to me when I first became a C.C.
12.XII.78
Eric St. Johnston

Sir Eric St. Johnston, CBE, QPM

*Her Majesty's Chief Inspector of Constabulary
for England and Wales 1967–1970*

Barry Rose (Publishers) Limited
LONDON & CHICHESTER
1978

First published 1978 by Barry Rose (Publishers) Ltd
Little London, Chichester,
West Sussex, England

© Eric St. Johnston 1978

 British Library Cataloguing in Publication Data

St Johnston, *Sir*, Eric
   One Policeman's Story
    1. St Johnston, *Sir*, Eric 2. Police-Great
     Britain-Biography
    1. Title
   363.2'092'4   HV7911.S/
   ISBN 0-85992-137-9

Printed in Great Britain by
Western Printing Services Ltd, Bristol

CONTENTS

FOREWORD 7

PROLOGUE 11

Chapter 1 Early Days 15

Chapter 2 The Metropolitan Police 35

Chapter 3 Oxfordshire 64

Chapter 4 Military Affairs 90

Chapter 5 County Durham 112

Chapter 6 Lancashire I 143

Chapter 7 Lancashire II 181

Chapter 8 Royal Occasions 204

ENTRE'ACTE 224

Chapter 9 Travelling Overseas 226

Chapter 10 The Imperial Defence College 244

Chapter 11 Overseas Again 253

FINALE

Chapter 12 The Home Office 261

EPILOGUE 297

Index 299

LIST OF ILLUSTRATIONS

Eric St. Johnston as HM Chief Inspector of Constabulary for England and Wales 1967–1970 frontispiece

between pages 34 and 35

Thomas Johnston, 1785–1866, great great grandfather

Thomas Johnston, 1815–1887, great grandfather

Thomas St. Johnston, 1851–1922, grandfather

Thomas Gerald St. Johnston, 1882–1966

Eric St. Johnston, 1916, 1929, 1934, 1944

between pages 162 and 163

Receiving the Baton of Honour, 1936

The King's Camp Staff, Balmoral, 1939

With Lord Londonderry, Victory Parade, Durham 1946

With Philip Allen, Police Training School, Plawsworth, Co. Durham

With Anthony Eden in Durham

With Harold Macmillan at the opening of England's first motorway

With Jim Callaghan, Home Secretary 1968

The original Lancashire Precepts of 1839

Eric St Johnston welcomes HM The Queen at Police Headquarters, Hutton 1954

With the Queen Mother

Inspection of recruits at the Police Training Centre, Chantmarle, Dorset

Inspection of recruits at the RUC Training School, Enniskillen, Northern Ireland

The Inspectors of Constabulary, 1969

Sir Eric St. Johnston as a member of Chapter General of the Order of St John

FOREWORD

by the Rt Hon Sir Harold Wilson, KG, MP

Some of the best autobiographies are not those which simply record the experiences and beliefs of an individual: they are those which illustrate the working or development of some great institutions, or some era in the history of a nation or the world. Thus Churchill's autobiographical volumes illumine events in British history, some of his peace-time writings the development of our social services, as do the memoirs of Lord Beveridge. Again Lord Reith's *Into the Wind* presents the authentic account of the creation and development of the BBC.

So with Sir Eric St. Johnston's volume covering a life-time in the Police Service at all levels. It is not only a revealing account of the career of a remarkable man, it tells us more than any documented, third-party history could hope to do, about the development of police work over an entire generation. More than that, it develops a theme clearly no less important to him, the concept of policemanship over a period of more than forty years, pre-war, war-time and post-war. For the generation he records, with close personal involvement, proceeds from the age of village bobbies, and early Metropolitan traffic duties, to the modern developments of highly advanced scientific technology both in the detection of crime and in traffic control, as well as unprecedented progress in man-management and training, processes to which he personally contributed as much as any single individual.

For an even wider readership it is a record of relations with democratically created police authorities, good and demonstrably bad, and because of these close relationships of the development of English local government in the most dynamic period of change and consolidation in our history, all from personal experience.

Sir Eric's own distinguished record itself reflects all these changes within the police service and within the national and regional authorities with whom he had to deal.

Foreword

He was one of the first graduate entrants, following Lord Trenchard's decision to recruit through the University Appointments Boards, and was posted to administrative duties in Trenchard's office. Again he was among the first crop of Hendon Police College products, whence he went on the beat in Central London. The fact that he had graduated in law and was a member of one of the Inns of Court was a further advantage in his manifold duties.

To his regret he had to resign his Territorial Army commission because he would be needed in over-crowded wartime London, and he rapidly became heavily involved in the new duties war demanded, including the management of War Reserve Constables and Civil Defence. Promotion then came quickly, and before the war really started he became – as the youngest candidate short-listed – the Chief Constable of Oxfordshire, at 29, a backward area in police terms, under-staffed and suffering from poor communications.

Oxfordshire licked into shape, he was posted to Eisenhower's Headquarters to plan the re-creation of the police forces in territories occupied by the Allies and the seizure of control of the German Police. Next – clearly one of the most exciting periods of his life – he became Chief Constable of Durham, and was able to enter fully into the rich and varied life of city and county: the University, the trade union movement, the Miners' Gala. The force had to be modernised, but he had the backing of the local authority and the able young officers.

It was clearly a break-through for him when after just six years he was appointed to one of the major police forces in Britain, that of Lancashire, a post he held for seventeen years. Appalling problems faced him, the territory of the county authority was honeycombed with independent police authority enclaves, large and small, over which the County Constabulary had no jurisdiction. Equally he had a police authority which knew it all, resisted reform and the modernising ideas of one of the most progressive Chiefs in police history, including the improvement of police housing. With crime becoming national, even international, while progress was slow in merging smaller authorities, others slowly accepted the Lancashire County ideas of better co-ordination.

It was the era of 'Z' Cars: Sir Eric helped to start the BBC series in Kirkby, in my constituency – the Newtown of the films. His modernisation of the traffic police system, and specialisation in new technologies, while encouraging good press relations began to be followed – and Lancashire together with London were among the foremost in applying the most sophisticated advances in science to the detection and prevention of crime. It was in those years that as

Foreword

Prime Minister I saw more and more of the work master-minded by the Lancashire Police under the leadership of Sir Eric.

He had his critics, not to say enemies – as well as having to contend with the police authority – and he took the daring step of putting his own individual, some would say idiosyncratic, evidence to the Royal Commission on the Police, rather than to rely on influencing the lowest common denominator basis of collective evidence through the Police Federation and Chief Constables' Association.

Not all the civil servants of the Home Office viewed his revolutionary ideas with enthusiasm, or would be happy to see him as either Metropolitan Police Commissioner or Her Majesty's Chief Inspector of Constabulary, a post which the Commission recommended should be created. It was Roy Jenkins as Home Secretary, despite some Home Office resistance, who appointed him Britain's HM Chief Inspector, a post he held for four years until his retirement in 1970, and his re-emergence on the international police scene.

From Lord Trenchard's office in Scotland Yard, therefore, to the highest position in the Service – the experience at home and abroad, North and South, war and peace, gives him an unrivalled authority to write this work on the theory and practice of policemanship.

HAROLD WILSON

HOUSE OF COMMONS,
April, 1978.

For J.

PROLOGUE

I cannot remember when I first decided to write these memoirs – the first incidentally ever to be written by an Inspector of Constabulary since the inception of the office in August, 1856. Indirectly I suppose my parents first started them for after their death I found neatly stacked in boxes all my school reports and every letter I had written to them during my school days and at University, and many that I wrote in later life.

When I began my career in the Police Service I did not, unfortunately, keep a diary, although I did keep copies of some of the more interesting case reports in which I was involved but luckily I have a fairly retentive memory. And, in later years whenever I went abroad I kept a detailed account of my travels and of the people I met. I also wrote up accounts of special events as they occurred but much to my regret I omitted to keep a diary during my army service in World War II. In the event, descriptive letters written home have helped to recall the incidents and excitements of those eventful and turbulent times.

At the end of my police career in 1970 when I was about to travel to Australia for several months, something had to be done with the very large amount of written material collected throughout my life – letters, diaries, reports, documents, newspaper clippings and photographs, all of which had to be stored. Through the years I had become friendly with the late Frank Elmes, a retired Superintendent of the Dorset Constabulary, a lively intelligent professional writer and a double Queen's Gold Medal essayist with whom I had first had correspondence about one of the weekly commentaries which he wrote so well for the *Police Review*. I asked him to examine these papers to advise me whether, in his view, there would be enough material for a book of some sort. He later told me, 'No. There isn't a book here. There's five or six.' I told him I had no

Prologue

intention of writing more than one and he agreed, during my absence in Australia, to put the papers in some semblance of order and collect together those that he thought would be useful in writing this book. For one reason or another, the book was not completed until six years later and I'm sorry he did not live to see the finished product, for he died in 1976.

As one gate closes another opens, for in 1975 I met Clifford R. Stanley, a retired Sergeant of the former Leicestershire and Rutland Constabulary, who has written some articles on police history and I invited him to take up the research where Frank Elmes had left off. This he did and I am most grateful for his diligence and good will.

On reading through the finished manuscript I am struck by the fact that so many people of whom I have recorded personal conversations or told anecdotes are now dead. Readers will have to accept my word that I have not been romancing. Words are inadequate, elusive things at the best of times and although the direct speech recorded may not be exactly the words used, it is a true mirror of their meaning. I do not pretend to have been as accurate as Hansard.

I hope I have not trodden on too many toes, nor destroyed too many sacred cows. There will be some readers who do not agree with my views and there are some lacunae in my story. I have refrained from recounting some incidents which would undoubtedly have been readable, either because it would have involved living people in a derogatory sense or because there are secrets which cannot be disclosed. I am answerable to the Official Secret Acts, while the draft manuscript has had to be examined at the Home Office before release for publication. Even so, I hope that this account of a policeman's life in different parts of England, including my tenure at the Home Office as a quasi-civil servant, and in particular my journeys abroad, will not only give an interesting and revealing insight into the life of a senior police officer, but will in a small way contribute to the history of the Police Service of this country.

I am well aware that in this book the first personal pronoun has been over-used, but it is difficult for it to be otherwise. For this is a very personal account of incidents and matters in all of which I have been personally concerned. It is a subjective record not an objective treatise.

This is a miscellany of reminiscences and in no sense a text book, but if in recording some of the incidents that have occurred, there shows through my philosophy in policing and the way in which the job should, in my opinion, be done it will perhaps be of some small

Prologue

value to young men of ambition who join the job and who want to reach the top.

ERIC ST. JOHNSTON

The Old Swan House,
Great Rissington,
Gloucestershire.

April, 1978.

The Coat of Arms of the Johnstons is derived from that of Bruce of Scotland. Eric St. Johnston's Arms, as approved by the College of Heralds are an adaptation —in layman's terms—by the addition of the Ox of Oxfordshire, the Lion Rampant of County Durham, the three Red Roses of Lancashire, and two barrels of the Vintner's Company of which he is a Liveryman.

ACKNOWLEDGMENT

I acknowledge with gratitude the patience and good humour of Delia Lawrance and Beryl Welch who deciphered my appalling handwriting and typed the manuscript.

Chapter One

EARLY DAYS

Since the beginning of the nineteenth century the city of Birmingham which many regard as the birthplace of the Industrial Revolution, has been a growing and thriving city, inhabited by sturdy, independent, hard working people, with no particular pretence to culture, but where many middle class people are born, go to school, work, marry and live respectable sensible lives.

The city has become prosperous, not because of any one trade or skill, but because of many. It has been described as 'a city of a thousand trades', and until recent years when the giants of Austins, Dunlops and Lucas arrived, it was essentially a business community built of small firms, where master and men worked close to each other, knew and respected each other and helped each other in any difficulties that might arise.

It has also been a city where much of the best of local government has been evolved and with a good record of municipal conduct, a lead being given by families such as the Cadburys, the Barrows and the Chamberlains.

It was to this city that my great, great grandfather, Thomas Johnston, came from Scotland a hundred and sixty years ago, and where four generations of Johnstons from father to son have since been born.

In 1939 there were no less than four Dr St. Johnstons, all related, practising in Birmingham, but now, alas, only one family of that name lives there. The Johnston family – it is, I believe, wrong to speak of clans in the Lowlands – were an ancient and prolific family in Scotland. They first broke into history in the 12th century as supporters of King Bruce. The family was a typical border breed, for ever fighting the English or indulging in feuds with their neighbours, which caused grief and suffering among the tenantry of Upper Annandale for generations. The bloody battle of Dryfe Sands in 1593 against the Maxwells, immortalised by Sir Walter Scott in his 'Minstrelsy of the Scottish Border', when the family was almost exterminated, was the last of the big border fights. After that, sporadic cattle raids took place and one origin of the 'Flying Spur' on the family crest was said to be the custom of placing before the Chief a spur with wings attached under a dish cover when the larder was empty, to signify that it was time to 'boot and spur' and start another raid.

In the family mythology, however, there is a better story: that while Bruce was in his cave near Gretna Green, hiding from the English soldiers and watching his spider go up and down, the Johnston of the day who lived nearby learnt that his hiding place was known to the English. Either because he did not dare write, but more probably because he was illiterate, he did not send a written message, but instead sent a small boy to the cave with a pie in which under the crust was a boot spur and two pigeons' wings. Bruce read the message correctly and escaped before the English came. When he became King he gave the Johnstons the right to wear the winged spur forever and to the Johnston who warned him he gave all the land that could be seen from the cave.

Whether this is true or not, it is a fact that Johnstons throughout the world – and there are many, as a glance at any telephone book in any English speaking country will testify – all proudly wear the crest – as I do – on our signet rings and on our silver.

My immediate forebears are descended from a branch of the family who lived at Bonshaw, Kirtle Bridge, a few miles north of Gretna Green.

If one drives north from Gretna Green along the A9 one can see across the fields to the west, by the side of the River Kirtle, a fortified tower to which was added in the 18th century, a house of considerable charm, known as Bonshaw Tower. For many generations it has been the home of the Irving family, one of whom in recent years was the late Sir James Irving, first Captain of the liner RMS *Queen Mary* and Commodore of the Cunard Shipping Line who, during the Spring of 1939, hit the world's news headlines when he docked the giant sized *Queen Mary* alongside Pier 90 of New York docks, unassisted by tugs, during a tugboat strike – the first time such an operation had ever been accomplished.

In the grounds close by the Tower is a small picturesque water mill, now derelict and unoccupied, where in the 18th century my four times great grandfather Thomas Johnston lived. For seven successive generations his male descendants have been christened Thomas. One of his grandsons, Thomas, the founder of the Birmingham branch of the family, decided as many Scots have done before and since, to seek his fortune in England. He walked south to

Early Days

Manchester making a living on the way selling drapery at roadside cottages. In the centre of Manchester he set up business, thrived, married a Derbyshire girl of 18, made some money and moved on to Birmingham where he made a respectable fortune by importing silks and linens from India and the Far East. I still have a sample of his office writing paper with its finely engraved letter head.

Thomas became Chairman of the Birmingham Water Works and was associated in other successful private enterprises, ending his life in a house he built, which later was for many years part of the Birmingham Mint. Soon after he arrived in Birmingham he formed the Birmingham Caledonian Society, the purpose of which was to assist Scotsmen living in Birmingham who needed help and advice. In 1839, after he had been Secretary for twenty-one years, all the Scotsmen in Birmingham by public subscription bought and presented to him a beautiful four-piece silver tea service of Regency design. I have one of the circulars inviting people to subscribe, a ticket of admission to the dinner when the presentation was made, and also a newspaper account of the dinner with a list of the fifteen toasts proposed, and synopses of the main speeches made, and – what is most important – I have the tea service.

The members of the Society then made him President and, after another twenty years, they had his portrait painted and presented to him. I have the account of those proceedings and the portrait hangs in my house.

The newspaper accounts of this presentation record fourteen speeches and replies, besides songs from eleven of the guests, and it ends,

> 'The evening was spent in the greatest cordiality and many other toasts given and songs sung. The company separated about 12 o'clock after spending a night full of fun and glee, yet so tempered by moderation that it might well bear the morning's reflection.'

This Thomas had five sons, all of whom except my great grandfather also named Thomas, became medical practitioners.

Charles, the eldest, was apprenticed at the absurdly young age of 15 to Edward Moore, Surgeon, Apothecary, for a fee of £99, later going to Samuel Cox's 'School of Medicine and Surgery', the forerunner of the Birmingham Medical School and now part of the University of Birmingham. He had the roaming spirit of the Johnstons and after qualifying he travelled much overseas; I have letters of his written while serving in the Portuguese Army, and later from Arabia and India. He was reported to be the first white man to travel through Abyssinia after which he wrote two very turgid and dull volumes entitled, *Johnston's travels in Southern Abyssinia*. I cannot help but feel that he left out all the interesting bits of the story. He eventually went to Durban in South Africa and there survives a letter to his father, asking him to send out some tools which he could not buy out there but needed in order to build a house. There is also another letter dated twenty months later saying that the tools had arrived. What he did in the meantime is not related, but it is an interesting commentary on the time taken for private communications in the 19th century when the mail went by sailing ship and stage coach.

George Johnston, the third of the sons, after qualifying as a doctor went out to Van Diemans Land (now Tasmania) on a migrant ship. I have one of his letters written to his parents describing conditions in the ship and remarking that 'The Captain is very pleased with me: only two people died on this voyage: eight died on his last one.' He then became MO at the convict prison but disliked the work because of the treatment of the prisoners and went on first to California and then to Vancouver Island where he is reported to have made a lot of money from land he won as a result of card debts – and then lost by the same means.

Yet another of Thomas's sons went to far off places. Alexander, the fifth son, arriving in Australia a little more precipitately than he desired for his ship was wrecked at the approaches to Botany Bay. He went on to Wellington, New Zealand, where he became the head of the hospital and helped to build the first theatre in the town – presumably the first in New Zealand. There is a hill behind Government House named after him, while his house, Goldisbrae, known as 'Johnston's Folly', for it has a very peculiar semi-circular design, has been a well-known landmark for many years.

Of the next generation Alfred went to the Polynesian Islands and there wrote and published five novels, some of them quite successful, before dying at the age of 32, while a great grandson, Reginald, achieved the greatest fame of anyone in the family. As soon as he had qualified as a doctor he obtained an appointment in the Colonial Medical Service; he was posted to Fiji, but soon transferred to the Administrative Service, and later was sent on promotion to the West Indies. He became Governor of the Falkland Islands and finally in 1926, Governor of the Leeward Islands, ending with a KCMG.

When I went to Antigua in 1970 to stay with the Governor, Sir Wilfred Jacobs, I met an elderly man who told me that he had known Reginald and his wife well. He added, 'he had an eye for the girls, and we always spoke of them as Randy Reg and Anxious Alice.'

Early Days

Reginald was a prolific writer and published a number of books about life in the Colonial Service. An interesting man who had served his whole adult life abroad, he managed in his official functions to combine great enthusiasm with old fashioned dignity, although his sense of humour was limited, which occasionally gave him an air of pomposity. After his retirement he did a great deal of research into the family history and it was from him that I was able to learn much of my Scottish ancestry.

Reg and Alice did not have any children of their own and probably for that reason they took a very great interest in and were most generous to the children of their relations. Because I wanted to join the Colonial Service, Reg took a particular interest in me and I shall always be grateful to him for his kindly advice and help.

My great grandfather Thomas who was born in 1815 a few months before Waterloo and died in 1887, the Golden Jubilee Year, did not become a doctor or travel as his brothers did because he was born with a serious speech impediment and except for some wood-turning, did little. Although born and living all his life in Birminghan he insisted on wearing the kilt, and from photographs I have of him, he must have been a very tall and handsome man.

Throughout the greater part of the 19th century we were known as Johnstons, but sometime in the last two decades of the century, some members of the family had their children christened with the name Saint and by 1900 all descendants of the original Thomas living in England had become St. Johnston. My grandfather was christened Johnston and only after 1900 do records show his name as St. Johnston, whereas my father's birth certificate of 1882 shows that he was christened St. Johnston. The origin of this self-canonisation is believed to be a sentimental visit paid to Scotland by my great grandfather Thomas shortly before his first grandson was born. He discovered that the old name of the county town of Perth was Saint Johnstone, the town of which the Patron Saint was St. John and this is still the name of the Perth football team playing in the Scottish league. When his grandson was born in 1851, he was christened Thomas Saint Johnston, and collateral branches of the family followed suit.

My grandfather Thomas had a strong yearning for military life, so strong indeed that he ran away from home at 16 to enlist. Eventually his parents managed to persuade him to return to civil life and he was bought out and apprenticed to a wine merchant. By diligence and honesty he was able to build up a successful wine importing business of his own, which was sufficient to keep him, his wife and eleven children in comfort.

He never, however, lost his love for soldiering, and despite the demands of a growing business, and his large family, (for my grandmother died at the early age of 44) he enlisted in the Warwickshire Yeomanry at a time when every man provided his own horses, the officers being the aristocratic landed gentry, and the non-commissioned officers and troopers yeoman farmers, businessmen and the like.

In due course, he became the Regimental Sergeant Major of the Regiment – a rank he held for twenty years during which time, year after year, he won prizes for shooting and swordsmanship. He was a big man physically and rode both at Queen Victoria's Diamond Jubilee procession, and at her funeral on seventeen hand horses. When he eventually retired in 1902 he was presented at a parade at Warwick Castle with an illuminated address and a large silver cup standing some thirty inches high, both of which I now have.

He lived in a very comfortable Victorian house in Kings Heath, a suburb of Birmingham, very close to Joseph Chamberlain's home, with good solid furniture, a large collection of Staffordshire figures in glass cases, and Baxter and Le Blond prints on the walls. It was not a smart suburb – though better than it is now – but was at that time on the perimeter of the City and very close to the country.

He liked to have his family around him and expected as many as were able to have supper with him on Sunday nights, and I well remember as a small child seeing some twenty adults sitting at the dining table with the grandchildren at a side table in the bay window.

He never owned a motor car, but kept horses and a variety of carriages, in one of which until he died in 1922 I was always taken to and from my preparatory school at the beginning and end of term.

Of his eleven children three died as infants, and of the eight remaining, five were daughters, of whom Daisy was the youngest, and three were sons, of whom my father Thomas Gerald was the youngest. Daisy and my father were closest in age and in many ways closest in affection too, but at the age of 16 Daisy incurred my grandfather's permanent anger because she ran away with, and eventually married, a printer my grandfather called a 'ping-pong playing wastrel', for he spent most of the time playing table tennis, to the detriment of his business affairs. My grandfather never acknowledged Daisy again and forbade his children to do so either, but my father surreptitiously continued to see them and to help them financially in a small way.

The result of this disliked union, my cousin Adrian Haydon, was for some years the runner-up in World Table Tennis Championships but he could never beat Barna of Hungary. When he died in 1973 *The Times* obituary notice describes him as 'one of the most remark-

Early Days

able table tennis players the game has ever produced.' He married his mixed doubles partner, and their daughter Anne Haydon, now Anne Haydon Jones became Wimbledon tennis champion and Wightman Cup captain, thus adding more lustre to the family annals.

My father Thomas Gerald was born in 1882, and after leaving school he went first into the insurance world, but later joined his two brothers in the family wine business.

My mother, a Ryley, came from a Coventry family of watchmakers, and my grandfather in the 1880s began manufacturing the new Safety Bicycle with pneumatic tyres. Many feel that this gave women and girls a new freedom by replacing the chaperon. In 1880, there were 230 Bicycle Clubs in this country, and grandfather Ryley did well financially from the national cycle craze, though during the slump of the 1890s he lost everything, mainly because of bad partners. However, foreseeing the immense potential of the newly invented motor car, which was beginning to make an appearance on our roads, he moved to Birmingham where, prevented by lack of capital from becoming a motor manufacturer, he set up as a factor of motor vehicle parts with my mother, Ethel, then a girl of 16, as his first and only employee. Like Topsy, the business, J. A. Ryley Limited, grew and grew becoming, with the passing of the years, one of the largest firms selling motor vehicle accessories in the industrial Midlands. A keen motoring enthusiast, grandfather Ryley bought in Belgium the patent rights of the first motor car in England to embody thermo-syphon water cooling hoping to manufacture it. This he named the Ryley Voiturette but, although we have a photograph of it, alas, the machine no longer exists.

Although an astute businessman, my grandfather had an obsession about his health and that of his family, and for long periods he practised vegetarianism. He was opposed to vaccination and refused to allow my mother to have her tonsils removed when she was ill with a severe throat infection, with the result that it spread to her ears and impaired her hearing for the rest of her life. Despite her deafness, my mother's enthusiasm for life never waned, and apart from bringing up her family and entertaining a great deal, she spent much energy and time on hospital and church work.

My parents were married in 1909 and lived in Kings Heath, close to my grandfather. I was born in 1911, and my sister Mary, shortly before war broke out in 1914. My father, who had just joined the Territorial Army, was called up, and one of my first recollections of him was being taken by my mother to see him being drilled at a local Territorial Headquarters. He had not been supplied with uniform and was wearing civilian clothes, with a military cap and khaki belt.

My father was wounded in 1916 and, after he had been demobilised, we moved to Moseley and, when my father's finances improved, we moved to Edgbaston where my parents remained for the rest of their lives and where, for many years, he was Treasurer and Churchwarden of Edgbaston Old Church.

Moseley tends to be made up of the homes of middle management, while Edgbaston caters for the wealthy idustrialists and the top professional people, especially on the Calthorpe estate with its many beautiful late Georgian and early Victorian detached houses with large gardens.

There is a saying, 'when you get on you live in Moseley: when you get honourable you live in Edgbaston: when you get honest you leave Birmingham altogether.' I have done all three.

Nevertheless, I am proud to call myself a Birmingham man for, although the City is scoffed at by many, if one has to live in a provincial town, Birmingham is as good as anywhere else.

There is an excellent University, a first class hospital and a good Art Gallery, the Warwickshire County Cricket ground, Moseley Rugby Football Club and two first division Football Clubs, are actually in the city, while the lovely countryside of Warwickshire and Worcestershire is close at hand.

My sister and I had devoted parents, and though in our early years there was little money in the family, we had a happy childhood spending our holidays either in Birmingham or at our cottage some five miles from Stratford-on-Avon, in the village of Aston Cantlow where Shakespeare's mother and father were married.

My parents always encouraged us to bring our friends home and many of our friends became friends of my parents, so much so indeed that my father was called 'Father' by a large number of people and my mother 'Bellemere' (a name given to her by my fiancée when they first met) by a large number of people. Long after I left home and my sister had gone to India, my parents' home continued to be a meeting place for young people who lived in Edgbaston and all through the war when petrol was short and social activities at a minimum, my mother ran a monthly dance known as 'The Dim-Out' first at home and then as the dances became more popular, at a local hotel.

My parents always regretted that they had been forced to leave school so young, and they were determined that Mary and I should have the benefit of what they termed, 'a full education', for which we will be for ever grateful. When we were young it was not easy for them to find the money to send us to preparatory schools, then public schools and ultimately, in my case, to Cambridge. To do this they denied themselves many luxuries and holidays to meet

Early Days

the cost of our education which must have been a great hardship to them.

In 1918, just before the end of the First World War, my parents sent me to a preparatory school on the outskirts of Birmingham. I was nearly eight years old and they felt I ought to be toughened up in some educational establishment where I would learn to live away from home and fit into a community of boys of my own age.

I soon settled down but cannot say that I had more than an average career, for I failed to get a scholarship to my public school, and was not even placed in the soccer and cricket teams. It was all the more surprising, therefore, that during my last year there, the Headmaster announced to the school that he intended to introduce prefects, the first to be the Captain of the Cricket XI, the second the Top Boy of the 6th and the third, myself!

At this school my interest in Mathematics was encouraged by two good teachers, and as the school was close to the Warwickshire County Cricket ground, I was able to spend many happy afternoons watching cricket. Although not much good as a player, I was at the time desperately keen and could recite the names of every member of every first class team and the batting and bowling averages of many of them.

In those days we did not have Test Matches at Edgbaston but the touring teams played Warwickshire, and I saw the famous 1922 Australian XI captained by Warwick Armstrong as well as the famous J.W.H.T. (Johnny won't hit today) Douglas, who captained England. Little did I think that in due time I should come to know and sit with many of my heroes of those days – Jack Hobbs, Herbert Sutcliffe, Frank Woolley and the like, when as old men they came to watch the Test Matches at Old Trafford.

In 1924 when I was 13, I went to Bromsgrove, one of the smaller public schools situated about twenty miles from Birmingham. The school's origins are unknown, but we received a grant from Edward VI in 1553 and as a consequence the place is steeped in tradition. While I was there the Headmaster was R. G. Routh, a man of strong character, personality and understanding who had a great formative influence upon my life. A magnificent preacher, R. G. ruled and guided his school in a manner for which all Bromsgrovians who knew him will ever be grateful. It was a good school in excellent surroundings and my five and half years there were extremely happy and valuable.

As soon as I arrived my father took me to my housemaster, who during the course of the interview, reminded me that a cousin of the same name had been Head of the House and he hoped I would do as well. This prompted my father to say, 'He's got to do better than that. I expect him to be Head of the School!' Everything went well for me at Bromsgrove. At 15 I obtained my School Certificate, and as I was already six feet tall I was lucky enough to get a place as a second row forward in the School XV and played for three seasons. In due course I became Head of the School, Captain of Games and in command of one of the two companies of the Officers Training Corps.

The widespread responsibility given to monitors at Bromsgrove was intended to develop latent powers of leadership, and I always feel that this proved to be a valuable factor in moulding my character. It gave me a sense of direction, and as my first real experience of man-management made me realise that I wanted to spend my life controlling and helping 'people' and not manufacturing or selling 'things'. At the Speech Day at the end of my last term, after all the prizes had apparently been given, the Headmaster announced that he had one further award to make. He then made a most complimentary speech about me, saying that I would long be remembered among the best of a long line of Head Monitors, and I was awarded a special prize.

Bromsgrove does not have a reputation for producing scholars – though A. E. Housman was educated there – but it has produced more than its fair share of leaders and as W. T. S. Stallybrass the well known Principal of Brasenose College, Oxford, said on one occasion at Speech Day, 'Bromsgrove and its produce have a reputation for virility. You find Bromsgrovians everywhere running things and running them well.' To prove his point, at a time when there were only twenty Colonial Governors in the British Empire – two of them were Old Bromsgrovians who were at the school in my time.

Whilst at Bromsgrove, I had become interested through the influence of R. G. in the problems of working class people in the Midlands, and a few of us from the school had been allowed to help in the running of a Boys' Club in Bromsgrove. For the first time in my life I came into contact with boys of a different kind from those that I had been used to, and I soon found what worthy qualities many working class boys possessed. Indeed, getting to know these lads was a salutary lesson. Many possessed gifts which shone through, despite their lack of opportunities to develop latent social and academic talent. Since then, I have never had any doubt about the need to improve housing conditions and standards of living and it grieves me that it still is hard for young people to shake off the handicap of a poor start. Social systems change all too slowly, and I have always tried to give the necessary push to young people as opportunity offered.

Early Days

In 1929 I was chosen to represent Bromsgrove at the Duke of York's Camp. Each year from 1922 until 1939, the Duke of York, later King George VI, invited 400 boys, between the ages of 17 and 19, half from public schools and half from factories, to join him at the Camp. Through the publicity given to the venture by the BBC, the press and cinema news reels, the camp later became a well known national institution. Hardly a public school remained unrepresented and hundreds of firms affiliated to the Industrial Welfare Society were associated with the Royal experiment. The Camps were unique, for every year the staff dealt with an entirely unknown force – every boy being a stranger to the camp staff and to every other boy. Writing of the success of the Camp as a breaker down of barriers, a public schoolboy said, 'One of the greatest experiences of my life. I now appreciate how the other man lives.' A Sheffield steel worker, confirming that the Camp was made up equally of public school and working boys, said he never could tell the difference. A Huddersfield boy wrote: 'I would not have believed that such a crowd would have become friends so soon'. At camp there were twenty sections each comprised of twenty boys, ten from public schools and ten from factories. Section leaders were appointed from Old Campers, and I filled this role at several successive Camps. Standard dress was shorts, T shirt and gym shoes, a levelling process which made it impossible to 'tell t'other from which'.

When HRH came to the camp, he was invariably accompanied by his Equerry, Sir Harold Campbell, and took a great interest in every aspect of camp life. He took part in all camp events, wearing shorts, sitting with us at meals and joining us in the popular evening sing song, and seemed thoroughly to enjoy his visits. He was, of course, treated with due respect – except when in possession of the ball during a peculiar game known technically as Foot and Hand Net Ball, but always referred to more accurately and graphically as Tooth and Nail. The Duke was friendly and amusing and the boys did their best to respond in the same vein. When under stress however, the Duke's stutter was at that time very bad, and his later mastery of his disability was a great personal achievement. I well remember on one occasion he was chatting gaily to a group of us outside the assembly tent and with no hint of difficulty, when the Camp Commandant told him that all was ready for him to address the boys. On the platform the Duke became speechless – unable for painful minutes to make any sound. The contrast was dramatic and the efforts needed later in his life successfully to overcome this disability and conduct great occasions must have been of Herculean proportions.

The Camp Chief, Captain J. G. Paterson, affectionately called

Pat by everyone was a big man, physically and mentally, with a remarkable personality of the kind to which others are instinctively drawn; he was the ideal Camp Leader. He died in April 1961 and in a tribute to him which I wrote for *The Times*, I said:

> 'To countless young boys who had the opportunity of attending the Duke of York's Camp – or King's Camp as it was later known – the figure, presence and character of the Camp Chief will be indelibly impressed on their memory, while those of us who had the privilege of coming back year after year as members of the staff learnt so much from watching and listening to the way in which Pat dealt so quietly and efficiently with the many administrative problems of running the Camp, and we never ceased to admire the way in which, through his influence, 400 complete strangers became overnight bosom friends.'

The last Royal Camp was held in August 1939, a month before the outbreak of World War II. By then the Duke of York had become King George VI and he found it impossible to spare the time to come to Suffolk where the camp had been for some years, so he invited us to Balmoral. Accommodation was more limited and only 200 boys could attend instead of the usual 400. We travelled up on an overnight train and after settling in at Abergeldie Castle, one of the Royal demesnes, all of us went to tea at Balmoral where the King and Queen and the two Princesses greeted us at the entrance. Each section leader had to introduce the members of his section. As we had only met the night before we had difficulty in remembering every name. Valiantly we did our best causing the King to remark afterwards, with a twinkle, that there 'seemed to be a remarkable number of Smiths and Jones at the camp.'

Camp routine was varied to suit the venue. Instead of competitive games there were walking expeditions, in parties over the glorious Cairngorm mountains. Inevitably, on the longest and most arduous climb to the summit of Loch Nagar, one boy got lost. Three Section Leaders, tough Scotsmen, Andrew Elphinstone, the Queen's cousin, Lord Malcolm Douglas Hamilton, later a Member of Parliament, and Donald Cameron – at that time Cameron the Younger of Locheil – did the trip again in reverse. To climb Loch Nagar twice in a day is no mean feat. It could have been in a better cause, for the lost boy walked into camp very shortly after the search party had left!

Each day the King joined one of the expeditions, and most days the Queen and the two Princesses came to the camp for a meal or the evening concert. On the last night the King arranged an enormous bonfire on a promonotory opposite Balmoral. Here the King, his family and all the rest of us, joined hands in a huge ring. Flames

Early Days

leaped and flickered, lighting up the walls of the castle below us, while the King's piper played 'Over the Sea to Skye' and 'Auld Lang Syne'. Most of the older people present guessed that war was near and that we boys at camp would soon be fighting men. It was a poignant moment for us all, the world was changing, an epoch coming to a close. Tears came unbidden to my eyes and I believe I was not alone. Within four weeks of breaking camp Britain was at War. How successfully the King had hidden from us the cares and worries which he must have been feeling as he climbed with us, told of his experiences, asked about our lives and joined in the teasing and leg-pulling in the best camp tradition.

In 1946 the question of re-starting the camp venture was brought up. Sir Harold Campbell was deputed by the King to take soundings from those most interested and he arranged a dinner party for the Camp Chief and five or six of us who were experienced Section Leaders. Anxiously we discussed the whole subject and, although we would have loved to see the Camps with all their revelries revived, it was not to be. Conscription had achieved far more nationally and effectively the Camp's primary objects of mixing up boys of differing backgrounds to enable them to recognise each other's qualities – the ultimate in a classless society. We could not, in all conscientiousness, recommend to the King the re-emergence of his Camps, and for me the decision was particularly disappointing for Pat had told me in confidence that he had asked to be relieved of future Camp duties, adding 'You have been chosen to succeed me.'

When I left school, there was another aspect of communal life which attracted me, for I immediately applied for, and was granted, a Territorial Army commission with the 68th (Warwickshire) Artillery Brigade, whose headquarters were in Birmingham. As a young battery subaltern of a horse-drawn gun unit – mechanisation had not yet arrived – I was in my element learning about man-management at the annual summer training camp and feeding, grooming, exercising and training the horses to work as a team pulling 18 pounder guns and ammunition limbers. There are few more exhilarating experiences than riding at the head of a well-turned out section of two gun teams and limbers, with the crunch of solid wooden, ironshod wheels on the road, the clattering hooves of the horses and the jangling of the gleaming, burnished harness. The Warwickshire Gunners proved their worth. One of the batteries – the 271st from Leamington – won, in 1932, the coveted King's Cup which was awarded annually to the most efficient Gunnery Battery.

In my last year at Bromsgrove, I failed to win a scholarship at Corpus Christi College, Cambridge, but I was accepted as a commoner. There I spent three very happy though undistinguished years, in my first year reading Mathematics, which was a mistake for I was not good enough, and then Law. I was very lucky for, at that time, Corpus not only had a distinguished group of Fellows, but I overlapped with a very intelligent and pleasant group of men, many of whom have reached the highest levels in their respective careers and as there were only 160 undergraduates we all knew each other.

Kenneth Pickthorn, a brilliant scholar, was the tutor and he later enjoyed a successful political career, which ultimately brought him a baronetcy for services to the House of Commons. Humphrey Mynors, the assistant tutor, later became Deputy Governor of the Bank of England, while from among my contemporaries of those vintage years, the college produced a Judge of the Court of Appeal (Lord Justice Lawton), a High Court Judge (Peter Foster), two Bishops (Kenneth Richards of Lincoln and Edward Roberts of Ely), a Colonial Governor (Sir Patrick Renison), two Ambassadors (Sir John Coulson and Sir Ronald Allen), two Headmasters (Sir Desmond Lee of Winchester and Lionel Carey of Bromsgrove), and a Commonwealth Prime Minister (The Hon Dudley Senanayake), while Marcus Sieff, Chairman of Marks and Spencers, Anthony Burney, Chairman of Debenhams and Nick Cayser, Chairman of the British and Commonwealth, all achieved great distinction in the business world and all now have titles.

My only friend outside Corpus was Nigel Balchin, who later became a distinguished author and scriptwriter. Nigel was an odd character with an intelligent, inquiring mind and a disconcerting habit of turning his upper lip inside out when he smiled, which was often. He kept copious notes of conversations that he had and would question all his friends and acquaintances about their dreams and, if they would discuss it, about their sexual thoughts and experiences. This was not for prurient reasons, but because of his scientific interest. In later life he told me that, with much regret, he was forced, owing to other commitments, to refuse a contract to re-edit and modernise Havelock Ellis's *Psychology of Sex*.

When we came down from Cambridge, Nigel first worked for the Institute of Industrial Psychology and then at Rowntree's as an efficiency consultant. He was pretty cynical about it all, saying that the work was mainly seeing a good idea in Factory A and selling it to the manager of Factory B. His first essay into professional writing was a series of articles in *Punch* under the pseudonym 'Mark Spade' on *How to run a bassoon factory or Big Business Explained* in which he said that to be a success one had to find a product which was cheap to make, in constant demand in times of boom and slump, quickly wore out and could not be repaired, e.g. beer.

In later years I used to visit him at his flat in Highgate where he lived with his first wife, Liz, (a thinly disguised character in one of his films) and at his oast house on the borders of Kent and Sussex where he lived with his second wife, and where he died much too young.

My tutor, Arthur Goodhart, was an American lawyer who later became Professor of Jurisprudence at Oxford, and ultimately Master of University College, Oxford. He was the kindest of friends, for whom I always had the greatest respect and I was glad to be able to keep in touch with him when I was in Oxfordshire. Our paths converged again in 1960 and 1961 when, as a Member of the Royal Commission on the Police, he was to hear evidence from me, his old pupil. Characteristically, Professor Goodhart declined to back the compromise solution preferred by the majority on the Commission and he supported my views by appending a dissenting report advocating a national police force, to which I shall return later.

Levees held by the Monarch are now things of the past, but in the 1930s young men attended levees much in the way that young girls were presented at Court. In 1930, while at Cambridge, I was summonsed to attend a levee at St. James Palace where, splendidly attired in the full dress uniform of a Lieutenant in the Royal Artillery (hired specially for the occasion from Moss Bros), I waited with several hundred others for what seemed an eternity. Groups of us were slowly shepherded through various state rooms by gorgeously attired court officials until we eventually arrived at the Throne Room. Here King George V attired in Naval uniform sat on the Throne, surrounded by his four sons and nodded impassively at each of us as our names being called out we advanced, halted, bowed, turned to the right and so left the royal presence. The bright colours of the Throne room and all those present, especially the multi-coloured uniforms of all the foreign military attaches was a sight that a young man would always remember.

Our termly college bills including University fees were of the order of £70. My father gave me £300 a year and a suit of clothes, and when I came down he cleared my overdraft of £100. So my University education cost him exactly £1000 and three suits, the most expensive of which cost £20 from a Cambridge tailor. I remember this well because he grumbled at me for my extravagance. The first two from his Birmingham tailor only cost £15 each.

At Cambridge I spent the time attending lectures in the mornings, playing rugger or cricket in the afternoons and in the evenings I played bridge or just talked, sometimes going to the cinema, the theatres, or the ballet. I entertained as far as my bank balance would allow, and I fear that I did little reading on my own.

I was not strongly interested in politics, but did go to political meetings of all three parties because I was trying to decide which party I wanted to support. I was brought up in a strong Conservative atmosphere, but I was already unhappy with the complacency shown about unemployment and bad housing.

Although not a fully paid up member of the Cambridge Labour Party, I used to attend their meetings more than others and on one occasion I was asked to go to a meeting at which, I was told, a bright new star in the Labour Party firmament was to speak. The meeting was held in a café and on the table stood an intelligent young girl who spoke with enthusiasm and lucidity about the aims of the Labour Party. I was much impressed. Her name was Jennie Lee, today the Baroness Lee, widow of Aneurin Bevan, and I little thought at the time that I should meet her years later in County Durham.

During my last year at Cambridge, I decided that I did not want to enter my father's business, despite an available and attractive opening, because I strongly wanted to work with, and for, people rather than things and, since I preferred an outdoor life, the Colonial Service seemed the answer to my problems. In this I was influenced by my father's cousin, Sir Reginald St. Johnston, of whom I have previously spoken and whom I met during my first year at Cambridge when he was Governor of the Leeward Islands.

A man of influence and foresight, he insisted that I should read for the Bar, and without the consent of my father or even firm agreement from me, he wrote to the Treasurer of the Middle Temple, a friend of his, and arranged my entry to that Inn of Court. In a short space of time I found myself travelling to London to eat my dinners. Examinations are not difficult, especially if one has done Law at University and it is an interesting experience. Many called to the Bar have no intention of practising though they make use of the qualification and experience in other ways. The number of practising barristers is small, only about 4,000, but they exercise a disproportionate influence on affairs. They fill exalted offices of the Crown: Lord Chancellor, Law Lords, Attorney-General, Solicitor General, Director of Public Prosecutions, Judges of the High Courts and most Recorders are barristers. Many become Circuit Judges, or Stipendiary Magistrates. Commissions of Inquiry are rarely complete without a barrister, either as Chairman or a serving member. Academic lawyers add their influence to that of the practising barristers when new legislation is under discussion. Because oratory is their trade, barristers make good Members of Parliament and, not least of their accomplishments, they are usually good after-dinner speakers and witty conversationalists. I unhesitatingly recommend any young man in search of an extra qualification which he will find interesting and who wants to further his career, to read for the Bar.

To become a barrister one had not only to pass the necessary examinations but it was also necessary to eat the requisite number of dinners. This was not a test of one's gastronomic ability, but a good rule just to ensure that students were attached to an Inn for a minimum period of time and so absorbed some of the atmosphere and traditions of the Inns of Court.

There are four student terms a year, each of which is approximately ten weeks in length. Before being called to the Bar one has to have kept twelve terms, and this is done by attending not less than six dinners each term unless one is a University undergraduate or graduate in which case only three dinners have to be eaten.

It has long been customary for students coming from the old colonial and commonwealth countries to read for the Bar in addition to whatever other subjects they may be studying. Since the Inns of Court are not residential for students, they need never come near the Inns of Court except to take their examinations and hence the practice is considered to be particularly important for those who come from overseas.

Although we sat on benches at long tables, we were divided into messes of four – two on either side of the table, and when one arrived one looked around for friends or others who looked congenial till one had collected a four and made up a mess.

We dined in gowns and paid seven shillings and sixpence for for our dinner, which consisted of soup, fish, meat and two vegetables, and a pudding. We were also given as much beer as we wanted, and there was one bottle of sherry and one of port for each mess. About once a fortnight there was a special night such as 'Grand Night,' when distinguished guests were asked to the High Table, or 'Call Night,' when those students who had passed their finals were called to the Bar; on such occasions each mess was given a bottle of champagne which could be exchanged for two bottles of claret. At the end of dinner, the snuff box was passed round. All this was included in the price of dinner, and if all this alcohol was not enough, I had one or two Cambridge friends who used always to find among the coloured students one or two teetotal Moslems to join their mess.

I made a number of friends through eating dinners and became friendly with Jack Simon, Eustace Roskill and Leslie Scarman, all of whom went on to high judicial office in later years, while Dudley Senanayake who later became Prime Minister of Ceylon was a Corpus friend also reading for the Bar at that time.

Apart from the slight advantage of being a barrister in my police career, I was very glad to have read for the Bar for it opened up to me a new cross section of life, and I learnt much from the friendships that I made, though I must admit that after eating dinners I often returned to Cambridge on the 10.0 p.m. train somewhat the worse for wear.

All too quickly my finals came and in a stupor of crammed learning and sleeplessness, I wrote my papers. When the results came out I found I'd got a mediocre Second in my Tripos and not a First as I and one of my law tutors had hoped. Acutely disappointed I went down from Cambridge. I know I had only myself to blame, for far too much time had been spent playing games, kissing the girls and enjoying the many social activities that pre-War Cambridge and London offered.

From that point of view I had done myself well but I was soon to come up against the harsher realities of life.

In June 1932 – the same month that I left University – I was interviewed for the Colonial Service by Ralph Furse, the Head of the Colonial Recruiting Service, who, during his long term of office (1930–48), showed a marked preference for young men with a public school background, a degree at Oxford or Cambridge, preferably not worse than a Second Class honours, and if possible, a blue or some other sign of athletic prowess. Usually about a hundred candidates were offered appointments in the Colonial Service each year but due to the financial crisis of 1931 and the severe retrenchment which ensued only fifteen of those who applied in 1932 were accepted, and I was sixteenth of them. For several weeks I was kept on a reserve list and was finally offered Bechuanaland. I did not want to live in Africa and when applying had given Malaya, Hong Kong and the West Indies as my priorities, in that order. Furse therefore advised me to wait and apply again the next year when the restraints would probably have eased.

With my father's somewhat reluctant agreement I decided therefore to mark time for a year hoping to obtain some part-time employment, and continue to study for my Bar finals.

There were also Territorial Army camp and parades to attend, while the Rugger season was looming ahead. From the age of sixteen onwards, I had been a member of the Moseley Rugby Football Club, which did not have the reputation that it has today, but even then we were considered to be a first-class club. During the Christmas holidays those members of the First XV whose homes were far away were not available, and each year I was lucky enough to be invited to fill one of the vacancies. Thus at a very early age I had the opportunity to play in first-class matches

Early Days

the Christmas fixtures being Old Edwardians, Northampton, and Bedford.

In 1932 I gained a regular place in the First XV and played in all matches through September and October, but when I went to London I could not continue, for in those days I worked on Saturday mornings, so I could not play for a club so far away. Indeed I could not afford the fare. Truth to tell, I had also for some unexplained reason, shot my bolt. I played better rugger when I was twenty than I did at any time after that though I was in 1932 selected for one North Midland Colts Trial.

Meanwhile, during 1931, Lord Trenchard, Marshal of the Royal Air Force, and one of the great figures to emerge from the First World War, had become Metropolitan Police Commissioner in succession to Lord Byng of Vimy. It was a period when things within the Force were not as well as they should have been, for corruption had been widespread and many of London's West End night clubs of dubious reputation which should have been prosecuted and closed, were flourishing.

Concerned as to how he could safeguard his Force from a repetition of the situation, Lord Trenchard with characteristic thoroughness, reorganised the entire Metropolitan Police Force. He imported officers of varying ranks from the Army to key posts and to ensure succession of such men of a wider and different background, upbringing and education, he decided to encourage University graduates to join the Force – an unprecedented step in the history of the Police Service of this country, and as things turned out, the most criticised of all his reforms and innovations. As the founder of RAF College, Cranwell, Lord Trenchard undoubtedly had in mind from the outset to inaugurate a Police College with a similar high standard of conduct and efficiency, which would ultimately produce a body of highly educated young men who, after concentrated professional training, would be eligible for the top posts before they were too old. As a first step in that direction he decided to introduce a sprinkling of young University men into the Civil Service Branch of the Secretariat at New Scotland Yard, the Headquarters of the Force. The Appointments Board at Cambridge wrote to tell me of this, and asked whether I was interested.

Criminal prosecutions had always interested me. Even during my school vacations, I had spent many long hours listening to policemen giving evidence in criminal cases and to some admirable advocacy in the Victoria Law Courts, Birmingham. Here I thought, was a heavensent opportunity of the possibility in later years, to have command of men and with it the responsibility of 'running a happy ship', which I had found so intriguing during the year I had been Head Monitor at Bromsgrove and as an officer in the Territorial Army. Clearly the opening presented a stimulating challenge. As my father's financial circumstances at the time were strained and I was conscious that to keep me unemployed for a further year would be a burden to him, I decided to apply, and attended an interview at Scotland Yard in October 1932 with H. M. Howgrave-Graham CBE, the Secretary of the Metropolitan Police. Along with three others I was offered and accepted an appointment as a Junior Executive Officer in the Commissioner's Office, at the princely sum of £168 per annum. I began my police career on the 1st November, 1932, twelve months after the arrival of Lord Trenchard and in that office were laid the foundations of everything that was to happen in my subsequent police career.

Thomas Johnston 1785–1866, great great grandfather

Thomas Johnston 1815–1887, great grandfather

Thomas St. Johnston 1851–1922, grandfather

Thomas Gerald St. Johnston 1882–1966, father

Above 1916

Right 1929

Below 1934

Below right 1944

Chapter Two

THE METROPOLITAN POLICE

The turreted warren of New Scotland Yard, the familiar red brick and grey stone building facing the river on the Victoria Embankment, a stone's throw from the Houses of Parliament, had been in constant use as the Headquarters of the Metropolitan Police since 1890. It was a somewhat forbidding building especially for a young man most unsure of himself, but on arrival I was ushered, with three others, into the presence of H. M. Howgrave-Graham CBE, who as Secretary to the Metropolitan Police was responsible for all the Civil Servants employed at New Scotland Yard, and I was immediately put at ease by his charming smile. During his 18 years in office, Howgrave-Graham, who enjoyed the equality of status of an Assistant Commissioner, served under five Commissioners and handled the vast correspondence which descended day-by-day upon the country's biggest police headquarters in addition to much of the administrative work of the Police. When I first met him he was standing with his back to the fire in a large room overlooking the Thames, with high ceilings and good mahogany furniture. I remember wondering even at the first interview how long it would be, if ever, before I had a similar office of my own. A man gifted with a strong sense of humour and a well developed power of observation, his administrative abilities were of a very high order. I shall always be grateful to him for the admirable and kind way in which he introduced me to the strange and alien world of the police, and for his expert advice and guidance as I carried out my new administrative duties, during what proved to be a very crucial and testing time in the history of the Metropolitan Police. The morale of the Force was at this time very low, due chiefly to the impact of the economy measures. Pay cuts, poor man-management, the utterly miserable working conditions of the police stations and especially the living conditions in the section houses which housed more than 4,000 single men — these were just some of a whole series of shortcomings and defects which were being given the immediate attention of the new Commissioner, with his well known customary energy and drive. This, and a host of other reforms, including a complete reorganisation of duties throughout the Force, concentrating on the essentials and developing the police organisation to such a pitch that it would work, as one national newspaper put it, 'with the sureness of a machine'.

Lord Trenchard denounced the cold, cramped, badly-lit section houses, which lacked even privacy as the men slept in cheerless dormitories. He made it plain that he was determined his men should have accommodation fit for human beings. Despite the national financial restrictions then prevailing – and many authorities thought economy meant saving expenditure at all costs – Lord Trenchard was given the go-ahead to launch an extensive building programme involving the erection of new section houses and blocks of flats with all the latest labour-saving devices. It was clear to everyone that under Trenchard rule at last, the long-awaited wind of change was blowing through the entire Metropolitan Police Force. But all these changes and reforms took time to achieve, and meantime the men were both critical and apprehensive. It was with this unhappy and uneasy atmosphere permeating the entire Force, that I entered the police service straight from University.

My initial face-to-face interview with Lord Trenchard to receive the equivalent of a papal blessing, took place during my first week of service. He was then 59, a striking man of aristocratic bearing and behaviour with a fierce energy. Tall and a magnificent figure when in dress uniform, he was a hard taskmaster, but intensely human and understanding, and bubbling over with infectious enthusiasm. Although we were awe struck by the man and his reputation, he kindly welcomed the four of us from behind a large polished desk in the centre of a spacious and gracefully furnished room – like himself impressive and inspiring. In a loud voice which literally boomed, he stressed the value of hard work and went on to explain the excellent opportunities which lay ahead, emphasising the fact that our primary duty as Officers, was to look after our subordinates properly – a point which came up time and time again during the course of his lectures at Hendon Police College. His message came over loud and clear and it became manifestly evident why he was known as 'Boom Trenchard'. Though often unable to express himself lucidly and sometimes even appearing inarticulate, his forceful character and powers of leadership drove all around him to the full extent of their energies, while his integrity inspired complete loyalty. Howgrave-Graham, who was of course in a position to observe Lord Trenchard closely wrote:

'His out-put was enormous. He was a ten-power man. He accomplished in four years more than anybody else I've ever met could do in a dozen years.'

Another writer put it this way, 'Few will ever match Lord Trenchard's record of achievement or service. Those of us, whether in the RAF or in the Metropolitan Police, who have followed along the routes which he laid down, willingly admit being in his debt', while 'Beachcomber' of the *Daily Express* facetiously remarked in one of his daily columns, 'the monthly re-organisation of the Metropolitan Police will take place weekly in future.'

A distinguished soldier, Lord Trenchard transferred to the newly created Royal Flying Corps as GOC, taking charge of air operations during the First World War. In April 1918, he founded the Royal Air Force and, as Chief of Air Staff, prepared for its role in the Second World War. In 1927 he was created the first Marshal of the RAF and on his retirement two years later, was appointed to the boards of several business companies. It was in that capacity that in 1931, against his own wish, he was persuaded by King George V to take over the control of the Metropolitan Police as successor to Lord Byng of Vimy.

For the first six months, the four of us were sent separately to work for one or two weeks in each of the departments of New Scotland Yard, in order to see what work was done and to meet the heads of all the main sections.

I was then posted to C2, the Department which looked after all the crime correspondence coming into or going out of the Yard. There were only four of us in this Department and, although crime was then much less than today, we were very busy; it did, however, give us the opportunity to read the very interesting and comprehensive reports prepared by operational police officers, which had to be forwarded to solicitors or to the Director of Public prosecutions.

At that time the Assistant Commissioner in charge of Crime was Sir Norman Kendal CBE, while his second in command, who eventually succeeded him, was Ronald Howe, who later became Sir Ronald Howe CVO, MC. Neither of them at that time officially had a Personal Assistant, but I became so in fact if not in name. Normal Kendal had practised at the Bar before his direct appointment as Deputy Assistant Commissioner in 1918. My first impression of my new Chief was of a formidable man with a clean shaven ascetic face, white hair and penetrating eyes, but when I got to know him better I found, beneath his grim exterior, a genial personality and a phenomenal memory. We had one thing in common, a love of cricket and most other sports and he used to invite me out to play tennis at his home at Gerrards Cross. His Deputy, Ronald Howe, was an elegant, dapper bachelor always immaculately dressed and perfectly groomed. His pleasant, easygoing manner and consideration for others made him a popular figure in the hierarchy of the Yard. The son of a distinguished journalist, he was a classical scholar of Oxford University, decorated for bravery on the Western Front during the First World War; qualified as a barrister, he had entered the Metropolitan Police in 1932 during Lord Trenchard's time in the rank of Chief Constable of the CID, after ten years in the legal branch of the Director of Public Prosecutions. Ronald Howe studied policing methods in America and most European countries and, for twelve years, represented Great Britain on the Executive Committee of Interpol in Paris and can claim much responsibility for its increased activities and universal reputation.

In 1953 he was appointed Deputy Commissioner and, after he retired in 1957, had a most successful career in business. From the outset Ronald Howe was most kind and helpful to me and we remained good friends until his death in 1977. From both Sir Norman Kendal and Sir Ronald Howe I learned much about methods of crime administration and in particular how to examine bulky case files and find quickly the vital part where a problem lay – an ability which was invaluable in later years.

In a strong-room next to the office in which I worked was kept the New Scotland Yard pornographic library and we had charge of this. When I first went to C2, the library was very untidy and unorganised, as material had, for a long time, just been stored in it without any attempt at a filing system. Geoffrey Richardson was another young executive who had joined the staff with me and who eventually became the Secretary – the senior Civil Servant at New Scotland Yard. For two weeks he and I sorted out and attempted to catalogue the contents of the library. Some of it was very innocuous, consisting of books sent in by members of the public, upon which no action was taken; some of it was just unpleasant filth, but other books were well-written erotic pieces, while the safe also contained some good classical 17th and 18th century literature, such as unexpurgated editions of *Gulliver's Travels*, as well as modern books such as *Lady Chatterley's Lover* and *The Well of Loneliness*. The theory was that we kept one copy of every book condemned for destruction by a magistrate, because it was often found that a book condemned under one name would reappear a few months later in a different binding with a different title.

The change in public opinion on the difficult problem of what is obscene has been so great that much of what was kept locked up in 1932 would today be openly sold on railway bookstalls. I have never felt that the test of 'what is likely to corrupt and deprave' is the correct criterion to apply. The test, I suggest, should be 'what is offensive to the man or woman on the Clapham omnibus', as the lawyers speak of the ordinary reasonable person.

My interest in rugby brought me into contact with a handful of rugby enthusiasts on the Civil Service staff at the Yard and together we formed a Rugby XV, calling ourselves 'The Comets', a derivation of 'Commissioner's Office, Metropolitan Police'. We competed in the Civil Service Cup Competition open to teams in the whole of the Civil Service and, to everyone's surprise – not least ourselves – we carried off the trophy in our first year in the competition.

I lived in lodgings in Courtfield Road, SW7, where I had dinner bed and breakfast for 30s. a week, but this was increased to 35s. a week after a short while.

I was not at all well off and was glad to fill my evenings with activities that did not cost money. Luckily I had two such interests – welfare work and the Territorial Army.

The depression of 1931 had now by struck the country with full force and more than two and a half million men were out of work. There were hunger marches from the provinces which led to angry street demonstrations when the marchers reached London. I volunteered to help to look after some of London's vast army of unemployed. There was a soup kitchen close to Waterloo Bridge on the south side of the river where each evening homeless men would converge for a bowl of soup and some shelter for the night. It was depressing work. Between 200 and 300 men congregated there and many were at the end of their tether, living like animals. Most were the worst dregs of London's outcasts, dirty, drunken, immoral and dissolute – but amongst these from time to time one came across men of a different sort – decent, respectable men, thrown out of work by the recession, had been unemployed for a long time through no fault of their own and had now spent all their savings. They were usually middle-aged men of the clerical type and had reached the stage where they could not think of trying to find a job and were concerned only with finding their next meal and the next night's lodgings.

A group of us led by J. G. Paterson, the Chief of the King's Camp, and Ashley Smith, a dentist, took the lease of an empty warehouse close to the soup kitchens. This we furnished with thirty beds and the bare necessities needed for men to sleep and have an evening meal. We invited suitable men from the soup kitchen to come to the Central Link as we called it (the link between starvation and a job) after we had checked their background. Men who came were our guests. We gave them a razor and toothbrush, a suit of clothes, shoes and shirt where necessary, and told them that for six weeks – but no longer – they would be our guests. We would give them a bed for the night: an evening meal: breakfast and a packed lunch. We also posted for them any letters that they wrote applying for jobs. We said that with that security they could concentrate all their efforts on finding a job and in fact over 85 per cent of them did find jobs within the time limit. There were some failures, of course. One or two were picked up by the police, while some just disappeared with the clothes we had given them, but we were satisfied that we helped a little, and certainly we had many letters of thanks from grateful men.

All the finance for this was supplied by *The Times* newspaper, whose manager, Williamson, was one of the helpers in the project.

The Central Link had a short but useful life and Paterson played a large part in the organisation and running of it. A strong, firm, leader, he had a complete contempt of snobbery, hypocrisy, disloyalty and slackness, and was always ready to help those who were down on their luck. Many men had cause to be grateful for the help, advice and friendship that he gave them.

It was impractical for me to continue to serve with the Warwickshire Brigade of the Territorial Army, and so when I went to London I transferred to the 90th (City of London) Brigade, R.A.T.A., whose Headquarters were in Bloomsbury, and of which the Lord Mayor was the Honorary Colonel during his year of office.

The Brigade – or rather my Battery – was most efficient since the Battery CO – Major Robert White – had been a regular gunner officer and the Adjutant of the Brigade. He ran us, as far as he could, as a regular unit and we were expected to parade two evenings a week throughout the year and to attend a weekend exercise at Bordon once a month. Because of his drive and enthusiasm we got into the final of the King's Cup in 1934 but on the day we were not at our best and did not win, though that year I won the Brigade Trophy for reconnaissance work.

I was very sorry that when I went to the Police College, the Metropolitan Police required me to resign my commission on the grounds that, in the event of war, police officers would be in a reserved occupation.

With two nights a week at the Central Link and two nights at Territorial Army Headquarters, my week was a busy one, but I did manage to find some time to read for the Bar examinations but it was not enough and, at the end of 1933, I had to fall back on my annual leave to find the necessary time to study for the Finals.

All my holiday I studied and my last three days were spent sitting the examination. It was a great relief that I passed and in April 1934 I was called to the Bar at the Middle Temple.

I was already starting to build up a wide circle of friends – all as impecunious as myself – and in particular I saw a good deal of my two Cambridge friends, Richard Marriott of the BBC and Pat Renison, who had by that time begun his distinguished career at the Colonial Office, which ended with him being the Governor of Kenya.

During those carefree days before the outbreak of the Second World War I was greatly influenced by Major General Sir Donald Banks, KCB, DSO, MC, TD, a Channel Islander and a man of distinguished appearance and exceptional charm, whom I had met purely by chance at a Territorial Army dance in London. No man could meet Donald Banks without being impressed. Good looking, with great charm and modesty he enjoyed a high prestige in military and civil circles. England has often in her history been served by great men and Donald Banks was one of them. He was a leader with a very clear and lucid brain who oozed integrity, enthusiasm and human sympathy. We became great friends and from him I learned much about successful techniques of administration; and he showed me how tremendous headway could be made, irrespective of the size or magnitude of a problem, by using the right approach, the right spirit of co-operation and enthusiasm. Noted for his personal courage at the age of 24 he was an acting Brigadier during the First World War with a DSO, an MC, and a Croix de Guerre. On demobilisation in 1919 he joined the Civil Service and soon became Private Secretary to the Secretary to the General Post Office and then to four successive Postmaster Generals. In 1931 he was appointed Controller of the Post Office Savings Bank, and in 1934, at the age of 43 he was knighted and became the first Director General of the Post Office. Always receptive to innovations and new ideas, he introduced TIM, 999, Greetings Telegrams and the neo-Georgian style of post office buildings, ultimately organising the first air mail service between England and Australia. In 1936 he became Head of the Air Ministry and his competency in that field ensured that our factories were put on a war footing and prepared to manufacture the Spitfires and Hurricanes which saved our civilisation during those dark autumn days of 1940.

As Deputy Adjutant General in the rank of Major General on Lord Gort's staff attached to the British Expeditionary Force in France in June 1940 and with a reputation for getting things done, he personally organised the evacuation from Boulogne at a time of much chaos. The Prime Minister, Mr Winston Churchill, was fully aware of Donald's vast potential and had a great opinion of him, asking him to form the Department of Petroleum Warfare. The success of PLUTO (Pipe Line Under the Ocean) and the more limited success of FIDO (Fog Investigation Dispersal Organisation), were the amazing result of Donald's resourcefulness, energy and ingenuity, which were devotedly aimed at the single purpose of winning the war. I have a lasting affection and respect for the memory of this outstanding personality whose career must be classed as brilliant.

But all this was in the future and at the time I first met him, he was head of the Post Office, working very closely with Sir Kingsley Wood, the Post Master General. Donald, with his wife Dorothy, lived in a large house north of the Park in Bayswater and I was frequently invited to dine there or to accompany them for weekends in the country. He had a daughter, Dawn, then a small girl but, at that time, no son and I am inclined to believe that it was because of this that he 'took me under his wing'. I was at the time 'deb-dancing' but through the Banks I received invitations to a number of official functions which I attended with them.

Meanwhile, in 1933 Lord Trenchard's famous Annual Report for 1932 was published by HM Stationery Office. It was the first intimation to the public of his intention to create a Police College and to acquire, as Lord Trenchard put it, 'for a Police Force a dignity and professional status which it had never enjoyed'. This was followed almost immediately by the issue of a Government White Paper in which the College and the equally controversial Short Service Recruitment Scheme were announced. The central feature of the new scheme was the selection and training officers who were to be recruited, partly 'by fairly rapid promotion for outstanding men who join as constables' and partly by 'direct recruitment into officer posts of men who have acquired good educational qualifications before appointment and are selected as suitable in respect of personality and physique.' Lord Trenchard's College Plan was headline news – *Punch* and cartoonists had great fun at the expense of the academic policeman. Much of the comment was favourable, although some sections of the press tried to bring in the class issue and others forecast disaster.

Within the Force the scheme was severely criticised by men who firmly believed that the creation of a so-called 'officer class' destined to fill the higher posts would lead to the exclusion of the experienced rankers: all but a few emphasised that the only way to learn police duty was in the streets and went on to add that it took many years. They chose to forget, or did not realise, that two thirds of the

College entrants were to come from the Force itself. In fact, during the life span of the College the overall figures were heavily weighted in favour of serving officers of the Metropolitan Police, for of the 197 who were selected for the College in the five years of its existence, 123 were serving constables in the Metropolitan Police and, of the 74 who passed the Open Examination or Selection Board, 18 were also serving policemen.

It was necessary to have the backing of Parliament and the Government and, after some lenghty debates in the House of Commons and the House of Lords, the Royal Assent was given to the Metropolitan Police Bill, authorising the formation of the new College.

There were to be three different forms of entry; and the first was by open competitive examination: secondly, there was selection based upon a candidate's qualifications, (rather on the lines of the conditions of Rhodes Scholars to Oxford) which took into account, not only the educational qualifications, but other qualifications: thirdly, there was selection from the ranks of the Police itself. Time showed that these three different forms of entry were satisfactory – balance being held between them. It has to be remembered that the Hendon Police College catered solely for the Metropolitan Police but, from the outset, the Home Office hoped that its influence would be felt by the provincial forces. In July 1937 at a Passing-Out Parade at the College, the then Home Secretary, Sir Samuel Hoare, said:

'I suppose that the founders of the College had very much in mind future developments and the hope that in time the College would become, not only an institution of the Metropolitan Police, but the Police College for the whole country and for the whole Empire.'

To hasten the opening of the College a country club at Hendon in North London was purchased and, after certain structural alterations and adaptations, this proved well suited for its new role.

It was clearly in the interests of Lord Trenchard and necessary for the success of the College, that he should appoint as Commandant a man, not only of exceptional ability, great integrity and strength of character, but with the gift of inspiration too – a hard man to find. Lord Trenchard wisely chose Colonel G. H. R. Halland CIE, OBE, who since 1931 had been Chief Constable of Lincolnshire, following distinguished service in the Indian Police, as Principal of the Punjab Police Training College. In 1938 Colonel Halland became first an Inspector of Constabulary and later Inspector General of Police in Ceylon, and he was succeeded as Commandant by Major (later Sir) John Ferguson CBE, who had enjoyed a distinguished career in the Army before becoming in 1932 a Chief Constable in the Metropolitan Police at Lord Trenchard's invitation. Appointed a Deputy Assistant Commissioner in 1935 and Chief Constable of the Sussex Joint Police in 1943, he finally became Chief Constable of Kent in 1946. Both Halland and Ferguson were admirably fitted to head the College. Eloquent and inspiring speakers, wise and courteous men but good disciplinarians, and with minds remarkable for their scope, they set the tone of the new establishment. Both belonged to an era which has sadly passed.

The first course of 32 students assembled in May 1934, a second course started in September 1934 and a third in September 1935 when the first course passed out. Originally courses were of fifteen months' duration, but this was later extended to eighteen months. In all six courses were held before the College, alas, was closed in 1939 on the outbreak of war.

One looks for turning points in all careers and 1934 was for me a very memorable year, for by then I was convinced that the best prospects for a career in the Police Service now lay through the new College at Hendon. When the scheme had first been announced I had consulted my superiors about making an application, but was advised to remain on the civil staff. I accepted the advice, which was well meant, but as time went on I realised that I was making a mistake and I therefore applied for a place at Hendon but, to my dismay, was turned down on medical grounds when they found in one leg a varicose vein, the existence of which was unknown to me. Declared fit after surgery, I applied again and joined the third course in September, 1935.

This particular course was made up of 34 students and I was one of the five University graduates selected. Nineteen had been chosen from serving members of the Metropolitan Police, eight from the results of a competitive Civil Service examination held the previous June, and two were Indian Police Cadets specially chosen by the Nawab of Bhopal, one of the great Hindu Princes of India. I soon settled down, working with beaver-like industry and playing with zest, so successfully that, after one term, I found myself appointed a Student Station Officer – a sort of prefect – and editor of the College Journal. I played most games for the College at one time or another and I thoroughly enjoyed my time there. The years at New Scotland Yard stood me in good stead for I knew most of the senior officers and I probably had more experience of police administration than any of the other students.

We were taught criminal law, studied the detailed procedures of the Metropolitan Police and listened to lectures given by experienced officers from practically every branch and department of the police and by experts from other civil service and defence departments.

We also made visits to police stations, courts of justice, the information room, the map room and the criminal record office, while the syllabus also included a course of driving tuition and car maintenance at the Metropolitan Police Driving School which had recently been opened adjacent to the College.

At that time there were no arrangements for attachments to other Forces in this country but, through the Commandant, privately I arranged visits in the vacations to the Headquarters of Birmingham City Police, to Manchester, Liverpool, and Lancashire, then in the throes of re-organisation by a new Chief Constable, Captain (later Sir) A. F. Hordern AFC. The choice of the Lancashire Forces was easy to make because I was at that time courting a Lancashire lass, who eventually became my wife.

Apart from the interest I naturally had in the organisation of the police forces I visited, the matter that struck me most was the appalling amount of unemployment in the Midlands and the North. I met married men aged 30 who had never worked since they left school some 15 years before. At each street corner in those ugly Lancashire mill towns one saw men congregating in groups, just standing, sitting or lounging with nothing to do. It made me feel strongly that the way of life in this country needed a radical re-organisation and I found myself out of sympathy with the political beliefs of many of my friends and relations.

At Hendon we lived well, for the building was comfortably furnished and the food excellent. We followed the lines of an army mess by dining in dinner jackets four evenings a week and were left in no doubt that we were 'officers', an elitist philosophy not previously encountered in the Police Service. Fifteen months swept by and in December 1936 we took our final examinations. By then the new Commissioner was Air Vice Marshal Sir Philip Game, a former Governor of New South Wales, who had served with Lord Trenchard at the Air Ministry; and he, accompanied by Sir John Simon, a former Attorney General and later Lord Chancellor, then Home Secretary, came to the College Passing-Out Parade on Saturday 19th December, 1936, when I was presented with the Baton of Honour.

It was while I was at the Police College that His Majesty King George V died and all members of the College were required to help police the route of the funeral cortege as it passed from the Palace to Paddington railway station on its way to Windsor. In 1935 the police arrangements for manning the route from the Palace to St. Paul's for King George V's Jubilee celebrations had been excellent, but then there had been plenty of time to make the necessary arrangements. On that occasion I had, as a Territorial Army Officer, helped with my battery to line the route in the City of London. The lack of advance planning meant that the police arrangements for the funeral were very inadequate, while it was not expected that more people would come to line the route, on a cold February day, than had come to watch the Jubilee procession in the previous summer.

I was given nineteen men and told to keep the large island at Hyde Park corner clear except for five hundred blinded ex-soldiers from St. Dunstan's. We were taken to see the route the day before and that night I told the Commandant that I could not do the job with a hundred and ninety men. One had to try, but on the day the whole operation was almost a disaster. People came from every direction in their thousands, and the route at Hyde Park corner was for a time completely blocked. We just, but only just, managed to clear a narrow path for the cortege, which eventually arrived at Paddington over an hour late. When the main part of the procession actually passed me I was jammed so tightly against the blinded men I was trying to protect that I could not turn to salute the coffin.

In January, 1937, I was formally attested as a police officer with the warrant number 125489 and the Divisional Number PC 640C. In common with all Hendon men who had not previously been serving police officers, I was required to spend eight months as a constable and four months as a sergeant before actually taking up the responsibilities of the rank specially created for Police College graduates, namely that of Junior Station Inspector. I was lucky enough to be posted to Vine Street in 'C' Division where I thoroughly enjoyed my first months working in the area rich in money, crime and vice.

In April of that year, while I was undergoing my practical training, I was married to Joanna Wharton, the daughter of an Oldham doctor and granddaughter of Daniel Orme, a Lancashire engineer who, as a young man, had invented both the first 'penny-in-the-slot' gas meter and also the Orme counter which can still be found in use on spinning and weaving looms in the older mills.

We took the lease of a first floor flat at Lancaster Gate, at a cost of £135 per year including rates, central heating and hot water. How cheap that seems, compared to present prices, but my income was only £200 a year plus £63 a year rent allowance. This, with my wife's allowance of £100 from her mother, was our total income and on this we lived adequately, though not well. We could not afford a motor car, but then none of our friends had one either and on special occasions we borrowed one from our parents. There was no television and evenings when I was off duty, which was not often, were spent playing bridge with Ted Dodd (later Sir Edward Dodd) and his wife, Eve. They lived close by and he was at that time a Station Inspector at Vine Street and technically my boss.

We paid our daily ten pence an hour to help keep the flat clean and, once a week, we went to one of the small but good continental restaurants that then existed in Soho, for a meal which cost 18s. for the two of us, plus 4s. for a bottle of claret. The postman called four times a day (if one posted a letter to a London address in the morning, it would arrive at its destination the same day) and the milkman twice. Both, like a policeman, worked a six day week.

Because of the awkward hours of work, it was difficult for us to mix socially with friends outside the police service and, as I worked six days a week, it was even more difficult to leave London and spend some time in the country. So our activities outside the police were much limited.

However, there were two evening relaxations which we much enjoyed although we could not really afford either. We joined the Gargoyle Club, then owned by David Tennant and his wife the actress Hermione Baddeley. It was at that time a very respectable night club – and not a strip club as it now is – with its large Matisse painting on the stairs, it was patronised mainly by actors and artists and we enjoyed the food, the dancing and the company.

We were also members of the Players Theatre, then in its original home in Covent Garden and it is difficult to believe that Leonard Sachs, now so well known to television audiences as the Chairman of the Victorian Music Hall programme 'The Good Old Days', was even then Chairman of the Players Theatre. This was a small and select club, the members mainly actors and intellectuals and the repartee between the Chairman and members of the audience was as witty and amusing as the show. The backbone of the performances were the permanent artistes, Archie Harradine, Joan Sterndale Bennett and Alec Clunes, but there were always one or two visiting artistes. Here we saw the first professional performance of Peter Ustinov, then a stripling of seventeen, who gave two magnificently contrasting performances, first as a retired female opera star making a come-back and then as the Bishop of Limpopo preaching to his flock.

Working a beat on foot as a uniformed constable in the West End of London was a very interesting and, on occasions, an amusing experience, though there were times in the middle of the night when it could be very monotonous. I am very glad that I did not have to do it for too long.

ONE POLICEMAN'S STORY

The hours of duty were, the early turn from 6.0 am to 2.0 pm, the late turn 2.0 pm to 10.0 pm, and night duty 10.0 pm to 6.0. am, all awkward times to fit into a normal social life. I was working when my friends were not, or off duty when my friends were working. Evenings when I was on early turn or on night duty, were spoilt either way because I wanted either to go to bed early, or had to leave home at 9.0 pm, while when on night duty sleeping and meal times were all upset. As a consequence we tended to live our social life with police friends who had similar awkward hours of work.

I soon realised what a wonderful disguise a police uniform is. Your friends pass you by in the street without giving you a second glance, and I was often on duty in Bond Street, Piccadilly or St. James Street where I saw friends shopping or going to their clubs, but they never recognised me until I spoke to them.

The man on the beat is now almost a thing of the past, but there is no doubt that on foot you see more than from a car, while people and particularly shop keepers can give valuable information to the PC if he stops and talks to them.

In the day time there was not a great deal of routine work to do except to keep the traffic moving and to prevent beggars and hawkers being a nuisance, but at night in the West End there was always something happening, drunks and fights, allegations of theft, prostitutes and beggars accosting passers by, were all prevalent in an area where revellers come to spend their money and predators come to take it away by any means fair or foul.

The year 1937 was Coronation Year and the West End became particularly crowded with large numbers of visitors both from home and overseas and these attracted many criminals to London. Crowds became dense and, for the first time, a loudspeaker was installed on Eros in Piccadilly Circus. Throughout Coronation week I was in charge of this, directing traffic and keeping pedestrians on the move. 'The only entrance to the Underground now open is in Jermyn Street. Keep moving please. Mind your handbags and your children.' I must have said it several thousand times.

While on this work I was interviewed by a young reporter working for the *Star* – a London evening paper now long since defunct – who wrote a piece about the University PC on Eros. Many years later – in the 1950s – I wrote an article for the *Field* on the problems of dealing with poachers in Lancashire. When I called to see Wilson Stephens, the highly successful editor, he then reminded me that he was that young reporter.

After the Coronation fever had died down I was assigned to what was colloquially called, 'The Prostitute Patrol', working from six o'clock in the evening to two o'clock in the morning. Our brief was to keep the streets clear of offences by prostitutes, drunks, beggars and the like, and we were expected to make at least one arrest each night. Usually we had made enough arrests by midnight to be given two hours off duty, so as to be ready to attend the court hearings next morning. The trivial charges were all disposed of in quick-fire routine, charges read, guilty pleas accepted, the briefest of evidence given, and the case disposed of 'Fined £2.' By and large we could rely on being released from Court by about eleven o'clock and home before mid-day with the afternoon free. What was more, there was a rule that anyone having to attend court after night duty was allowed four hours off duty at a convenient time. So with taking two hours off duty each night and being given a 'credit' of four hours for attending court on the following morning, by the end of the month I had a credit of some 48 hours, which gave me a week's leave on full pay.

In the thirties the licensing hours were much shorter than they are today. Restrictive laws are a stimulus to ingenuity and in no direction was greater ingenuity exercised than in attempting to clothe with a show of legality the sale or supply of intoxicating liquor outside permitted hours by the so-called 'Social Clubs' which had sprung up in London, particularly in the West End.

Associated with these bogus clubs were the Bottle Parties and, during the autumn of 1937 I was attached to the Clubs' Office and spent some time assigned to law enforcement affecting Bottle Parties. These bottle parties owed their existence to the fact that one could not legally obtain a drink after 11.30 pm and, to get round the legislation, club owners devised a system whereby in theory members consumed their own drink which had previously been purchased during licensing hours. The rules were that members gave their orders by telephone during permitted hours to a club official and he passed on their requirements to a firm of licensing victuallers which, in turn, reserved and marked the ordered drink in the name of the customer. When the drinks were asked for a boy messenger was sent to make the necessary collection. This was the procedure commonly carried out by the reputable establishments at this time.

There were, however, many other Clubs which were conducted with an entire disregard of the liquor licensing laws and where the only qualification necessary was a well filled wallet. Once admission had been gained to an establishment of this kind, and an entrance fee paid, a bottle of whisky, gin or whatever was taken from the Club's own stocks and appropriated in the name of the customer for which he paid a very high price. It was considered desirable to prevent prominent and foreign pleasure seekers from being fleeced by the unscrupulous individuals running these clubs, so I was sent to investigate these dubious establishments. While some of these clubs were amusing and gay, most were really very dull and uninspiring.

One of the bottle party clubs which I was required to penetrate and keep under observation was the El Morocco Club, run by the ex British and World Welterweight, Ted Kid Lewis. My instructions were to gain admission on a night when it was to be raided. I knew this would not be an easy matter and so to allay suspicion I was authorised to take my wife Joanna, two girls friends and a male colleague in my mother-in-law's large Daimler car. Joanna and I assumed the name of Mr and Mrs Hadley-Wood – actually the name of our golf club – and using this ruse we gained access. I did not tell my companions that the doorman, a thoroughly unpleasant individual had previously been convicted for serious bodily assault upon police officers who had entered his domain by subterfuge. As luck would have it, very few people patronised the club that evening and this made our small party conspicuous. The ex pugilist and his wife invited themselves to our table, made quite a fuss of us and in the process consumed much of our drink. Promptly at two o'clock in the morning the police raided the premises and the Lewis's friendship changed instantly to visible hatred as they realised our true identity. Anticipating violence, my wife and the two girls dived under the table and refused to emerge until they had been assured it was safe for them to leave the club under police protection. Shortly afterwards I was officially commended by the Commissioner for this work but to me securing the admission of police officers under such undesirable conditions was a dispiriting experience, although the only way in which offences of this kind could be detected.

As a constable, alone in the evenings and at night, I soon learnt to have confidence in myself and found out when it is wiser not to see anything and to look the other way. It is not necessary to be officious and often, if one steps in when an argument arises, particularly among people who have had some drink, one only makes matters worse. The older men were wise in keeping a restraining arm on us younger, more hot-headed men.

There were the regular respectable people on the streets that we came to know, such as the LCC street cleaners, for in those days the streets of the West End were regularly washed at night. We got to know the truck drivers coming through every night on their way to Covent Garden and the voluble early morning char-women on their way from Fulham or Lambeth to clean the offices in the West End. I met some good cockney types with interesting stories of life to tell and there was much leg-pulling, not only with these people, but among the policemen themselves.

One very cold February night with snow flurries, I was in Regent Street when I saw a black shape in a door way and, shining my torch in it, much to my surprise I saw it was a live cormorant. Calling the man from the next beat, we caught it and wrapping it in a policeman's cape, we took it to the station where the sergeant on duty was a bad-tempered, uncouth and unpopular man. It was our responsibility to deposit found property with the Sergeant, so we took him the somewhat unusual parcel and placed it on his desk. 'What have you got there?' he gruffly demanded.

'Some found property, Sergeant.'

'What is it?'

'One live cormorant or shag' we said, taking off the cape and letting the bird waddle up and down on his desk, making its messes. The Sergeant's reaction was to be expected. 'Take the f—ing thing out of here!' was the least unprintable expression he used.

Eventually we had to get the police van to take the bird to St. James's Park and return it to the lake there. Whether the necessary entry was ever made in the Found Property Book I do not know, but the Sergeant never again spoke nicely to me.

I feel I scored a right and left, for shortly afterwards I found a live lobster in Jermyn Street in the early morning but this never got to the police station for it had fallen off a van taking fish to a nearby restaurant and I was able quickly to restore it to its owners.

In 1937 the great houses of Park Lane were disappearing as demolition gangs moved in and large hotels took their place; but Londonderry House remained and here Lord and Lady Londonderry gave glittering receptions attended by politicians, statesmen, ambassadors and the whole establishment of London. In particular, they always gave a reception for the Government of the day on the eve of the new session of Parliament.

In the autumn of 1937 when I reported for duty one day, the Sergeant in charge of the relief said, 'PC 640, you've been to a University. Have you got a white tie and tails?' And when I replied that I had, he said, 'Right boy, Londonderry House for you tomorrow night. Be there at 7.30 pm and report to the butler. Look after the guests at the Government reception.'

So on the following evening, together with an older Detective Sergeant, I arrived at the stipulated time. The Sergeant had been before and we walked through all the reception rooms, noting the entrances and exits and the positions of back stairs. At 8.00 pm we were shown to the servants' hall by a flunkey. In a private room a uniformed maid served us a good dinner with a very good bottle of claret in which the housekeeper joined us. The butler came in from time to time for a quick drink, but as the Londonderry's were entertaining friends to dinner, he was not able to dine with us.

At 9.00 pm we went upstairs to await the arrival of the guests. Shortly before 10.00 pm Lord and Lady Londonderry, with the Prime Minister and Mrs Neville Chamberlain, stationed themselves at the top of the stairs and received the guests as they arrived. Lady Londonderry was a magnificent sight, a good-looking woman wearing, not only a tiara, a beautiful necklace and earrings, but also a large stomacher made entirely and solely of large diamonds.

Among the guests were a number of my friends and I must admit that, not only did I enjoy the party, but I do not really think I helped in any way to add to the security of the house or those present that evening!

Little did I think at that time that thirteen years later my wife and I would go as guests to Londonderry House on the day before Lady Londonderry, as the wife of the Lord Lieutenant of County Durham, presented my wife at court.

I was also detailed to be the Police Constable outside the door of Lord Belper's house in Berkeley Square when their daughter, the Hon Lavinia Strutt, left to marry the Duke of Norfolk and I vowed to myself that one day when my daughter was married, I would have a policeman outside the door – and I did.

Both the Duke of Norfolk and Lord Londonderry were much amused when, years later as a Chief Constable, I told them these stories.

On other occasions I was assigned for protection duty, known at Vine Street as being 'On the Gun', at the home of the Duke of Abercorn, then Governor of Northern Ireland. I was given specific instructions to see that no unauthorised person came within a certain distance of the Duke, for ever since the assassination in London, outside his house in Eaton Square, of Field Marshal Sir Henry Wilson, Chief of the Imperial General Staff by Sinn Feiners in June 1922, it had been the practice of the Metropolitan Police to guard the Duke whenever he was in London.

The Constable assigned to this particular duty was issued with a Webley and Scott automatic pistol and a sealed envelope containing the requisite ammunition. There was an element of farce in the compulsory signing of a receipt certifying that one had received a SEALED envelope containing so many rounds of ammunition, then on return from duty, one had to return the envelope still sealed. Inconceivable but true.

After eight months training as a Constable, I then had four months as a Sergeant. I reported for duty one evening as a Constable and was instructed to report the following evening in the rank of

The Metropolitan Police

Sergeant. I was given some sets of chevrons which I took home and gave to Joanna, asking her to sew them on my uniform, ready for wear that evening, with no more instruction than that. I then went off to court to give evidence. Joanna had no idea where the stripes should go and proceeded to walk solemnly round the streets of Paddington with my jacket over one arm, stripes in her hand, looking for a policeman. At length she met a constable and asked him the vital question, 'Where should a Sergeant put his stripes?' The constable replied gallantly that he would like to tell her but perhaps he'd better not. I must add that the stripes were sewn on in the right place eventually.

In January 1938, on completion of my practical training, I was posted to Walham Green Sub-Division of 'B' or Chelsea Division, in the rank of Junior Station Inspector. I had hoped I might be sent to a much more glamorous district, for the sub-division consisted of the Borough of Fulham, with a population of 160,000 inhabitants, mostly working class living in squalid 19th century Victorian property. Fulham had then (and still has) a strong Socialist Council, progressive in its ideals and active in the interests of those it represented. Any adverse feelings I had previously entertained about my new posting were soon dispelled when I realised the many varied and interesting aspects of police work Fulham presented, for the West End and the fashionable and prosperous districts of Mayfair and Kensington with their large houses were within easy reach of Fulham's criminal fraternity.

Street bookmakers abounded in those densely populated streets. The Borough included the football grounds of Chelsea and Fulham Clubs, as well as Earls Court and its skating rink, boxing tournaments and International Motor Exhibitions. These were the days when the masses flocked to Earls Court to listen to the inflammatory speeches of the Communist and Fascist Party leaders, which led to clashes of a kind not seen in this country since the Chartist disturbances of the mid 19th century. They were a confounded nuisance to the police because, on each occasion, precautions had to be taken lest the opposing party should attempt to break up the rally. As a police Inspector, I had on numerous occasions to spend the whole of Sunday afternoon, either on duty at the meeting, or waiting in reserve with a large number of policemen, in case trouble broke out.

Several times I heard Sir Oswald Mosley speak and each time I was most impressed with his air of confidence and leadership and the way he addressed the meetings. Although one might not agree with all he said, I could not help but admire his lucid style and the way he marshalled facts and arguments. I always felt that he would have made a great success at the Bar; he was a great orator but, at the same time, I felt that he was devoid of any human sympathy. Little did I think at that time that in a very few years he would come into my life again during the War.

Before 1939 there were 200 police officers in the Walham Green Sub-Division and I was second-in-command of the station. The men on the whole were a good crowd a typical cross-section of the sort of men to be found in any police force. In my role as Deputy Sub-Divisional Commander I worked closely and harmoniously with them, though I was careful always to keep myself a little aloof. During the football season Saturday afternoons were reserved for football at the Chelsea or Fulham grounds, according to which team was playing at home. My chief always attended on duty and in uniform for he enjoyed the game as a bonus. Arrests were made from time to time but trouble, when it did come, flared up spontaneously and had not the heavy overtones of violence, premeditated and deliberate, which has marred football in recent years.

My chief, a man of happy and carefree disposition, was nearing the end of his service and did only the minimum that was required of him. His daily routine never varied. In the office promptly at nine he completed his paper work by 10.30 am, then after a quick stroll round part of his domain he went to the canteen at 11.15 am and there he stayed drinking beer and playing darts until 1 pm, when it was time for lunch in his quarters. He reappeared at 4 pm to sign letters or reports made ready for him and that, by and large, was the end of his day's work, except for a late look in to see all was well in the station. Content to leave in my hands the real supervision of the men and the operational control, he let me plan and conduct my own campaign of duties and strategy to deal with the petty yet chronic police problems of the district. I found this a great mental stimulus and much to my liking and later it became apparent just how much I had benefited from this extra and unexpected bonus of responsibility. It was a most enlightening experience and I never begrudged the long hours that the responsibility demanded.

There was, at that time, a great deal of bad housing in Fulham and many of the houses near the police station were bug-infested. On a hot summer's night many families would sleep on the steps leading up to the house rather than in their bedrooms.

Yet on the edge of all this poverty and squalor there was the smart Hurlingham country club, with its two polo pitches, tennis courts, croquet lawns and swimming pool. We saw numbers of large chauffeur driven cars travelling to the balls held at the club and, in the early morning, strings of polo ponies were exercised in the streets and one knew that more money was being spent on each pony than was available to feed a whole family in many of the houses they passed.

I remembered what I had seen of poverty in Birmingham as a youth and in Lancashire when I had visited that county and it strengthened my belief that the country was bound up with the fortunes of the Labour Party.

At that time Joe De Palma was Mayor of Fulham. He was a strong supporter of the Labour Party and he and I had many discussions on the future of England. In 1938 the Conservative MP for Fulham died, and Dr Edith Summerskill, now a Life Peeress, stood for the first time in the Labour cause.

I was in charge of the police arrangements to cover the meetings which were very well attended because women candidates were then a rarity and it was before the days of T.V. She greatly impressed me and there was much jubilation in Fulham when she was elected.

I have had, of course, to be careful not to show the colour of my political skin, but even a policeman can have his opinions and beliefs and although I have always had many friends in the Conservative Party and also some who were Liberals, I have at heart been a supporter of the moderate leaders of the Labour Party though in recent years I have become disenchanted with the pressures of the Left Wing.

One of the most unpleasant jobs that a police officer has to do is to break the news to someone that a husband, wife or child has been killed in a motor accident. I have said many times that the quoting of accident statistics rarely brings home to people the tragedies that occur daily on the roads of this country. The most important statistic is the figure 'one'. When someone related to you or someone you know well loses their life in an accident, then the true meaning of accident statistics is really impressed on the mind.

While at Walham Green I was called to a fatal accident where a bus had knocked over and killed a cyclist on his way home from work. It was, I fear, entirely the man's own fault for, in a moment of thoughtlessness, he had turned off the main road into the side road in which he lived. After I had sent the body to the mortuary and obtained particulars from the driver of the bus and the witnesses, I had to break the news to the dead man's relatives.

I had obtained his name and address from documents in his pocket and I shall never forget the next half-hour. I called at the next door house and asked the woman the circumstances of her neighbours. She told me that they were a very respectable happy couple who had no children and that the husband was about to retire and they had just bought a bungalow at some seaside town on the south coast.

Together we went to the next house and, as gently as possible, broke the news to the woman that her husband, whom she was expecting home for his evening meal, would not be coming home again. The tragedy really hit me when I noticed his meal waiting for him on the table in a spotlessly clean living room. Ever since, that scene has been as clear in my mind as it was almost forty years ago – quite the most unhappy moment in the whole of my police career.

It was not necessary for me to attend the post mortem on the body but, because I anticipated that sooner or later in my police career I would have to attend one, I went to the mortuary on the next day and asked the pathologist if I might be present. As my attendance was not required – except to identify the body to the pathologist, I could walk out when I wanted to do so.

The pathologist was a young man, just starting on a career which was to be very successful, for his name is Keith Simpson, today the Professor of Forensic Medicine at the University of London. He was most kind and helpful to me, explaining the procedure and the work he was doing and I have many times since been grateful for that early introduction into the interesting but less aesthetic side of police work.

Following the halcyon days of Munich in 1938, the international situation had deteriorated so rapidly that it became necessary to prepare the police machine for war conditions and a new branch was set up at Scotland Yard for this purpose. Shortly afterwards I was appointed Police Liaison Officer to the Fulham Borough Council and this involved the additional duties of ARP planning and organisation for the Sub-Division. During this hectic period the First Police Reserve of retired police officers was reactivated and steps were taken to establish a second Reserve comprising full-time paid Special Constables, as well as a Third Reserve of War Reserve Officers – men over 30 recruited for the duration.

On the morning of Sunday, 3rd September 1939, when Neville Chamberlain's disenchanted voice announced over the radio that once again we were at war with Germany, events moved with astonishing rapidity. Many of our peace-time duties disappeared and we soon found ourselves making a general sweep of the enemy alien population, as well as enforcing the new black-out lighting regulations and sandbagging and strengthening police stations with large baulks of timber. All car head-lamps had to be hooded while lighted street lamps became a thing of the past. Barrage balloons floated in the sky to foul enemy aircraft, while National Registration cards and gas masks had to be issued and carried.

At Walham Green we had to recruit very quickly 250 War Reserve policemen and among those that I recruited were the whole of the Chelsea and Fulham football teams, but they did not prove very amenable to discipline and we soon got rid of most of them. Having recruited the men, we had to set up training courses and it was some time before we even had uniforms for them. All through the winter of 1939, there was really insufficient work for them and many were allowed to return to their ordinary peacetime jobs on the understanding that they would come back to us when required. The difficulty with police work is that it needs men who want to do the job. It is unwise – and indeed unsafe – to have men in police uniform with police powers who do not want to be police officers. Conscripts will not do: we must have volunteers.

Unfortunately, whilst at Walham Green I suffered badly from the behaviour of the Superintendent in charge of the Division. The Division was divided into three Sub-Divisions, each of which at that time was under the control of a Sub-Divisional Inspector and each had a Hendon College man as second-in-command. We Hendon men were inexperienced but hard-working and enthusiastic, but for some inexplicable reason the Superintendent seemed to enjoy finding fault with everything we did, calling our attention in writing to every error, however small. Each Wednesday it was the duty of the three Sub-Divisional Inspectors (one of whom incidentally later became Sir Charles Martin, the Chief Constable of Liverpool and one of HM Inspectors of Constabulary), and the three Station Inspectors, as we Hendon men were called, to report to the Superintendent's office to collect in cash the pay for the men of the Sub-Division. Before being given the money however, we were required to stand to attention in the Superintendent's Office, while he harangued us, sometimes for as much as an hour, about the sins and omissions of the men of the Division. The trouble was that he was a paper man who had spent most of his service in office work, and he had no ability to manage men. He loved detailed clerical work and spent a great deal of time when he visited the Station reading and examining with great care all the books relating to the running of the Station. The Occurrence Book, the Charge Book, the Lost and Found Property Register all were given his rapt attention and any faults found – and there usually were some of a minor nature – were commented on in red ink in the margin. A sour individual, he never had a kind word to say to any of us, nor did he ever compliment us on any good piece of work. Basically, I believe, he was unsure of himself which was probably the root cause of the trouble. Because I had a better education than most of his officers I became the special target for his continual criticism, to such an extent that I had to receive medical treatment for anxiety neurosis. The breaking point came after a very successful raid on Walham Green Social Club, which I had organised when instead of praise, I was questioned about the accuracy of some minor expenditure I had incurred and reclaimed, with the implication that I was cheating.

There is within the Police Service a Discipline Code which it is the responsibility of all serving policeman to observe. Should there be a breach of any section, the alleged offender can be punished by the Chief of Police, the punishment ranging from dismissal, through demotion or a pecuniary fine, to a caution for minor offences. Most of the sections of the Code deal with neglect of duty, discourtesy to the public, conduct prejudicial to the good name of the Force and so on. One section very rarely used, deals with the offence of a senior officer using 'overbearing conduct to a subordinate'. Fully aware of this important section, I eventually submitted a short report to the Deputy Assistant Commissioner in charge of the District, alleging overbearing conduct on the part of the Superintendent – the first and only time during the whole of my police service that I have known this section to be invoked by anyone. The report had to go through the Sub-Divisional Inspector to the Superintendent and thence to the Deputy Assistant Commissioner. When the Sub-Divisional Inspector saw the report, he became a frightened man. He begged me to tear it up saying it would be the end of my career – while he feared for his own position too. I was, however, adamant as I had already made up my mind to resign from the police service rather than continue to be treated as I had been. Three days later I was told that the Deputy Assistant Commissioner wanted to see me in his office at Hyde Park Police Station. This was it! The die was cast. The Deputy Assistant Commissioner at this time was Jack Nott-Bower. He treated me very kindly, asking me to explain in detail what was troubling me. I was with him an hour and unburdened my soul to him. He was most sympathetic and, at the end, at his request I agreed to withdraw the report and accusations and leave the matter in his hands. A few days later I was given a message, 'Would I kindly call to see the Superintendent at his office that afternoon?' This in itself showed a change of attitude for previously the modus operandi had been an abrupt instruction to be at the Superintendent's office at a specific time. On arrival at his office I was invited to sit down. He told me that he understood I had withdrawn my accusation, and that the Deputy Assistant Commissioner had discussed the matter with him. He said he would like to know what had gone wrong in our relationship and why I thought he had treated me badly. Feeling that I had everything to gain and nothing to lose by being frank, I began by saying I had served in the Division under his command for two years, that I had been in his office each week during that period and that this was the first time he had invited me to sit down. I then told him straight that he didn't treat any of us properly and that all his officers not only disliked him but were frightened of him. I cited a number of occasions when he had in my opinion treated others, as well as myself, badly, and I said that because of the lack of trust he had engendered, his officers did not confide in him and certain matters were happening in the Division, which would cause trouble for him should they ever come to light. He tried to get me to be more specific but I refused to be drawn further, saying I was not a tale-bearer, but suggested however, that he ought to keep a wary eye on the work and behaviour of some officers in the Division. Throughout the interview I was most careful to be courteous and the Superintendent took it all meekly. We parted by shaking hands and with him saying he hoped we would be friends in the future. I was asked to keep the conversation confidential and this I did, merely informing my own Sub-Divisional Inspector that we had had an amicable discussion.

From then on the Superintendent was a changed man in his treatment to all of us. Every Wednesday there were chairs in his office for our weekly conference and whenever he visited Walham Green he had a smile and a cheerful word for the officer on duty. A year later came the sequel. A telex message was received at Walham Green saying tersely that SDI 'X', SI 'Y' and Inspector 'Z', all of Chelsea Sub-Division, had been suspended from duty while certain disciplinary charges were investigated, and that Station Inspector St. Johnston was to report for duty at Chelsea forthwith to take charge of the Sub-Division.

The officers concerned had not been guilty of any heinous offences, but the Officer in Charge of the Chelsea Sub-Division had wanted to retire at the outbreak of War and had not been allowed to do so. He then became slack and only did the bare minimum of work taking no interest in seeing that the job was done well or that the men were properly supervised. Moreover, he was in the habit of having drinking sessions with his cronies late at night in the police canteen, and on one or two occasions they had girl friends with them whom they had later taken home in police cars – even on one occasion when no other transport was available, in the police van used to transport prisoners. When this was discovered, they were suspended from duty, and I had to take charge of the Sub-Division.

It was all too clear from the outset that much needed to be done to improve the efficiency of the Sub-Division. This was not difficult, for everything was in poor shape. On the first evening I discovered that the afternoon shift of some sixteen constables who were supposed to be on their beats until 10.00 pm, were all in the police station by 9.30 pm, spending the last half hour pretending to be writing reports, but in fact, just sitting gossiping and smoking or drinking in the canteen.

The books in the station in spite of the attention of the Superintendent, were badly kept and I soon discovered that there were serious discrepancies in the treatment of found property deposited at the station.

Outside the station police work was very slack, and many street offences were being overlooked. In my first month in the Sub-Division I personally walked into eight clubs in plain clothes had a drink and walked out again, proving that they were nothing more than unlicensed public houses.

I had a happy two months getting things straight and the men, though not liking the stiffening of discipline on which I insisted, were becoming to appreciate the changes, for all policemen however much they may gripe, basically like 'a well run ship'.

On the BBC's 6 pm news bulletin of Tuesday, 14th of May, 1940, when the invasion of our islands seemed imminent, the new Secretary of State for War, Anthony Eden, the late Lord Avon, announced the formation of the Local Defence Volunteers, whose title was later changed to the Home Guard; he appealed for men of all ages from 17 to 65, to offer themselves for enrolment at their local police stations. The response was immediate and within twenty-four hours, 250,000 men had enrolled. In the early stages, the Government were unable to supply arms to this new force and so that at least some of them should have some sort of weapon with which to repel the German invader, Eden appealed at the same time for the gift or loan of shot guns, rifles and ammunition. Even the Imperial War Museum at Lambeth was asked to supply machine guns and rifles of the First World War from their show cases. Inevitably there was an urgent need for some kind of uniform to protect the newly enrolled volunteers from being arrested as spies, and within days armbands bearing the letters 'LDV' were issued as a temporary measure.

Within an hour of the broadcast, we had a queue of people, all in a great and embarrassing surge of patriotism, lining the steps of the station stretching along into Lucan Place. Intermingled amongst them was a good number of middle-aged and elderly men, and a considerable sprinkling of elderly ladies, bearing an odd assortment of arms. Every widow of every Indian Mutiny survivor seemed to live in the police area and the whole scene seemed like an apparition from the distant past as these determined daughters of the pioneers

The Metropolitan Police

of the 19th century British Empire resolutely advanced upon us with every sort of rifle, muzzle loader, elephant gun, shotgun revolver, pistol, blunderbuss, fowling piece and even spears. I sorted the queue, separating those who wished to hand in weapons from the men who were volunteering to use them. All this took some time for no prior warning had been given of the appeal: each weapon had to be examined, a description noted and a receipt given, while detailed personal data had to be carefully taken from the volunteers. During this process, I caught sight of a short, dapper military-looking figure, wearing a black bowler hat and carrying a rolled umbrella, patiently waiting in the queue. Amongst these people he stood out. Sensing there was something special about him I engaged him in conversation and asked his name, 'Gough', he replied. Guessing his identity I exclaimed, 'Are you General Gough of the 5th Army?' He said he was and taking him along to a waiting room I told the Superintendent that I had found just the man to run the Chelsea LDV. As soon as Eden had made the announcement, the Commissioner had instructed Superintendents by teleprinter to organise the LDV on police boundaries and to find suitable civilians with military experience to run the units. At first, the Superintendent thought I was romancing, but he was pleasantly surprised when I brought General Gough into his room. I was of course too young to remember much of that earlier War but Gough of the 5th Army was a legendary figure, just as Bomber Harris and Montgomery were in the Second World War.

In common with many other young police officers who were later released to join the Armed Service, I began in the early months of the War to experience a sense of frustration. I had a nagging feeling that I ought to be doing more. But then suddenly, almost overnight, my whole life changed. On a Sunday, just after Dunkirk in June 1940, I was patrolling in Kensington when I met, by chance, Colonel Halland, formerly Commandant of Hendon Police College and by now one of Her Majesty's Inspectors of Constabulary. I had not seen him for some time and we stopped to talk. Inevitably I voiced the feeling of frustration which was worrying me and my growing conviction that with my military training in the OTC and Territorials, small as it was, I should be involved in some more active role in the war effort. Out of the blue Colonel Halland asked, 'How would you like to be Chief Constable of Oxfordshire?' I was dumbfounded but delighted at the prospect. Colonel Halland went on to explain that the Oxfordshire Force was part of his inspecting responsibility. The force had been lagging behind in war preparation and policing in general and only that week he had persuaded the Chief Constable to resign. Age and failing health had caused the

Chief to neglect his duties just at a time when energy and drive were most needed. To me it was a wonderful suggestion, opening out vast possibilities. I said as much and Colonel Halland promised he would see the Commissioner the next day and broach the matter at the Home Office. Things moved in a whirl from then on but it was not quite as straightforward as was first thought. While the Oxfordshire Standing Joint Committee and the Home Office, because of the urgency, were happy to accept Colonel Halland's advice, the Commissioner refused to do so, saying that he would select the officer he considered best for the job. The Oxfordshire Standing Joint Committee therefore decided to advertise the post. I applied and with five others was put on a short list for interview the following Monday.

On the Saturday night before the interview, however, I had been called to a rough house in a Chelsea pub when I had had to arrest the drunks and for my efforts had been kicked in the face. I thus appeared before the Oxfordshire Standing Joint Committee at the County Hall, Oxford, with a badly swollen face and I felt sure that the Committee, consisting as it did of twenty-four very aristocratic country squires, would not want as their Chief Constable someone who got himself mixed up in public house brawls, even in the course of duty.

I found that I was the youngest person to be interviewed and the decision was very much in the balance. Of the other applicants, two were Chief Constables, Arthur Young, Chief Constable of Leamington, who later became Commissioner of the City of London Police, the other Colonel R. G. B. Spicer, CMG, MC, Chief Constable of the Isle of Wight, Commissioner of Police in Kenya and later Inspector General of the Palestine Police. Also applying for the post was Captain G. E. Banwell OBE, MC, who, after a distinguished background with the Police in Burma, was then an acting Inspector of Constabulary, later to become Chief Constable of East Riding and then of Cheshire; the fourth was another Hendon College man, John Skittery, a former schoolmaster who later became Chief Constable of Plymouth. It was he, I knew, that the Commissioner had recommended for the appointment as he was older than I and senior in rank. Sizing up the opposition, I decided my ill-timed facial damage must put an end to any slight chance I might have had.

The Oxfordshire Standing Joint Committee consisted of 24 gentlemen – 12 county councillors and 12 magistrates, who all looked very elderly and austere and as it was my first interview of this kind, I found it something of an ordeal. But I managed to bring a smile to their faces and it was this, I feel, that turned the scales. After we had all been interviewed, to my utter surprise, I was

The Metropolitan Police

called back and told I had been chosen. In retrospect it is clear that the Committee was taking a substantial risk. My police experience was very much less than that of any of the other candidates and I had not held an independent command. Guided by even the best of behind-the-scenes recommendations, the Committee was still taking a chance.

They were anxious to have their new Chief Constable in office at the earliest possible moment and so following a drink with Major Feilden, the Chairman, the Earl of Macclesfield, the Chairman of the County Council and the Clerk Mr G. Scott, I returned to London to tie up loose ends, and by special permission of Sir Philip Game, I started work as the 5th Chief Constable of Oxfordshire on the Thursday – three days later – at a salary of £650 a year and a rent allowance of £125 a year. By then my face was resuming its normal appearance and my Metropolitan Police career was over.

Chapter Three

OXFORDSHIRE

Early on Thursday, 11th July, 1940, at the age of 29 I sat down at my desk to begin my work as Chief Constable of the County of Oxfordshire. Dunkirk was a recent disaster and miracle, invasion seemed possible at any time. Everywhere there was feverish activity. A shattered army had to be revitalised and re-armed, an alarmed but resolute population had to be mobilised for total war. So far my own part in the war effort had been infinitesimally small. At Chelsea I had had the command of some 500 police officers, but here in Oxfordshire the Constabulary consisted of only 156 men and two women, while our responsibilities were so much greater. The main differences for me lay in the extent of authority of the Chief. In the Metropolitan Force command wound upwards through a plethora of ranks before reaching the Commissioner. At any time it had been possible for me to say that the problem was too big and pass it on upwards, but in Oxfordshire I might have anticipated Harry S. Truman with a desk notice, 'The buck stops here.' Not that my problems were on the Truman scale, but for me young as I was they were enough.

The Headquarters of the Oxfordshire Constabulary was a nineteenth century militia barracks adjacent to the Prison in the centre of the City of Oxford, which had its own police force independent of the County.

The building was antiquated, dark, dismal and very badly furnished. On the ground floor there were offices for the Chief Constable and his Deputy, a telephone room and two general offices, while on the first floor were two further offices. This was all the accommodation, but since the whole staff consisted of the Chief, his Deputy, a Superintendent who also had command of a Division, an Administrative Superintendent, an Inspector, a Sergeant and four Constables, it could be considered adequate. There were no civilian clerks and no typists. The general office

Oxfordshire

contained a few filing cabinets, and a mahogany dining table at which the Superintendent and two clerks sat with one typewriter.

There were no specialist departments, not even a CID, but after pressure from the Home Office a Special Branch Officer had been appointed to each of the five Divisions to deal with allegations of Fifth Columnists. There was no police wireless, but at that time very few forces had this facility, nor were there any traffic patrol cars, the only vehicles the police possessed being six Hillman Minx cars, one for each Division, and one for use by Headquarters personnel.

Police problems in Oxfordshire before the War were doubtless not great, but nothing had been done to gear the force to the very different tasks imposed on it by the War. It was precisely this failure that had made the Home Office insist on a change of Chief Constable.

At Headquarters there was also residential accommodation – if it could be so called – for six constables. This was quite appalling. It consisted solely of one dormitory and a kitchen-dining room. The dormitory contained six iron bedsteads with the minimum of bedding, and behind each bed there was a coat hook on the wall where a man could hang his suit. Beside each bed the men had provided themselves with a wooden tea carton which, when placed on its side, provided them with a bedside table and a container for their clothes. There were no chairs and no covering on the floor. In the kitchen the only furniture was an old wooden table and two backless forms, while the kitchen plates, cutlery, pots and pans, were such that I quickly had them consigned to the dustbin. Conditions in the police stations throughout the county were not much better, but the rural houses provided for constables were of good design, due to the personal interest of the Chairman, Major Feilden, who was very interested in the provision of better houses for everyone living in the rural villages in the county. The only trouble was that my predecessor, Captain Arbuthnot, firmly believed the rural constable must keep himself aloof and apart from the villagers, so he had persuaded the Standing Joint Committee that the police houses should be built outside the village, preferably on the nearest main road. As a consequence, many of them did not have electric light or water closet lavatories, while baths were filled from coal fuelled coppers situated in the ground floor bathroom.

The Chief Constable of a small force, as I soon realised, leads a lonely life at the office. Although he has a staff to support him they are not usually of high calibre, and though loyal and hard working, cannot give him mental stimulus. He can, of course, consult the Clerk of the Standing Joint Committee but he is also the Clerk of the County Council and a busy man who does not anyway know the technical details of police work.

There is also the Chairman of the Standing Joint Committee, but he is a layman, and it is best if the Chief Constable does not involve him in the day to day running of the Force. I was very lucky in that I could not have had a kinder man to help me as Clerk of the Standing Joint Committee than Gerald Scott, happily still alive. He was wise and helpful, without in any way trying to interfere with my responsibilities and he always respected the independence of the Chief Constable.

On my very first morning at the office I took an intriguing telephone call from Superintendent Hugh Cameron, the King's Private Detective, whom I had known at Balmoral in 1939. He first wanted to know whether my telephone was fitted with a scrambler device so that secret conversations could be carried on without fear of someone listening to them. I told him I had no such contrivance, whereupon he cagily inquired if I was aware of certain engagements in the near future. I expressed my ignorance and he then advised me, as a matter of urgency, to call upon Air Commodore McNeese-Foster at RAF Abingdon. Guessing the purport of the mystery, I telephoned the Air Commodore and arranged to see him that afternoon, when he told me that HM the King was to make secret visits to a number of Bomber Stations in Oxfordshire in four days' time.

I hastily made the necessary police arrangements and at 10.0 am on the day, I was at Bicester Station when His Majesty arrived. He was received by Air Chief Marshal Peter Portal, then Air Officer Commanding Bomber Command and later Chief of Air Staff for most of the war. He was to become Viscount Portal of Hungerford, KG, GCB, OM, DSO, MC, and after the war I came to know him well. He presented to the King firstly the Air Commodore, then myself and finally the Station Master.

Owing to the suddenness of my appointment I had had no time to obtain a uniform and didn't possess even a bowler hat. Everyone in the entourage wore uniform of one kind or another so I stood out in my civilian attire and wearing a black homburg, then all the vogue for civilians in London. We started for Bicester aerodrome and apparently on the way the King asked Portal who I was and when Portal told him, he asked, 'Why isn't he in uniform?' Portal replied that he was prepared to answer for the sins of Bomber Command but not for those of the Police.

While enjoying a coffee in the Officer's Mess, after the parade at Bicester, Portal told me through an ADC that I'd better explain myself to His Majesty. This I did and told him why I did not have any uniform. The King laughed, wished me well and added, 'But I've seen you before.' I then reminded him that I had been a member of his Camp Staff and had been at Balmoral only ten months previously, which led to a conversation about the Camp, and in particular, the climbing of Lochnagar, the King's favourite mountain.

The visit went off well, save that on the way home the King's car went so fast that the escorting Hillman Minx, which was all that Oxfordshire had for me to travel in, was overtaken by the King's Daimler, which finally disappeared from sight; but not before the second police car full of CID officers following at the rear, had driven into a ditch, luckily without injury. All's well that ends well, for on the strength of this episode I was able to persuade the Standing Joint Committee to authorise the purchase of one or two more powerful cars, one of which was a Daimler for my own official use.

There was another sequel. Six months later the King, accompanied by the Queen, came to visit an evacuated London school living in huts near Henley-on-Thames. On arrival, the King was received by the Headmaster and myself, for in war-time the Lord Lieutenant was not always informed of Royal Visits and was not responsible for the necessary reception arrangements. As the King greeted me, this time in uniform, he said, 'Hello Chief Constable. I'm glad to see the uniform fits well,' and turning to the Queen he remarked, 'The last time I came to the County the Chief Constable had only just arrived and didn't have a uniform.' I've often wondered whether this was a feat of memory or whether Cameron had reminded him of the Bicester visit. I shall never know.

On another occasion HM The Queen came to the County to look at some hospitals. This time we were entertained to lunch at 'Tusmore', the home of Lord Bicester, the Lord Lieutenant. There were only eight of us sitting at a square table and the Queen sat next to Lord Bicester, while I sat next to Lady Bicester. Almost as soon as the lunch began Lady Bicester said in a jocular way, 'Well I hope, Chief Constable, you've still got my photograph in your criminal records!' Thinking she had been involved in some minor motoring prosecution, I replied that we didn't take photographs for minor offences. To everyone's surprise she retorted, 'Well, it wasn't so minor. I did six weeks in Holloway!' She then confessed to having been a militant suffragette and she regaled us, with much humour, of her experiences in prison. The Queen was much interested and amused for I don't expect she often lunches with someone who has 'done time'.

On my second morning in Oxfordshire, my opposite number, Charles Fox, OBE, Chief Constable of Oxford City Police, called to see me. Charles Fox, whose police service dated from before the

First World War, had also been appointed Chief Constable as a young man and was, therefore, able to appreciate the difficulties of my position. I found in him a kindly and wise counsellor, who went on serving Oxford until his retirement in July 1956, after more than 25 years as Chief Constable of Oxford.

Although there was a very great difference in our ages, I soon became very friendly both with my Chairman Major Feilden and with Lord Macclesfield, the Chairman of the County Council, lunching with them several times a week at the County Club which was then situated in the Mitre Hotel. Although strong minded men who knew what they wanted, they were wise counsellors and friends and supported me in all that I was trying to do in the County. Major Feilden was a wealthy man who lived at Cokethorpe, a beautiful 18th century house, near Witney, and he had long been associated with local government in Oxfordshire. His son, Major General Sir Randle Feilden, became after a distinguished military career, Senior Steward of the Jockey Club, and he has probably done more for racing in this country than anyone else over the past thirty years.

It was a great loss to the county and to me when Major Feilden died. He was succeeded as Chairman of the Standing Joint Committee by Lord Macclesfield, who frequently asked me to visit him at Shirburn Castle, his moated home near Watlington. He was a big bluff man and a fierce critic of all Government departments in general, and of civil servants in particular. J believe he really enjoyed doing battle with them. If there was any delay in obtaining a reply from the Home Office, he had always one answer, 'Send them a telegram, Chief, and demand a reply by return.' I did as he wished but don't remember that it ever did any good.

One of the first questions I put to my staff at Force Headquarters concerned the training of recruits. At this time there was in England no such thing as standardised police recruit training, and methods were completely haphazard, varying greatly from Force to Force. To my dismay Oxfordshire virtually had no system at all. In such a small force recruiting was usually done singly as vacancies occurred, and the unfortunate lone recruit was attached to Headquarters for three months, during which time he was required to attend to the daily cleaning chores and to man the telephone throughout the night for which purpose a bed was provided for him in the telephone room. Although he was encouraged to buy a copy of Moriarty's Police Law, no one insisted he should study it. When I asked what happened if a recruit refused to buy such a text book I was blandly told, 'That's not yet happened, Sir. A man is usually quite keen when he joins'. A recruit received no lectures or organised training of any kind; at best a man of an inquiring mind could pick up a fair amount of knowledge by observing what went on at Headquarters and by asking questions. At the end of his three months, inquiring mind or not, a recruit left Headquarters to walk a beat as a fully-fledged policeman, while another recruit was taken on to go through the same process of little learning and much labour. On recruit training, Oxfordshire rated a zero.

There was similar neglect in Force organisation with no specialised departments, no detective, traffic or war departments. I found that the gas respirators and anti-gas protective clothing issued in bulk to all police forces in March, 1939, were, in July 1940, Dunkirk and invasion threat notwithstanding, still lying in their original cartons, the respirators not even assembled. I found filed away the main Home Office directive circular, issued in November, 1938, advising Chief Constables on the necessary preparations for War. Scribbled in the margin by the then Chief Constable were the words, 'We do not want anything in Oxfordshire. Perhaps, however, we should get another typewriter!' And the extra typewriter, not very useful for fighting on the beaches or even in the Oxfordshire lanes, was the sum total of all the preparation which had been made. Blind faith in Britain's ability to muddle through could reach no further.

My predecessor, Captain E. K. Arbuthnot, had served with distinction in the Royal Navy, commanding fighting ships during the First World War. He had been Commodore of Convoys in 1918, when he was awarded the DSO, and was three times mentioned in despatches.

He had, however, a reputation for being a tough disciplinarian, and he disliked spending any money on the police. I discovered, for instance, that the blankets in the single men's quarters were worn-out. Army blankets from Cowley Barracks, which he had obtained when the Army was selling them.

On my first day at the office he invited me out to a café in the town for lunch, and urged me never to go to the office in the afternoon. 'Start as you mean to go on. The men don't want you about the place all the time. Your job is to recruit the right men and to maintain discipline. Let the Superintendents run the force.' Needless to say, I didn't take his advice.

The Standing Joint Committee was surprised when I asked them for a uniform allowance for Arbuthnot never had a police uniform. The story is that he once attended the Annual Inspection of the Force by HM Inspector of Constabulary – much to the latter's indignation – wearing plus fours.

In the store room I found two tin trunks containing the most lovely Edwardian dresses. These, I discovered, belonged to his first wife, an actress, and he was loathe to take them away because he didn't want his second wife to know that he had kept them. I believe he had them destroyed and I now wish I had asked him to give them to me, because, apart from their beauty they would today be valuable.

A new Divisional Police Headquarters had been built in Banbury in 1938, and while externally it had pleasing elevations, and had been built in natural Cotswold stone, the internal planning was appalling. When I entered a large entrance hall I was confronted on the left with one door leading to the men's lavatory and a second door marked, 'Witnesses'; on the right was a door marked, 'Women's lavatory', and a second door labelled 'Police Office'. Inside the last was an old-fashioned high Victorian police counter at which was standing a Constable (later Superintendent Johnson and a very good opening bat for the County Police Cricket XI), a Constable sitting at a desk and a Superintendent sitting at another desk wearing a cap which looked like the kind worn by prison officers in Victorian stage melodramas. This was the Superintendent who was in charge of the Division – a very small one totalling only 30 men. He rose to greet me, and after I had introduced myself, and spoken to the two Constables, I suggested to the Superintendent that we adjourn to his office. 'This is my office,' he said, and when I replied that I thought it was the General Office, he told me that there was only one police office in the whole building and that he did all his work sitting here. He then conducted me round the rest of the Station. In a room immediately behind the General Office was a telephone booth, a gas cooker, a scrubbed and unpainted kitchen table with no cloth or other covering on it, and two benches. A policeman was frying some bacon on the cooker and was about to have a meal. 'This is the Charge Office,' said the Superintendent, and I then discovered that it was the only place where men could take their refreshments, or where the single men who resided in the Station, could sit when off duty. From the Charge Room a corridor led to the cells, which could only be described as palatial compared with everything else in the building. There was also a staircase leading to the single men's quarters on the first floor. In each of the six rooms there was an iron bedstead and a chair. The rooms were unused except one, which had been sparsely fitted up as an office for the newly appointed Special Branch Officer, the only specialist officer in the Division. On this floor there was also a combined bathroom and lavatory with a high level flush system and a long chain handle. There was no linoleum nor any floor covering in any of the rooms. This was the total accommodation provided for the police in a Station built only the previous year.

In addition there was a court room and a Magistrates' room with its own lavatory facilities, and in the same building quarters for the Superintendent, an Inspector and a Sergeant. The Borough Bench sat once a week and the County Bench once a month. Before I left the Station I instructed the Superintendent to take over the Witnesses' Room as his office, buy himself office furniture in town and have a telephone installed. Such was my inexperience and brashness that I never thought to consult either the County Architect or the Magistrates' Clerk on the matter. But I did tell the Chairman of the Police Authority what I had done and I asked him to speak to the Chairman of the two Benches who used the Court. No protest at my action ever reached my ears. But what an indictment of all concerned this was. It is unprofitable to apportion blame, but I suppose that not only my predecessor but also the Inspector of Constabulary who had passed the plans on behalf of the Home Office must bear responsibility for this appalling situation; the reader must, however, remember that at that time very few people in the country had any experience of building police stations.

Unfortunately for my predecessor, a few weeks before my arrival there had been an extensive military operation by Canadian troops in the county, searching for two suspected trained German saboteurs, rumoured to have been dropped by parachute over Oxfordshire in the Henley-on-Thames district. This had led to such repercussions that Winston Churchill, the Prime Minister, became personally interested and sent Field Marshal Ironside and his ADC, the Duke of Marlborough, to investigate the matter. The whole operation was badly handled owing to excessive zeal on the part of a Canadian Army Lieutenant and it ended with apologies all round and the War Office offering to pay heavy compensation. The panic began when an elderly woman walking in the country near Stoke Row reported that she had seen objects dropping from the sky and as a consequence, the whole area was combed by police and military units. At this time the Canadian Forces had their Headquarters at Shotover House, near Oxford. The security officer on the General's staff who received the message about the incident immediately left for the Henley district and as he was passing the golf course at Huntercombe, he saw sitting under a hedge, a young man of rough appearance wearing military uniform. The officer stopped his car, went to him and said that he suspected him of having just been dropped from an enemy aircraft. The man said that this was correct, and was at once taken to the Canadian Headquarters and closely interrogated. The 'spy' said that he was a Welshman who had been captured by the Germans in the Dunkirk retreat. As an ardent Welsh Nationalist he, with others of similar political aspirations, had volunteered for training as a saboteur, to be dropped in England to attack vital installations. He named another Welshman who had dropped with him and claimed that their orders were to contact a Mr James Florey of Manor Farm, Hardwick, near Witney, who would furnish them with materials and instructions. German refugees working on the farm were in the plot and would help. All this was plausible and his story seemed to be confirmed, when on arrival at the farm some Germans were found to be working there. The Canadians decided to occupy the farm and, fearing armed resistance, mounted a military operation on a suitable scale. The Headquarters Police Inspector, though a little late in the inquiry arrived at the farm before the Canadians and without the slightest difficulty arrested the three German male workers and the German woman who cooked for them. Unaware of this development the officer commanding the Canadians was surprised at the lack of opposition but went on to occupy the farmhouses. Searches and spot interrogations revealed nothing. Mr Florey, his wife, and the employees were completely dumbfounded by the thunderbolt which had struck them. They were taken to Canadian Headquarters and all the occupants of the farm were taken into custody. The Canadians decided the second saboteur would probably come to the farm that night and a strict, silent vigil was kept. Morning came but no saboteur. The Police Inspector presented himself at Shotover House where the by-now rampantly suspicious security officer decided the Inspector too must be one of the gang and placed him under armed guard, from which ignominious situation he was rescued by a Colonel from MI5 who had heard by chance that a man claiming to be a detective was in custody. To add to the confusion a young cyclist was arrested as the second saboteur because, when questioned, his surname was by a coincidence exactly that given to the Canadians by the man who had started the trouble. Like the Inspector, the youth was rescued from captivity, this time by a police officer who knew him as a permanent resident, under military age, and working as a butcher at Goring. Interrogation of the anti-hero of the story went on for hours and manfully he held on. Apart from the Canadians no one by now was prepared to believe him. His underclothing and boots were British army issue, and he had no identity documents or articles of value on him. Efficient German spy organisations were most unlikely to drop into England an agent so meagrely supplied. Gradually the suspect tired and at last admitted to being a deserter from a searchlight battery in the Midlands and that he had once worked for Mr Florey. In due time he was identified by one of his NCO's and that was almost the end of the saga but not quite. Mr and Mrs Florey were released from custody to find that troops occupying the farm had stolen some of their property and caused much damage to the farm house. As to the anti-hero, he explained he was aggrieved by the rough handling he had received from the Canadian security officer who had made up his mind at the outset that he had caught a spy, and so the deserter decided, with the aid of a little local knowledge and much mischievous inventiveness, to reinforce the Lieutenant's conclusions. Mr Florey behaved with admirable dignity and restraint throughout; the War Office tried to make amends with an apology and an offer of compensation but Mr Florey was sensible, and magnanimously would only accept enough to pay for the damage caused to the farm house.

The Home Office had for some time been unhappy about the police command in Oxfordshire and this incident was the last straw which led to pressure on my predecessor to retire.

My own troubles were not helped by the Superintendent in charge of Administration at Headquarters. I realised very soon that there was something odd about him. He would come into my office and just stand and stare at me before handing over his papers or letters and would walk out without a word. I found his behaviour disconcerting and the signs indicated mental illness of some sort. The Superintendent had been an applicant for the Chief Constable's post when I was appointed and though not considered for the job he resented my appointment. His dislike was obvious when I spoke to him and he gave the impression that my presence as Chief was unwelcome and unjust. Altogether the situation was difficult and mildly sinister. After suffering for some time the depressing effects of this man's actions and ill-concealed hostility, as I had no confidence in the Police Medical Officer, a local general practitioner, I consulted the doctor in charge of a mental hospital on the outskirts of Oxford. By arrangement he telephoned me for police assistance. I responded by asking the Superintendent to deal with the inquiry as it was an important matter requiring the attention of a senior police officer of experience. The Specialist and Superintendent talked for a couple of hours, at the end of which he was persuaded to remain at the hospital as a voluntary patient. At the end of six weeks, however, he discharged himself, presenting me with a difficult legal problem as the power to compel the resignation of a man on medical grounds was by no means clear. After much consultation and advice from the Home Office, I was able to secure his retirement on full pension but to a young, newly appointed Chief the whole incident was unwelcome and distressing and it was a decision which a few months earlier in the Metropolitan Force I should not have had to make. In tiny Oxfordshire the buck stopped when it reached me.

The Superintendent later committed suicide and several days after his death, I received through the post an envelope containing a newspaper account of the inquest; written across it were the words, 'You killed this man.'

Poor training and administration did not mean that the men serving in the Oxfordshire Constabulary were of poor quality. Many of them were very good indeed and welcomed new leadership and the firmer sense of direction they so badly needed. Within weeks I was able to build up a team of four or five men to form the basis of a re-organised Force. Of these the most notable was Sergeant Ralph Buckingham, whom I found in charge of Burford Police Station and who flung himself energetically into his new duties, soon making his mark as the Inspector in charge of the War Department. Promoted Divisional Superintendent of the Witney Division in May, 1942, he distinguished himself by his courageous action in an aeroplane crash and this brought him the King's Commendation. In August 1945, he was seconded to the British Police Mission in Greece and later became the Deputy Chief Constable of Oxfordshire and was awarded the King's Police Medal.

By the time I submitted my first quarterly report to the Standing Joint Committee, less than three months after my appointment, I was able to say that a War Department had been set up, war stores checked and issued, training in air raid precautions was well under way and plans drawn up to clear the strategic roads for use by the military, or for the passage of refugees. A Special Branch to deal with the problems posed by aliens, disaffected nationals and others likely to interfere with the war effort, had also been established and was proving its worth. Liaison with Air Raid Controllers, local authorities and the military had been arranged and the Special Constabulary although woefully ill-equipped had been galvanised into active life. Everywhere there was a need for training and more training and rapidly, yet painfully, the Force hauled itself up by its own bootstraps. Women were recruited to take over indoor jobs; War Reserves were recruited to take the place of the young constables who were now being called into the Armed Services. The times were hectic and full of movement. By 1941, Oxfordshire had a properly organised CID, a Traffic Department, a War Department and a Special Branch. We had even evolved a pigeon post for use should communications break down for there was no police wireless in those days.

In 1940 speed in re-organising the police was essential. Almost all that was left of the British Army was manning the beaches to resist the expected invasion, but there was a reserve stationed in North

Oxfordshire

Oxfordshire and East Gloucestershire ready to go immediately to the point where the invading forces landed. We in Oxfordshire had to be ready to give these men our assistance and I quickly had to prepare a plan to close the main roads to all but military traffic. An additional problem was the presence of many thousands of evacuees from the Isle of Wight and the South coast. Many of these were living in poor conditions in the rural villages and the situation was aggravated when their numbers were increased by the bombing of London which started in September.

A typical example of our duties is that one evening at 6.0 pm, we received information that a special train had left Dartford, Kent with 1,500 evacuees and would arrive at Oxford in the early hours of the morning. The train had to be met, 'buses provided, and billets found for all the evacuees – no easy task, but we did it.

While the Battle of Britain was taking place a bombing raid was made on the RAF Station at Brize Norton and the satellite landing ground at Stanton Harcourt. This was part of the Luftwaffe's attempt to knock out aerodromes as a prelude to a more general assault. Seven men were killed, hangers, and buildings damaged or burnt out. The first call for help came directly to me and I arrived at the scene soon after the attacks. I was appalled by the chaos. It was not the damage which was frightening, but the *mélange* of independent, part-time fire fighting units all arriving haphazard and too late, many with incompatible equipment. Early raids such as this exposed the deficiencies of the voluntary brigade system and led directly and quickly to the formation of the National Fire Service.

A few weeks after the bombing of Brize Norton, the Regional Liaison Officer for MI5 came to see me to tell me in great confidence that the Germans were proposing to drop agents in the United Kingdom by parachute, and that the first was expected to arrive between Oxford and Thame within the next few days. The public was well aware that agents had been dropped in continental countries and so we were able to emphasise the general warning without raising any suspicions that we had intelligence information; but I did send a special message to all men working east of Oxford. In the event the agent arrived by parachute on the 6th September, 1940, just over the border in Buckinghamshire where the police were also on the alert. His instructions, as we found later, were to inform Germany of the effects of the blitz on Birmingham. He was easily picked up by the police, for on landing, a strap holding his radio transmitter snapped, the apparatus hit his head and he was mildly concussed. I went over to see him in the cells at Aylesbury. He was a Dane who spoke fairly good English, which by a curious coincidence he had learnt whilst living with a family in Kings

Heath, Birmingham – in the very next street to the one where I was born.

The day after this agent's capture – Saturday, 7th September, 1940 – was a very notable day in the War, for that evening London suffered its first blitz. During the Battle of Britain, the Germans attempted to destroy aerodromes and deal a fatal blow to the Royal Air Force, but they had failed and so the enemy now tried to break the spirit of London by sustained and concentrated night bombing. The dockland to the north and south of the river, became a red glare, a glowing map reference for the relays of Dorniers, Heinkels and Junker bomber aircraft which throughout the next three months flew en masse over London amid the roar blast and thundercracks of of anti-aircraft batteries dropping their high explosive and incendiary bombs indiscriminately.

Although at that time no bombs were dropped on targets in Oxfordshire, we were indirectly affected for immediately many tens of thousands of refugees evacuated themselves from London and tried to find safety in the country villages. Many homeless made straight for Oxford and the City became a seething mass of humanity all looking for accommodation. One day after a meeting at County Hall, I was making my way, in uniform, through the crowds accompanying Lord Macclesfield and Major Feilden to lunch at the Mitre, when suddenly there were shouts of 'Mr St. Johnston, Mr St. Johnston,' and I saw, descending from a flat lorry of the type used by greengrocers, a whole motley collection of London Cockneys. They were the Huggins family who had for generations kept street stalls in the North End Road, Fulham, selling fruit and vegetables. The younger ones were true London barrow boys and they had been a confounded nuisance to me at Walham Green, for their stalls and barrows overran the roadway and obstructed the traffic, while there was running warfare between the family and the police.

But on this occasion all faces were wreathed in smiles and I was surrounded by the family shaking me by the hand saying, 'Nice to see yer, Sir. We'd read you'd become a Top Cop. We always knew you'd get on. Good luck to yer.' Then they all scrambled back on to the lorry as the traffic moved on. I was very touched, but my two companions wondered whether I had the right sort of friends.

At that time the population of the County was growing fast. Before the War there were 120,000 but by 1942, this had risen to over 200,000. This increase alone put an almost intolerable strain on police manpower, and we were hard pressed to find men to carry out the many additional tasks placed on our shoulders, while much ordinary police work had to go by the board.

In 1940 when I went to Oxfordshire there were only four aero-

Oxfordshire

dromes in the County – Bicester, Heyford, Benson and Brize Norton but by the end of the War there were, including emergency landing strips, over twenty.

As a consequence, we had a large number of RAF service men in Oxfordshire and though they were usually well behaved, there were occasional problems and I sometimes said that life for the police would be easier when the County became one big aerodrome. Benson, now the Headquarters of the Queen's flight, was then the Headquarters of PRU (Photographic Reconnaissance Unit) and I visited it fairly frequently. The members of this unit were the most courageous men I met during the war. On the day after a raid, it was the PRU's task to fly over enemy territory and photograph the damage.

Their aircraft were unarmed wooden Mosquitos, and the flight had to be done in broad daylight at 35,000 feet. Speed and height were their only defence; small wonder that both pilots and navigators lived in a high state of tension, and each day, more faces were missing from the Officers' Mess.

Although there were about a thousand Special Constables in Oxfordshire when I assumed command, they were virtually untrained, and none had been issued with uniform or organised on a county basis. All had the rank of constable and wore only arm bands with here and there a peaked cap of First World War vintage. Cohesion and training was completely lacking and to assist in their re-organisation and co-ordination of the work and training, I appointed Major F. W. Cole MBE, to take charge and for the first time instituted Divisonal Commandants.

Supplies of uniform and equipment were speeded up and all ranks had to be trained in police and war duties, for there were many new offences and restrictions imposed by the Defence Regulations. Eventually, uniformed and well trained, they gave valuable service where it was most needed, especially in mounting guard at places vulnerable to sabotage. They protected important railway junctions and armament factories, and kept the roads clear for the heavy volume of military convoys, first, those of our defending forces and later vehicles providing equipment for the invasion forces assembled on the South Coast. The Regular Police owe them a great debt of gratitude for their assistance and good comradeship.

The shortage of manpower during this crucial period of ever-increasing commitments, was a constant source of concern, but in March 1941, I suddenly received an unexpected bonus. Although there were then no such personnel as Women Special Constables, the Home Office had agreed that Chief Constables could use women on a part-time basis as drivers and as telephone operators; and I was considering trying to recruit some women in Oxfordshire when I received a visit from Sir Ralph Glynn, who was at that time Member of Parliament for the Abingdon constituency. Because it was thought possible that the Germans might effect a seaplane landing on the Thames as part of their invasion force, he had formed a flotilla of Home Guard to patrol the Thames comprised of men who owned river cruisers and they were to be assisted by some thirty women to act as couriers driving the crews by car to their craft and to provide cooked food on board. The women, all married with family commitments which prevented them volunteering for full-time work, were most enthusiastic. They had bought themselves navy blue uniforms, blouses and caps and already had some semblance of discipline. Now, however, Sir Ralph had received specific instructions from the War Office that the women were to be disbanded as it was contrary to the Geneva Convention for them to be be employed in what was considered a combatant role. I didn't quite see the point of this argument, because women were at that time being used in similar roles in the Armed Forces. However I did not argue this when the unit was offered to me en bloc. It was, for me, manna from heaven, and in no time all of them were transferred to the Women's Auxiliary Police Corps (WAPC).

I told Mrs Wilder, their efficient and enthusiastic Commandant that I wanted her to arrange that there should be seven women in each of five Divisions, each with one Divisional Commandant and six drivers. Each driver was to arrive in her own car at the Divisional Headquarters at 9 am, one day a week for general driving duties as required by the Superintendent. The Divisional Commandant was expected to ensure that there were no absentees and stand in herself if no substitute could be found. We had to recruit a few additional women to fill the Divisions of Banbury and Bicester, which were not close to the Thames, but I believe that all whom we recruited stayed with us until the end of the War, and all certainly gave magnificent, devoted, and efficient service. They were educated women many of whom had interesting backgrounds and they could be relied upon to use their own initiative. When our manpower difficulties worsened as the war progressed, I asked for and received two days work a week from each woman, one day driving and a second working as telephone operators at Divisional Headquarters.

It is perhaps invidious to mention names, but Sir Miles Thomas, now Lord Thomas of Remenham, has recounted in his autobiography, *Out on a Wing*, how much his wife, Hilda, enjoyed her time in the Women's Auxiliary Police Corps as Commandant of the Banbury Division. Mel Russell Cooke, the daughter of

Captain Smith of the *Titanic* ran the Witney Division, Elaine Brunner who now owns Wotton House near Brill ran the Wheatley Division, while Marley Raphael of Stanton Harcourt, Celia Johnson the actress, Viscountess Harcourt, and Jeanne Stonor, now the Dowager Lady Camoys, all gave their time unstintingly. I am glad of the opportunity, all too late, to pay this tribute to a body of women who gave valuable assistance to the Police in Oxfordshire during World War II. They were a unique group and I regret never arranging for the whole unit to be photographed, and that I did not put forward any of their names for a decoration. Their work ought to have been officially recognised in some form or another.

As part of the preparations for work under war conditions, plans had been made in London for the recruitment of a number of wives of serving police officers to work in Metropolitan Police Canteens. My wife was one of those who volunteered. In due course she was invited to join a select group for work in a canteen used exclusively by the staff of MI5, our counter-intelligence organisation, where all personnel were required to pass a strict security check.

Much later it was disclosed that the place of their employment was to be of all places, Wormwood Scrubs Prison, which had been cleared of its inmates to make room for the Headquarters of MI5. By the time war started, my wife was expecting our first child, Caroline, and after a few weeks of canteen work her doctors advised her not to continue. When we moved from London to Oxfordshire we had difficulty in finding a suitable house, mainly because the County was so full of evacuees. Eventually we found a home in the attractive town of Woodstock near Blenheim Palace, home of the Duke and Duchess of Marlborough. It was a modern house which, though not beautiful or entirely satisfactory, suited our requirments.

I was aware that in the event of London being seriously bombed, MI5 would be transferred from Wormwood Scrubs to Blenheim and early in September 1940, the Prison was hit during a heavy air raid on London and the move to Blenheim was given top priority. The security of MI5's Registry of Files was essential and I was asked to undertake responsibility for the removal of these documents from Wormwood Scrubs to Blenheim – a job admirably carried out by twelve strong Oxfordshire constables.

Before the concentrated bombing of our provincial cities started in the Autumn of 1940, the Germans sent over lone aircraft on special missions, and it so happened that on the night MI5 arrived at Blenheim, a raider put a stick of bombs right across the park close to the Palace. Living so close, I heard the explosions and hastily dressing I went to the Palace relieved to find that no damage had been done, although my first reaction had been to praise the accurate knowledge of the German Intelligence Service. In fact, it was pure coincidence that the raider had released his bombs over the park.

Later it was thought that the intended point of attack had been the Aluminium Works at Banbury, a few miles north east of Blenheim. Shortly afterwards, there was an attempt during the afternoon to bomb the works, which was vital to the nation's war effort at that time as it was producing over half the country's aluminium for the manufacture of Spitfires and Hurricanes. To mislead the enemy, a dummy factory made of wooden material from the pavilions and stands of the Royal Show held in Warwickshire in 1939, had been constructed a few miles from the real factory which was carefully camouflaged with dummy trees and bushes on its roof. To give the decoy an air of authenticity, a number of old motor car bodies and other worn out machines were placed in the vicinity. When a lone raider planted a stick of bombs across it and for good measure, dropped another bomb on Banbury Railway Station scoring a direct hit, that evening the German radio announced that Britain's war effort had been seriously affected by a successful raid on factories in the Banbury area. We were glad they thought so, and the truth was not disclosed until after the War.

In 1942 our son Thomas Andrew, was born – the seventh generation in direct line to be christened Thomas. Thus another interest was added to our homelife, though with rationing of food, the lack of petrol and the blackout, life was not easy for my wife.

Provided that one was not taken prisoner or wounded, almost every man must admit that the period of the war was an interesting and on the whole enjoyable, period of his life, while for unmarried girls or married girls without children, it was a time of fun. But for married women with small children, life was tough. There were difficulties in finding enough food and adequate clothes, little petrol was available for cars, inadequate public transport and little social life, while if the husband was away in the Armed Forces there was also the constant fear for his safety.

Most of the MI5 staff were accommodated in Colleges in Oxford and travelled daily to Blenheim by 'bus, whilst the canteen staff were lodged in a house in the spacious park adjoining the Palace. My wife was asked to rejoin her old colleagues but was by then helping the Duchess of Marlborough to run a British Restaurant in Woodstock.

The Marlboroughs kept one wing of the Palace for their own occupation and since the petrol shortage and restrictions meant that people were not able to travel far for social purposes, we were frequently asked to dinner. We played tennis and croquet at the

Palace and I shot there in the winter. Knowing, as I did, so many members of the MI5 staff now living in and around Woodstock, we had as pleasant a social life as the war and police work permitted.

One of the real pleasures of being a County Chief Constable has always been the invitations to most, if not all, of the big houses of the county. Here evidence could be seen of generations of occupancy by the same family. To be entertained at such places as Blenheim, or Tusmore, the home of Lord Bicester, the Lord Lieutenant, or Stonor where Jeanne and Sherman Camoys have until recently lived and upheld the Catholic traditions of the Stonor family throughout the centuries, was for me a great thrill. Three other large houses close to Woodstock were Glympton, at that time occupied by the Barnetts, Kiddington, Mr Gaskell's home and Ditchley where the Trees lived. We visited all of them from time to time and I shot there each year. The most beautiful was Ditchley, the lovely home of Ronnie Tree which had been tastefully decorated and furnished by his wife, Nancy, and it was a house that I visited frequently for there the Trees entertained Winston Churchill each month at the full moon, since those responsible for his security had decided that Chequers was too easily recognisable from the air. Winston, wearing his famous siren suit with a zip fastener up the front, would come for the weekend, bringing with him his Chiefs of Staff and others, British and later American, connected with the war effort. All this has been well and delightfully recorded in Ronnie Tree's book, *When the Moon is High*. The Army provided a guard for the Prime Minister but I also arranged for a few CID officers to ensure privacy. It was no easy task, for apart from the Prime Minister's personal staff, there were also many private visitors, for the Prime Minister busy as he was, still liked social life to go on around him. It was not at Ditchley that I first met Winston Churchill but at Bladon, when he came to attend the quiet family funeral of his aunt. I remained discreetly in the background but after the service, the Duke of Marlborough introduced me to the Prime Minister. It was a time when things were going badly for England and he seemed, and must have been, a worried man. He asked me how old I was and when I told him I was 29, he looked at the ground and shaking his head said, 'Yes, young men have to carry a lot of responsibility these days.' I had the presence of mind to answer, 'Well, Sir, some older men carry much more', and he replied with a smile, 'Well, perhaps you are right.'

War tends to change the character of policing quite drastically. Personal selfishness diminishes in the face of national danger and younger people who get into mischief can be drafted while crime diminishes in gravity as other offences take precedence. Sensitivity to actions likely to imperil the nation or fellow-citizens is tremendously heightened. Blackout regulations were very well obeyed during the 1939–45 war, because irate neighbours were apt to shout, 'Put that bloody light out', long before police or air raid wardens got round to it. Foreign accents or even foreign names gave rise to suspicion, which though usually unjustified, and often irrational, did make it very difficult for spies who were less than perfectly rehearsed to escape notice. Special Branch work demanded of its practitioners a highly analytical approach not required in any other class of police work. Over 99 per cent of material collected by Special Branch officers was useless but the remaining 1 per cent was vital.

German-born housewives, for example, had a hard time. Reports would come in claiming that such a woman was pro-Fascist, anti-British or pro-German. Remarks made by her would be quoted to prove the informant's point. When analysed these remarks usually turned out to be the kind of protest which comes naturally to people when they hear sweeping condemnations of their own race. 'All Germans are not like that', or 'I find it hard to believe that German soldiers behave so badly', are defensive remarks provoked by the statements of others. It was the need to balance reason against emotional, though not unpraiseworthy, sentiment which made Special Branch work so delicate. One has to look very hard to find the occasional grain of truth in all the chaff of suspicion. Once a firm basis of disloyalty or disaffection had been established, subsequent inquiry and assessment became easier. In the interim we had to waste a great deal of police time searching for some solid basis of truth in many of the stories that came to us.

Prejudice had built up, not without good cause and hatred had arisen for those otherwise loyal British subjects who had openly espoused the Fascist-Nazi cause. Sir Oswald Mosley's controversial and dangerous politics sprang from his impatience with what he saw of the ineffectual fumblings of democracy. He, his followers and sympathisers, were left completely vulnerable to government precautionary action, suspicion and contumely when war broke out between Great Britain and Nazi Germany. In normal circumstances imprisonment without trial is abhorrent to the British people. Nevertheless in a state of war, and particularly when invasion became a real threat, virtually the whole population accepted the decision that those likely to help the invaders should be taken into custody.

Each Chief Constable had a list of those he proposed to arrest the moment invasion became imminent. On my arrival in Oxford I asked to see the 'lock-up' list. The Headquarters Detective Inspector produced the document with three names typed on it, the top one being Unity Mitford, then resident in the County. I asked for the files in conection with this matter. The Inspector looked at me and said, 'Well, it's Unity Mitford, Sir. Hitler's girlfriend; of course we must lock her up.' I said that I fully appreciated the stories that had been told about Unity Mitford, and it might well be true that she had been Hitler's mistress, but I had no definite evidence of that fact and wished to know on what evidence we were proposing to lock her up. The Detective Inspector again repeated that everyone knew she was Hitler's girlfriend and quite clearly it was necessary to lock her up if an invasion took place.

I did not feel we had any right to take her into custody merely on the strength of newspaper reports, and I was surprised to find that we did not have a file of evidence of this girl's association with Hitler and with the Nazi Party.

Although we had nothing in our files in Oxford, I felt sure that the appropriate authorities in London would have a complete dossier on her but, to my surprise, I discovered that there was no official file in London, it being assumed that the Oxfordshire Police, in whose area the girl lived, would have the necessary papers.

I therefore made up a file by obtaining copies of newspaper cuttings from the library of a daily newspaper, and after consultations in London it was decided that I should see her father, Lord Redesdale. I wrote to him saying that I would like to discuss with him the situation about his daughter's affairs in Germany and he invited me to meet him at Boodle's, his London Club. We met there and I could not have had a more delightful hour's talk with a most charming benign gentleman. He was supposed to be the prototype of Uncle Matthew of his daughter Nancy Mitford's book, 'The Pursuit of Love', written after the war, but he showed none of these symptoms to me.

At the beginning of our conversation he said, 'Chief Constable, my daughter Unity has been front page news in the National Press for four years, yet you are the first official who has had the courtesy to come to discuss the matter with her father. I shall be delighted to help you in any way I can.'

He told me that she had gone to Germany at the age of 16 and had quickly become enamoured of the discipline of the Nazi Party. Because of her connections in this country, she obtained an introduction to Hitler and immediately fell under his spell. Undoubtedly Hitler was flattered by the fact that this daughter of a very old aristocratic English family took an interest in him, and there was no doubt that on her part, it was a schoolgirl's hero-worship. Lord Redesdale told me he did not believe that Hitler had at any time been on terms of intimacy with his daughter and indeed, when she returned from Germany she had been medically examined and found to be virgo intacta. Hitler had merely regarded her as a young devotee, interesting in that she was English and of an aristocratic family, but other than that, no different from the thousands of other young devotees he had in Germany. Unity visited Germany a number of times between 1936 and 1939 and, from time to time, was seen in the company of the Fuehrer. She was in Germany at the time that War broke out, but there is no evidence that Hitler saw her in the months before the War started or at any time after it began. She evidently felt strongly the impossibility of her position for in October 1939, in a public park in Munich, she shot herself in the back of her head. Her injuries were not fatal however, and after a short time in hospital, Hitler arranged for her to be sent to Switzerland. There, her family found her and brought her back to England where she lived with her mother in a small cottage at Swinbrook in Oxfordshire. Unity was under the medical care of Professor Cairns, the Professor of Neurology at Oxford for as a result of her injury, she was just like a child, simple and easy to get on with, and obviously of no importance to the war effort on either side.

As a result of what Lord Redesdale told me, I asked if he would agree that I should confirm the story of her present mental condition by interviewing Professor Cairns, but I pointed out that the Professor would, as a matter of etiquette, not discuss her case with me unless he had her father's approval. Lord Redesdale there and then wrote to the Professor and a week later I saw Professor Cairns and discussed the matter with him. Having heard his diagnosis of the girl's condition, I immediately had her struck off the suspects' list though whether I was right to do so is a matter of opinion. Quite clearly she was still in the minds of the general public, a danger because of her association with Hitler; and in the event of an invasion it might well have been in her own personal interests for us to take her into custody to prevent her becoming the victim of an assault or even lynching by indignant British people. However, I felt that on the evidence before me, there was no reason why we should lock her up and I was supported in my decision by MI5. Unity eventually died in 1948 and is buried in the churchyard at Swinbrook, one of Oxfordshire's most attractive churches. It was a church to which my wife, Joanna, and I frequently went and which I use now. When Joanna died in 1974 she was buried in the same churchyard.

During the course of the discussion with Lord Redesdale, his son, Tom Mitford, joined us. Tom was at that time, an officer in the Army, and I was very impressed with him. He was a most delightful young man who, alas, was killed in Burma shortly before the end of the War.

Oxfordshire

As leader of the British Union of Fascists which supported many of the Nazi ideals, Sir Oswald Mosley was imprisoned during the early part of the War under Regulation 18B of the Defence Regulations. Diana, his second wife and a sister of Unity Mitford, was imprisoned with him and they spent all but the first few months together in Holloway Prison.

When the threat of invasion had receded in November 1943, both were released and allowed to live with Pamela Jackson, another of the Mitford sisters, at Barford St. John in North Oxfordshire, but were kept under police supervision and could not leave the house without my permission. I met them at Deddington Police Station, to which they had been brought by the Metropolitan Police, and took them to Barford St. John and posted a Constable to live in the house, more to protect them from the attentions of the Press than to ensure their security.

Oswald Mosley had suffered from phlebitis while in prison and he certainly was not well while in Oxfordshire. He was very silent and seemed morose so I really cannot say I gained any impression of him as a man. But one could not help being impressed with Lady Mosley who was very good looking woman, a delightful conversationalist, with a first-class brain and a lively manner. When I asked her about conditions in prison, she said the first six months had been the worst, because they had to keep their cell doors open, and she disliked intensely both the smell and the noise of prison life. Subsequently, however, when she was allowed to keep her cell door shut, and of course, after she was allowed to live with her husband, she found conditions not at all bad. They had been allowed to read whatever they liked and she told me that as a result of her time in prison, she had been able to do something which she would not in any other circumstances have been able to do. She read every book in English, French or German on Hellenic culture, and she felt she could now regard herself an expert on that particular subject.

When after a few days I went to Barford St. John to see how the land lay, I found Diana Mosley and the Constable in the kitchen sharing the washing up and knew that all was well, but two weeks later I received a call from the Home Office asking me as a matter of urgency to move the Mosleys elsewhere. I was told that Derek Jackson, Pamela's husband, was engaged on important secret work for the Admiralty at Malvern and he had been forbidden to spend the weekend with his wife while the Mosleys were there.

It so happened that the previous day I had called at a charming small country hotel, the Shaven Crown at Shipton-under-Wychwood where the proprietress had told me that because of the severe petrol rationing, she had no one in the hotel. At my request she agreed to give the Mosleys a detached suite of rooms, where they lived quietly for some months until they eventually found a permanent home in Wiltshire.

Oxford City has long been dominated by two great rival powers, the University and the motor car factories. The story of the late Lord Nuffield's progress from a small cycle-repair business to the pioneering of mass production methods for motor car bodies is a milestone in our lives for he gave many thousands the pleasure of cheap, reliable motoring. In 1910 he was the first to design a low cost car for the man in the street, and in 1912 the first Morris Oxford went into production. He subsequently built up the firm of Morris Motors Limited at Cowley, Oxford, acting as Chairman until 1952, when a merger with Austins created the British Motor Corporation. Lord Nuffield made numerous gifts to charity, founding Nuffield College, Oxford, and in 1943 the Nuffield Foundation, which reflects his interest in medical and social research. I met Lord Nuffield on numerous occasions and always found him a modest, retiring man, pleasant in all his dealings with others.

One sunny day in November 1941 when General de Gaulle came on an official visit to Oxford, the University authorities gave an afternoon reception for him at Balliol. Charles Fox and I were invited and we both went in uniform. As we left, we saw Lord Nuffield sitting at the wheel of the small Morris he was accustomed to drive, for he was a simple and unpretentious man. He kept pressing the starter button to no effect and so we offered our help. 'Just give me a push,' he said. 'It will start in a moment.' We were not keen to do so, but he was most insistent. I asked whether he had petrol and offered to look at the carburettor and the points, but he said that we couldn't as it was a secret engine and the bonnet was locked. He adamantly refused our repeated offer to take him in one of our cars or to arrange for his car to be collected and kept on asking us to give him a push. So, as many important people were leaving the reception they were greeted with the sight of two Chief Constables in uniform pushing the greatest British motor car manufacturer in a very small motor car along the Broad, but all to no effect.

Suddenly Lord Nuffield slammed on the brakes and explained, 'Oh I know. It's all your fault. You have advised us to immobilise our cars. I've a secret switch,' and pressing a switch underneath his seat, he started the car and drove away with a wave of his hand.

I did not have as many associations with the University as I would have wished, for I have always envied those who live as academics at Oxford or Cambridge. The quiet calm of University life has a strong appeal although had I ever had the brains to achieve a Fellowship I would probably have soon found life too dull; it was a case of the grass on the other side of the road looking

Oxfordshire

greener. But it was a matter of great regret to me that, while living in Oxfordshire and working in the City, I was not asked to be a member of a College. However, in those years, I did receive invitations to dine on Sunday evenings at most High Tables and much enjoyed the erudite conversation of my hosts and their eminent guests.

I dined several times with W. T. S. Stallybrass, the Master of BNC, who on one occasion was bubbling with glee because his butler had just provided the necessary evidence for the police to arrest a well-known Oxford black marketeer. This individual had evolved a simple method of obtaining his supplies. Ascertaining that food from the USA was arriving at Bristol docks and being brought from Bristol to London by train via Oxford, with the aid of dishonest railway employees, he unhooked in Oxford the last truck of each consignment. This was moved into a siding, whence the contents disappeared into his warehouse nearby.

Two other incidents that occurred in Oxfordshire during the war are worth recounting. About 9.0 pm one evening in the early Autumn of 1942 the Superintendent at Witney telephoned to my home to tell me that a matter had come to his attention which he felt I ought to know about immediately. He came over to my house, bringing with him a number of military maps marked 'TOP SECRET' showing a piece of coastline. All the place names were Arab or French and there were certain red lines across the map with numbers attached to them. He told me that a Constable cycling along the main A.40 between Burford and Witney had found them scattered along the roadside over a distance of about a mile. I telephoned the night duty officer at MI5 Headquarters at Blenheim and took the maps to him. He promised to make inquiries and, in the middle of the night, he telephoned and asked me urgently to have a detailed search made at daybreak as some maps were still missing. I now forget the exact figures but I think we found 28 in all and that 33 had been missing. The maps had been improperly packed and had been lost from a vehicle taking them from Cheltenham to London. I later ascertained that they were maps showing the landing beaches to be used in Operation 'TORCH', our invasion of North Africa which was launched in November 1942. What negligence on someone's part!

A second incident of less potential danger was reported by one of my constables, Francis Cowan. At midnight on the 15th May 1941, the constable was cycling to his home in Tetsworth along the main London to Oxford road. In the dim light cast by his hooded lamp he saw in the gateway of a field a completely naked man. At first the constable assumed he had a mental case on his hands, but the naked man, although in some distress and apparently exhausted, was quiet and sensible. The constable gave him a coat, took him to to his house, which was not far away and, after providing food and warmth, waited for explanations. Patrick Murphy told how he had come from Southern Ireland to Liverpool, evading all the stringent checks and restrictions, in order to get a job as a fireman, or, if that failed, to join the Army. In Liverpool he met some other Irishmen who said they were going to London and could find work for him too. Next morning two car loads of Irishmen set out from Liverpool to London. Murphy recognised one of his travelling companions as a man with a bad police record for violence. The nearer they got to London the more worried Murphy became. At last he plucked up courage to ask what job he was to do in London. They told him they were going to loot bombed buildings and wanted him to assist as a 'look-out'. Murphy declared vehemently that he would do no such thing, whereupon the car was stopped and one of the party pulled out a pistol and ordered Murphy to strip. Stark naked he was pushed out of the car and he had climbed a gate into a field waiting for darkness. He was, on his own admission, an illegal entrant and while he was held in custody before being sent back to Ireland, every effort was made to check his story but with little success. The man of violence was identified but we could not find him while a fruitless search was made for Murphy's clothes. Whether the man told us the truth or whether there was another explanation, we shall never know.

As the reader will have gathered, my stay in Oxfordshire was full of interest and greatly broadening my conception of police work and my understanding of human nature. Coming from the Metropolitan Police I was always conscious of the smaller scale of Forces in the provinces. The advantage of the compulsory amalgamations in South East England for war purposes sparked off thoughts which have never left me and I gave some thought to the position in Oxfordshire. I was leading the County Force of some 200 men and women just a little larger than that commanded by my good friend, Charles Fox of the Oxford City Police. The City Police had a much better Headquarters than the County Constabulary and probably had more to give in an amalgamation. It was clear that both Forces would benefit from sharing the same Headquarters, the same communication systems, the same training facilities, criminal records, administrative branches, CID, Traffic and War Departments. Military convoys moving about Oxfordshire frequently passed through the City of Oxford necessitating a liaison effort which a single command would eliminate. Similar savings in time,

Oxfordshire

effort, and cost could be found in almost every branch of police activity. What was not so easy was how to resolve the personal problems of leadership which would arise. I committed my thoughts to paper and in it suggested that Mr Fox should be Chief Constable of the amalgamated Force, on the grounds of his seniority, experience and the amount of expertise his Force would bring to the merger and this would leave me for military service. I sent the memorandum to the Home Office and I hopefully showed my paper to Charles Fox. To my surprise he vehemently disagreed. He was proud of his small, efficient Force, proud of its connection with the ancient University, and did not want to exchange his compact command for a larger, looser organisation. I was not completely discouraged but recognised that to persuade the two Police Authorities to agree to a marriage of convenience, would require the full support of both Chief Constables. Military events forced me to leave the position at stalemate but the amalgamation I proposed in 1943 finally became part of a wider merger in 1965.

Chapter Four

MILITARY AFFAIRS

By the Autumn of 1942 it was clear that Hitler was no longer a threat to this country and everyone's thoughts were now concentrated on how to win the War rather than how to avoid losing it. The tempo of police work had slowed down. I had completed the reorganisation of the Oxfordshire Force, as far as possible in the circumstances, though there was more that I would have done had bigger resources of money, men and material been available. I like to think, however, that I was running a tight little ship, the Police Authority were satisfied, the public had no complaints – certainly very few came to my notice – and the personnel in the Force were happy in their work.

In November 1942, Operation TORCH was launched. This was an operation, planned from London, in which English and US Forces landed in Morocco and attacked the Germans in North Africa on their western flank so that they had to fight on two fronts. A month later the German 6th Army was encircled at Stalingrad. It was clear that the next step would be an attack on the enemy in Europe and I badly wanted to be in it. Since I had come to Oxfordshire in 1940 I had been fully occupied, and knew I was doing a useful job, but now I became restless and felt as a young and physically fit man I should be making a bigger contribution. So, in January 1943, after consulting my Chairman, who was now Lord Macclesfield as Major Feilden had died, I put out some feelers in the Home Office but was told that it was policy that Chief Constables must stay at their posts. Not to be put off, I asked for an interview with Mr Herbert Morrison, the Home Secretary, but received a reply that Sir Alexander Maxwell, the Permanent Under Secretary of State at the Home Office, would see me. I had not previously met him but I found him charming, friendly and sympathetic to my request. At the same time he held out no hope that the Home Secretary would change his views and I returned to Oxford somewhat crestfallen

But within twenty-four hours there was a message asking me to return to see Sir Alexander Maxwell again.

On this occasion he had with him Sir Frank Brook, DSO, MC, one of the four HM Inspectors of Constabulary and the most senior one in terms of service. He was a strikingly handsome man with a full head of white hair and blue eyes which usually had a twinkle of laughter and mischief. This was my first encounter with him and I immediately recognised him as a man I could like and respect, and he was to prove one of the most formative influences in my police career.

An Inspector of Constabulary for eighteen years and, before that, Chief Constable of the West Riding of Yorkshire for seven years and previously Chief Constable in turn of Southport and Nottingham, he had gained much distinction in the field during the First World War. In August 1914, he was a Sergeant in the KOYLI: by 1918 he was commanding a Brigade. He won the MC in 1917 and the DSO in 1918 and, in addition to receiving the Croix de Guerre, he was mentioned in Despatches and Cited in French Army Papers.

Sir Alexander Maxwell told me that since our interview the War Office had informed him that planning for the invasion of Europe was now starting and because of the problems that the Armies would face in coping with the civil population they required the services of a number of senior police officers. The Home Office had selected a number of Chief Constables to attend a training course at the Civil Affairs Staff Centre at Wimbledon and they now wanted a Chief Constable to join the team at the War Office making plans for the invasion. Sir Alexander asked whether I would like the assignment and I accepted with alacrity. He said that Sir Frank Brook would be available for consultation and thus began a most interesting chapter of my life and with it a very close and warm friendship between Sir Frank Brook and myself, which lasted until his death in February 1960.

When I returned to Oxford and told Lord Macclesfield of the offer, he readily gave his approval for me to undertake the work and it was agreed, between the Home Office and the Oxfordshire Police Authority, that I would for the time being continue as the Chief Constable of Oxfordshire and the County would be responsible for my salary. It was also agreed that all expenses of my travelling to London and accommodation there, would be met by the War Office.

So on Monday, 1st February, 1943, I found myself in a room in Whitehall furnished simply with two desks, two chairs and a filing cabinet and on my desk a directive, 'Prepare a plan to control the civil population when the Allied Armies re-enter North West

Europe' a task which was certainly a challenge for a young man of 32 especially as I was told that my responsibilities would include not only the police, but also the fire, prison and civil defence services under the umbrella name of 'Public Safety'.

To assist me initially I was joined by Detective Inspector Harold Suttling of the Metropolitan Police, an experienced Special Branch officer who had been nominated by the Commissioner at the request of the Home Office. We got on well but I did not find him an ideal planning officer. Loyal, intelligent and friendly, he had done invaluable work in operational matters, but he was not staff-trained and was much better suited in an operational role than as a planner.

The work involved two widely different kinds of conditions – the liberation of friendly territory from German occupation, and the occupation by the Allied Armies of enemy territory: each called for different policies, while there were many factors outside the realm of law and order which would have to be dealt with.

It was accepted that the whole of continental life would have broken down, food would be extremely short, there would be no transport of any kind and hundreds of thousands of homeless people of many nationalities would have to be handled, while it was believed probable that in their retreat the Germans would take with them all the able bodied police and firemen. A daunting prospect but not insurmountable.

My first task was to try to assess the number of trained policemen we would require to carry out the work in the field once the plan had been made and the invasion started. In theory, of course, this was putting the cart before the horse for one should have made the plan first, then assessed the numbers required, but I knew that it would take time to find the men and give them the necessary training. So I took the number 500 off the top of my head and, knowing that in the police forces there were many physically fit and efficient policemen in the ranks of Inspector and Sergeant who wanted to play an active part in the fighting, I suggested to the Home Office that we should call for volunteers and take the best 500. This was agreed, and there was no shortage of volunteers. We selected about 20 Chief Constables and Assistant Chief Constables, who were then sent on a course at the Civil Affairs Staff College at Wimbledon.

To deal with a large number of lower ranking officers, we borrowed Peel House, the Metropolitan Police Training School in London which was then lying empty. We put Arthur Young, who was then still Chief Constable of Leamington, in charge and we gave each man a two months' course on the duties we expected he would have to undertake. On each course we arranged to have a few Army Officers found for us by the War Office hoping the policemen would gain something by absorbing a little of the military atmosphere. At the end of each course the officers went back to their forces to await the time for their call-up.

Generally it was agreed that Chief Constables and Assistant Chief Constables when called up would be given the rank of Lieutenant-Colonel, Inspectors were to become Majors, and Sergeants, Captains or Lieutenants.

In the Summer of 1943 while we were in the middle of this training, I received a message that Lord Rennell of Rodd wished to see Sir Frank Brook and myself urgently. When we met at the Home Office he told us that he was responsible for the planning for Military Government in Sicily and Italy when those countries were invaded in the very near future, and that it was essential that he should have a number of police officers to take part in the invasion. He asked us to supply him with 60 men and someone to take command of them. It was, as I remember, a Thursday afternoon and he said that he wanted them to fly out on the following Monday morning. We told him that this was quite impossible because the officers who had been trained had returned to their forces and had not yet been commissioned. Sir Frank and I decided that the only way to obtain 60 officers quickly was to ask for all of them from the Metropolitan Police and this we did. Men were selected, commissioned, provided with uniform and they left for North Africa within the week. To take charge of them we nominated Arthur Young and he was commissioned and given the rank of Full Colonel. All those who went made a valuable contribution to Military Government in Sicily, not only in the field of Public Safety but in the wider areas of Local Government, Transportation, Food Supplies and so on.

My responsibilities not only included planning to resuscitate the public safety services in the countries to be liberated, but also plans to seize control of the German Police, the SS and the Gestapo as well as their Fire, Prison and Civil Defence Services and to decide what should take their place. In making these plans I had also to consult with other planning sections who were dealing with food, and displaced persons, and to negotiate a dividing line between the responsibilities of the military police and civil affairs public safety officers.

At first the group to which I belonged was called the War Office Planning Team but in August 1943 we were amalgamated with an American planning team and the whole given the name of COSSAC (Chief of Staff Supreme Allied Command) the officer in charge being Lieutenant General Freddy Morgan, a jovial intelligent man whose only decorations at that time were the General

Service and Victory medals of the First World War, though in due course he became General Sir Frederick Morgan, KCB, and given a number of foreign decorations. Our Headquarters was established at first at Norfolk House, St James's Square, W1, the staff consisting of officers both British and American from all three Armed Services. I was the only person in the building in police uniform and this proved to be an advantage for no one knew exactly what rank was my equivalent in the Armed Services and therefore I was able, though I did not often take advantage of it, to consult people of the highest rank.

Among the Americans who came was O. W. Wilson who appeared from the Italian theatre of war to be my Deputy, and this started a close friendship which lasted until his death in 1960. He was a professional police officer who at an early age had been appointed Chief of Police of Wichita, Kansas, but who in 1938 had become Dean of the School of Criminology at Berkeley in the University of California. I was very glad to have his help for he was able to contribute first hand practical knowledge of the problems that had existed in Italy while the Allied Armies were fighting in that country.

Other specialist sections were making their own plans and the general plans had to be adapted to the particular circumstances and laws of the countries to be liberated, while the plans for Germany were quite different from those for the Allied countries. We therefore, set up separate subsidiary planning staffs for each country, and I had to supply two public safety officers – one English and one American – for each 'country house' as they were called.

We established the general policies at Norfolk House and then the officers in each house adapted those plans for the particular circumstances of the country for which they were responsible, working closely with the exiled government of the country, also situated in London.

The general organisation of COSSAC and subsequently SHAEF (Supreme Headquarters Allied Expeditionary Force) was based on the American system. We had five separate divisions – G1 responsible for Military Formations, G2 for Intelligence, G3 for Operations, G4 for Services and Supplies and G5 for Civil Affairs and Military Government.

At first the Officer in Charge of G5 was Major General Sir Roger Lumley,[1] who had been a Member of Parliament and Governor of Bombay.

After a short time he was replaced by Lieutenant General

[1] later the Rt Hon the Earl of Scarborough KG, PC, GCSI, GCIE, GCVO died 1969.

Grasett, later Lieutenant General Sir Edward Grasett, KBE, CB, DSO, MC. He was a Canadian with a very strong personality, just the sort of man to have as one's Commanding Officer, for he was wise, objective in his assessments of men and ideas, and strong minded in supporting anyone whom he believed to be right.

The general policy at SHAEF was that where the Head of any division or branch was English his deputy would be American, or vice versa.

General Grasett's deputy was an American, Brigadier General Frank McSherry who took a particular interest in the planning of Public Safety matters, while my immediate superior officer was Colonel Tom Henn, in peace time a very popular Fellow of St. Catherine's College, Cambridge. By coincidence he was a younger brother of Colonel W. Henn who was Chief Constable of Gloucestershire.

Tom had no knowledge of police affairs and so I was in the lucky position of being able to run my own show without fear of interference, although Tom and Frank McSherry were at all times available for consultation.

As the planning proceeded, differences of opinion at the political level on our relations with the exiled governments complicated matters.

France was particularly tricky for at that time there was a strong difference of opinion between the Americans and the British. One took the view that we ought to deal with General de Gaulle as the outward manifestation of the resistance movement, while the other side held that it was not for the allies to pre-empt the future government of France and we should not appear to give de Gaulle close support as the French people would not necessarily recognise him as their political leader.

Although not a party to the political discussions, I knew about this strong difference of opinion, and thought that Churchill was backing the Committee of National Liberation while the Americans were supporting de Gaulle but when I read Churchill's book on the Second World War I discovered that I was wrong and it was the other way round, though I know that Churchill found de Gaulle most difficult to work with.

We had to write a manual for use by public safety officers in the field, and as a consequence of these changes in policy, the Public Safety Manual was re-written no less than four times.

When we first wrote the manual we said, 'On entering France you will do so and so'. Then we were told that we must re-write the manual saying, 'When you enter France you will assist the French Authorities to do so and so'. Subsequently we were told to re-phrase it again, saying 'When you enter France, if you find that the French Authorities have not done so and so, you will assist them and advise them to do so and so'; fourthly and finally we were ordered to word it so as to make clear that we would only take action if the French failed to do so.

Other sections had also to re-write their manuals but because of the continual conflicting instructions, none of them were ready by D Day, and the only manual that was printed and distributed to the Civil Affairs officers in the field was the Public Safety Manual.

Right up to the last minute we were firmly instructed not to discuss the details of our planning with the exiled French Government in London and this certainly caused us difficulties and embarrassment.

For instance, at one moment shortly before D Day, I discovered that the French Government in exile had arranged for the production of quantities of brassards decorated with the Cross of Lorraine, to be handed to people they proposed to make police officers. When I reported this to General Grasett he instructed me to do all I could to persuade the French not to use such brassards, since this was the emblem of General de Gaulle. I did my best but I was quite sure that the French would not listen to me, and in the event they did not.

About a week before D Day, however, the picture changed and we were then told that we could co-operate with the exiled Government. I was made Chairman of a small Sub-Committee which was to discuss with representatives of the exiled Government the plans that we were making to help re-start the French Public Safety Services.

On asking the French what assistance they would require I discovered what I had long suspected; the French themselves had already made extremely detailed plans and chosen the men whom they intended to put in charge of the various governmental activities when areas of France were liberated.

Owing to the expansion of the staff at SHAEF we were moved from our offices in Norfolk Square and in November 1943 I found myself working from some very insecure offices in a building in Victoria Street. At that time I was still a policeman going back to Oxford each weekend to look after the affairs of the Oxfordshire Constabulary.

About 3 o'clock on the afternoon of Friday, 26th November, 1943 – that date will always stay in my mind – Tom Henn walked into my office with a large sealed envelope which he put on my desk and said, 'Eric, read this over the weekend and let me have it back; you'd better look after it carefully.' I went on with the work I was doing and shortly before I packed up to catch the 6 pm train to Oxford I opened the envelope, and discovered to my absolute amazement that it was the complete detailed plan for the invasion, giving code names for the beaches, the numbers of troops and divisions that would be landed on each day, and a whole appreciation of the various alternative dates on which the invasion with the code name 'Overlord' could be launched. I sealed the envelope and went to Tom's room only to find that he had left. As I had no safe in my office I put the file in my despatch case and took it back to Oxford, hugging it closely the whole way. On arriving home I did not tell my wife what was in the despatch case but insisted on taking it up to my bedroom and putting it under the bed. On Saturday morning Tom Henn telephoned me from Cambridge to ask what I had done with the parcel, as he was somewhat concerned about its safety. I replied that I was sitting on it and was going to keep sitting on it until I returned it to him on Monday morning in London.

When I returned it I wrote a memorandum to the Chief of Staff saying that I thought it was entirely unnecessary and a threat to security that I should have seen the plan and that we ought to adopt 'a need to know' basis for letting people see it. All that I needed to know at that time was that the invasion would take place in France rather than any other country and even that was not essential.

It is believed that probably as many as 2,000 people knew the details of the invasion plan by the end of December 1943, and as many as 10,000 by the 1st June, 1944, yet the Germans never had any inkling of the plans that we had made, neither the date nor the place that the invasion would take place; this says something for the ability of people to keep their mouths shut in important circumstances.

By December we knew that General Eisenhower, at that time in charge of the Italian theatre of operations, had been appointed Supreme Commander, and we anticipated his arrival at Norfolk House immediately after the New Year, when COSSAC would change its name to SHAEF.

Freddy Morgan then told me that he thought I ought now to get into military uniform so I was commissioned as a Second Lieutenant on the General List on one day and promoted to Full Colonel on the next.

On Monday, 6th January, 1944, we were told that Ike had arrived and wished to see the whole of his staff in a room on the top floor of the building. This was an empty room which had last been used for some social activity on the Saturday night and was not exactly clean.

ONE POLICEMAN'S STORY

Some 80 of us were in the room when Ike walked in, with an ADC who carried a chair. Ike stood on the chair, put his hands on his hips, looked around with those wonderful blue eyes and a great beaming smile and said, 'Gentlemen, I've just come to say hello', and with his personality and demeanour he had from that moment onwards our complete support, respect, loyalty and affection. He spoke quite briefly saying he had read the plan that we had prepared and he congratulated us all on the amount of hard work that had gone into it, and added that if he altered the plan at all, it would be because he was able to persuade the American and British Chiefs of Staff to allow him more men and equipment than we had estimated we should be allowed to have when making the original plan.

In the following five months I saw Ike from time to time, but the only other occasion on which he called the whole of his staff together was two days before D Day when most of the Headquarters staff had moved to Bushey Park. On that occasion we were again told that the Supreme Commander wished to meet his staff and we met in a large cinema where there must have been some 400–500 officers present. On the stage were serried ranks of one star, two star and three star Generals, and when Ike walked in he looked around in exactly the same way as he had on the first occasion and putting his hands on his hips he said, 'My, how the family's grown', a remark which was only appreciated by the 80 of us who had been present at the first meeting.

By April 1944 all 500 police officers had been to Peel House and the time had come to call them up. They were commissioned and placed in waiting units in different parts of the country, the main one being at the Grand Hotel at Eastbourne where I went from time to time to give the men last minute instructions.

It so happened that the Americans had very few professional police officers on whom to call for Public Safety work, but when the plans had been made we found that we did not require as many as 500 Public Safety Officers for the British area of operations and so we were able to supply British police officers not only for the Italian Theatre, but also to join American Civil Affairs detachments.

In the event this proved to be most successful and since the calibre of some Civil Affairs Officers, particularly in the American detachments, was not as good as it should have been, the British Public Safety Officers in many cases formed the back-bone of the detachment.

It was at the hotel at Eastbourne that I first met W. J. H. Palfrey who was at that time Chief Constable of Accrington, a small Borough Force in Lancashire. His first two Christian names were

Military Affairs

William John and in the Police he was always known as Bill, but for some reason, when he was in the Army he was always known as John and since I first knew him in the Army I always afterwards called him John Palfrey.

I was immediately impressed by his personality for he was forthright, lucid in expression and very enthusiastic and it was clear that he had a very orderly mind. When, therefore, we were asked to nominate a British Public Safety Officer for the American detachment going into Cherbourg, the first large city we expected to liberate, I chose John Palfrey for this job.

After D Day when Cherbourg was liberated, the American detachment worked most efficiently, setting up a local government to deal with the many problems that arose in the town which had been badly bombed by both sides. I heard how very well Palfrey had performed in all this taking on much good work outside the field of Public Safety so, when later we were making plans for the liberation of Paris, I was very glad to hear that his detachment had been nominated to be the Civil Affairs detachment for Paris, for I was confident that in Palfrey we should have someone who would be of the greatest assistance to the Paris police and my expectations were fulfilled. It could not be known at that time, of course, that in due course John Palfrey and I would work together very closely in Lancashire for many years.

By early August it was clear that Paris would be liberated some time that month, and I decided that it was time I paid a visit to France to see how plans had worked out in practice, and in particular, to see whether the Paris police needed any assistance.

To move about in the rear of the battlefield one required to have written orders giving the necessary permission to requisition transport, accommodation and food. Having told the appropriate department of my proposal, I received the necessary written authority. All the document said was, 'You will proceed to the continent of Europe by aircraft "Sunrise" and will return to England when your mission is completed.' Sunrise was the code name for one of the air ferry services that had been established and ran at that time between Northolt and an airstrip outside Caen. With such wide and vaguely defined orders as these, the liberated part of Europe was now wide open to me; I could go anywhere, requisition a car and a driver at any time, free petrol, accommodation and food were all mine for the asking at any military installation, and I could stay as long as I liked.

It was expected that Paris would be liberated sometime about Wednesday, 24th August, so I arranged to fly over to France on the previous Sunday. At 8.0 am I arrived at Northolt in bright sunshine to find waiting for the 'plane a number of war correspondents who were to cover the liberation of Paris. We were then told that owing to fog at Caen the flight was delayed. There was no food at Northolt and at 12 noon we were put in a 'bus and sent for lunch to the military mess at Grosvenor House, returning to the airfield at 2.30 pm, where we waited until 5.0 pm, only to be told to come back the next day. Monday dawned bright and clear but, as on the day before, we sat on the aerodrome all day, save for our luncheon excursion to Grosvenor House.

By this time the war correspondents were getting very tense that they were missing a good story, but we heard that General Bradley's First Army was meeting more resistance than had been expected and this cheered us all up for it meant that the liberation of Paris would be delayed.

At last on Tuesday, the 23rd we got away. During the wait I had become friendly with Ed Murrow, the well known American broadcaster, and at Caen he and I requisitioned a jeep and a US driver and visited various detachments in the field. We were impressed by the way in which the French civilians had so quickly taken charge and were, as far as circumstances allowed, re-establishing normal life. All the bodies of soldiers, civilians and the carcasses of animals killed in the fighting had long since been removed and buried, but every village we came to showed signs of severe damage caused by the allied armies as they drove back the Germans. Some towns such as Vire, had been completely destroyed by allied bombing, and we drove through narrow alleys made by bull-dozers as they piled up the rubble eight to ten feet high on either side of the streets.

When we arrived in Le Mans we learnt that there would be further delay before the Germans left Paris, and so Ed and I parted company as I wanted to visit Angers where, thirteen years earlier, I had tried to learn the French language. I also wished to make the visit because this is where they make Cointreau which we had not seen in England for a long time, and I knew that a case of it would be well received at home.

Angers had been liberated with little damage by Pattons 3rd Army, and when I arrived there, soon after 12 noon, I was told that the distillery was closed until 2.0 pm.

While looking for somewhere to eat, I was accosted by a man who told me in English that I was the first English officer they had seen in the town. I was taken to meet the Mayor who, after several celebratory drinks, insisted that I should be his guest at lunch. We went to a good restaurant and soon the party grew. Throughout that afternoon, the entente cordiale was sealed and re-sealed and about 5.0 pm, I was poured in a comatose condition into my car and my faithful driver drove me back to Le Mans. Not until the next day did I realise that I had forgotten the Cointreau.

By chance that same day I met Geoffrey Webb, a Professor of Arts at the Slade School in London, who was in charge of the Fine Arts and Monuments Section of SHAEF. Geoffrey was with a US colleague from the Food Section and all three of us decided to go into Paris together in two cars. We were an oddly assorted trio but felt we had got our priorities right. I was going in to see that law and order were functioning, the American to see that there was enough food and Geoffrey Webb to see that the Venus De Milo, who would outlast all of us, was unharmed.

We learned that de Gaulle was at Rambouillet, and that he expected to enter Paris on Friday evening or Saturday morning when he would go in procession to Notre Dame. We decided to try to join the procession and arranged that if we got separated, we would meet at the Hotel du Louvre where I had stayed before the War.

We did get separated and I was held up in the mass of military traffic all making for Paris, but eventually on the Saturday afternoon I found myself close to the Petit Palais in the Champs Élysées. It was a lovely afternoon and the crowds had turned out in force. Every car was packed, not only with soldiers but with civilians – mostly young girls with flowers in their hair. At one moment I asked my driver whether I had as much lipstick on my face as he had. Suddenly there was a fusillade of shots and the crack of a tank gun. One moment all was jollity and fun, the next everyone was lying on the ground trying to work out where the shooting was coming from and whether we were in danger.

Paris had been liberated by the US First Army assisted by the French, and as far as I knew there were no British troops in the city. When the firing stopped, I went into the Petit Palais exhibition centre where much to my surprise I found Kenneth Younger, later Sir Kenneth Younger, KBE, a prominent Labour MP, whom I knew to be doing intelligence work on the staff of 21 Army Group. He had with him several British soldiers, and was very angry because one of his men looking out of a window had been shot in the shoulder by a US soldier. No one really knows quite what happened, but someone had said that there were German snipers on the roof of the Crillon Hotel and trigger-happy US soldiers had started firing indiscriminately. There is now a plaque in the square close to the Rue de Rivoli commemorating the death of the civilians who, alas, died amongst the celebrations that afternoon. The scars caused by the shells are still to be seen on the walls of the Crillon Hotel.

That evening I met Geoffrey Webb and the American at the Louvre Hotel which was closed, dark and dismal. The manager said he had no food, heating or light, but he could let us use a suite on the first floor.

I had assumed that Paris would be a scene of gaiety that evening, but the Parisians had just undergone a week of terror expecting that there would be a battle for the city. Although the Germans had eventually withdrawn without a fight the restaurants were still shut and there was little or no food. The streets were dark and the whole place gloomy and unfriendly.

We had brought with us our own cooking gear and food, but we had no drink. While we were preparing our meal, two girls appeared, dressed in trousers and blouses, wearing military belts with guns at the hip and FFI brassards denoting that they were active resistance fighters. They said that their FFI flag was flying from our balcony and that they had come to collect it. We learnt that they were actresses from the nearby Comédie Francaise and when we asked if they knew where we could get a drink, they invited us to come with them to the Theatre. We went in through the stage door and in a room behind the stage we were shown stacked cases of champagne and brandy, ostensibly guarded by a rather beautiful fair-haired young boy, who was lying on a settee fast asleep.

Carrying a case of brandy and two cases of champagne we returned to the hotel with the two girls and we hardly noticed the air raid on the city that night, when Les Halles – the Covent Garden of Paris – was burnt out.

The next morning I went to Police Headquarters to meet M. Luizet, the newly appointed Prefect of Police and formally presented the congratulations of the British Police to the French Police on the magnificent way in which they had helped to defend Paris, even though many of them were shot by the Germans before they left.

M. Luizet assured me that they were not in need of any assistance, and once again I was impressed by the calm efficiency with which they were carrying out their plans so obviously prepared in advance by de Gaulle and his staff officers.

I then went to the offices of the Chase Manhattan Bank in Rue Cambon, which I knew was to be the Headquarters of the SHAEF Mission to Paris, and there I met John Palfrey and his team, who had come in to act as liaison officers with the Paris Police. With his usual efficiency he was already well organised and had made contact with some of the leading people who were organising civilian life in the various arrondisements.

Satisfied that the French Police were quite capable of looking

Military Affairs

after themselves, and realising that they really did not need any help from us, there was no reason for me to stay in Paris, and so on the Monday I found an airstrip and an aeroplane and flew back to England.

Back in England I learnt that SHAEF was to move to Granville in Normandy and there we went in September, living for a short time in caravans among the sand dunes.

From Granville I was recalled to England to appear before the Durham Police Authority to be appointed Chief Constable of that County.

My life during the great adventure of the turbulent liberation of France had been so hectic that I barely had time to keep in touch with internal police affairs at home. I did however, receive the Police Review each week and letters from the Oxfordshire Police Headquarters kept me in the picture to some extent, while I always called at the Home Office on the few occasions when I returned to England. I was aware that Harry Studdy (later Sir Henry Studdy CBE, KPM), a former Indian Police Officer and Chief Constable of Northumberland from 1935 to 1943 had been appointed Chief Constable of Durham but after only eighteen months in office had moved on to the West Riding of Yorkshire. I had heard, too, that the Chief Constable of Hertfordshire had resigned earlier in the year, which left both Durham and Hertfordshire without Chief Constables. Advertisements inviting applications for both posts had appeared in the national and police press during the summer of 1944, but at this time I had not given much thought to my future in the Police Service and certainly never considered applying for either the Durham or Hertfordshire appointments. Indeed, now that the Allied drive was relentlessly rolling on towards Germany, I was looking forward to the realisation of our plans for military government; but this was not to be. When I returned to the United Kingdom after the liberation of Paris, I called at the Home Office to see Sir Frank Brook, who told me that there had been a very disappointing number of applicants for both the Durham and Hertfordshire posts. He added, 'Both positions are to be re-advertised and the Home Office want you and Arthur Young to apply for them.'

Sir Frank went on to explain that the Durham Police Authority would require the successful applicant to take over the Force fairly soon, and in any event before the end of hostilities as the new Chief Constable had to be ready, if the necessity arose, to deal with any disorder in the Durham coalfields which might arise when the reorganisation plans of the coal industry were made known, for there was already some talk of nationalising the industry and it was not known what the reactions of the miners would be if this did not happen.

After taking counsel with Joanna, who was still living at Woodstock with our two young children, I did decide to apply for both appointments, and I asked Sir Roger Lumley, to act as one of my referees. As he lived at Lumley Castle in County Durham I felt I could not have better support.

The Durham appointment carried a salary of £1,450 a year while that of Hertfordshire was only £1,000 a year, and because of this, the Home Office arranged that the Durham Police Authority should interview candidates on the Monday, while Hertfordshire would interview on the Thursday. Arthur Young also applied for both appointments and he flew over from Italy, while I came from Paris for the two interviews.

Feeling very uncertain as to whether I was doing the right thing, I boarded a train for the North. My spirits sank to the lowest point on my arrival in Durham for it was a gloomy day and all the dull buildings presented a dour and unfriendly outlook to a stranger, despite the magnificent and breath-taking beauty of the Norman Cathedral overlooking the town. To make matters worse, the hotel to which I had been directed was very old fashioned and uncomfortable (how different today), while the interviews were to take place in the Old Shire Hall, a monstrous, ugly edifice of bright red brick contrasting unhappily with the 18th century brown brick buildings of the Old Elvet.

Besides Arthur Young the other candidates were Bill Willis,[1] the then Chief Constable of Bedfordshire, George Banwell,[2] who had been on the short list with me for Oxfordshire and was now Chief Constable of the East Riding, and Harold Golden,[3] who was Chief Constable of Shropshire. We were all friends and on the morning before the interview we walked up to look at the Cathedral. I immediately fell in love with it, and I made a silent resolution then and there that if I was appointed Chief Constable of Durham I would bring the Force to the Cathedral as soon as the War was over for a Victory Service.[4]

The interviews took place at the Old Shire Hall at 11 am.

---

[1] later Commander W. J. A. Willis CBE, MVO, KPM, HM Inspector of Constabulary.

[2] later G. E. Banwell CBE, Chief Constable of Cheshire 1946–1955.

[3] later Lieutenant Colonel H. Golden OBE, Chief Constable of Wiltshire 1946–1963.

[4] This I did in September, 1945, when some 700 policemen with their wives and children, accompanied by the Lord Lieutenant and civic dignitaries from the County, attended a service of thanksgiving and remembrance for those who had lost their lives. It was a moving sight.

Although we were all friends it is inevitable that on such occasions a somewhat apprehensive and uneasy atmosphere prevails and this was not even dispelled by the warm welcome we received from Kenneth Hope, the Clerk of the Police Authority. We were interviewed individually, in alphabetical order. The Police Committee in Durham consisted of 12 Councillors appointed by the County Council and 12 Magistrates appointed by the Magistrates at their annual meeting at Quarter Sessions. The 12 Councillors were all members of the Labour Party and most had been in the pits. The Chairman of the Police Authority, Lord Barnard, CMG, OBE, MC, whom I was later to know very well, surprised me by asking very few questions preferring no doubt to watch my reactions to the questions put to me by his colleagues. One or two Councillors asked in their quaint Geordie accent, which I later came to love so much, when I could start if I was offered the job, and Sir Frank Nicholson, CBE, also a Magistrate and a Deputy Lieutenant of the County, posed the question, 'Do you think you will like living in the North?' I replied though I had never lived anywhere north of Birmingham, I knew that the people of Durham had a reputation for friendliness, that I considered myself adaptable and believed I could settle down and enjoy life in this part of England.

Eventually, after everyone had been interviewed, there was a short pause, and then I was called back, offered the appointment and pressed to say that I would begin my new duties not later than 1st January, 1945. I promised to consult my General in France, and provided he agreed, to ask the Home Office to accelerate my release from the army service.

Following a short discussion with Lord Barnard, Alderman Thomas Benfold, CBE, JP, Chairman of Durham County Council, and Alderman J. W. Foster, OBE, JP, his Vice-Chairman and Chairman of the Finance Committee, I returned to my hotel and lunched with the other candidates, still uncertain as to whether I was the lucky or the unlucky one of the five.

Afterwards I was introduced to John Wright, the Acting Chief Constable of the County, who took me along to see West House, the official residence of the Chief Constable of Durham, a converted 18th century farm house on the outskirts of the City. I was not impressed by its condition and felt that Joanna would not be happy living in it.

I returned to Oxfordshire feeling anything but elated at my success, told Joanna what had happened, sent a letter withdrawing my application to the Hertfordshire Police Authority and returned to France.

General Grasett was not particularly pleased to hear of my

success but said that he would not put any obstacles in the way of my release at the end of the year. It was, in many ways, a convenient time for me to leave the Army, for all the plans for the military government of Germany had been completed.

From Granville we moved to Versailles where we set up our offices in the grooms' living quarters over the Palace stables. At SHAEF life only began if one's rank was higher that that of Colonel. In ordinary regimental life even subalterns had batmen, and cars were easy to come by, but at SHAEF only one star generals or higher had batmen and motor cars. It's all a matter of relativity. Colonels and Majors were two-a-penny in that rarefied atmosphere.

I had been offered the use of a beautiful apartment in Avenue Foch, one of the most expensive parts of Paris. This belonged to a wealthy American friend who used it before the war whenever she was in Europe. Throughout the war it had been occupied by a German General who had kept it in immaculate condition and had even added a grand piano.

As I was a mere Colonel, I had no means of transport to and from Versailles, so the Brigadier, who was my immediate superior, shared it with me, and together we had a happy and most elegant home for the next four months. Each day his car took us out to Versailles in the morning and back into Paris in the evening, and his batman looked after us.

I cannot say that I made much constructive contribution to the Allied war effort during the following months. The work of helping liberated countries set up their own public safety services was the responsibility of the Army Group and Armies as they implemented their own plans in accordance with the directives which we had drawn up at SHAEF and issued before 'D Day', while the plans of the exiled governments proved adequate to deal with the problems that arose.

Directives had been prepared and issued to the Army Groups for seizing control of the German Police and other services and re-organising them on non-Nazi lines. We understood that detachments of military government officers were being trained in the field to undertake these duties when the fighting units reached Germany.

Of course, from time to time there were problems referred back to SHAEF for us to solve but they were of a minor nature mainly dealing with the supply of uniforms and vehicles for the public safety services.

SHAEF was only concerned with issuing directives on what should be done during the initial stages of our entry into Germany, while hostilities continued. This was known as the stage of 'unrolling the carpet'. Once an armistice had been declared, responsibility for the control of Germany would pass to the Control Commissions. The real planning for the final situation in Germany was a matter for the members of the Control Commission; in this the British and Americans worked separately, not being integrated as we were at SHAEF, for each of the Allied nations would have its own area to administer in accordance with the directives issued by the combined Chief of Staff. At the last minute, it was agreed that the French would have a Zone, but I had no contact with their planning officers, and there was no contact with the Russians until we reached Berlin.

I was not really concerned with any of this, though I did keep in touch with Colonel Halland who was in charge of the Public Safety section of the British Control Commission but as he was still working in London we rarely met.

The personnel for work on the Control Commission had been recruited separately and Colonel Halland had arranged for a number of police officers still at home to join the Commission as civilians at the appropriate time, while I had given him the names of men working in Civil Affairs whom I believed might wish to stay on in Germany for some considerable time. These were mostly men who saw no prospect of promotion for themselves in the British Police after the war had ended.

I did have one operational matter to deal with soon after Paris was liberated. M. Luizet, the Prefect of Police, took the view that while there were still Frenchmen detained as prisoners of war, or as civilians in Germany, there should be no jollifications in Paris. He decreed that while restaurants could be open for certain limited hours, the theatres, cinemas, and especially the night clubs, should remain closed. This did not suit the owners of these establishments, the citizens of Paris or the Allied Forces – especially the Americans. It was my job to represent to Luizet on behalf of the Allied Forces that he should relax his rules in this matter. In this I managed to succeed, and night life started once more. The owners of restaurants and night clubs, who form a strong and closely knit union, were of the opinion that John Palfrey and I had persuaded Luizet to change his mind and as a consequence, restaurants and night clubs were free for us throughout the time I was in Paris – a very satisfactory state of affairs.

At SHAEF my main preoccupation was to argue with the G1 Division who dealt with the allocation of military personnel about the responsibility for dealing with the concentration camps as they were uncovered. This was at first considered work for

Military Government Officers and, therefore, the responsibility of G5, but from the outset I had said that the task would be beyond our capabilities, and that the military units must do it. 'The soldiers are there to fight the Germans, not to do welfare work', was the argument I met, and while we were in England I lost the battle. But as we got nearer to Germany, and Intelligence reports started stressing the appalling size and seriousness of the problem that the Allied Armies would encounter, those in G1 who had originally opposed me agreed that they would have to accept responsibility and in due course they issued a directive that specific Army Units would be allocated for this work, though they were at the time thinking in terms of companies, and not of the battalions and even the brigades that were eventually required.

On Armistice Day, Winston Churchill came to Paris and he describes his visit in his book, *The Second World War* as follows:

> 'At eleven o'clock on the morning of November 11 De Gaulle conducted me in an open car across the Seine and through the Place de la Concorde, with a splended escort of Gardes Republicains in full uniform with all their breastplates. They were several hundred strong, and provided a brilliant spectacle, on which the sun shone brightly. The whole of the famous avenue of the Champs Elysees was crowded with Parisians and lined with troops. Every window was filled with spectators and decorated with flags. We proceeded through wildly cheering multitudes to the Arc de Triomphe, where we both laid wreaths upon the tomb of the Unknown Warrior. After this ceremony was over the General and I walked together, followed by a concourse of the leading figures of French public life, for half a mile down the highway I knew so well. We then took our places on a dais, and there was a splendid march past of French and British troops. Our Guards detachment was magnificent'.

I was lucky enough to have a seat on the dais, which was a small one, and it was a thrilling sight to see the Prime Minister walking down the Champs Élysées and standing on the dais acknowledging the cheers of the crowd.

During this time I also paid visits to detachments in the field and as soon as Lyons was liberated and Patton's 3rd Army had linked up with the 6th Army coming up from the South, Major Fouliquies, the French Liaison Officer at SHAEF took me with him on a tour which included some of the Cote Rotie vineyards where he was well known. As a consequence, the trip became more of a gastronomic excursion than a military visitation.

Lyons situated on the confluence of the rivers Rhone and Saone was not much damaged during the War, but when they retreated the Germans had attempted to blow up all the twelve bridges over the two rivers and had destroyed eleven of them. The bridges are the very arteries of the city and though the Americans had quickly built a temporary bridge over the other river, the delays to traffic were appalling and we were glad to be away as soon as possible.

On a second tour I went up to Brussels to the Headquarters of 21 Army Group, going first to Luxembourg and then through the Ardennes, an area which two weeks later was to be the scene of the counter-attack by the Germans, which for a time seriously held up the advance of the Allies.

In Brussels, alas, I met an unfriendly reception, as I believe did all SHAEF officers. Indeed some cynics at SHAEF considered that the fights we had with 21 Army Group were much more bitter than the fight against the Germans.

The attitude of the staff with whom I had to deal was that once we had issued our directives, it was their job to implement them as they thought fit and we had no right to interfere. I said that I had not come to interfere, but only to see whether our directives were being carried out, and if there was any way in which I could help.

At first I was told that I could not even visit detachments in the field in the British area of responsibility, but I insisted on this, and eventually, with bad grace, the necessary arrangements were made for me to go to Lille where the Army Group was holding the pool of Public Safety Officers who would eventually be allocated to units entering Germany. I am glad I went, for there I found a mood of great frustration as the men were just sitting doing nothing, and had not even been issued with the training manuals we had prepared in England, and which were in the hands of the staff at Army Group Headquarters.

Very angry, I returned to Paris to ask my General to write a strongly worded letter on the matter to Army Group, which resulted in the manuals being issued and a proper training school for the men being set up.

The unwillingness of Army Group Headquarters to co-operate was exemplified by the fact that I received a letter from the Head of the Police Division at the Home Office, saying that he had heard some excellent work was being performed in the field by Civil Affairs Officers who were members of the British Police, and that he would be glad if I would let him have any reports on the matter so that he could brief the Home Secretary. I wrote to the Head of Public Safety at 21 Army Group Headquarters to ask his help and received a reply that it was contrary to the policy of the Army Group to ask for such information from detachments in the field. I was quite sure that this was not the policy of the Army Group, but merely the views of the individual concerned, and I asked my General to deal with the matter at a higher level. The question was still unresolved when I returned to England, but I fear that because of this we never obtained records of the many incidents of extremely good work in the field carried out by police officers.

Some years later I was approached on the matter by Mr F. S. V. Donnison who was at the time writing that part of the Official History of the War which dealt with Civil Affairs and Military Government, and I published a request in the Police Review asking for any private records that officers may have kept. Very few answers were received and it was most unfortunate that at the outset we were not advised to keep war diaries, for there is no doubt that an interesting and valuable story could have been told.

Another matter at SHAEF under discussion at that time was the so-called 'non-frat' order. There were those at SHAEF who were of the opinion that because of the appalling atrocities committed by the Germans before and during the War we should, on entering Germany, ostracise the civilian population. To implement this they proposed that an order should be issued to the troops stating that fraternisation with the Germans was forbidden, and that there should be no social contact between the troops and the civilian population. With hindsight it seems almost laughable that serious, intelligent, grown men should have made such a proposal, but at the time feelings were running high, and the idea was strongly canvassed.

From the outset I strongly opposed the whole idea on the grounds that even if such a policy was desirable in theory, it was totally unworkable in practice. Soldiers were human beings and as soon as the fighting was over they would want to talk to the girls, give sweets to the children, and enjoy such home comforts as they could get in their leisure time. The arguments waxed fast and furious for a time, and in the end no such directives were issued from SHAEF, although I believe that some of the first units to arrive in Germany unsuccessfully tried a policy of non-fraternisation for the first few days.

The arrest and trial of war criminals was another matter we discussed at the time that provoked a difference of opinion. It was, I believe, during the Boxer Rebellion at the turn of the century that the Army Commanders were issued with a directive, 'You will seize the body of "X", and he will be executed!', with no question of a trial. Such a course was canvassed by some at SHAEF and I must admit that I was sympathetic to that point of view, as I feared that if there were a trial, those found guilty would in later years by regarded as martyrs. I now realise that I was quite wrong and that the result of the Nuremburg trial which I attended for two days has

Military Affairs

not been to make Goering and the others into the war heroes of their age.

With these and other discussions, the days of my military service came to an end, for on the 22nd December after a stupendous farewell party at our apartment in Paris, I flew home to spend Christmas with my wife and children in Oxfordshire, and after the holiday went North to start a new and exciting period of my life.

Subsequently Sir Frank Brook sent me a copy of a letter he had received from Brigadier General Frank McSherry, in which he said:

> 'Colonel T. E. St. Johnston departed from this Headquarters yesterday, and leaves a big hole in our organisation. I want to take this oppotunity to express to you my sincere appreciation, and that of SHAEF as a whole, for making Colonel St. Johnston's services available to us during the past months.
>
> During this period we were making plans for Civil Affairs in six countries to be liberated, and for Military Government in Germany. Colonel St. Johnston's understanding of Public Safety matters, his forceful manner, his initiative, and tireless energy have contributed a great deal to the preparation of superior plans for Public Safety. The actual carrying out of these plans in France, Belgium, Luxembourg, and Germany have proven their soundness and adequacy. We are indeed extremely fortunate to have had the benefit of Colonel St. Johnston's service during this period.
>
> You may be assured that Colonel St. Johnston will be greatly missed, and I personally, and all the officers in this office wish him every success in his new appointment and in his future work.'

Though this was the end of my time as a soldier there were a few sequels. In 1945 the European War ended and in the following months I was notified that I had been awarded the OBE (Military Division) for my work at SHAEF, while later in the summer I was summoned with a number of others to the French Embassy, where I was kissed on both cheeks by the Ambassador and invested as Un Chevalier de La Legion d'Honneur, and awarded the Croix de Guerre Avec Palme. I am very proud to have this honour, but in all honesty, I feel that the only valuable assistance I gave the French was to get their night clubs re-opened.

Chapter Five
COUNTY DURHAM

Durham was and is a fascinating county in which to live. It is immensely varied with its shipbuilding and heavy engineering on the Tyneside: huge chemical plants like ICI in the South East: the mining industry in the East: the wealthy and almost feudal county landowners living on good farm land amid beautiful rugged scenery in the West; while in Durham City at the centre brooding over the whole county, stands the magnificent Cathedral, built in a superb natural defensive position on a high rock in a horseshoe bend of the River Wear, close by the Castle which is now part of the thriving University.

'Half Castle, half Church of God', the Cathedral was described by Sir Walter Scott. Built in the supreme expression of Romanesque style which dominated Europe from the 10th to 12th centuries and acknowledged to be the greatest masterpiece of Norman architecture in Great Britain, it marks the site where almost a thousand years ago, devoted followers of St Cuthbert, who brought Christianity to the North of England, built the Saint's last resting place and whose cross adorns heraldic devices throughout the county.

The long western limb is the magnificent nave, 400 feet in length, one of the finest in Europe. Begun about 1096 and finished in 1133 its enormous spiralled and fluted pillars are of great grandeur and never failed to excite me whenever I entered the building.

For centuries the whole of the North East of England was physically isolated from the rest of the country and it became a separate enclave under the aegis of the powerful Bishops of Durham. For hundreds of years these so-called Prince Bishops enjoyed considerable independence, ruling as monarchs of Durham, administering their own courts, exercising the right to pass the death sentence and raising their own armies to guard the Scottish border. It was not until 1832 that their privileges were abolished and the revenues of the Bishopric transferred to the Crown. Bishop Van Mildert, the last of the Prince Bishops, founded Durham University – the first in England after Oxford and Cambridge – and handed over Durham Castle for University use.

Coal had brought wealth to the county and had lined the pockets of wealthy pit owners, but at a price of much hard work for poor wages for the majority while mining, a dirty and dangerous occupation, cost many lives in disease and accidents.

In the 1930s when as a result of the economic slump there was no work in the shipyards, nor was coal required elsewhere, there was great poverty and much unhappiness in the county. At Tow Law, for instance, a pit village high on the hills, the only two men in employment were the postman and the village constable.

The county's plight was mainly brought to notice by the famous Jarrow March, when hundreds of men walked from Durham to London to bring their plight to the notice of those living in affluence in the South.

But the war had changed all this and there was work and prosperity by the time I arrived in 1945, though I found that many of the older generation were still bitter about the way in which they believed the country had forsaken them and turned a deaf ear to their cries for help, and there was a grim determination to ensure that the bad old days should not return when paradoxically peace might bring unemployment once again.

The Durham Police Headquarters which I had inherited was a singular unlovely two storey Victorian building situated in the centre of the City opposite the Assize Courts and Durham Prison, and it was much too small and totally unsuited for modern police administration. Old and out of date, the offices of the Chief Constable and Headquarters Departments were on the upper floor, while the operational Police Station for Durham City was on the ground floor. The facilities were hopelessly inadequate; the Headquarters was frankly described by my predecessor in a letter he wrote to me as 'a disgrace'.

My own office was dingy, gloomy and poorly furnished, but because of war-time shortages, I had to put up with it. For twenty years from 1922 until his death in October 1942, the Durham Constabulary had been commanded by Bradford-born Sir George Morley, an Oxford graduate with a Law degree, who had joined the Royal Irish Constabulary in 1898, as a cadet. He rose to the rank of District Inspector and then became the Chief Constable of Hull in 1910. He was a real character and the many stories about him lost nothing in the telling. I liked the tale of a meeting at the Home Office which was attended by George Morley who was seated next to a civil servant who in pursuance of his secretarial duties was scribbling assiduously during the meeting and George Morley asked him what he was doing. 'I'm writing up the minutes,' he was told. George Morley inquired how he was able to do that before the business was transacted. The civil servant replied, 'I know in advance what everyone's views will be.' 'How do you know what my opinion will be?' asked George Morley. 'Oh!' was the reply. 'That's easy. I've just written it. I've said Sir George disagreed.'

He cared nothing for his own comfort and even had two garden deck chairs in his sitting room. When I lived in the same house I invited to stay with me a Home Office Official who was coming to Durham on official business, and I suggested he should bring his wife. 'No thank you', he replied, 'I knew your home when George Morley lived in it. In the guest room were two beds and the only way I was able to keep warm was to pile all the bedclothes from both beds over me.'

George Morley was very keen on shooting, but alas, was notoriously an unsafe shot and a somewhat dangerous driver. People therefore did not like driving with him or being at the next stand to him when shooting. It is said that once he turned up at a shoot without any cartridges, and when another gun was asked to lend the Chief Constable some of his cartridges, he replied, 'No thank you, I don't want to be shot with my own cartridges.' But apart from his failings and eccentricities, George Morley was greatly loved not only by his own men, but by everyone he met. He was a kindly and generous man, and having no children of his own he was particularly good to other people's young families. He had however, old fashioned ideas about a Chief Constable's responsibilities. Soon after I took office in Oxfordshire I sat next to him at a conference at the Home Office. During the course of the meeting I made some remarks about something I had seen when visiting the scene of a murder. After the meeting George Morley, in the kindest possible way, remonstrated with me about attending the scene of a crime. 'Your job', he made plain to me, 'is to administer the force. Let me advise you not to deal with operational matters. Leave those to the practical policemen.' I did not suggest that I considered myself a practical policeman but his attitude was typical of County Chief Constables of his generation.

Because of war restrictions when Harry Studdy took command in 1943 he was unable to take steps to modernise the force, so that I found it in 1945 very much as Geroge Morley had left it.

As I had done on arriving in Oxfordshire, I spent the first days at Headquarters getting to know the personnel and their various duties and acclimatising myself to the new organisation. During the war years the Force as everywhere had been subjected to a 'freezing order', which stopped recruitment, or retirement except on medical grounds. The men remaining in the Force found themselves faced with more difficult and complex situations than ever before but despite the added work of enforcement of emergency laws, heavy civil defence commitments and a host of other strange tasks they managed very competently.

The shortage of trained manpower had been accepted by the Police Service as an inevitable condition of war. Although an ageing, undermanned Force diluted with many partially-trained Special Constables and temporary war-time policemen, I soon found some first rate men and the main pillar was John Wright, the Deputy Chief Constable, whose great service to me is worthy of record. He was one of the best types of administrative officers. I found him most helpful and obliging. His wide experience of Durham's police affairs over the whole of his time at Force Headquarters revealed a close and constructive interest, and he was meticulous in his paper work, helped by a long and accurate memory.

When Harry Studdy left, Wright was offered the appointment of Chief Constable before it had been advertised, but refused it on the grounds that the County ought to have a younger man and someone with police experience elsewhere.

I was very lucky to have such an experienced second-in-command who approved the appointment of a Chief able to bring in new ideas. John Wright was made an OBE in 1949, but sadly died nine days after he had retired in September 1953, on completion of 45 years' service.

After making myself familiar with the Headquarters personnel and the organisation, I made a tour of inspection of the entire police district to assess the situation throughout the County especially where buildings, equipment and personnel were concerned. Generally speaking, I was unhappy on all three counts. Buildings were poor, badly in need of repair and inadequately furnished while equipment was woefully short and in every way run down. The Superintendents were old and most of them tired and narrow minded in their outlook and almost all the younger men in the Force were away either in the Armed Forces or in essential industry, and it could be said that the Force was only just ticking over.

One startling aspect of my new command that I had never encountered before, was the general untidiness in the men's personal appearance. It was, of course, difficult to get new uniforms during the war years but although many were well worn I felt that this should not have prevented them from being cleaned and pressed. Durham people are not militarily minded and the constables slouched rather than stood and while disciplined, spoke to me almost as if of equal rank. What did and still does appeal to me, was their most likeable smile and the way they looked you straight in the face. I soon realised that it was necessary to identify myself with them before they would open up and talk, but their language and dialogue was strange to my ears and at first I had difficulty in understanding what they were saying. For all that, they possessed in varying degrees, warmth, wit, kindness, generosity and great strength of character while their imperfections gave spice to the dullness of perfection. From the start I felt a great liking for them and it became a love which I have never lost.

I later discovered that the general untidiness of the men was all part of the Morley technique. George Morley was a rugged individualist who ran the Force as he conscientiously thought fit. He was a great believer in the village constable being identified with the village inhabitant. Since Durham people in the pit villages could not afford to be smart in their dress, George Morley did not insist that his men should be smartly turned out.

George Morley's views were in sharp contrast with those of Captain Lionel Lindsay, OBE, MVC, Chief Constable of Glamorgan. A bantam-sized policeman and a fanatical exponent of the keep-fit movement, he particularly liked imposing uniforms and tall, smart, powerfully built men, preferably ex-guardsmen, not less than six feet tall, a condition of appointment which was only waived if a candidate had exceptionally sporting prowess, especially on the rugby field.

A strange man in many ways, he nevertheless produced a fine police force with a splendid record of smartness, discipline and efficiency. He was a firm advocate of the maxim that smart men ought to have smart uniforms and he introduced a military-style uniform fashioned on that of the Guards, with helmets of the striking military pattern of the vogue of the 1860 period, resplendent with fine mesh silver chain, in place of the leather chin strap, bright silver coloured helmet badge and surmounted by a ball and knob on a gleaming metal screw stem. Captain Lindsay was strongly of the view that his officers must, at all times, be the outward visible embodiment of the law in action, and after Durham, I found a drive through a village in Glamorgan, a most striking contrast, and with my military mind, I knew which I preferred.

But whatever my feelings might have been in this direction, I could not put the matter right in the short term and I had to carry the men with me in this matter. So for the time being I had to be content with things as they were and sit down and plan for the future. In many ways this suited me for I was able to start with a clean sheet, decide what I wanted and what my priorities should be as soon as the war ended.

In 1945 the Force had 1,119 officers, but 288 men were away in the Armed Forces, their places being taken by Temporary Constables and War Reserves. I had not previously had the command of such a large number of men and as they were spread all over the County I felt I must quickly get to know something of their problems and abilities so that I could assess their worth individually and collectively, so that the right men could be selected for promotion, when many of the senior officers retired at the end of the War.

It was also vital to ensure that any changes of organisation to be made should have the support of the majority. To do this I offered a financial prize for the best essay written by any member of the Force, suggesting alterations he would like to see made in the Force. Some sixty papers were submitted, five or six of which were of a very high standard indeed. Apart from producing a number of good ideas the essays quickly showed me the ambitious men with constructive ideas to offer on post-war planning. The most outstanding of essays was written by Sergeant W. E. Hogg[1] then in the Traffic Patrol and as everyone spoke well of him I promoted him to the rank of Inspector and placed him in charge of the newly formed Organisation and Training Department including Welfare and Housing. His first assignment was to make a precis of all the suggestions put forward by the contributors and many of the ideas were incorporated into our plans for the future.

I was very concerned about the housing situation of the members of the Constabulary. It was an acute problem, for no police houses had been built for many years. Durham, like many other Forces at this time, was woefully short of the number of houses we required and what we did have, were of a very poor standard. First priority for the Housing Department, with the active help of the County Architect, was to design a house which conformed to the limited dimensions laid down by the Ministry of Health at the time. A three bedroomed council house was then restricted to a maximum floor space of about 900 square feet, but for police houses we were allowed 1,000 square feet – small enough in all conscience for the requirements of policemen who tend to be of large stature, as often are their children. We were therefore faced with the problem of having either two very small living rooms or one large one. I was in favour of the latter but encountered some opposition.

I had heard that before the War the Police Authority of Stirlingshire in Scotland, had built some police houses with one big living

[1] later W. E. Hogg OBE, QPM, Deputy Chief Constable.

room fitted with windows at each end which they called 'Sunshine Houses'. It seemed a good idea to see if they were suitable for Durham, and by arrangement, a small party of us, including a representative of the Police Federation, drove to Stirling. The first house we saw was occupied by a couple with young children, who told me that they would have preferred a house with two separate living rooms however small, so that they could keep their best furniture and china out of the reach of the sticky fingers of their children. In the second house lived an older couple with a teenage daughter, and when I remarked that not having young children likely to damage their furniture, they would probably prefer one large room, 'Oh, no', I was quickly told, 'we would much prefer to have two rooms. You see, we have nowhere for our daughter to do her courting.'

In spite of these views the design the County Architect and I put to the Durham Police Authority for their approval, recommended a police house with a large living room. We further planned and recommended that each town in Durham should be ringed with houses spaced in pairs and fours on all the main roads leading to the towns – two in each locality to be complete with office accommodation. All these ideas, however, were then just paper plans, and two years were to elapse before the first of these new style police houses made their appearance. In all, 250 were erected to this particular design during my six years in Durham, and whenever I return to the County, it still gives me a real sense of pleasure to see their pleasing elevations.

Another matter which required urgent attention during this period was to prepare for the return of members of the Force who were serving with the Armed Forces or in industry. It had been agreed by the Government that on the cessation of hostilities, civil policemen would be given accelerated demobilisation and the 288 Durham policeman away at the time would require some sort of rehabilitation training before they resumed operational police duties again. I had met Canon Evelyn Brayley, Principal of Bede College, an Anglican Teachers' Training College, which was situated in Durham City and which had been used for other purposes during the war years. The college was of modern design, adequately furnished and an ideal place for our purpose, so with the approval of the Police Authority, a short lease of the College buildings was arranged. Here as soon as hostilities ceased and the men came back to civil life, we gave them a course of training to remind them of their civil police responsibilities and duties while it gave me a chance to get to know the men and for them to get to know me.

Canon Brayley and his wife, Isobel, became great friends of

ours, and later we frequently visited them when he became a Canon of Worcester living in the beautiful house beside the Cathedral, so often shown in pictures opposite the County cricket ground. He was a popular man and it was in a slightly blasphemous joking manner that his students used to say of him, 'Give us this day our Brayley dead'.

The offices at Headquarters were so poor that better accommodation had to be found at once. At that time the building of an entirely new Headquarters was out of the question, and there was nothing suitable for conversion in the city of Durham. At Aycliffe, fifteen miles south, in a war-time Ordnance Factory which was being converted into a Trading Estate, we found that the administrative block consisting of some sixty vacant offices, would be an excellent temporary stop-gap and the Police Committee agreed that we should take a lease of the premises for fifteen years, but only after some fierce debate and strong opposition especially from Alderman Tom Benfold, the Chairman of the County Council and Vice-Chairman of the Police Committee. He felt it quite wrong that the police should move out of the county town so far away from the county administrative offices. It was the only occasion that a recommendation of mine in Durham was put to the vote, when the Committee finally agreed to the proposal by 16 votes to 6. The move took place in February 1947, and later when the Home Secretary opened the new Headquarters, Alderman Benfold, who was officiating in the place of Lord Barnard, said in the course of his address, 'You will all know that I bitterly opposed the move from Durham to Aycliffe. I thought it quite wrong that the Police Headquarters should be moved out of the county town. Now that the move has taken place and I have seen the great improvement in the working conditions for the personnel, I want publicly to acknowledge that I was wrong to oppose the move and the Chief Constable was quite right to persist in his recommendations.' It was a handsome gesture which I greatly appreciated. Tom Benfold was an elderly man who had spent most of his life below ground as a miner. A sturdy individualist, only just over five feet tall with a slightly bowed back, he was nevertheless, a figure of authority. A strong supporter of the Labour Party, he had his principles and was not always prepared to toe the party line. Indeed after I had left Durham, he offended his colleagues when he resigned owing to their insistence upon a closed shop for all council employees. In due course he was awarded the CBE and made a Deputy Lieutenant for the County and well deserved both those honours.

Once the move to the new Headquarters at Aycliffe had been agreed, the next thing was to do something to improve the training facilities for the Force. The Home Office had through a Committee of Chief Constables in the North East agreed to set up a Regional Training School for recruits at the war-time Miners' Hostel at Plawsworth. Bede College had catered for the short term problems of the Force but something more permanent was required, and my concern was to give those serving in the Force training on a regular basis, and for this purpose the Police Committee agreed to buy Harperley Hall, a Georgian residence in a beautiful position at the entrance to Weardale. We acquired the place for the absurd price of £2,000 and we spent some £6,000 on alterations and decorations. For this sum, plus £2,000 for furniture, we had an excellent school able to accommodate thirty students and here members of the Force have ever since received systematic training which has been of value to them and to the Force throughout their career.

When I first went to Durham there were no policewomen in the Force. This I felt to be a serious omission and in January 1946, I obtained authority to employ thirteen policewomen, one Inspector, two Sergeants, and ten Constables. Policemen are for the most part very conservative animals and at first the girls were treated with great suspicion. That they were soon accepted by most, if not all members of the staff, was due to the tact and persuasiveness of Sybil Finlay, BEM, the Inspector in charge, who had previously served in the Sunderland Force. Nothing succeeds like success and as soon as policewomen started doing good work, they began to be accepted as a valuable addition to the Force.

Soon after the first woman had been trained and sent on to the beat, I noticed in the crime returns that we were having a good number of purses stolen from women's shopping baskets in Darlington on market days. The local Superintendent and the Head of CID assured me that everything possible was being done to arrest the thief. When I suggested that they should employ a policewoman in plain clothes to keep watch in the market, they demurred saying, 'There is nothing she can do that we can't do,' but I pointed out as they had not caught the culprit at least she couldn't do any worse. So with obvious reluctance they accepted my instruction and called for the services of a policewoman. About four o'clock on the afternoon of the following market day the Superintendent telephoned me to say that the policewoman had caught the person responsible and that he thought I ought to know the thief was the wife of a prominent Alderman in the town. Inevitably there would be much publicity given to the arrest. I asked the Superintendent and the Detective Inspector to bring the policewoman to my office at once and when they arrived I asked her to tell me how she had managed to make the arrest. She explained that as the thief usually took two or three purses each day, she had reasoned that she would want to examine the contents for money and that the best place to do this was obviously the women's lavatory in the market place. With this in mind she had given the woman attendant ten shillings to take the morning off and had deputised for her, keeping at the same time a sharp eye on the visitors. When the woman concerned came in for a second time within a very short space of time, she sensed this was the thief and entering the next cubicle, she stood on the seat, looked over and saw the suspect taking money out of a purse and putting it in her handbag.

I turned to the Superintendent and the Detective Inspector who looked shamefaced while the story was being told, and merely said to them, 'When I suggested you should employ one policewoman you said that there was nothing a woman could do that you couldn't do. Could you have done that?' The story got around as I meant it should, and it sold the value of policewomen to the Force in a way no series of lectures could have ever done.

While we were in Durham we lived at West House, the Chief Constable's official residence. It was an 18th-century farm house on the outskirts of the City overlooking the Cathedral which we used as our parish Church.

No one living as close to this magnificent building as we did for five years, could fail to fall under its influence. It stands so strong, so solid and so proud that to me it epitomises all that is good about England.

Soon after our arrival Joanna and I were invited to lunch with the Dean, Dr Cyril Alington and his wife Hester, a member of the famous Lyttelton family. Though of an older generation they took to us kindly, making us both most welcome and in the course of time we came to know them well. Both were remarkable people. Dr Alington who had been Headmaster of Eton for 17 years and before that Headmaster of Shrewsbury, was a successful writer of detective stories and also of a number of hymns. His wife was very much loved and respected, and a good friend to many. They had two sons and four daughters. One son had been killed in the war and their other, Giles, a Fellow of University College, Oxford, we came to know well, but, alas, he died while we were still in Durham. He was a great friend of Harold Wilson, whose son Giles is named after Giles Alington. One daughter, Lavinia, married Roger Mynors, Regius Professor of Classics at Oxford, and the twin brother of Humphrey Mynors, my tutor at Corpus, while another daughter, Elizabeth, married Alec Dunglass.

From time to time the younger Alingtons came to stay and often when that happened, Joanna and I were invited to lunch with the family at the Deanery. I much liked Alec Dunglass, but I must confess that I never imagined that one day he would, as Alec Douglas-Home, be Prime Minister of England and I don't think at this stage of his life, he did either.

When we arrived in Durham, the Dean kindly allocated me a Canon's stall. For services we all sat as a family in the choir, but as only men are allowed to sit in a Canon's stall in the top tier, Joanna was thereby relegated to the pew below. Directly opposite was the Bishop's Throne, a very high stone structure, reputed to be the highest in Christendom, beneath which at ground level there was an enclave containing a pew which was used by Caroline and Andrew 'sitting in the fireplace', as they called it, where Joanna and I could keep a watchful eye on them. To my regret, on my last visit the pew was no longer there. Among the Canons at the Cathedral at this time was Michael Ramsay, later Bishop of Durham, and more recently Archbishop of Canterbury. We knew him well. His sermons were very erudite and above the young heads of Caroline and Andrew who invariably stepped quietly out from under the throne and away through a side door before he started.

Many fine special services were held in the Cathedral organised quite brilliantly by Dean Alington who was a great showman. One of them, 'Friends and Benefactors Day', sometimes irreverently called, 'The Feast of St. Cyril', is most memorable. To these services civic dignitaries from the whole county were invited and in solemn procession took their seats on one side of the nave while a second procession headed by the Vice Chancellor of the University and professors attired in their academic robes sat on the other side. The choir was filled with ecclesiastics wearing their canonical regalia and the Dean, dignified with a head of white hair, clad in a 13th-century gold and green cope, walked with a pronounced limp, propelling himself down the aisle of the main nave in a rocking motion, accompanied by two small choir boys holding open the sides of the cope to enable the beautiful green of the richly decorated vestment to be seen. The stall usually allocated to me was on these occasions required by a visiting Canon, but Dean Alington kindly invited me to sit beside him and share his seat high in the choir next to the nave, the cynosure of all eyes of the 2,000 worshippers in the Cathedral.

At the first of these services that I attended the guest preacher was Bishop Arthur Headlam, a former Regius Professor of Divinity at Oxford, who had only recently retired from the Bishopric of Gloucester and returned to live in his native Durham. When he stepped into the high pulpit it was clear to all that he was suffering from a very bad cold. Suddenly he sneezed and out came his false teeth in full view of the packed Cathedral. Dexterously catching them with one hand he returned them to his mouth in a flash. Without the flicker of an eyelid the Dean, a keen cricketer, remarked out of the corner of his mouth, 'Jolly good catch for 84.' Sitting in our highly placed seats and eyed by everyone, I had the greatest difficulty keeping a straight face, but this is not the end of the story. In catching his teeth the Bishop broke them and to keep them in position in his mouth, he had to hold them in with his thumb while at the same time rubbing his streaming nose with his forefinger. In such a difficult and trying situation he preached a sermon in his cultured gentlemanly voice on the theme of 'Wisdom', and it was a sermon which could only be described as vitriolic. In the course of his address, looking down on the impassive face of Sir James Duff, the Vice Chancellor of Durham University surrounded by all the academics in their full regalia, the Bishop made the following acid comments:

> 'You call yourself the University of Durham. You are not interested in furthering the cause of wisdom. You are only interested in the number of degrees you get each year.
> 'You ought not to call yourselves the University of Durham. You ought to call yourselves "The Polytechnic of the North of England". '

The academics were not amused but most of the others in the Cathedral were.

After the service, at the big tea party given by the Dean in the magnificent 16th-century Monks' Dormitory, everyone was talking of the incident when a jovial Archdeacon with a twinkle in his eye, came up to me saying, 'Wonderful, wonderful. How lucky you were. You could see, I couldn't. I sit on the pulpit side, such a pity! Such a pity! We shall talk about this for years'. Barchester Towers in real life!

Durham has for long been a County renowned for the number of real individualists or characters who live there, and there are many good stories told about them.

When we first went to Durham the Bishop was Alwyn Williams, formerly Headmaster of Winchester. He was a kindly and friendly man but not very inspiring, and a pale successor to the famous Herbert Hensley Henson who had retired to live in Norfolk and whose memoirs, *Retrospect of an Unimportant Life* Joanna and I had read, and much enjoyed long before we knew we were going to Durham. When I got the job, Joanna wrote to him and thus began a correspondence between them which was terminated only at his death. Several of his letters to her have been reproduced in a book of his letters compiled by Canon Brayley. The Bishop always wrote with a quill pen and Joanna used to collect goose feathers for him. It was a matter of great regret to us that we never met him, but petrol rationing was still in force until our last few months in Durham – it only ended in June 1950 – and we could not make the long journey.

He was a remarkable man and the stories about him are legendary. He once attended a meeting of the Moral Welfare Council in Durham which consisted of a number of well-meaning matrons who tut-tutted over the troubles the unmarried girls got themselves into, and did indeed give practical help when needed. As he left the meeting he shook his head and was heard to say, rather sadly, 'Scarecrows on the field of virtue.'

Hensley Henson was an ascetic and disliked the pomposity of showmanship. It is the custom of the Archbishops of Canterbury to have their portraits painted and hung in Lambeth Palace. Cosmo Lang, had his portrait duly painted and at a meeting of the Bishops at Lambeth Palace showed it to them. When asked what he thought of it, he replied, that he didn't like it, and that a friend had told him that it made him look a vain and pompous prelate. Hensley Henson was heard to mutter, 'I wonder to which of those epithets does he object?'

A third story is told of a visit he made to Sandringham, to preach the Royal Sermon. Just before he left Durham one of his Suffragan Bishops fell ill. Hensley Henson disliked this man who worshipped the material things of life as much as his religion, but felt that out of charity he must visit him. He was somewhat nauseated to find his sick colleague lying in his four-poster bed in his linen sheets in great luxury surrounded by groups of servants. At the dinner at Sandringham, Queen Mary was talking of a visit she had made to a London theatre and among the plays she had seen and enjoyed was, 'Pigs in Clover'. 'Have you seen "Pigs in Clover", my Lord Bishop?' asked Her Majesty, and Hensley Henson was reported to have absent-mindedly replied, 'No Ma-am, but I've seen Bishop . . . in bed.'

My police authority consisted of twelve Councillors, all strong Labour supporters, and twelve Magistrates all of whom were landed gentry and supporters of the Conservative Party. But in the Police Committee, politics never entered into the discussions, and each side respected the other's views.

My Chairman was Lord Barnard, who owned 20,000 acres, in West Durham. Although a simple man in his habits, he and Lady Barnard lived in almost feudal splendour at Raby Castle, where it was said that it was 150 paces from the kitchen to the dining room.

County Durham

Tea was served in the Great Hall – a huge and draughty chamber which luckily had an enormous fire burning in the hearth near to which a tea-table was placed. Lord Barnard used to sit in a leather watchman's-chair into which he was apt to disappear from time to time. When the family went out hunting the doors were opened and the horses brought into the Hall so that their riders could mount them indoors.

From a Chief Constable's point of view, Lord Barnard was the ideal Chairman of a Police Authority. He was always available for consultation: he gave wise advice and never interfered. I always went to Raby Castle two days before the quarterly Police Authority meetings, to discuss the Agenda with him, and at the meeting he let the Chief Constable go through the Agenda with the Committee, and rarely spoke. Such was the respect that the Labour Councillors had for him that he was unanimously re-elected each year until his death in 1964.

Though not on the Police Committee, nor a member of the County Council, the over-riding influence in Labour affairs in the County was Sam Watson, the Secretary of the Durham Miners' Association. He, and his wife Jenny, became our two greatest friends in the County, and I admired him as much as any man I've ever met. He came up the hard way going into the pits straight from school, working below ground and remaining there until 1936 when he was elected to an administrative position in the Durham Miners' Association. Highly intelligent and a voracious reader with a very retentive memory, he was also full of commonsense, and could quickly see to the core of any problem.

He was greatly respected by everyone in the Labour Party, and his advice was much sought by Ministers in London especially by Clem Attlee, the Prime Minister. On frequent occasions I have been sitting in Sam's house in the evening, when the Prime Minister has telephoned to discuss some matter with him, and there is no doubt that had he been prepared to move to London he would have been an influential member of the Attlee cabinet. But Sam loved his Durham coalfield and the pitmen, and felt that he could do as much good for the county and the country by remaining on the side lines.

He was a member of the National Executive Committee of the Labour Party of which he became Chairman in 1949 and a member of the Court of Durham University from whom he received an Honorary DCL, in 1955. He was also a Magistrate and a Deputy Lieutenant and a CBE.

It was a great loss to the county and to the country as well as to all his many friends when he died at the age of 67 in May, 1967.

My period in office in Durham coincided with the Attlee Government of 1945–51, and in Durham at that time we had no less than five members of the Cabinet. Ellen Wilkinson, Minister of Education (though she died in 1947), J. Chuter Ede, Home Secretary, Manny Shinwell, Minister of Fuel, Jack Lawson, Minister for War, and Hugh Dalton, Chancellor of the Exchequer, while William Whiteley was Chief Whip. I met them all, save Ellen Wilkinson, frequently at various social gatherings, and especially at Sam Watson's home, and was glad to do so because I much sympathised with their ideals and views. Much of Labour's national policies were developed in Durham and as they talked freely to me, I learnt a great deal of the political thinking of the day.

A unique operational matter with which the Durham Constabulary is concerned is the policing of the Durham Miners' Gala, which takes place each July in the city of Durham. Originally started in the 19th century as a protest meeting of all the miners in the Durham coalfield against the believed machinations of the owners, it became after the War a great day to celebrate the miners' achievement of their long-sought nationalisation of the industry.

On the day of the Big Meeting, as it is known, the city which had a population of less than 30,000 is closed to wheeled traffic from 8 am to midnight, for into the city come over 100,000 people. The pitmen of each colliery arrive by coach bringing with them their band, and their lodge banner, large and beautifully designed silk tapestries depicting various advancements in the mining industry or portraits of prominent leaders. Borne by six men, and accompanied by their wives and children they march in disciplined but unmarshalled procession through the narrow streets of the city, past the County Hall and on to the old Race Course by the river bank. On the balcony of the County Hotel the national leaders of the Labour Party, especially those connected with the coal industry, stand waving to the crowds.

When the Labour Party is in power, the Prime Minister usually attends along with four or five members of the Cabinet. Over the years many prominent people in the Labour Party have climbed to the platform on Gala Day and spoken to the vast crowds assembled to hear them. They included in my time, Ernest Bevin, Stafford Cripps, Aneurin Bevan, Herbert Morrison, Hartley Shawcross, Hugh Gaitskell, Michael Foot, Dick Crossman and Hector MacNeil, as well as the Prime Minister.

On the evening before the Day, Joe Shaw, a prominent farmer in the county, always gave a dinner for the official guests and afterwards we would go to Sam Watson's house where the party went on till late, when it gave one an opportunity to meet all the official guests, while on the Saturday evening after the celebrations were over those who stayed on used to come to our house. The Prime Minister was always very complimentary about the police arrangements and on one occasion in the course of his speech said that he believed no large crowd of people anywhere in the world was policed so well by so few policemen – which says as much for the behaviour of the crowd as it does for the police.

One's first impression of Clem Attlee was that he was a very diffident man; 'A sheep in sheep's clothing' as someone once unkindly said. I don't think that he liked social gatherings and he certainly had little small talk. While all the guests and local officials gathered at the County Hotel before the speeches, he would be found standing quietly in a corner, and more than once I have rescued him from behind the door. But beneath this meek outward appearance, one could see that there was iron in his constitution, and I was always impressed by the respect and affection that the senior members of the Government had for him despite the great difference in their educational backgrounds.

Whatever members of the Conservative Party may have thought of him, Nye Bevan was great fun to meet. Emotional but with a very quick intelligence and wit, he was an excellent conversationalist and with him the discussion and arguments waxed fast and furious. But of them all, the one I liked the best was Hector MacNeil and it was a tragedy that he died so young for had he lived, he was destined, I feel sure to have held with success one of the great Offices of State.

Of the local MPs, I came to know Jack Lawson much the best for after the retirement of Lord Londonderry, Jack went to the House of Lords and became Lord Lieutenant of the County. He continued to live, as he always had done, in a terraced pitman's cottage, and as he did not own a car, he was always supplied with a police car and driver for his official duties. He was a simple man and a good man. I remember him saying to me on one occasion 'Chief, you know, men like Will Lawther and I have given our lives to fight for a place in the sun for the miners, but we are getting old and now our goal has been reached, the difficulty is to find intelligent young men to take our places. The pay at the coal face is now so good that they would sooner go down the pit rather than go into politics.'

Sam Watson was aware of this and for many years he ran educational classes on Sunday afternoons when selected young pitmen were encouraged to attend and where they were taught constitutional law, Trade Union policies, and the like to fit them to take part in the political life of the country. From time to time I used to lecture to these classes on the place of the policeman in society, and continued to do so after I had moved to Lancashire.

When I went to Lancashire Sam asked me to get to know Joe Gormley of whom I had had never heard as he said that one day he would be a very influential figure in Trade Union politics. So I invited Joe Gormley to lunch at Police Headquarters and he gave a dinner for me at Bolton to introduce me to some of the Lancashire colliers, but I never got as close to them as I did to the Durham pitmen.

Lord Londonderry, the Lord Lieutenant, was another of Durham's personalities of this period, and an extremely pleasant and kindly man. He had held high offices of State but had been severely criticised for his friendship before the war with Ribbentrop, the German Foreign Minister. He had houses in London and Northern Ireland, but his main county seat was at Wynyard in County Durham. Unfortunately, Lady Londonderry did not like the North and I do not remember her coming there. Lord Londonderry however came up to the county frequently, and to me he always appeared a lonely man. On more than one occasion after some civic reception in Durham, I would ask him back to West House for a drink and often he stayed to dinner apparently pleased to be asked.

Durham has an Assize Court and four times a year two Judges of the High Court came to the City and were duly treated, as was proper, in royal fashion. They were accommodated in beautiful but not very comfortable rooms in the Castle. It was customary on the opening day of the Assizes for the Mayor of Durham to call to pay his respects at 10.0 am, for the Chief Constable to arrive at 10.15 am; and for the Vice Chancellor of the University, to present himself at 10.30 am. Usually the Judges were very courteous, but on one occasion I inadvisedly said that I hoped they had had a comfortable night, which caused one Judge to say, 'How can we be comfortable in this place? The beds are impossible: the food arrives cold (the kitchen was some way from the dining room) while the students resident in the Castle sleep overhead and make a great deal of noise.' In a cowardly way I repeated almost the same remark Air Chief Marshal Portal once said to the King of me, 'I'll answer for the crimes of the County, but I can't answer for the omissions of your hosts, the University.' As I left, the Vice Chancellor walked in, and I just had time to warn him that he was in for a bad time.

It so happened that the High Sheriff for that year was Douglas Nicholson, the Chairman of the largest brewery in the county, and someone who has throughout his adult life given much public service to the County. He obtained expert advice and with the consent of the University authorities, considerable improvements were made for the comfort of the visiting Judges.

It is the duty of the High Sheriff to provide transport for the Judges to the Assize Court. Douglas Nicholson was a very fine horseman, and a keen coach driver, and at the first Assize that he attended in the role of High Sheriff, he produced at the Castle his own coach and four to convey the Judges to the Assize Court. It was a fine sight as the coach on its steel wheels, with mounted police outriders, rumbled over the cobbles out of the Castle and down the hill through the streets of the City, but Lord Goddard, the Lord Chief Justice, was not amused when he heard of it and the High Sheriff received a written rebuke. 'I will not have my Judges treated as a circus turn'.

Lord Goddard only came to Durham once whilst I was there and I was very glad to meet him for he was a great character and a strong and outspoken Lord Chief Justice, who, whatever Bernard Levin may have thought and said in his unkind attack in *The Times* after Lord Goddard's death, had done so much to uphold the rule of law in this country. I asked Lord Goddard to talk to one of my training classes and this he did. When in a speech of thanks I remarked that he didn't often come to Durham and I suspected the reason was that he had heard of the discomfort of the lodgings he interjected, 'You young ruffian. You shouldn't say that.' I always feel I am the only person that the Lord Chief Justice ever called a ruffian who didn't get a term of imprisonment.

In the six years I was in Durham we had no less than six cases of murdered prostitutes – always a most difficult type of murder inquiry to investigate, owing to the number of casual acquaintances this sort of woman, by necessity had. We were lucky enough to be able to solve all six cases, but as there was still capital punishment at that time, and as Durham juries were notoriously soft hearted, the verdict was usually one of manslaughter.

The first of these cases began when some boys playing on waste ground at Catchgate, a colliery village in North Durham, some fifteen miles from Newcastle, found the body of a woman hidden under a pile of cardboard sheets. She had been strangled with her head scarf, and I soon discovered that immoral women in Durham who wore head scarfs were a poor insurance risk, for in five of the six murders of this kind, death had occurred by this means. At first we were unable to identify her, but eventually owing to a tattoo mark on her wrist, she was identified as a low class prostitute from Newcastle who had disappeared a week before.

We had to discover how she had come to be so far away from her usual haunts, as well as the identity of the man she had been with so we decided to appeal to the public for help. This was long before the days of television and we resorted to a large poster campaign, not relying just on police notice boards but putting the posters in public houses, railway stations and bus stops between Newcastle and Catchgate. The poster in large red and black lettering was most effective. This form of publicity has been used many times since by other forces, but I believe this was the first time it was done.

House-to-house inquiries by a large number of detectives were instituted at the same time with the result that within a few days four people were traced who provided some enlightening statements, saying that they remembered seeing a woman in a drunken condition at Newcastle railway station boarding a train for Catchgate accompanied by a man.

At the same time we had a stroke of luck – and luck is always necessary in murder investigations. We learned that on the evening of the day in which the woman had disappeared, a constable had stopped a man at Gateshead near the bridge over the River Tyne. The man had in his possession a handbag which he said he had just found, and two stones which he said he was carrying to defend himself from the repetition of an attack made on him the previous night. The constable took possession of the handbag and after ascertaining the man's name and address let him go as he was a seaman on a ship sailing in the early hours for Norway. The handbag was found to belong to the dead woman and the man's description tallied with that given by the witnesses at the railway station. We realised that the seaman had been about to throw the handbag weighted with stones into the River Tyne, thus disposing of a vital piece of evidence.

Two weeks later his ship berthed again in England and the man was duly questioned, charged with murder and convicted. All this may sound fairly easy but many hours of hard, painstaking work had to be put in by thirty detectives working round the clock. Hard work and a flair for nosing out the vital witnesses and an element of luck are all necessary ingredients of a murder investigation.

Of the other five of these murders two are in the best detective story tradition. The case of the murder of Eva Mordue at Leadgate, a colliery village close to the town of Consett, may be of particular interest.

Colliery villages tend to be connected to each other by mineral railways which are often used by pedestrians walking from one village to the next. At noon on a Sunday in May, 1947, a man exercising his dog discovered in a cabin beside a mineral railway line the body of a half-naked girl with severe facial injuries and strangled with her head scarf. She was soon identified as Eva Mordue, a local girl of known immoral habits. She had left home at 6.0 pm, and had been seen in the local public house and later at a dance hall in Consett that evening. Despite our best endeavours we could not, however, find anyone who could say with certainty with whom she had been associating that evening. The type of people with whom she mixed were of low intelligence and not helpful to the police. A shovel was missing from the cabin as was her purse. There was a large army camp in the vicinity on the west side of Consett, and many soldiers from the camp had been in the town on the Saturday night. It was important to find both the shovel and the purse and for this purpose four squads of a Sergeant and ten policemen, were instructed meticulously to comb all the area surrounding the murder scene. They worked assiduously all day, Monday, Tuesday and Wednesday until on the Thursday an old man was traced who had found the shovel on some waste ground some distance from where the murder had taken place. Eva's purse was also found on an allotment close to a narrow public path in the same vicinity.

I am quite sure that we only kept the men working and their morale up because we looked after their welfare. We ensured they were provided with transport from their homes to the murder scene and back again at the end of the day. Dry clothing was also provided for it was raining most of the time, and a hot, substantial meal was served to them at midday. Men will work if they are properly looked after and this was proof of that maxim.

The value of the discovery of the shovel and purse lay in the fact that they had been located on the east side of Leadgate, which inferred that the murderer was not a soldier, the murder having been committed on a dark night on a narrow path between buildings. We knew that the troops were strangers to the district and their camp was situated on the opposite side of the town. On the Saturday evening following the murder, the town centre of Consett was sealed off after the public houses and dance halls had been closed, and all young people in the town were rounded up, their names and addresses taken, and their movements on the previous Saturday were all checked. Two thousand young people were interviewed and two thousand statements taken, all of which were laboriously checked and double checked. Nothing was too much trouble, no line of inquiry was too tenuous to be pursued, no stone was left unturned, but we were no nearer to the solution of the problem.

Three weeks later I decided to call a conference not only of all the senior officers involved in the inquiry, but to include everyone actively engaged in the investigation and also every policeman who worked within ten miles of Leadgate. With maps and diagrams the senior officers recounted in detail all what had been done. This helped to satisfy ourselves that we had covered every possible angle of inquiry and also had the indirect effect of raising morale of the local policemen for they now felt that they were more deeply involved being asked to help, and not merely being used as tools. They were encouraged by the interest of their Chief who wanted to hear what they had to say.

As a result the conference it was found that six men had been interviewed who could not satisfactorily account for their movements. At the meeting it was suggested that since the victim had been so severely injured the clothing of the six men should be given to the staff of the Forensic Science Laboratory at Newcastle-on-Tyne, for them to make a microscopical examination, to ascertain whether there was any blood on them. We also asked all present to name anyone living in their respective districts whom they thought was the type of person who might have committed a crime of this sort. A number of names were put forward and all but one had already been interviewed by the CID. One elderly policeman, however, working a country beat seven miles from Leadgate, mentioned the name of Albert Nixon, a bad tempered pitman of a violent disposition. The constable said that he had closely interrogated Nixon who admitted being in Consett during the evening of the crime but that he left in the company of his brothers and they confirmed his story. Although the CID knew of Nixon's reputation they had been unable to trace him, as he and his family had moved from one colliery village to another. His name was added to the list of suspects and after the conference detectives collected the clothing of the seven men. Twenty-four hours later we received a telephone call from the Forensic Science Laboratory saying that 36 specks of the blood of the same group as the murdered woman had been found on Nixon's clothing. He was brought in and when faced with this unassailable evidence, admitted he was the man we wanted.

The other case worth mentioning was the murder of another woman of known immoral character whose body was found hidden under some sheets of corrugated iron at the edge of a refuse dump, strangled as usual, with her own head scarf. Her handbag was close beside her, open and empty. The woman was well known in the locality and our problem was to find with whom she had been on the night she was attacked. A search of the area was made particularly difficult owing to the general debris found on rubbish tips, but by careful organisation all the ground nearby was carefully scoured and in some long grass some fifty yards away the contents of the dead woman's handbag were found close to a flattened area of grass. Nearby, hidden in the grass, was found a home-made petrol lighter which proved to be the key to our problem.

Photographs of the lighter were quickly made and distributed to thirty officers who were instructed to make a house-to-house inquiry of everyone living within five miles of the murder scene. A few days later we found a publican who told us that he had seen this particular lighter being used by a pitman in the bar of his public house. When we eventually found the man he admitted his responsibility for the murder and told us the usual story that the woman had asked for payment after intercourse had taken place and this had caused him to lose his temper.

These cases were an unhappy result of the great increase in miners' wages that took place whilst I was in Durham. What many of the girls did freely in the days of poverty, they demanded payment for in more affluent days of the miners, but the girls were so unsophisticated that they did not get paid before the act. The quarrel that ensued afterwards when the man refused to pay was the cause of five of the six deaths we investigated.

These six cases provided the material for a lecture with slides, entitled, 'Investigation of Murder in a County Force', which for some years I gave to each course at the Police College and also on invitation to members of other Forces and legal societies.

The Army is under an obligation always to give aid to the Civil Power whenever a Chief Constable so requests and on two occasions while in Durham I had to ask the Army for their help.

The first call to help was at the scene of a serious railway accident. My wife and I had arrived home late from the Zetland Hunt Ball in 1946 and I only seemed to have just put my head on the pillow when the telephone beside my bed rang. It was the officer in charge of the Information Room, to say that he had just received a message that the London to Edinburgh express was derailed at Brownie Colliery, and that there were a great number of casualties.

He had already called out the Ambulance Service and the Fire Brigade, and wireless police cars had been diverted to the scene. I instructed him to warn the Hospital to expect casualties and asked him to request the local military camp at Brancepeth to send me 100 men with vehicles. I hastily put on some uniform over my pyjamas, pulled on a pair of gumboots and drove quickly to the scene. As the accident had occurred only a few miles from my house I was one of the first rescuers to arrive.

It was six in the morning and very cold and dark, and it was an eerie sight to see, across a ploughed field, a railway coach sticking up into the air at an angle of 45 degrees on top of another coach. Both coaches were still showing interior lights and some passengers had started a bonfire with broken pieces of coachwork and were huddled round the fires trying to keep warm. Some were already walking across the field and making their way towards the nearest town. All were shocked and apprehensive and had no idea whether they were in England or Scotland, let alone which county. Worst of all were the moans and screams of those trapped in the wreckage and still conscious.

The accident had been caused by the derailment of a goods train travelling south on the up-line, when some trucks had overspilled on to the down line in the path of the express. The engine had overturned killing the driver and fireman and the first five coaches had telescoped. All the casualties were in these coaches.

I soon found the guard who to my surprise was able to tell me the exact number of people on the train – 477. Luckily it was emptier than usual for an international rugby match was to have been held in Edinburgh that day, and many of the regular passengers had decided not to travel anticipating the train would be crammed to capacity. At the last moment, owing to severe weather, the match had been postponed and so the rugby spectators were not after all on the train.

When I arrived two doctors were already doing their best to reach the trapped passengers, while the ubiquitous press were hovering around. I grabbed one press man and asked him to let me have the names and adresses of anyone seen doing any meritorious, or dangerous rescue work. I set up an Incident Post and as more rescuers arrived we began to establish a little order out of the chaos. Buses ordered by the station master at Durham came to collect the uninjured passengers to take them to Newcastle and ambulances arrived to take the injured to hospital.

It was just getting light when the army arrived and the sight of one hundred disciplined men in uniform doubling to the scene did much to raise morale. Some were detailed to carry the injured on stretchers to the ambulances in the road some 300 yards away, whilst others were directed to transfer the mail and newspapers from the train on to their lorries and take them to Newcastle.

Three Inspectors were sent to make a complete reconnaissance of the whole length of the train and they reported that the sleeping compartments while upright, had been derailed, but I inadvertently forgot to inquire whether any VIPs were on the train. About an hour later while I was drinking a mug of hot coffee from the police canteen, I saw walking sedately towards me the Home Secretary, Mr J. Chuter Ede, and his private detective, both dressed in black Homburg hats and black overcoats, somewhat incongruous figures in that bizarre setting. The Home Secretary was his usual urbane self, and when I asked him if he was all right he replied, 'Yes. I was woken up by the noise and the jolting and I guessed we were off the rails', and added, 'I've been off the rails before!' I replied, 'Shall I tell your political opponents that?'

He had a mug of coffee with me and discussed the situation and then he went on his way to South Shields in a police car.

By this time some bodies were being brought out of the wreckage and were taken to a local chapel which we used as a mortuary. As the body of a woman was being placed on a stretcher, I noticed a handbag on the ground nearby, and told the ambulanceman to put it on the stretcher alongside the body as it probably belonged to her. One can usually identify the body of a man from the contents of his pockets or wallet, but once a woman is separated from her handbag, it is often difficult to ascertain her identity.

By lunch time heavy lifting gear had arrived from York which enabled us to reach the casualties still trapped but alive. Most of the police work was over except the collection and identification of the bodies in the first coach some of which lay there for as long as twenty-four hours, piled on top of each other and for some time inaccessible. After what I saw that day I made a firm resolution never to travel in the first coach of a train.

One more misadventure in connection with this appalling railway accident remains to be recorded. In the goods train there were several damaged trucks laden with valuable merchandise including whisky. As a precautionary measure against looting, I asked the Army to unload the trucks and move the whisky cases to a nearby warehouse. Despite the precautions, at the end of the day two young soldiers were found unconscious in one of the damaged trucks surrounded by empty bottles of whisky. Rushed to hospital, stomach pumps were quickly applied but it was too late to save the life of one of them.

In all, eleven persons were killed and sixteen taken to hospital for injuries of one kind or another. This was the first serious accident which had occurred in this country since the war and when the new Police College opened at Ryton-on-Dunsmore in June 1948, I gave a lecture outlining in some detail the police action we had taken at the scene of this railway accident and the lessons we learnt. This was subsequently used as a model by many Chief Constables and formed the basis of their instructions to their Forces on disasters of this kind.

The second time that we needed the assistance of the military happened when a large timber yard at West Hartlepool caught fire. Fanned by a strong sea breeze the fire rapidly took hold; and when I arrived it was obvious that the local Fire Brigade could not cope with the situation. I telephoned the County Fire Chief, a man of great experience in his own field, and explained what was happening and how it was obviously being inadequately handled. He told me that while he could send additional fire appliances and fire crews he was unable to interfere because West Hartlepool had its own Fire Chief which precluded any personal direction on his part. However I persuaded him to attend and also took upon myself the responsibility of calling out the Army to assist with making fire breaks, while after I had telephoned the Home Office and spoken to the Chief Inspector of Fire Brigades, he instructed the County Fire Chief to take charge. The fire burnt for three days and we had to organise the evacuation of ten dwelling houses which at one time seemed to be in danger of being engulfed. Luckily, at the last moment the wind changed and the houses were saved. Here again, the Home Secretary, Mr J. Chuter Ede, turned up and took a great interest in the way the Police and Fire Service handled the situation.

The aspect of a Chief Constable's job I enjoyed most, was the responsibility for the men's happiness and every day when I came to my office I wondered what problems in this field I would have to handle. Men who had done well had to be seen to be congratulated; men who were in trouble had to be helped; men who had broken the Discipline Code had to be dealt with, while vacancies had to be filled and the right men promoted.

Whenever I heard that the son of one of my constables had been awarded a place at either Oxford or Cambridge, I asked the officer to bring his son to my office for me to offer my congratulations. On more than one occasion when I said to the youth that after he had obtained his degree I hoped he would join the Durham Constabulary, a shocked look appeared on the fond father's face, and he answered, 'Oh, No, Sir. He's not going to join the Police. He'll do better than that.' It is sad that in the eyes of so many, even policemen, the Police and a university career have so long been regarded as incompatible.

Superintendents were always under strict instructions to let me know immediately if any man under their jurisdiction was in any personal or family trouble so that we could consider what assistance could be offered. One afternoon a Superintendent rang me up to say that the wife of a Sergeant stationed in a rural area had suddenly left him. Apparently, the Sergeant had gone on duty at six o'clock in the morning leaving his wife in bed and the house in normal condition. When he returned home in the afternoon he found that his wife had gone taking with her all the furniture save the kitchen table, one chair, a set of cutlery, one plate and one cup and saucer, and upstairs in one bedroom, she had left the curtains, a single bed with one pair of sheets, one blanket and a pillow and towel. Except for these items the house was completely empty. I told the Superintendent to send the Sergeant to see me and when he came into my office I rose, took him by the hand and put my hand on his shoulder to commiserate with him. To my surprise, stepping backwards, the Sergeant said, 'Don't be sorry for me, Sir. This is the happiest day I've had for 25 years!'

Apparently she had been a real scold and given him a bad time throughout their married life. The Sergeant I must admit was a meek individual and she had bullied him unmercifully. He told me that when they got married she demanded his wage packet each week and from it she gave him half a crown pocket money. When he was promoted to Sergeant and he gave her his increased pay packet, she increased his pocket money to five shillings.

Another story of matrimonial strife in Durham, is that of a very efficient smart, young constable who had joined the Force just before the War, and on being called up for National Service, eventually was given a commission. At the end of the War he rejoined the Police and was regarded as good potential material. After a year, however, he resigned and on making inquiries, I was told that the reason for it was that his wife considered herself demeaned by her husband's rank of constable after six years as an officer in the Armed Forces, and she had persuaded him to leave the Police Service. About twelve months later I saw the man at a police dance, and when I said how glad I was to see him he answered, 'I can't keep away; I love the Police: will you have me back?' I told him I was not prepared to discuss this at a police dance but that if he really wanted to return he should write to me. This he did and shortly afterwards I saw him in my office and discussed the matter. I said that I thought every one was entitled to look over his shoulder once, but not more than once, and that if he came back he must be prepared to stay. In answer to my question he assured me that his wife would accept his decision and I then gave him some advice, saying that it seemed to me that his wife was ruling the roost too much. I went on to say that if he was to live a happy life he must help himself and concluded, 'Wives at times need putting in their place, and sometimes even need a spanking', meaning this in a figurative sense.

He came back to us and when six months later I was in the Division to which he had been posted, I asked the Superintendent how he was getting on. 'He's settled down very well,' said the Superintendent and with a twinkle in his eye added, 'You know, he took your advice, Sir.' When I asked what he meant he replied, 'Well Sir, I understand you told him to go home and give his wife a good thumping. This he did and she's been a different woman ever since.' I was horrified to learn the PC had taken my remarks literally but I'm glad to say that in later years the constable was promoted, completed his 30 years efficiently and is still, as far as I know, happily married, though ever since I have always been more careful how I have worded any advice I gave to a man in trouble.

One morning I arrived at Headquarters just as two motor patrol constables were leaving. Both seemed in such a mood of despair and frustration that I asked what was troubling them. 'We've made the worst arrests in the whole of our career, Sir.' Intrigued I asked them what had happened, and much to my amusement this is what I was told.

They had been driving southbound on the Great North Road, when they saw in front of them a motor hearse displaying red and white limited trade plates and apparently carrying a coffin draped in a grey blanket. Their interest was further aroused by the clothes the driver was wearing – hardly in keeping – they thought, with the sombre black attire of undertakers. Aware that the regulations did not allow vehicles driven under this kind of licence to carry goods, they could not decide if a coffin was 'goods' within the meaning of the Act, and not wishing to make fools of themselves, they discussed the various exemptions on this sort of thing as they drove along. Suddenly the hearse had to pull up for some obstruction, and their surprise the blanket covering the coffin sagged in the middle. Overtaking and stopping the vehicle, they told the driver they wished to examine the coffin. Looking most apprehensive the driver removed the blanket to reveal two wooden packing cases, containing butter and tea, between which lay a number of sides of bacon. As food was severely rationed at the time – the officers promptly arrested the driver and took him along to the local police station. There the whole story came out. The driver was the manager of a Ministry of Agriculture Hostel in an isolated part of Lincolnshire, and was returning from a holiday spent with his brother, a garage proprietor, at Newcastle-on-Tyne. From his brother he had bought the hearse for eventual conversion to a van to use for collecting and transporting foodstuffs from the nearest town. While in Newcastle – he had decided to buy his month's supply of tea, sugar and bacon using food coupons all of which he had with him. As the vehicle was not licensed his brother had allowed him to use the trade plates and they had decided to disguise the food stocks in such a way so as to create an impression of a coffin, in the belief that the Police would not stop a funeral hearse. Neither of the two constables believed the story, but much to their chagrin, they had, through a series of telephone calls, just discovered they had been told the truth and nothing but the truth.

In March 1950, Sir Archibald Hordern CBE, AFC, KPM, the Chief Constable of Lancashire died, and even before the funeral more than one person in Durham said, 'Well, I suppose you will be leaving us and going to Lancashire.'

I went to Preston for the funeral. Archie was a very popular Chief Constable and for long had been regarded as the leader of the Chiefs of Police in this country. His funeral was very much a State occasion with some 500 policemen marching from Headquarters to the Church in front of the coffin. The coffin bearing his sword and full dress cap was preceded by a police constable bearing his medals on a purple cushion and by another constable leading his police horse with boots reversed, whilst some forty Chief Constables and Assistants lined the church yard.

After the funeral, at a buffet lunch at Headquarters, Sir Frank Brook said, 'We won't discuss the matter today but you must apply for the job when it is advertised.' I returned to Durham with a heavy heart to discuss the matter with Joanna. We were extremely happy where we were, and although the house was not all that could be desired, we had made it comfortable. We loved the County and the City and we had many friends there, while I had a happy force running efficiently, and I knew that I was popular both in the Force and with the public. I had outside interests and especially could get in the winter all the shooting I wanted.

In addition I was, by then, not only a member of the Territorial Association in which I was closely interested, but I was also on the Council of one of the Colleges of the expanding University and I had been unofficially approached about filling the next vacancy on the Court of the University; and yet I felt I must try to go to Lancashire. For one thing I had set my eyes on the Metropolitan Police Commissioner's job in due course and felt, probably wrongly with hindsight, that I would not stand any chance of that appointment if I remained Chief Constable of Durham, while if I first made a success of commanding England's largest provincial force it would stand me in better stead. I also felt that it was a challenge, as I had visited Lancashire frequently, and I knew that although on the surface it appeared to be a very efficient Police Force, underneath there was a lot wrong that needed to be put right. Moreover, if I did not move now there might not be another opening for many years. I was just 39 years of age and unless I moved soon, I would probably continue to serve in Durham until I could retire in 21 years time when I reached the age of 60. I had already been in Durham for over five years and to be Chief Constable of one force for twenty-six years would be bad for the Force as well as for me.

I discussed the matter with Lord Barnard who neither encouraged me nor discouraged me from applying, merely saying, 'We will be sorry if you go.' I then talked it over with Sam Watson, who actively discouraged me, saying that there was a man's job at all times to be done in Durham, 'and if it is the extra money you want, we will get Joanna made a member of the Board of the Peterlee New Town', plans for which were then being prepared. Finally, when I asked Sir James Duff, the Vice Chancellor, to act as one of my referees, he surprised me by uttering an unacademic expletive and added, 'We don't want you to leave and I think you are making a mistake. You won't like it there; I know, I have lived and worked there.' How right he was.

Finally, to add to my discomfort, after I had submitted my application, I met the Home Secretary, Mr J. Chuter Ede, at a function in the County, and when I told him of my plans he said, 'Well, if that is what you want, you must go, but you won't be happy as you are here.' Of those who applied, five of us were called up for interview the other four being –

> Captain F. R. J. Peel, Chief Constable of Essex, a descendant of Sir Robert Peel, later Sir Jonathan Peel, CBE, KPM.
> G. E. Scott, Chief Constable of Newcastle on Tyne, later Sir George Scott CBE, KPM, Chief Constable of the West Riding.
> John Skittery, OBE, Chief Constable of Plymouth, a Hendon contemporary who had also been shortlisted with me for the Oxfordshire appointment.
> Colonel J. D. Stewart, Deputy Inspector General, Special Police Corps for Germany who had been a Chief Constable in Scotland.

The interviews took place on the 4th July, 1950, and at the end of the morning I was offered the appointment which then carried with it a salary of £2,700 per annum plus allowances. I was invited to stay for lunch in the County Hall and while waiting an oldish man with a limp who was a stranger came up and asked, 'Have you lived in the County before?' I said I had not, and he then asked, 'Do you suffer from rheumatism?' 'No, I replied. 'You will, you will,' he said and limped off!

I returned to Durham with mixed feeling, elated at my success and with the thought of the work that lay ahead, but very sad knowing all that we were giving up. On my arrival home I found that the children had decorated the garden gate with flags and a large notice in childish writing, 'WELCOME HOME, CHIEF CONSTABLE OF LANCASHIRE'.

I remember little of the next two months save that there seemed to be an endless round of farewell parties given both by the police throughout the county and by many friends. Finally on 30th

September, 1950, the whole family lunched at Headquarters and as we left we found all the Headquarter's staff, men and women, lining the drive, and driven by my driver, PC Rae Smith, and accompanied by my secretary, Muriel Nicholson, both of whom had asked to come with us, we went down the drive with tears freely and unashamedly running down our faces.

I add only two postscripts.

The *Police Review* that month made the following comment on a report that had been written on the postwar reconstruction of the Force:

'In brief, from whatever angle the post-war re-organisation and modernisation of the Durham Constabulary is considered in retrospect after four years of reconstructive effort the record of achievement shows very substantial progress.

The Durham County Police Authority and their Chief Constable have cause for much satisfaction in the measure of success that has rewarded their efforts to date.

As it turns out this is probably the last report which Colonel St. Johnston will make to the Durham Authority. It is a record of which he may well be proud and it should give him no small encouragement in facing the still heavier tasks and responsibilities to which he has been appointed as Chief Constable of the County Palatine'.

The second postscript is a story told to me some time later by Tommy Bradford,[1] a Durham friend, who was also a member of the Police Authority, and who had many friends among the pitmen. The story exemplifies the loyalty and friendship of the miners to one they liked.

Soon after I arrived in Lancashire, there was a very severe storm off the coast at Fleetwood, as a result of which the sea-wall was breached. This was a serious matter as much of the town is below sea level, and we had to move the patients from a children's convalescent home and make plans for a more general evacuation of the inhabitants of the town. At the same time, as the storm gave no sign of abating, convoys of lorries were organised for work day and night bringing hard core from inland quarries to close the gap, the scene being lit by strong arc lights. The BBC's television outside broadcast units were in their infancy, and much coverage was given by them to the scene.

On the second evening, while I was on the sea wall close to the breach watching operations with the Engineer in Charge, the

[1] Sir Thomas Bradford, DSO, MC, whose three brothers were killed in the First World War. Two were awarded VCs, the third an MC.

television commentator mentioned that I was there, and a miner watching the programme in a club in a Durham pit village was heard to remark, 'There's no need for them to worry: the water won't get in: the Chief's there: that bugger's better than King Canute.'

Chapter Six

LANCASHIRE I

Durham was such a warmly hospitable county that it would have been easy to forswear ambition and settle in that congenial atmosphere and company for the rest of my police career. Easy for some, that is, but my restless nature was eager for fresh experiences, new trials, and stronger challenges.

Those who aspire to positions of power and responsibility usually prefer to take over a position where they know there are improvements to be made. Oxfordshire presented just such an opportunity and Durham another, though for different reasons. Lancashire was a much more formidable challenge, not only because of its greater size, but because I should have to live up to the reputation of my predecessor, and his popularity with members of the Force and with Lancashire people generally; I would also have to prove myself master of a situation where most members of the Force were keen and brimful of ideas, believed themselves fully efficient and the leading provincial force in more than numerical strength. And yet I had reason to believe that all was not well and that much needed to be altered.

Such were my thoughts when on the 1st October, 1950, still under forty years of age, I took command of the largest police force in Great Britain outside London.

Until the radical re-organisation of county boundaries in 1974, Lancashire had for many centuries been one of England's largest counties, stretching a hundred and ten miles from North to South and over eighty miles at its widest parts. Within its boundaries lived over five million people – more than the whole population of Scotland. For the purposes of local government, in addition to the area for which the Lancashire County Council was responsible there were no less than seventeen Cities or County Boroughs of which all but one, Bury, had their own separate police forces. The Lancashire Constabulary, with an establishment of over 3,000 personnel, policed the Lancashire County area and that of the County Borough of Bury, and in this area there lived over two million people.

The Lancashire Constabulary, created in December 1839, was one of the first County Constabularies to be established under the 'permissive' Police Act of that year. Until then, nearly all the county areas were policed by a mixture of parish constables and paid and voluntary special constables. Supervision was provided by Magistrates and occasionally by the appointment of a Head Constable. The first Chief Constable of Lancashire, Captain John Woodford of the Rifle Brigade, served for seventeen years, just about matching my own service as the eleventh in line of Lancashire Chiefs. Woodford who in 1856 became the second Inspector of Constabulary to be appointed, followed the pattern set by the first Commissioners of the Metropolitan Police by defining the task of his Force of New Police as the prevention of crime and the protection of life and property. His charge to the Force, reproduced in poster form and exhibited at all police stations in the county in 1840, has survived and can be seen on page 9.

Since the 1930s the Constabulary had a national if not an international reputation for progressiveness and efficiency, and this was mainly due to the character and work of my predecessor, Sir Archibald Hordern who had succeeded Wilfred Trubshaw in August 1935. Archie was originally a soldier during the First World War but transferred to the Royal Flying Corps, and by the end of hostilities he had been awarded the Air Force Cross and mentioned in despatches. After the war he was attached to the Shropshire Constabulary for some years before being appointed Chief Constable of the East Riding of Yorkshire in 1926. In 1934 he took command of the Cheshire Constabulary, and twelve months later he was appointed Chief Constable of Lancashire.

Archie, a bachelor, was an extremely popular man. Kindly and thoughtful towards others, he was the type of Chief who commands loyalty without conscious effort and thus a difficult man to follow; I was under no delusions as to what lay ahead on that score. Tall and good-looking with a smart military bearing, he was also a good and forceful speaker and lived for the Police Service, having few outside interests, though in the winter he shot a little and when at home, which was not often, he interested himself in woodwork of a fairly basic kind. He had a domestic staff of four, and a police driver, all of whom worshipped him.

Since the end of World War Two, he had been much involved in the national affairs of the police and was for some years spokesman for the Chief Constables in all negotiations with the Home Office.

Because of these commitments he spent a great deal of his time in London, where he was a regular resident of the Royal Automobile Club in Pall Mall. When he was in Lancashire, in order to catch up with the avalanche of paper-work on his desk, he often worked in his office the whole evening and expected his staff to do likewise. Small wonder that a sigh of relief went round Headquarters when it became known that the new Chief was a married man with a family, and the remark was passed, 'Perhaps he'll go home at the end of the day at a sensible time.'

While still working in Durham I had visited Archie fairly frequently at the Lancashire Police Headquarters at Hutton near Preston to discuss various problems affecting the police and he had indicated that he hoped I would succeed him in due course. I usually stayed with him when we talked police affairs late into the night and I found myself in general agreement with him on most matters, but in the years before he died I noticed that he was becoming more and more impatient and even querulous at times about the Home Office and County Hall in Lancashire; he did not, however, seem to be failing in health and it was a great shock to all of us when, after a short illness, he died in April 1950.

In spite of the Force's reputation for efficiency, on my visits to Hutton I had seen signs that all was not well during Archie's last years. The whole place seemed to be untidy, and through talking to senior officers I found a lack of co-ordination and at the same time, an atmosphere of arrogance. Many senior officers seemed to imply, 'We are Lancashire. We are the best. We know better than you.'

Archie's fifteen years in Lancashire had been marked by hard work and a willingness to experiment which was quite outstanding. A great innovator, he was also a great believer in giving men their heads to try out new ideas. As a result, Lancashire had pioneered a number of new ideas of a mechanical type to help police in their operational duties. The introduction of photographic, fingerprint, modus operandi and printing departments had been notable advances but the most useful were Lancashire's experiments with the use of VHF wireless for police work. Unfortunately much experimental work was duplicated. For instance the Traffic Department was carrying out similar experiments at the same time as the Radio Branch, each working separately in their watertight compartments.

Throughout the County the eighteen Divisional Superintendents were all allowed to run their own Divisions very much as they thought fit, and were encouraged to try out any new ideas which occurred to them. All this was entirely admirable but the system, if it could be called such, suffered from a lack of control and supervision, while there was no one to ensure that a good idea developed by one

Division would be introduced throughout the Force. No one evaluated the experiments and some were allowed to continue long after it was obvious they were of little use. One example that comes to mind is that I found eight different types of electric torches were being bought independently by different divisions and departments.

Because of Archie's frequent absence in London, the day-to-day running of the Force was largely left in the hands of the Deputy Chief Constable, Walter Thornton, who is happily alive and well today at the age of ninety-two. He was a strong character though somewhat austere, and a man of great integrity, and a fervent admirer of Lancashire and its Police Force. I had every reason to be very grateful to Mr Thornton – no one in the Force in later years ever called him by his Christian name – for in 1936, when a student at Hendon Police College, I had spent part of the Easter holidays visiting the Lancashire Constabulary and although I was only a very young student Inspector, Mr Thornton, even then an Assistant Chief Constable, had taken the trouble to spend two whole days showing me round and discussing with me police administration in general. I learned a great deal from him in a very short time.

When Archie died in March, 1950, Mr Thornton had become the Acting Chief Constable, and by the time I arrived in the following October, he had been running the Force for six months. He was then approaching sixty-five and although I immediately asked him to continue and serve as my Deputy. he said that he wished to retire at the end of the year. In my heart, much as I liked and respected him, I was glad he had made this decision, for I knew that much had to be changed and that at his age and with his experience of such long standing, though he might have approved in principle, he would not take kindly to the new broom.

Before I came to Lancashire I had, as a precautionary measure, spoken to several officials at the Home Office about the situation there, and the only advice I had been given was to watch out for County Hall. 'They', I was told would do all they could to get the Police under their control, and I was advised whilst working with them, to ensure the independence of the Chief Constable in operational matters. Mr Thornton was very much anti-County Hall and although I was determined to keep my independence, I was anxious to maintain good friendly terms with the officials and the Police Authority and I felt my task would be easier if Mr Thornton was not there.

To replace Mr Thornton I felt there was no alternative but to recommend to the Police Authority the appointment of Mr A. E. Waddington, who was an Assistant Chief Constable. He had joined the Lancashire Constabulary in 1920 and had been an administrative

Lancashire I

police officer throughout his career. While hard working and very knowledgeable on every aspect of administrative police affairs, he possessed no knowledge of nor indeed ability for operational police work; he did however, have an encyclopaedic knowledge of all that had gone on in Headquarters for many years, and was a good foil for me as he was a very cautious man and was continually waving red flags, so that I had to think twice before embarking on any new scheme.

To fill the vacancy caused by his promotion, I had quickly to assess the qualities of those in the rank of Chief Superintendent, and I had no doubt that the man to appoint was W. J. H. Palfrey, at that time in charge of the Leigh Division, and who had, as I have recorded in an earlier chapter, served with me so efficiently during the war in Europe. When he volunteered for military service he was Chief Constable of the small Borough of Accrington, but when he returned from War service as a Lieutenant Colonel, he found his Force about to be merged with the Lancashire Constabulary. Though it must have been a hard decision to take, John Palfrey, to his credit, wisely agreed to continue even though it meant stepping down in rank, and he became a Superintendent in the Lancashire Constabulary, serving successively in command of the Blackburn, Bolton and Leigh Divisions. Apart from the fact that I already knew his worth, he had the advantage from my point of view that he had served elsewhere, and therefore had a broader outlook and wider experience than those who had served only in Lancashire.

Born in Devon and originally a Portsmouth policeman, Palfrey had come North and adapted himself well to Lancashire life. He spoke bluntly and to the point, and had drive and initiative. His judgement was generally good, but there were times when his enthusiasm ran away with him and he had to be ridden on a tight rein.

In due course when Waddington retired in 1962, Palfrey was appointed Deputy Chief Constable, and when I eventually left Lancashire, Palfrey succeeded me. Though, with many people he was a popular Chief Constable, it has always been my view that he was a better No. 2 than No. 1 in peace time.

With the work load that we had at Headquarters and with the plans that I had in mind, there was need for another Assistant Chief Constable, and I also wanted someone to help me look at the Force with completely fresh eyes.

I was aware that Jack Waldron, who had been senior to me at Hendon Police College, was still a Superintendent in the Metropolitan Police, and I knew him to be an intelligent, hard working and pleasant man, although not a close friend of mine. Educated at

Charterhouse and Cambridge, he was a direct entrant to the first term at the Hendon Police College. He had, during the War, been one of four who had helped re-organise the Police in Ceylon, but on returning to London he had been given no further advancement. I felt that he was being wasted in London, and in any case I knew that as a Berkshire man, he was very anxious to take command of that Force when in due course the Chief Constable retired. I therefore suggested to the Police Authority that Waldron should be appointed as an Assistant Chief Constable in Lancashire. To this they agreed and he came and worked beside me for three years, giving the most enormous amount of help. I did not give him any departmental responsibilities but asked him to be responsible for regular Inspections of the Departments at Headquarters and the territorial Divisions of the Force. When I went to a division I could only spend a short time there, but if I could sense that there was something wrong, Jack, at my request, would spend a week or even longer in the division to ascertain what changes were needed, and would then put matters right. This he did impeccably and with great tact so that he became extremely popular.

He was also a good athlete and was responsible for setting up a unified Sports and Social organisation in the County, for as in most things in Lancashire, there had been good Sports and Social Clubs in some divisions but not in all. The new Club came into being in January, 1952, when ten sports sections were enthusiastically supported by the interest of over ninety per cent of the Force.

In 1954, Jack became the Chief Constable of Berkshire and four years later he returned to the Metropolitan Police as an Assistant Commissioner. He ended his career as Sir John Waldron, KCVO, Commissioner of Police for the Metropolis, 1968–1972, when he was succeeded by Robert Mark, who had begun his police career as a constable in Manchester.

The situation which I faced on arrival was quite different to that which I had encountered in Oxfordshire and Durham. In my first two commands everyone in the Force had appreciated that they were badly organised and inefficient. In Lancashire however many changes that I suggested met with resistance and often open resentment. If I did something popular, I was given no credit, for 'Archie would have done that anyway'. If I insisted on something they did not like, I was met with, 'Archie would never have done this'. The successor to a popular man always bats on a sticky wicket.

During the three months that Mr Thornton was with me, I asked him to carry on with the routine work while I spent my time visiting and inspecting the eighteen divisions and the two hundred police stations, to assess the situation and get to know the men, and for them to get to know me. On the whole I found much that I did not like, and, as one senior officer told me later, 'When you arrived, you found the Force like an overripe peach. It looked all right on the surface, but everywhere you squeezed it your thumb went in' – a very apt analogy.

Many of the seventeen separate County Borough Police Forces, whose strengths varied from 150 to 300 men, were islands in the midst of the County Police area. Indeed, of the eighteen Lancashire Divisions, no less than five had their Headquarters in the middle of towns that we did not police. The larger City forces of Manchester and Liverpool were on the perimeter of the County and did not affect the situation to the same extent, but many of the criminals living in those cities operated in the county area.

Furthermore, the boundaries of the smaller towns did not contain the whole area that should have been the sole responsibility of one police force or one Local Authority. The urban areas had long ago spilt over into the County, and in the built-up areas of the suburbs, we frequently found that one side of the street was in the County Borough, while the other belonged in the County, which meant that two separate police forces had the responsibility for law and order in the same street.

This made it all the more important that I should have good relations with the Chief Constables of these smaller forces. I therefore made it my business during my first month in office to call on each of these Chief Constables. I am sorry to say that not everywhere did I receive a favourable reception and was sometimes met with obvious suspicion. Archie had been openly critical of them and they assumed I would be of the same mind. One Chief Constable greeted me with the words, 'Well, have you come to take me over?' Another, who did not even rise from his seat when I was taken into his office, merely said, 'Well, what do you want?' I must say that I was not impressed with the calibre of many of them, but we were colleagues, and at Regional Meetings of Chief Constables, they had every right to state their point of view and where necessary, each had an equal vote with me. So I was anxious to be on friendly terms and desired to place the resources of the Lancashire Constabulary at their disposal where necessary.

But it took a long time to overcome the suspicion and apprehension, and while some Chief Constables became good friends, others, I fear, remained aloof and difficult throughout the time I was in the County.

Although the City of Lancaster is the county town of Lancashire, Preston because of its more central position and easier communications, has for a long time been the administrative centre. This is unfortunate, for Lancaster is a much more pleasant area in which to live and work. But since the County Council has from the outset had its Headquarters in Preston, so the Police Headquarters has also been there, and when Archie became Chief Constable, it was housed in a very poor Victorian building close to County Hall.

One of Archie's first moves was to recommend to the Police Authority that they should provide better accommodation and he persuaded them to buy the Hutton Hall estate, consisting of a pretty Queen Anne house badly extended in the 19th century, surrounded by sixty-five acres of land, situated on the outskirts of Preston in a suburb by the name of Penwortham. Although acquired by the Lancashire County Council in 1937 and used for police purposes, it was not until 1939 that it was finally bought for £16,000 by the Police Authority.

The Hall and estate had been owned since the 18th century by the Rawstorne family. The house was in a very derelict condition and it was much too late to restore it. But it had, however, an appealing historical background for me. Interested as I am in shooting I discovered that it was here, in the early 19th century, that pheasants were first bred in this country for shooting. All this is faithfully recorded in a book called *Gamonia*, which was written in 1837 and re-printed in 1939. In the last century the estate abounded with game but, alas, by the 1950s all had gone, as a result of the attentions of animal and human predators, both common in these parts.

The County Architect had drawn up a very grandiose scheme for a Headquarters to be built adjacent to Hutton Hall. The first phase of this was to be the Headquarters of the Traffic Department, since Lancashire was taking a leading part in the Home Office Experimental Motor Patrol scheme throughout the country, known to the general public as 'The Courtesy Cops'. The Exchequer financed the whole programme and the Force received an augmentation of over 300 men, to enable the scheme to be run without taking men from the normal policing of the county. In April, 1938, a Police Motor Driving School was formed as part of the Home Office Scheme, the cost again being borne by the Exchequer.

The new Traffic Department Headquarters was completed just at the outbreak of the Second World War in September 1939, and it was hastily converted to become the administrative Headquarters of the Lancashire Constabulary, which it has remained ever since. I would have liked to build a completely new Headquarters for the administrative staff and thus allow the building to revert to its original use as a Traffic Department, as Archie had intended, but other priorities prevented it.

When Archie first arrived in Lancashire there was no house for the Chief Constable, and at his request the Police Authority bought 'Holme Mead', a house in Penwortham, close to Hutton Hall. The house had been built about 1910 in the worst possible style, in bright Accrington brick. It consisted of two reception rooms, a large kitchen, six bedrooms and two bathrooms, but had the great advantage that the previous owner had built fifteen extremely good stables in the grounds, and so these were available for use by the Mounted Branch Headquarters of the Force, which had previously been quartered in very poor stables in Preston.

Although Archie Hordern lived alone, he considered the house too small for him and he persuaded the Police Authority to build on to it a very large drawing room, sitting room and study on the ground floor, with two suites, each containing a double bedroom, dressing room and bathroom, on the first floor. This was the house my family and I were expected to occupy. It contained no less than ten bedrooms and four bathrooms and had sixty-five windows, for which we certainly hadn't the money to provide curtains.

It was, therefore, generally agreed between the Police Authority and myself, that as soon as we could find a suitable alternative house we should move. The difficulty was that in Lancashire there were very few suitably sized houses with any character, and as my wife and I were both very interested in architecture and had quite a few good pieces of 18th-century furniture, we did not want to move into any of the modern 'boxes' available and which the Chairman of the Police Authority thought suitable for us.

After much searching we eventually found an extremely pretty, early 19th-century stone vicarage, set in a beautiful position on the side of a hill on the edge of the village of Longridge, ten miles north of Preston. There we moved in 1954. Regrettably by that time, the disagreements that had arisen between the Chairman of the Police Authority and myself over the vexed question of a suitable house, had permanently soured our relationship, and gave rise to much difficulty and trouble.

For the first six months of my command, the Chairman of the Lancashire Police Authority was a sick man who lived in Anglesey and whom I saw very rarely. Indeed, he was ill and absent on the day I was appointed. When he retired he was succeeded by a County Councillor and later Alderman, who remained Chairman for the whole of my last sixteen years as Chief Constable of the County.

It is sad but true that with him I never enjoyed a friendly or happy relationship. He clearly disliked my independence and disapproved of many of my actions. From the outset, meetings with him were unpleasant and full of tension for I felt that he mistrusted my motives in much that I was trying to do. We had the most disagreeable discussions and arguments, and though in the end I usually got what I wanted for the Force, it was at the cost of much nervous energy and unhappiness.

He was a man who worked very hard for what he believed to be right in County Council affairs and he liked to be at the centre of everything. He was politically in a strong position so that although many sympathised with me and some even tackled him in private about the attitude he had adopted towards me, no one was prepared to take my part in public debate. It was the custom in Lancashire that the party in power should nominate the Chairman of the County Council and the Chairman of all the committees, while the other party nominates the Vice-Chairmen. It is, of course, accepted in this country that the police should be kept out of the political arena, and for this reason, irrespective of whichever party was in control, the Chairmanship of the Police Authority never changed. In the circumstances this situation was not helpful and it was unfortunately aggravated by the fact that I did not have the friendship and support of the official who was Clerk to the Police Authority throughout the last fifteen years that I was in Lancashire. Although I know that in other matters the Clerk and the Chairman had their disagreements, both appeared united in their stand against me.

The main purpose of a Police Authority is to appoint a Chief Constable and provide him with the money, buildings and equipment to run the Force efficiently, relying on the qualified officials, namely the Chief Constable, Clerk, Treasurer, and County Architect for professional advice in their respective areas. Each member of the Committee can also put forward public opinion and any grievances which come to his knowledge, and thus ensure that the Force properly and efficiently serves the people who live in the police area.

I do not want to imply that the Chairman of the Lancashire Police Authority was not prepared to ensure the efficiency of the Constabulary, but before he would recommend his Committee to approve any expenditure, there was always a battle to persuade him that it was really necessary. During the seventeen years that I was Chief Constable of Lancashire, the Police Authority built a hundred new police stations of varying sizes and increased the number of houses they owned from one thousand to two thousand five hundred. Before I left, the Police Authority had also started to build a Training School which is probably the best of its kind in the country. Much was achieved, but to get projects of this kind agreed by the Chairman was always a struggle and the negotiations took a great deal of time and effort.

Obviously the Chairman of a Police Authority should not just rubber-stamp any scheme for improvements put forward by a Chief Constable; there must be careful consideration of each matter of policy, and as major schemes involve much expenditure, a Chief Constable must be able clearly to justify his proposals on the grounds of improved efficiency in relation to the cost incurred. To do this, however, full and free consultation based on mutual trust between the Chief Constable and the Chairman of his Police Authority, is essential. This was greatly lacking in Lancashire, and it was a sad contrast to the happy relationship that I had enjoyed with Major Feilden and Lord Macclesfield in Oxfordshire, and with Lord Barnard in Durham. In Lancashire, I also greatly missed the close association, both professional and social, that I enjoyed with the Clerks of those two other counties.

Not all the fault lay with my Chairman, for I am sure that I handled him badly and should have humoured him more. It was a straightforward clash of personalities and the unhappy relationship dragged on for sixteen years. There was no reason why he should resign his position, to which he was re-elected every three years, and there was no reason why I should resign my appointment, for it was, after all, my career and my bread and butter. But undoubtedly it was bad for the Force and I suspect it was bad for the personalities of both of us. I do know that it had a permanently damaging effect on my home life, for I used to arrive home tired and bad-tempered and then lie awake half the night wondering what trouble was brewing for the next day. Later I learnt that there were many at County Hall who were of the opinion that Archie had been too independent, and so before I arrived, there had been a determination to try to clip the wings of the new Chief Constable.

It has been said that in operational matters a Chief Constable is answerable to God, his Queen, his conscience, and to no one else. The legal position is that in operational matters the Chief Constable is independent, and it is important that he should remain so, and his independence be observed.

Unlike all county officials the Chief Constable is not a servant of the County Council. All police officers are Crown Officers administered locally, as Mr Justice McCardie averred in 1930 in his famous judgement in *Fisher v Oldham Corporation*, when an attempt was made to maintain that police officers were servants of the Local Authority. In fighting this battle of independence, I felt that I was fighting for an important principle, and that if I gave in, it would adversely affect my successors as well as me, and indirectly affect my colleagues in other Forces. But in fighting for this principle it was not my intention to refuse friendly advice or ignore guidance and help.

The senior officials at the Home Office were well aware of this struggle behind the scenes, for I kept them fully informed, and I knew that the Chairman, who was frequently in London, visited the Home Office from time to time, to tell them his side of the story.

Although the civil servants privately sympathised with me in my difficulties, it was no easy task to persuade them openly to support me. I got the impression that the Home Office was inclined to sit on the side-lines watching the situation carefully but not appearing to take sides. Indeed, the civil servants' primary concern seemed to be to ensure that the Home Secretary did not become involved, and particularly that he was not embarrassed. Furthermore, if someone had to go to the wall, it was much easier to lose an individual than to lose a Police Authority.

During my ordeal I had frequent consultations with Sir Frank Brook whose valued friendship, sage advice, sound judgment and tremendous support were of great help to me. He always advised me to go on doing the job as I thought fit and not to give way on any major matter of principle, but, on the other hand, he told me to be prepared to give way on trivial issues.

It was a great blow to me when Frank Brook retired in 1953 for it was at the height of my troubles with my Chairman. Despite the differences in our ages, we had been close friends since I first met him in 1943. We stayed at each other's houses, he knew my family well and I knew his. He used to talk to me in great confidence about his problems with other Chief Constables and about the future of the Police Service as he saw it. As he had no office and little secretarial assistance, he used my office and secretary and I would draft memoranda for him. After he retired we continued to see each other frequently and I often consulted him. He died in 1960, much beloved by many.

Frank Brook and Donald Banks, of whom I have written earlier, have had a greater influence on my life than anyone else. Born within a year or so of each other, they were similar types. Both had a distinguished record in the first World War and both were a great success in their chosen professions. Both had the same ideals, and both did all they could to help and encourage young men who came into their orbit.

When I went to Lancashire, I was surprised to discover that there was no such thing as regular weekly Orders to the Force informing everyone of appointments, promotions, transfers, resignations and the like. This I immediately started, and as there was at the time a considerable amount of re-organisation taking place, with men being moved from one job to another, the knowledge of the number of transfers taking place caused some consternation though in fact a good number of the transfers were on paper only and did not mean that the men actually moved house. I was soon amused to learn, however, that the Weekly Orders had been re-named 'The Gospel According to St. Johnston,' the first verse of which reads, 'Thou shalt take up thy bed and walk.'

With over three thousand men and women working from two hundred police stations in such a large county, it is important not only for a Chief Constable to get to know and be known by the rank and file, but if there is to be cohesion and a uniform policy throughout the Force, it is equally important that there should be lucid, well written and comprehensive instructions and guide lines on which the operational officers may work. I found that the lines of communication were blurred and often non-existent, while the Standing Orders to the Force consisted of a large number of memoranda, some short, some long, some recent and some going back many years in the history of the Force.

As soon as I had completed the main lines of the re-organisation at Headquarters and in the Divisions, I felt that the task of re-writing orders to the force must be tackled. It was a mammoth task and one that had been attempted before, but without success. I gave the task to one man, Inspector J. Holden, and, basing these orders on the Metropolitan Police Orders which have stood the test of time so well, and including the relevant contents of the myriad of memoranda, he produced, two years later, a set of Standing Orders which as much as anything else gave to the whole Force a cohesion and was the basis for really efficient concerted administrative and operational work.

One matter that concerned me at the outset was the poor standard and condition of police buildings in the county, and the state of many of the houses in which policemen were living, was appalling. To deal with the problem, I inaugurated, as I had done in Durham, a Housing Department. Owing to the lack of money at that time there was not much that could be done to provide new police stations, but priorities could be decided and plans made, while a great deal, could be done to improve the living conditions of policemen.

First we made a survey of each of the thousand houses that were owned by the Police Authority, dividing them into three categories. 'A' consisted of houses good enough for a policeman to live in: 'B' were houses good enough for policemen, if certain improvements were made, such as modernisation of the kitchen or the provision of an inside lavatory: category 'C' houses were for disposal as soon as possible. The results of the survey proved my first impressions, for we found, as far as I can remember, that there were forty-seven policemen living in houses without any bathroom facilities at all, while no less than one hundred and fifty lived in houses without an inside lavatory.

We then set about improving the 'B' class houses and at the same time we bought a number of good properties and purchased sites for new houses. All this took time and inevitably there were many frustrations and delays, and despite the greatest help and co-operation from the County Architect, five years elapsed before we were satisfied in general with the housing conditions in Lancashire, though even then there were properties which had to be improved.

My slogan in the police has always been 'efficiency through the kitchen sink'. One cannot have an efficient force unless its members are happy, and on the whole they will not be happy unless their wives are content. Since a Chief Constable has very dictatorial powers of being able to require a policemen and his family to move at a moment's notice to any part of the county, and to any house supplied by the Police Authority, it is important that the house should be a good one. Moves in the Police Force are a constant source of worry and concern to all. Although the Police Authority now takes responsibility for most, if not all, of an officer's removal expenses, his wife has to find new shops, and the children have to change schools, which interrupts their education, while often new uniforms have to be bought, and all of them have to find new friends. For the efficiency of the police force we need to be able to move men from place to place, and indeed it is often in a man's own interests in order to give him a wider experience, but at the same time one must alleviate as far as possible the problems that such moves create for policemen and their families.

For this reason I was always very keen that the wife should feel that when she moved she was going to a house of which she could be proud, and since so much of a married woman's time is spent in the kitchen, it is particularly important that she should be proud of her kitchen and feel it is one in which she enjoys working. I know from letters received and remarks made how much this policy was appreciated by the men in the Forces of which I had command.

Although nothing could be done immediately to provide new or better police stations, I was determined that we should deal at once with the general untidiness that I found in and around Headquarters and in almost all police stations throughout the county. At the first Superintendents' Conference I announced that November 1950 was to be a spring cleaning month, and every room in every station was to be examined to ensure that everything in it was in use and usable. All broken furniture – and there was much of it – had either to be repaired or thrown away. All yards and gardens had to be cleared of rubbish and in particular, attics and unused rooms in police stations where single men had once lived had to be cleared of old papers, unused furniture and equipment. I cannot say how many tons of rubbish were disposed of throughout the county but I do know that we sold four tons of scrap iron found lying in the grounds at Headquarters.

At the same time we worked out a list of priorities for replacing most of the two hundred police stations in the county, and we started to press both the Police Authority and the Home Office for the necessary funds. As the Stretford Police Station had been destroyed during the War, permission had already been given to start the construction of a new Divisional Headquarters on an excellent site opposite the Lancashire County Cricket Ground and close to the Manchester United Football Ground. For some reason the Home Office allowed us to build this to a higher standard than any other for many years.

In due course other Divisional, Sub-Divisional and Sectional offices were built during the seventeen years I was in Lancashire, and this made a great deal of difference to our efficiency. It was interesting to see how the morale rose and the general behaviour of the men improved when they worked from a modern aesthetically pleasing building in which they had pride.

One of the first pieces of paper placed in front of me when I assumed command of the Force, was a memorandum addressed to the Clerk, asking the Police Authority to approve the expenditure of £1,500 for the repair of the roof of the prison in Lancaster Castle, that historic landmark which overlooks the River Lune. When I asked what had this to do with us, I was told that in 1930, the then Chief Constable, Wilfred Trubshaw, being dissatisfied with the provision made for the training of police recruits, had taken a sixty year full-repairing lease on the prison blocks in the Castle owned by the Duchy of Lancaster. This had not been used as a prison since 1913, and very little in the way of repairs and renovations had been done before the advent of the Police Training School. Throughout his regime and until 1938, all recruits of the Lancashire Constabulary, and many from other forces, were trained inside the erstwhile prison, sleeping in prison cells and dining in the halls of the four main convict blocks.

When Archie took over, he immediately recommended to the Police Authority that a better Training School should be provided, and a 19th-century house, 'Stanley Grange', situated at Hoghton, twelve miles from Preston, was bought specifically for training purposes. Fourteen wooden huts were erected in the grounds for use as classrooms and dormitories, and another larger hut was built next to the house, for dining facilities.

Although this accommodation was a decided improvement on the prison, it was still not good enough, but was all that we had when I arrived in 1950. One of its main deficiencies was the lack of lavatories for the dormitories, with the result that any man caught short during the night, whatever the weather, had to leave his hut and walk across ten to fifteen yards of open ground to reach the latrines. In spite of this and other drawbacks, men who had been to Stanley Grange were very much attached to the place, chiefly because of the friendly atmosphere and the traditionally good meals provided by an excellent cook.

Since the opening of Stanley Grange, the prison buildings at Lancaster Castle had not been used by the Force, save for two rooms used as store-rooms and the early 19th-century laundry which dealt with the sheets and towels from Stanley Grange.

The prison was of considerable historical interest because there is still in existence the cell in which George Fox, the founder and martyr of the Quaker movement in this country, was imprisoned in 1660, and there were the dungeons in which were incarcerated the Lancashire Witches made famous by the historical novel of Harrison Ainsworth. There was also still in existence in the prison block, the condemned cell, the execution shed, and the drop, and I suspect I am the only Chief Constable in the country, who has had those implements of execution under his charge, while even today in the dock of the Crown Court, also in the Castle, there is the branding iron with which all persons were once branded with the letter 'M' for Malefactor when convicted of felony.

Though we had not used the prison as a Training School since 1938 we continued to be responsible on a full repairing lease of the buildings until 1990. In 1950 the Prison Authorities were becoming concerned with the lack of provision for the increasing prison population. With this in mind, I saw Philip Allen who was in charge of the Prison Department at the Home Office and suggested we should assign our lease to the Home Office. After the usual legal negotiations, this was finally agreed, and since then Lancaster Castle has once again been an operational prison. I much regret that before signing the lease, I did not have photographs taken of the execution shed and early 19th-century equipment in the laundry, for they would be museum pieces today.

Amongst the stores at the Castle, we found a considerable number of old documents relating to the Lancashire Constabulary of the Victorian era, and these were sent to the County Archivist.

Lancashire I

There was also in the store, an old bath in which Dr Ruxton had dismembered his wife and nursemaid after he had killed them in a house opposite the town hall in Lancaster. The case was a *cause célèbre* in 1935 when the dismembered bodies of two women were found scattered along the sides of a gorge near Moffatt, Dumfriesshire. By some excellent police work the crime was eventually brought home to Buck Ruxton, a Parsee doctor and he was found guilty and hanged at Strangeways Prison, Manchester. The bath, a crime exhibit, was held by the police and later stored in Lancaster Castle.

It so happened that the day before my visit to the Castle, I had been inspecting the stables of the Mounted Branch and had noticed that there was no drinking trough for the horses. Ruxton's bath was the answer. It was sent to Holme Mead where it still stands to this day, as far as I know, surrounded by a low brick wall, but it is doubtful if any of the young policemen bringing their horses to water are aware of the macabre origin of the trough.

In Lancashire about 150 Constables and 35 Sergeants were promoted each year as vacancies arose, and when I first arrived I was appalled at the method of selecting men for promotion. On my second day there, the Assistant Chief Constable, Mr Waddington, brought to me the personal records of five or six constables. He told me that there was a vacancy for a Sergeant in a certain division and that we had to decide who should be promoted and sent there. I was asked to choose from six personal files placed in front of me the man I thought was most suitable. When I inquired why these particular constables had been suggested, I was told that their respective divisions had not had a promotion for some time and so it was their turn to have one. I was not happy about this haphazard method of selection, but as there were more pressing matters to attend to I looked through the records and decided which man seemed to be the best on paper, suggesting him for promotion. A few days later, Mr Waddington again came to me with the personal files of six other men for promotion to Sergeant. When I inquired what had happened to the records of the earlier five who had not been chosen I was told that they had had their chance, and as I had not selected one of them, there were other equally good fish in the sea, and was advised to choose from the fresh batch. This extraordinary 'hit and miss' method was clearly most unsatisfactory and at the first Superintendents' Conference I made it clear that the whole system of promotion in the Force must be more methodical and fairer to the men concerned. I therefore instituted a system of Promotion Selection Boards. Today this may sound all too obvious, as the system introduced at that time has since become more or less universal throughout the Police Service; in 1950, however, it was a real innovation.

I must admit that I have had more sleepless nights on the question of promotions than over anything else in the whole of my Police Service. One must think not only of the man but of his wife and children also. I could always imagine the tension that must exist in the man's home on the day on which he is to appear before a Promotion Board, the wife lovingly pressing his suit or uniform, kissing him fondly good-bye and wishing him the best of luck. Should she and her husband be ambitious people, she knows that so much will depend on the way in which he presents himself to the Board. If he gets promotion it will not only mean more money for them but higher social status for the family, while the man himself will be more contented in his job.

In making promotions, one cannot always be right. Some men who deserve promotion will probably 'miss the boat', for one reason or another. The important point is not to promote a man who does not deserve promotion. I hoped that the safeguards we built into the system, involving the submission of periodical personal reports which were always carefully considered by the Board, prevented that happening.

In 1950, only one member of the Lancashire Constabulary had been appointed a Chief Constable in the previous twenty years. This clearly was most unsatisfactory. With the type of young men that we had in the Force and with the type of experience that we could give them in such a large and varied county I was sure we could train a number of men to become Chief Constables of other Forces, especially of the smaller Borough Forces in Lancashire. With this in mind I asked my Superintendents to recommend not more than three Constables of potential in their respective divisions whom they regarded as being particularly bright. After considering their recommendations, twelve young men were short listed. Their personal files were marked in the top right corner 'BYL' – Bright Young Lad – and this number was increased from time to time. The Personnel Department were instructed to ensure these young men were considered for any vacancy in the Force which would give them wider experience, and it was emphasised that during the next five years each of them must be given the opportunity of serving not only in the uniform branch, but also in the CID, the Traffic and Administrative Branches. Subject to passing the necessary qualifying examinations, they were then promoted as quickly as possible to ascertain whether they instinctively possessed the qualities of leadership. A few turned out not as good as originally thought but on the whole the experiment worked out well.

Knowing what benefit I had derived from being office boy/staff officer to Sir Ronald Howe at the start of my police career, I had always determined that when I reached high rank, I would have a young man of potential as a staff officer, and the best of the BYLs were chosen for this. In all I had eight in Lancashire. Each stayed with me for not more than two years, during which time he sat in on most of my conferences. These Staff Officers had to prepare briefs and meet all my visitors, and they had the opportunity to examine all files as well as being present when all matters of policy were being discussed and decisions taken. They heard the views of senior officers, not only of the Lancashire Constabulary but of other forces, and there is no doubt that as a result of these opportunities they became better and more knowledgeable policemen. The practice of having a young man attached to a senior officer is unusual in the Police Service, although it is common in the armed forces and other organisations. At least ten of those who had the opportunity of serving with me, have gone on to become Chief Constables and Assistant Chief Constables and it is regrettable that few other police chiefs have tried to do the same thing.

When the University of Lancaster was formed in 1964, I arranged with the Vice-Chancellor with the consent of the Police Authority, that three Constables a year should go to the University to take a degree, and it is good to record what a success this has been. Those who went gained much by meeting people outside the Police Service, while the University told me that the police students, usually older than the rest, were a stable influence among the undergraduate population. Furthermore they all did well in examinations and were awarded good degrees.

Although I was in Lancashire for over sixteen years and in County Durham for less than six, I always felt closer to my men in County Durham than I ever did in Lancashire. This was due to the enormous amount of administrative work in Lancashire, which made big inroads in one's time and meant that I was unable to visit policemen in their own homes as often as I had in Durham. My diary records that while in Durham I had been in the houses of over 400 policemen and had actually sat down and had a cup of tea with the policeman and his wife. By the time it came for me to leave Lancashire I doubt whether I had visited 100 houses in this way. I have always regretted this, because it is important that the Chief should know his men, and they get to know each other and to understand each other's point of view much better if they meet informally.

Another factor that restricted my visits of this kind was the inevitable involvement in national police affairs. For the first two years I refused to serve on any committee which necessitated going to London as I wanted to concentrate on my new job. But I was then appointed to the Traffic Committee which met from time to time to consider any legislation proposed in connection with Road Safety, and in addition I was frequently consulted by the Home Office on one matter or another, while the affairs of the Association of Chief Police Officers increasingly took up one's time.

Though I had to curb the enthusiasm of various members of the Lancashire Constabulary who were experimenting with different types of equipment, I was careful, nevertheless, not to stop altogether the formulation and introduction of new methods of policing but steps were taken to see that any new schemes were controlled and watched and, which is equally important, stopped if after a fair trial, they were not successful.

Much of the experimental work at Headquarters was the responsibility of a small team of specialists directed by Sergeant, later Inspector, Douglas Smith, who could be relied upon to make anything in the shortest possible time; the squad was composed of policemen who were skilled craftsmen – plumbers, carpenters, electricians, signwriters and the like – and they were all enthusiastic and inventive.

The first innovation introduced by this squad was the establishment of a specialised squad of men who were trained as underwater divers by Ian Fraser VC, using the techniques of frogmen in the Royal Navy. We had a great deal of water in Lancashire. In addition to the long coastline and a number of rivers and canals there were reservoirs, lakes, and many quarries filled with water, while each cotton mill had its own small reservoir, a relic of the days when steam provided the power.

We frequently found that when some person was reported missing there was water nearby which had to be searched, and here the body was often found. These stretches of water provided easy disposal for stolen safes, minus their contents, of weapons used in crime, stolen vehicles and even explosives. They were also the dustbins of the local inhabitants, who threw into them old bedsteads, broken bicycles, glass and coils of wire, which made diving ventures hazardous as well as being far from pleasant. Our underwater teams, however, achieved such success that they were called upon to visit the Police College and other police forces to give demonstrations, and since then many other forces have followed our lead by establishing their own diving teams.

The Lancashire Police had long prided itself on the efficiency

Receiving the Baton of Honour, December 1936 from Sir John Simon, Home Secretary

[*T. H. Everitt & Son*

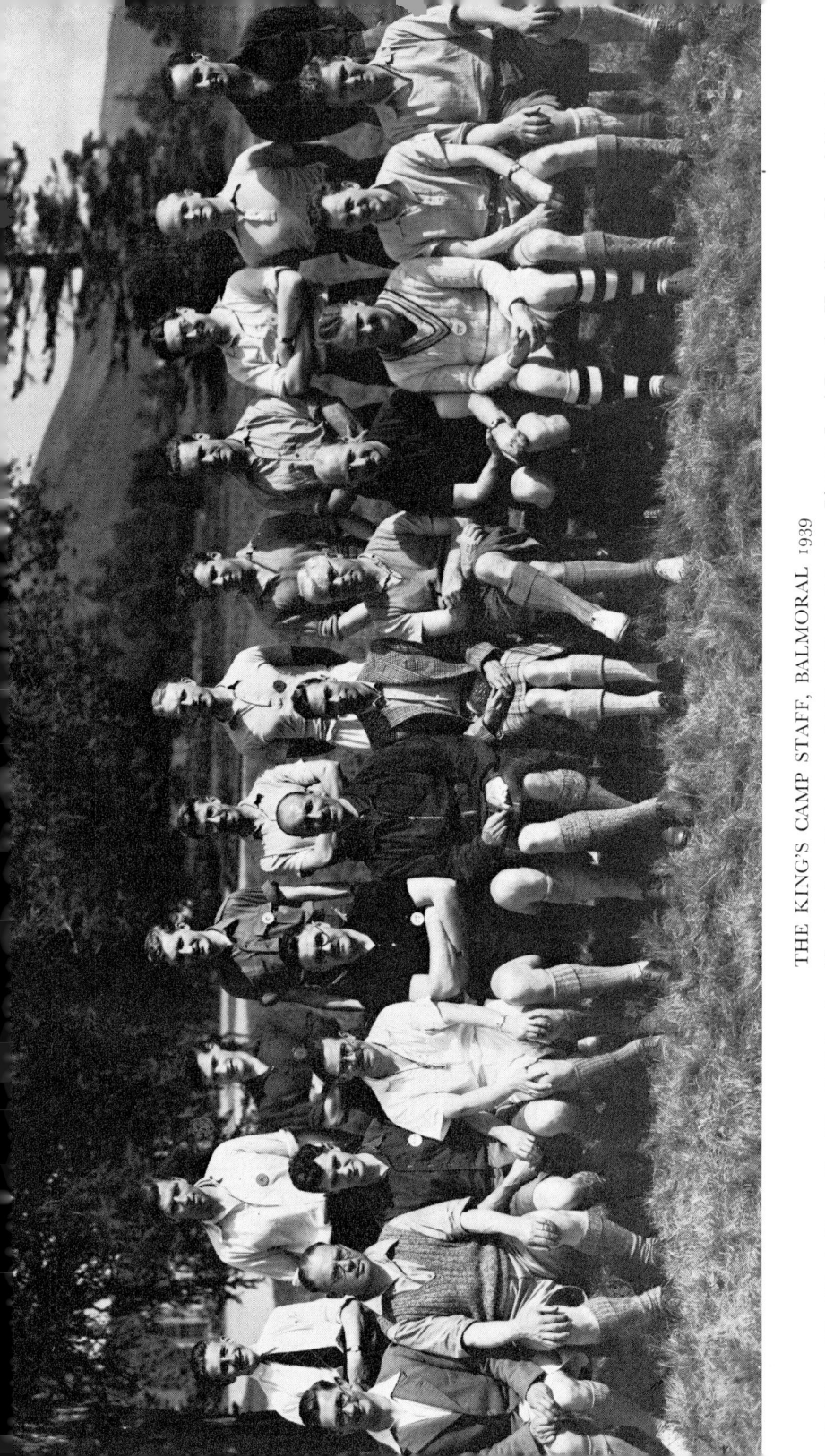

THE KING'S CAMP STAFF, BALMORAL 1939

Back Row The King's Piper, Alec Stirratt, Yellowlees, Hon. Andrew Elphinstone, McPhail, E. St. Johnston, Biggart, Lord Douglas Hamilton, Edward Shackleton, Cameron of Lochiel, Rowland Harper

With Lord Londonderry, Victory Parade, Durham 1946   [*Northern Echo*]

With Philip Allen, Police Training School, Plawsworth, Co Durham, 1947

With Anthony Eden in Durham
Newcastle Chronicle]

With Harold Macmillan at the opening of England's first motorway [*Lancashire L.*

With Jim Callaghan, Home Secretary 1968

COUNTY OF LANCASTER  CONSTABULARY FORCE.

THE FOLLOWING MAXIMS

Are to be strictly observed and borne in mind by the Constables of the Force:—

1. Constables are placed in authority to PROTECT, not to OPPRESS, the PUBLIC.
2. To do which effectually, they must earnestly and systematically exert themselves to PREVENT CRIME.
3. When a Crime has been committed, no time should be lost, nor exertions spared, to discover and bring to justice the OFFENDERS.
4. Obtain a knowledge of all REPUTED THIEVES, and IDLE and DISORDERLY PERSONS.
5. Watch narrowly all Persons having NO VISIBLE MEANS OF SUBSISTENCE.
6. Prevent VAGRANCY.
7. Be IMPARTIAL in the discharge of duties.
8. Discard from the mind all POLITICAL and SECTARIAN prejudices.
9. Be COOL and INTREPID in the discharge of duties in emergencies and unavoidable conflicts.
10. Avoid ALTERCATIONS, and display PERFECT COMMAND of TEMPER under INSULT and gross PROVOCATION, to which all Constables must occasionally be liable.
11. NEVER STRIKE but in SELF-DEFENCE, nor treat a Prisoner with more Rigour than may be absolutely necessary to prevent escape.
12. Practice the most complete SOBRIETY, one instance of DRUNKENNESS will render a Constable liable to DISMISSAL.
13. Treat with the utmost CIVILITY all classes of HER MAJESTY'S SUBJECTS, and cheerfully render ASSISTANCE to all in need of it.
14. Exhibit DEFERENCE and RESPECT to the MAGISTRACY.
15. Promptly and cheerfully OBEY all SUPERIOR OFFICERS.
16. Render an HONEST, FAITHFUL, and SPEEDY account of all MONIES and PROPERTY, whether intrusted with them for others, or taken possession of in the execution of duty.
17. With reference to the foregoing, bear especially in mind that "HONESTY IS THE BEST POLICY."
18. Be perfectly neat and clean in Person and Attire.
19. Never sit down in a PUBLIC HOUSE or BEER SHOP.
20. AVOID TIPPLING.
21. It is the interest of every man to devote some portion of his spare time to the practice of READING and WRITING, and the general improvement of his mind.
22. IGNORANCE is an insuperable bar to promotion.

J. WOODFORD,
Chief Constable.

The original Lancashire Precepts of 1839

Eric St. Johnston welcomes
HM The Queen at Police
Headquarters, Hutton,
1954

With the Queen Mother

[*Weekly News*

Inspection of recruits at the Police Training Centre, Chantmarle, Dorset

Inspection of recruits at the RUC Training School, Enniskillen, Northern Ireland

The Inspectors of Constabulary, 1969 [*Ron Francis*]

Sir Eric St. Johnston as a member of Chapter General of the Order of St. John

[*Bassano and Van Dyk*

of its Traffic Patrols, for, with the Metropolitan Police and the Essex Constabulary, we had, as I have said, started in 1936 the Home Office 'courtesy cop' scheme, concentrating on educating the motorist to be a good driver, rather than just prosecuting whenever an offence was observed. By 1950, however, the whole motor fleet was in a sorry state with no fewer than twelve different makes of cars, many of them needing to be replaced, while there was no cohesion in the work of the patrols.

Having obtained the consent of the Police Authority to renew the cars and vans, the whole of the Traffic Department was reorganised, and for the first time in any force, a number of women traffic patrol officers were included.

I always encouraged my men when on traffic patrol to remain stationary as much as possible. A patrol travelling along a road is only seen by the drivers of a few cars immediately in front or behind him, while drivers going in the opposite direction know that he cannot observe their standard of driving or speed and so take no notice.

A police car stationary on the road and facing outwards is seen by many more drivers, while the officer can observe the traffic travelling in either direction and he can, if it is a single carriageway road, move quickly in either direction should the need arise.

There is, moreover, the financial saving. If every car in an eight hour tour of duty is stationary for an additional hour a tour, in a fleet of 500 traffic patrols on the road for two tours of duty a day, there is a saving of some 1,000 gallons of fuel daily.

When replying to the Toast, to 'Lancashire', at the annual dinner in London of the Society of Lancastrians I had remarked that the County was being strangled economically and socially by the appalling road system that we suffered, and eventually the first motorway in Great Britain was built around Preston, when Harold Macmillan, as Prime Minister, came up to open it.

Although much preoccupied with many national and international problems, the Prime Minister fulfilled a heavy day of engagements in Preston. When I thought that we were coming to the end of the programme, I was annoyed to find that he had been persuaded by the Chairman of the local Conservative Party to go to a tea party of Old Age Pensioners before he left. When he arrived at the party he climbed up the steps on to the stage looking a tired old man, and I remarked to Julian Amery, the Prime Minister's son-in-law, that it was unfair to inflict this extra chore on him. Julian replied, 'Don't worry, Eric, he's acting: he is associating himself with his audience.' I didn't really believe this and when we arrived at Warton Aerodrome, owned at that time by the English

Electric Company Limited, I was even more annoyed to find that two of the company's aircraft, the latest versions of the Canberra and the Lightning, had been brought alongside the Prime Minister's aircraft, and that the Prime Minister was invited to inspect them.

He walked briskly to the aircraft, climbed into the cockpit, and looked almost as young as the pilot who was explaining the controls to him.

I thought of this incident as I read Alec Douglas Home's charming book, *The Way The Wind Blows*, for he records that Macmillan once remarked, 'Of course, when a man becomes a Prime Minister, he has to some extent to be an actor.'

When he climbed into his own plane with one or two secretaries, having bid us goodbye, he had already opened one of the red dispatch boxes and was reading documents before the doors of the plane were even shut. The way of a Prime Minister is hard.

During my first visit to the United States in 1953, I was very impressed by the police use of radar for checking the speed of vehicles, and when we found that despite our best efforts, the number of accidents in Lancashire was continuing to rise, I asked the Police Authority to agree to the purchase of one American radar set. When this arrived we invited the Press to see a series of demonstrations of its use, and then on 1st August, 1957, radar for police purposes was first put to use in Great Britain on the highways of Lancashire; eighteen days later, after hearing the evidence of a technician and seeing the equipment in operation, Magistrates recorded a conviction for exceeding the speed limit.

This was, at the outset, an extremely unpopular move with the motoring public and their organisations, and we were of course challenged by the AA in the Courts. However, we won our cases and radar has become an established weapon in today's police armoury.

Although we had only one instrument and many thousands of miles of road in Lancashire, the knowledge that we were using this equipment had a dramatic effect on the speed of vehicles throughout the county, and as a consequence, there was a considerable reduction in the number of accidents.

In January, 1958, after six months use, the number of casualties in the country as a whole had risen by 7 per cent, while in Lancashire we were able to record a reduction of 8 percent. Alas, this good record did not persist, for later when motorists began to realise that there was not a radar machine round every corner, speeds increased once more and so did the accidents. But it was proof to us that speed is a very considerable factor in causing accidents.

Fully aware that the life blood of policing was rapid

communications, my predecessor had, by 1936, established a VHF Radio Station on a hill in the north of the County, with a 20 mile range and in contact with two cars which used two-way radio telephony. At the Grand National in the following year, two-way radio was used for the first time to help control the traffic. Further wireless stations were established and by 1939, there were 140 wireless cars in the county.

In this field the Lancashire Constabulary and the Home Office had long been at loggerheads. When Lord Trenchard became the Metropolitan Police Commissioner in 1931, wireless for the police was very much in its infancy. Speech over a short distance, from station to car or vice-versa, was not then technically possible, so Morse with all its disadvantages was introduced. At this time no provincial police force had wireless of any kind, but when Archie Hordern came to Lancashire, he found in the Force two good radio technicians, Frank Gee and Keith Eve. He encouraged them to experiment, and in a very short time they had developed, albeit in a rudimentary form, a system of speech telephony for police cars.

In the meantime, the radio engineer whom Lord Trenchard had introduced into the Metropolitan Police had moved to the Home Office to start radio for the provincial police. He was way behind the times and long after Lancashire had police telephony he refused to admit that it was a practical proposition. By the end of the War in 1945, when few provincial forces had wireless of any kind, Lancashire had progressed from amplified modulation to the more sophisticated frequency modulation which had the advantage of greater clarity and less background noise. The Home Office continued with the old-fashioned system and pressed Lancashire to adopt a system compatible with theirs, but the Police Authority fully supported the Chief Constable in his refusal to toe the line.

When I arrived in Lancashire, I made my own independent assessment of the situation, as far as a non-technical person could do so, and I was soon satisfied that the Lancashire system was in every way better than that of the Home Office. In 1950, however, we could not broadcast to the cars from Headquarters. We had three transmitter stations high in the hills and messages were passed by telephone to operators at the transmitting stations, who then broadcast the messages and received the replies. Apart from the delay that this entailed, there was also a great expenditure in manpower, not only in manning the transmitters, but also in the time spent travelling over rough hill tracks to and from the transmitter stations. Many times the operators were snowed in for days on end, and we had to keep emergency stores of food and bedding at the stations.

I therefore encouraged the radio branch to improve the situation and in 1951, Sir Frank Brook came to Hutton to open our operations room from which, by remote control, we could communicate with police cars throughout the county. The Home Office accepted but never really forgave us for our independence. However the very fact, that we were independent and progressive made the Home Office technicians try all the harder. Competition is no bad thing.

But of all the innovations that we introduced into Lancashire during the time I was there, undoubtedly the one which has had the most lasting effect on police technology was the introduction of personal radio.

I am a great believer in the traditional methods of policing in this country. If one could only have a policeman on his feet in every street in every town, the amount of crime and public disorder would be minimal. Of course this is not practicable but the fact remains that once policemen are taken off their feet and put into motor cars, they do lose touch with the public. However well marked the police car may be, they are not seen by pedestrians in the same way and therefore not available for the passing of information from the public at large to the policeman.

Although we have to provide policemen with motor cars, I am a great believer in the slogan, 'Policing off Wheels: Not on Wheels', that is to say the car should be used for getting from police hazard A to police hazard B, but when the man arrives he should get out of the car and be seen on his feet, readily available and accessible to the members of the public. But human nature being what it is, the man tends to sit in the car, mainly because the car has a radio and he is listening to any messages being broadcast. He feels that if he leaves the car he will be losing his efficiency and will no longer be able either to call for help or be called to help a colleague in difficulties. As one policeman put it to me, 'Whenever I leave my car, I feel I may be losing the opportunity to save a life or catch a criminal.'

For this reason I came to the conclusion that we must attach the wireless to the man rather than to the vehicle, so that even when away from his car he was still in contact with his station. During the War years soldiers had what was called 'walkie talkies', but these transmitting/receiving sets were very heavy and had to be carried in a pack on the man's back and were therefore impractical for police work. During the summer of 1961, however, I heard that the Motorola Company of Chicago in America had produced a much smaller transistorised transmitter and receiver, and with the consent of the Police Authority we bought ten of these sets and conducted an experiment with them in the busy industrial town of Chorley, where some 40,000 people lived. Each man on the beat was provided with a set and almost at once we found they were a tremendous advantage. A Sergeant sitting in his office was able to talk to his men, who could also talk to him wherever they might be. Not only did we achieve considerable success in the detection and conviction of criminals but we found from the point of view of morale that the men were well satisfied.

The American equipment was still too heavy, and very expensive for each set weighed 47 oz and cost £250, so I asked Superintendent Gee, whether he could construct a set which weighed less than 16 ozs and from which messages could be sent and received over an area of seven miles in urban conditions. He promised that he could design and produce a set to these requirements within six months, and six months to the day he put the set on my desk. We called the set LANCON (Lancashire Constabulary) and after due trials enough were manufactured to our design by the General Electric Company to allow every policeman in Lancashire to have one when on duty. Thus we became the first Police Force, not merely in this country but in the world, where policemen had the means of being constantly in touch with their police stations irrespective of their locations, and it revolutionised methods of police supervision.

As a result of our experiments other commercial firms began to work on the project and eventually a set slightly smaller than LANCON was produced and bought by the Home Office for general police use. Thus Great Britain became the first country in the world to provide individual radios for police patrols as standard equipment, and subsequently personal radios have been adopted throughout the world.

In 1968, after I had left Lancashire, the American Express Company offered a prize of $1,000 for the most useful invention made by any police force in the world in the fight against crime and this was won by the Lancashire Constabulary for the invention of personal radios. This was international recognition for the part we played in what was certainly the most exciting development in police communications in recent years and probably the most important technical innovation made by any police force anywhere this century.

The third main innovation to improve police efficiency introduced by the Lancashire Constabulary were the Panda Cars, and these too have now been adopted by police forces throughout Great Britain.

We introduced them because of the serious problem that we had in finding enough policemen to cover adequately the fast-growing town of Kirkby, on the outskirts of Liverpool. After the war the Liverpool Council found themselves in great difficulty in finding enough space within the city to build modern houses to replace the appalling slums that existed. The Council therefore bought a large stretch of ground in the country, close to the village of Kirkby which was owned by the Earl of Sefton, and there in 1950, they started to build a very large housing estate.

Normally a housing estate is built near an area which has shops, public houses, churches and places of amusement, but apart from a church and one public house there was no place of public resort in the old village of Kirkby and it was a serious criticism of the planning of Kirkby that no thought had been given to any aspect of planning except housing. We therefore had the absurd situation of a place where at one time 30,000 people were living, without a single shop to meet the needs of housewives who had to rely on the visits of a number of mobile shops from Liverpool. To worsen matters, there were no cinemas, no youth clubs and no playing fields.

The people sent by the City Council of Liverpool to the new houses at Kirkby were all working class people, the majority of whom had lived in slum areas the whole of their lives and who were, to say the least, very anti-social, so there were many police problems.

On the basis that there should be one policeman to every thousand members of the population, on the normal average of four people to a house, there should be one policeman living in each 250 houses built. As it is cheaper to build four houses at a time and as the police were of a better class than most of the residents in Kirkby, it was decided that it was a better proposition to build four police houses together, and so we arranged that for every thousand houses put up in Kirkby, four police houses should also be built.

It was interesting to see the way that better living conditions improved the standard of living of those who came to live in Kirkby. When the first thousand houses were built, the surroundings looked like a battle field strewn with broken glass, bricks and stones, and with rubbish dumped everywhere. The children were dirty and extremely badly behaved, while the gardens were for the most part unkempt and over-run with weeds. The men we sent there and their wives and children particularly hated the place and there was much hostility between the local people and the police.

But on returning to the same locality two or three years later, it was refreshing to find a very remarkable change for the better. The streets were clean, the children better behaved and much more presentable and many of the gardens were well kept. They were still the same people, but the better conditions in which they were living improved their standard of life. They had raised themselves up by their bootstraps.

Nevertheless, Kirkby still had a very bad reputation for juvenile crime, especially vandalism, due largely to the high spirits of the younger generation, aggravated by insufficient recreational facilities. Although we had divided the town into eleven beats we were unable to find enough policemen to send to Kirkby, and we had at the most only six uniformed men patrolling the town at any one time, and this in a community which had risen to 60,000 by 1963. We decided the foot patrol beat must go, and in May 1965, the eleven foot patrol beats were re-organised into five mobile beats patrolled throughout the twenty-four hours by a policeman in a car, only the pedestrian shopping precinct being covered on foot. More important, each man carried in his pocket a personal radio which enabled him at all times, whether in the car or out of it, to keep in touch with his station, so that wherever he was he could summon speedy help or be directed to the scene of any incident.

The motorised beat constable also had the advantage of being able to cover a much larger area and he could also speedily double back on his tracks, thus giving added surprise attention to vulnerable property.

Mobile beat policing is not a panacea for all our ills, but it was a method by which we were able to make the best use of available manpower. The scheme was a success and in an article I wrote for *The Times* I was able to say that:

> 'In the last eight months of 1965, compared with a similar period in 1964, there was a decrease of 31% in the number of crimes reported to the police, whilst the detection rates rose from 29% to 37%. Cases of damage fell by 53% with a detection rise from 9% to 21%. The number of street accidents was reduced by 16%'.

During my visits to the United States I had noticed that in many American cities their police patrol cars were black with a white door on each side, upon which was painted the word 'POLICE' surmounted by the town's coat of arms. This was conspicuous and effective so I suggested that we should paint white the doors of each of our patrol cars in Kirkby, adding the words 'LANCASHIRE CONSTABULARY'. To make them even more conspicuous, I suggested we should continue the white line right over the roof above the two front doors, thereby dispensing with the traditional navy blue or funereal black which until then had always been the colour of police vehicles. To distinguish these patrols from the ordinary crime cars, I suggested that they should be painted a light blue colour, a choice influenced incidentally by my Cambridge University background. I was later told that when my instructions reached the motor workshops, one of the mechanics remarked, 'Have you heard the latest mad idea of the Chief? He wants the

Kirkby cars to look like bloody pandas.' Thus the name 'PANDA CAR' was born.

I am firmly convinced that painting police cars in unusual colours is a good idea, for just as the helmet of the policeman although in many ways outmoded, makes the man conspicuous in a crowded street, so on the highways a coloured police vehicle can be more easily spotted. All are essentials in our main duty of the prevention of crime. Police cars should only be inconspicuous when they are attempting to detect crime, not when they are trying to prevent it.

In the same way, we in Lancashire were the first police force in this country to use on our Motorway Traffic Patrol Cars the very unaesthetic combination of orange and red colours. We had already had the distinction of being the first force to use white traffic patrol cars, but very soon we were dismayed to discover that many motor manufacturers were offering white as one of their standard colours, and this put an end to the conspicuousness of Lancashire's all-white police traffic vehicles. Not to be thwarted, the traffic workshop staff came up with the novel suggestion of painting the vehicles in orange/red colours similar to those used on RAF training 'planes and the Royal Aircraft of the Queen's Flight, scientists having found that these colours were the most effective in poor visibility. The Traffic Superintendent asked my permission for one patrol car painted in these appalling colours to work the M6 Motorway for a period of three months. After the car had been on the road for a few days, I decided to find out from the driver what impact the vehicle was making on the public. The driver seemed very pleased with the effect and when I remarked how I personally disliked the awful colour, adding, 'Well at any rate I don't think we shall find the public using these colours as we did with our white cars,' he replied with a twinkle in his eyes, 'Don't be too sure, Sir.' He then went on to explain that after he had been on the road for about two days, an elderly motorist had stopped him to inquire the source of the paint. When the police driver asked why he wanted to know, the motorist told the suprised patrolman that his wife had seen the police car and liked it so much that she wanted their saloon car painted the same colour.

Today this colour scheme has been adopted by most police forces in this country for their cars patrolling the motorways, though instead of having the whole car painted orange/red, many have just a coloured strip horizontally along a mainly white car.

In 1959, R. A. Butler, then Home Secretary, announced the appointment of a Royal Commission to inquire into the organisation of the Police Service. The Association of Chief Police officers set up four committees to prepare evidence to be given to the Commission, and I was appointed Chairman of the Committee dealing with Police Establishments. This has always been a difficult problem. Some years earlier the Metropolitan Police had under a committee chaired by Sir Arthur Dixon, CB after his retirement from the Home Office, attempted to find a rational formula for ascertaining the number of policemen required in a particular area; they had eventually proposed a most complicated mathematical formula that was really not of much practical use. In theory, of course, two towns of the same size should have the same number of policemen, but when one examines the facts in detail it becomes apparent that there are special circumstances within each town, relating to the type of population, the amount and type of industries and amusements there might be, and so forth, which affect the number of policemen required. One is never comparing like with like. We did our best to prepare a paper of value for the Committee, but I was never satisfied that we found a satisfactory answer.

When the reports of the four committees were considered by the Association of Chief Police Officers, I was much disturbed to find that we proposed to tell the Royal Commission that, on the whole, we considered the Police Service to be efficient; what especially worried me was the view that police boundaries did not need any radical alterations, only a few changes in points of detail in one or two areas.

For many years I had held the opinion that the organisation of the police in this country was inefficient. Boundaries of Local Government took no account of the changes that had taken place in the distribution of population and industry since the 19th century and were therefore badly out of date, and I considered it fundamentally wrong that police boundaries were always coterminous with local government boundaries.

In many parts of the country, especially in Lancashire, surbuban areas on the perimeter of towns which had their own force were policed by the county force. The people who lived in those suburban areas went into the local town for their higher education, work, shopping, amusement and hospital treatment, while it was the criminal fraternity from those same towns who broke into their property. Police boundaries must take into acount these facts and not be influenced by out-of-date local government boundaries.

At the time the Royal Commission was sitting, there were 126 separate police forces in this country, many of them much too small to be efficient in this day and age. I argued the issue before the full Conference of Chief Constables but had no support, chiefly because most Chief Constables present were in charge of small forces and my proposals naturally made them very prickly about the prospect of losing their jobs. I therefore asked that I should be allowed to submit a minority report attached to the main report to be submitted to the Commission. The Chief Constables present would not agree to this, so I argued that I felt this left me free to give evidence quite independently to the Royal Commission. This upset a number at the meeting, but the Chairman, Sydney Lawrence, the Chief Constable of Hull, afterwards a good friend of mine, supported me.

I therefore wrote a 16,000 word memorandum outlining my criticisms of the organisation of the Police at that time and making a number of constructive proposals. The memorandum was bound in a pink cover and irreverently referred to afterwards by Joe Simpson, the Commissioner at that time, as 'Eric's Pink-'Un', partly because of the colour of the file cover and also because of the radical views it expressed. It was duly submitted to the Royal Commission and in addition I sent a copy to each Chief Constable in the country. Some reacted furiously as the memorandum recommended, *inter alia*, the abolition of all small forces in the country and the establishment of either a national Police Force or a series of large police forces based on an amalgamation of counties, and a number of large urban forces.

Written evidence for the Royal Commission was required by the end of December, 1960, and I reasoned that if the Commission wished to question me about my evidence, they would do so after meetings with all the many official bodies such as the Home Office, the Association of Chief Police Officers, the Police Federation and Local Government Associations. It was, therefore, very unexpected when on 16th January, 1961, Tom Critchley, the Secretary to the Commission and a former principal private secretary to R. A. Butler, telephoned to ask me to come to London to appear before the Commission early in February. When I said that I was very surprised to hear this, for I had anticipated that the Commission would hear evidence from all the official bodies before they came around to mavericks like myself, he told me that the Royal Commission had read all the written evidence sent to them and that they were so impressed with my views that they wished personally to question me before they called upon the many official representatives.

I was to have gone alone, but at the last minute, Dick Pratt, the Chief Constable of Bedfordshire, who had similar, but not identical views to mine, offered to come with me. Thus the two of us gave our own independent evidence before the Royal Commission. It was a very interesting experience, but for me, not unique, as I had given evidence before the Royal Commission on Gambling some years earlier.

We had a very favourable reception and though I was asked many questions, I did not find anybody who disagreed with my views. I happened to be on fairly close terms with four members of the Commission, which helped. I had met the Chairman, Sir Henry Willink, QC, Master of Magdalene College, Cambridge, on several occasions before and had a high regard and respect for him, while I knew well Arthur Goodhart, my Cambridge Law Tutor, Alistair Hetherington, the Editor of the *Guardian*, and Charles Burman, a friend from childhood days and who had been Lord Mayor of Birmingham in 1947 and knighted in 1961.

Although I was very unpopular with most of my colleagues for offering independent evidence, I felt the issue was of such importance that I ought to express my views, and that I was justified became clear when the Commission's Report was finally published, for many of their recommendations followed the lines of those I had made.

The Royal Commission on Police held its inquiry in two parts, dealing first with the levels of police pay compared with people in other occupations, and when the Police Federation gave oral evidence on the first occasion, I went to London to hear their Parliamentary Adviser, Jim Callaghan, MP, then a back bencher, state their case for them. He did it magnificently and one would have thought him a trained barrister of high calibre and great experience. He was lucid, a master of his case, and he exhibited both intelligence and charm. When the hearing was over, I introduced myself and we agreed to meet again.

Shortly afterwards there was the annual dinner of Chief Constables, to which I invited Jim Callaghan as my guest. Unfortunately he could not come but I was rebuked by two of the old school of Chief Constables for inviting him, such was the attitude in those days towards the Federation. I replied that I had asked him partly because I liked him and partly because I was sure that he would have an increasing influence on police affairs, and that as such he should get to know and to hear the views of Chief Officers of Police as well as those of lower rank. I added, 'some day he will probably be Home Secretary'. I did not have the prescience to add, 'and also Prime Minister'.

Some time later he came to Lancashire to attend a political meeting. I heard that he was coming and he accepted my invitation to lunch when he visited Hutton. There, with a number of senior officers, we had a most agreeable discussion on police problems and again I found him knowledgeable and wise in his judgment.

Incidentally, Alistair Hetherington was, I know, equally impressed with the way in which Jim Callaghan spoke before the Royal Commission and I believe it was largely because of this that the *Guardian* came out in support of Callaghan for the leadership of the Labour Party after the untimely death of Hugh Gaitskell.

During my first week in Lancashire, to my great discomfort, the Lord Lieutenant of the County, Earl Peel, was in the dock at Liverpool Assizes facing serious charges of contravening the Building Regulations then in force. He had been appointed Lord Lieutenant of the County in 1948 and lived in a charming country house called 'The Hynings', near Carnforth, with his wife, Kathleen, and two sons. He was a wealthy man who held a number of business directorships and until 1948 had been Deputy Chairman of the London, Midland and Scottish Railway Company. On becoming Lord Lieutenant, he felt his home was inadequate to meet the needs for entertaining, associated with the office, and he applied for permission to improve the mansion by building extra bathrooms and fitting expensive antique panelling into the fabric of the dining-room. The post-war building regulations forbade building of this kind unless written permission was given, and this was refused.

For reasons quite inexplicable to their many friends, Arthur and Kathleen, in spite of this refusal, gave orders for the extensions and renovations to be carried out. As might be expected, the matter reached the ears of the Authorities and the Director of Public Prosecutions asked the police to make the necessary inquiries. All this had occurred before I came to Lancashire and on my arrival Lord Peel had already been committed for trial. At the Liverpool Assizes in October 1950, before Mr Justice Lynskey, he pleaded guilty to being a person at whose expense unlawful work had been carried out without a licence, and was fined £20,000 and £5,000 costs, a large amount of money in those days.

Arthur and Kathleen afterwards became great friends of ours and were extremely kind to us during our stay in Lancashire. They were most charming; everyone regarded them as people of the greatest integrity, but they were a little unworldly and I can only believe it was this unworldliness which caused them to commit such a foolish offence.

Arthur had to resign the Lord Lieutenancy of the County, and the Earl of Derby was appointed to replace him. The Chief Constable and the Lord Lieutenant are very often required to meet and discuss county matters, especially in connection with Royal Visits, and though I saw a good deal of Lord Derby during my time in Lancashire and we were much closer in age, I never became as friendly with him as I had with the Lords Lieutenant in Oxfordshire and Durham.

To be Lord Lieutenant of a County the size of Lancashire, is almost a full-time job, and Lord Derby, who has always identified himself strongly with the County, carried out his duties impeccably. Lancashire had 26 mayors, and 110 local authorities each with a Chairman, so there was much to be done by Lord Derby, who for instance, made a point of visiting each mayor every year. The situation has now greatly changed since the re-organisation of Local Government, for this has to a great extent meant a break up of the geographical County of Lancashire. Merseyside and Greater Manchester have taken enormous bites out of the County and there are now three Lord Lieutenants carrying out much the same duties that previously Lord Derby performed on his own.

Harold Wilson had been a Member of Parliament for the constituency of Huyton on the outskirts of Liverpool since 1950 but I did not meet him until I had been in Lancashire for two or three years. When we did meet we became friendly and I have always liked him. After 1964 when he first became Prime Minister, I saw a good deal of him because I felt that it was important that as Chief Constable I should see that the Prime Minister of England was properly looked after. Whenever he was in Huyton, unless I was otherwise engaged, I went down to meet him. He worked extremely hard and I was always very impressed by the assiduous way in which he looked after the affairs of his constituency, despite the tremendous responsibilities of a Prime Minister of this country. His stamina seemed to be inexhaustible, for whatever the national or international problems he had at the time he always seemed to be physically alert and mentally relaxed.

Nevertheless, on more than one occasion I remonstrated with him, saying that as the Prime Minister of England he should not spend so much of his energies on attending minor functions in his constituency, but he always replied that the first essential of any good politician was to keep in touch all the time with the grass roots and that anyone who failed to do this could not govern successfully.

On one occasion at least however he overdid it, when we had to investigate the murder of a small child in Huyton and before I could stop him he had gone to commiserate with the mother. At the time we were fairly certain that the mother had killed the child, but we did not find the necessary evidence to arrest her until two days later.

Often I have known him travel on the afternoon train on a Friday from London to Liverpool, where on arrival he was met by Mr Smith, his agent, and taken to some Labour Party 'do' in

Huyton. He would be extremely friendly and affiable to everyone he met and never seemed in a hurry to leave at the end of a function. When he did go, he returned by car to the Adelphi Hotel in Liverpool, and he would then catch the midnight train back to London. Not infrequently I would take him back to Liverpool, where in his private suite we would sit talking, and on these occasions I learned, in confidence, a great deal of his views and thoughts on matters of immediate political interest and importance. At times he was also very outspoken about his colleagues with whom he had to work.

In 1965 I had personally to make some very discreet and confidential inquiries on behalf of Lord Wigg and Lord Goodman, and a little later Lord Wigg asked me to see him again. On this later occasion he told me that the Government had set up a broadcasting service in Botswana in order to give the Rhodesian people the British Government's point of view on the dispute between Great Britain and Rhodesia over UDI. The British were afraid that the Rhodesians might cross the border and sabotage the wireless station, and to prevent this Lord Wigg asked me to supply him with a team of police dogs and handlers to guard the premises in Botswana.

After consultation with the Chairman of the Police Authority, we agreed to do as he wished but for a limited period only, the main purpose of the men going out being to train the local people and their dogs in this specialised work. Three members of the Lancashire Constabulary were sent to Botswana, along with their dogs, for a period of four months. Nothing was said about their mission at the time as it was thought politic to keep the whole matter secret.

While traffic on the Lancashire roads was heavy every day of the year, it was exceptionally heavy on the day that the Grand National was run at Aintree on the outskirts of Liverpool, while every Saturday and Sunday of the summer months motorists and coaches came in their thousands to Blackpool.

Before the advent of television, over 100,000 people came each year to watch the Grand National, the greatest steeplechase in the world, and this caused great problems for the Lancashire Police. In spite of the difficulties of the road system, however we prided ourselves on the speed with which vehicles could be parked and that there was very little delay in departure when the racing was over.

The course, which was owned by Lord Sefton, was held on a long lease by a company controlled by a formidable figure in the person of Mrs Mirabelle Topham. Her husband's family had been lessees of the race course and had been responsible for running the National for many years, but by the end of the war, Mrs Topham's husband was no longer able to take charge and so his wife took over. A large woman in every sense of the word, she was a great character and I got on well with her, although members of the racing fraternity were very hostile to her. She was a good organiser but had a poor team around her, and we in the police gave her a great deal of assistance in matters not strictly within the scope of our responsibilities. As I was so busy, John Palfrey looked after everything at Aintree and it was his duty as Assistant Chief Constable in charge of operations to ensure that all went smoothly for the Grand National.

Apart from the very big crowds, usually at least one member of the Royal Family attended as well as many highly placed personalities from home and abroad whose safety called for special police attention. The course is situated on the very edge of the City of Liverpool in an area abounding with criminals and, as a safeguard, we always provided a strong police contingent to prevent the course being taken over by hoodlums from Liverpool.

I had a luncheon room on the course in which I was able to entertain Home Office officials and Chief Constables of other forces, while we also had a control room on the roof equipped with television and police radio and from which we could see the whole course and the car parks.

The traffic going to and from football matches on Saturday afternoons in the winter also caused us much work, for in the geographical county we had in some years as many as nine First Division League teams, and while individual forces policed the grounds, much of the traffic came through the county area.

In the early 1950s the Manchester United Football Club was at the height of its fame, and we were horrified when it was announced on the BBC news on the evening of 6th February, 1958, that the whole team together with their Manager, Matt Busby, had been involved in a serious air crash while taking off from Munich Airport on their way home from Belgrade, where the team had won through to the semi-finals of the European Cup. On take-off in appalling weather conditions the 'plane would not lift off and at the end of the runway it smashed through the perimeter fence and hit an unoccupied house. A port wing was ripped off, causing the 'plane to spin round like a top until it hit a wooden hut stored with oil and petrol and finally came to rest among some trees, minus its undercarriage and tail.

I immediately telephoned Fred Waddington, Chief Superintendent of the Stretford Division, and asked him to fly to Munich to help in any way he could. I told him to go in uniform and liaise with the German police. This he did and everyone was delighted with the help he gave. He was able to identify the dead men and collect and bring back all their personal possessions. He was also able to visit the injured in hospital, when it gave them great comfort to see a familiar and friendly face in the strange surroundings and the unhappy circumstances in which they found themselves. The Manchester United Directors paid all his expenses and they much appreciated the spontaneous gesture we had made at a time when they were in so much trouble.

Altogether 23 lost their lives, including eight Manchester United players, three club officials, eight sports writers and two of the crew. Amongst the seriously injured was Matt Busby, who though initially suffering from serious injuries, eventually made a complete recovery. When he was well again, Matt, courageous as ever, continued to give much valued service to football in general and to Manchester United in particular and it was a great delight to all his many friends and admirers when he was knighted in 1968.

Ensuring that holidaymakers travelling by road could reach Blackpool at weekends during the summer months was also a real headache for us. It was estimated that some four million visitors came to Blackpool each year and most of them came by car or coach. Controlling this traffic before the motorways were built entailed a very considerable use of manpower and many Lancashire policeman had to give up their weekends to work. Hold-ups caused by broken down vehicles and accidents created havoc, for traffic was so dense it was often difficult, if not impossible, to get a police car to the scene of of the trouble. I have no doubt that police should use helicopters much more and we did experiment with them in Lancashire but at the time the cost was prohibitive.

Traffic to and from Blackpool was at its worst during September and October when over half a million people came to the town each weekend to see the Illuminations.

Spread over five miles of the promenade, the Illuminations consist of some 500 scenic designs and features made up of some millions of coloured electric lamps. The designs mainly depict fairy tales and stories from history and are automatically motivated.

During the illuminations many coach operators arranged that each 32 seater coach should bring 64 people to Blackpool each weekend. Leaving the industrial Midlands at six o'clock on Friday evening when work was over, the first coachload arrived in the town about 10 pm., when the occupants were allocated lodgings. The coach then returned empty overnight to its place of origin, and on the Saturday morning, with a different driver, brought its second contingent to Blackpool, arriving at mid-day. At midnight the coach returned through the night to its starting point with its original occupants, mostly in a very alcoholic condition, the second coach-load occupying on the Saturday night the same beds – hopefully with a change of sheets, – that the first contingent used on the Friday night. The coach then returned empty to Blackpool on the Sunday morning, and that evening returned with the second contingent, ready for work on the Monday morning.

All this was good for trade in Blackpool but unfortunate for those who lived on the roads through which all this traffic had to pass, but the situation has been much improved once the M6 motorway was built, and the Blackpool spur completed, and the police traffic problem has been greatly alleviated.

This festival of lights is a 'must' for everyone at least once in a life-time, and each year we invited to stay with us friends from the south who had never before visited Blackpool. Our drill was always the same. We would go to the first house of the Revue at the Opera House which was always a very well staged show, and most amusing. We would then dine in the French Restaurant in the Imperial Hotel, probably one of the best restaurants in the North of England. Afterwards we would motor slowly down the five miles of the flashing pagan festival of lights, ending at the Amusement Park, where Leonard Thompson, the owner, would meet us and arrange for our party to be taken round the various amusements. By eleven o'clock in the evening, when we arrived, the equipment had been running all day and the wheels were hot, with less friction, and everything was just a few miles an hour faster. The Big Dipper, the Grand National, the Mouse Run and other horrific features we visited in turn, before returning home, eating fish and chips on the way. It was always a really happy Lancashire way of spending an evening.

My wife and I were usually invited by the Mayor for the official switching on of the lights which was performed each year by a different person, usually a well-known personality from Show-biz, though on some occasions politicians or overseas diplomats have been asked to perform the ceremony. One year the guest celebrity was Jayne Mansfield, the American film actress who was later killed in a road accident, and I sat next to her at dinner before the ceremony. This lady, it will be remembered, was renowned for the size of her bosom, but when I first met her, it did not seem more prominent than that of others of her sex. However, while I talked to her, whenever a photographer hove in sight, and she seemed to be able to see them out of the back of her head, with a dextrous flip of her bra everything fell forward, while she unconcernedly went on talking. The moment the photographer disappeared, everything went back to normal. I found talking to her was a most unnerving experience, though I must say she did not have anything very intelligent to say.

Among the more well-known actresses who came to Lancashire while I was there was Marlene Dietrich. I had first met her in Paris in 1944 when Noel Coward had introduced me, and together they had taken me to a private party given by Susy Salidor at her famous night club.

In the early 1960s Marlene was billed for a week at the Opera House in Manchester, and being in that city on business one afternoon, I called at the theatre and was able to get a seat for that evening. When the show was over, I went backstage to renew my acquaintance with Marlene, who pretended she remembered me and accepted my invitation to dine at the Midland Hotel. As soon as we entered the Midland, anyone who has ever met me greeted me as a long lost friend, in order to be introduced to her. We sat in the Octagon Room for a drink while the maitre d'hotel hovered over us. When he asked her what she would like to eat, she replied, 'I know what I would like, but you will not have it in Manchester. I would like some lobster.' When I said I was sure they would have lobster, she said, 'Well, but it won't be fresh and I only eat fresh lobster.' I said I was sure she was right and suggested she made another choice. When the meal had been ordered I asked a friend of mine, who was sitting nearby, to look after Marlene while I slipped out to see Monsieur Cottet, the Manager, and ascertained from him that they had a live lobster in the kitchen. I therefore arranged that the Head Waiter would bring it to our table during the first course, and with due solemnity and much amusement in the restaurant, the Head Waiter duly placed a very large, live wriggling lobster in front of us on a silver plate. The City of Manchester once again preserved its reputation for efficiency.

I must add that Marlene was very good company and though she has been the adulation of millions for many years, I did not find her conceited or off-hand: on the contrary she was a delightful dinner companion and a good and interesting conversationalist. The following week she was in Liverpool and my wife and I were invited by the management to meet her at a small reception, but on that occasion Bobby Charlton, the famous England footballer, was there and she was more interested in him than in a Chief Constable.

Chapter Seven

LANCASHIRE II

Probably one of the best known and popular BBC programmes during the past fifteen years has been the 'Z' Car series and its successors, 'Softly, Softly', and 'Task Force'. The Lancashire Constabulary was very closely associated with the first of the series, 'Z' Cars, which was based on the work of our fleet of special crime patrol cars which we set up in Lancashire in 1958. The cars, all equipped with two-way radios, gave a twenty-four hour cover, but carried no police signs and were placed at strategic points throughout the county.

There was much controversy over the first 'Z Cars' programme, 'Four of a Kind', televised on the 2nd January, 1962, and great publicity was given to the part the Lancashire Constabulary had played in the matter. The BBC's account of the start of the 'Z' Car series was the subject of an article in the *Radio Times* on the tenth anniversary of the first programme, but my side of the story has never been told.

One day in October, 1961, John Palfrey and Chief Superintendent W. Roberts who was in charge of the CID, told me that the BBC had asked whether we would be prepared to help them in a series of programmes they proposed to make. They thought that, successful as the programme 'Dixon of Dock Green' had been, it was rather too paternalistic and they now wanted a programme showing some of the more difficult and 'aggressive' work that policemen had to do. They also wanted to move from the man on the beat to the man in the motor car, and they admitted that as the ITV programme 'Coronation Street' was attracting big audiences in the South of England, they wanted to compete by launching a new programme based on working-class life in the North of England.

They had, therefore, come to inquire whether we would be prepared to help them make a series of programmes based upon the work of our crime car crews, of which they had recently heard.

I felt that this would be good public relations for the police in general and for Lancashire in particular, and so I agreed to the proposal. We suggested that the series should be based on police activities in the new town of Kirkby, near Liverpool, where we were experiencing trouble of various kinds and we invited the BBC representatives to visit both Kirkby and our Information Room at Headquarters. When they came, they told us that they were thinking of calling the series, 'Crime Patrol', but after seeing our Information Room and demonstrations of the wireless control of a crime car they quickly changed their minds. We had eighteen divisions in Lancashire each of which was identified by a letter of the alphabet and each radio car in the division had a number prefaced by the letter of its division while traffic cars which operated from Headquarters had a number prefaced by the letter 'T' for Traffic. When we started the crime cars, which also came under Headquarters control, we decided that we could not use the prefix 'C' for Crime since over the air 'C' and 'T' could not be clearly distinguished, so we went right to the end of the alphabet and called our Crime Cars, 'Z' cars. This so took the fancy of the BBC that they immediately said they would call the programme 'Z' Cars. They were also much taken with the set-up of the new police station at Kirkby, which they adopted as a model for the police station of New Town in their programme. Kirkby was a Sub-Division of the Seaforth Division, an area surrounding Liverpool, and the BBC decided that the home of 'Z' Cars should be in the Seaport Division.

We then supplied the BBC with several real life stories. Within a month they came back to us with six scripts which were vetted to ensure accuracy and avoidance of technical errors, and in due course we loaned them a certain amount of police equipment and uniforms. They also bought a number of Ford motor cars which they equipped in exactly the same way as our Crime Cars. I personally did not read the scripts, but was informed that after a few amendments had been suggested and accepted, they were satisfactory, and I did not bother any more about it. Policemen, however, are not used to reading television scripts and they certainly do not understand that however a script is written, the whole atmosphere can be changed by a skilful producer.

The first episode introduced the main characters of the series and when the programme was shown we found to our horror that the producer had included details which, in our view, altered the whole atmosphere. In particular, he had portrayed the wife of a policeman as a slut with dirty face and hair in disarray, who ate in a most uncouth manner, using mugs, not cups and saucers, on the table. Another scene showed a policeman stopping a car and asking the driver who had won the third race, while a third showed a policeman dancing in an alley to music coming from a public house. To make things worse, at the end of the programme an announcement appeared, out of the kindness of the BBC, declaring that the programme had been produced with the assistance of the Lancashire Constabulary, thus giving the impression that it was a quasi-documentary film.

I realised that there would be a real storm in the Police Service over the programme and I immediately telephoned the Clerk to the Police Authority to tell him I was going to London the following morning to protest to the BBC. I caught the early morning train to Euston and at the BBC I met Stuart Hood, Controller of television programmes, who incidentally was the author of a delightful book of his experiences in Italy during the Second World War, called *Pebbles from my Skull*. There was nothing I could do except register a strong protest and get the BBC to agree that future transmissions would not screen any acknowledgement of the assistance given by Lancashire Constabulary. In all fairness, I must say that the views of the police were not shared by the press and the reviews were uniformly favourable, praising the producers and script writers for their 'realism'.

I then went to the Home Office, where by chance I met Sir William Johnson, an old friend of mine who was then the Senior Inspector of Constabulary, and therefore in many ways the Senior Police Officer in the country. It was not very pleasant to hear him say to me, 'Eric, you must realise that you are this morning probably the most unpopular man in the Police Service.' My feelings can be imagined.

However, the storm soon blew over, the programme became increasingly popular, and we had more requests from the BBC for assistance. Although the script of the first programme was so distasteful to policemen, we did find that the subsequent programmes portrayed the police in a better light. They showed the need for policemen to be tough and firm when dealing with unpleasant and unco-operative people, and the police usually, but not always, won through in the end.

One character that has been a subject of much discussion, was Inspector (later Chief Superintendent) Barlow played by Stratford Johns. Many viewers objected not only to his off-hand manner, but also his brusque treatment of his men. When I was asked what I thought of his character portrayal, I confirmed that I had certainly known policemen like him and that in the various episodes he was a very good 'audience irritant' who kept the interest of viewers, though there were many who thought he was not a good advertisement for the police. Indeed, when I talked with a Grammar School Headmaster about interesting some of his best boys in a Police career, he exclaimed, 'How can I possibly suggest to parents that they should send their boys into the Police when they are treated in the same way that Inspector Barlow treats his men.' Through the years however I believe he has become a much loved character of the BBC programmes. Certainly Stratford Johns, who was earning the Equity minimum wage when 'Z' Cars first started, became a wealthy man as the result of his association with that programme.

The BBC were so pleased with their success that at one time while the budgeting cost of any programme produced was in the region of £3,500 per hour, they were allowing £14,000 an hour for 'Z' Cars.

On the financial side, neither the Lancashire Constabulary, nor as far as I know, any member of the Force ever received a penny from the BBC or anyone else for the great help that we gave them. All we ever got was a great welcome when any of us went to the BBC Headquarters. Other people felt they did very well out of the programme. A member of the Ford organisation told me he thought the use of Ford motor cars in the series was worth in terms of public relations, £100,000 per year.

When the hundredth episode was filmed the BBC wrote to say that they would like to come up to Lancashire and give a dinner for everyone in the Lancashire Constabulary who had been connected with the programme. I invited them to Police Headquarters for lunch and on 6th March, 1964, Sir Hugh Carleton Green, Director General of the BBC, accompanied by Mr Kenneth Adams, the Director of Television, Stratford Johns, Frank Windsor and all the main characters from 'Z' Cars, as well as Elwyn Jones and other script writers and producers, all came to Hutton. We arranged a demonstration of police work, and showed them some of our specialised equipment, and the day was made all the more memorable when Stratford Johns bravely volunteered to be chased by a police dog as he ran away. We gave all our visitors lunch at Headquarters and that evening at a country hotel near Preston, the BBC gave a dinner party for about 100 members of the Constabulary of various ranks. Any sore feelings there may have been in the past were certainly buried that night.

During the summer of 1965, the BBC felt that the time had come for a change in the programme and as we in Lancashire were running out of authentic material from which they could write their scripts, they decided to transfer the whole programme to Bristol and to base it on the work of the Regional Crime Squads, which had then been introduced nationally. But they took with

Lancashire II

them the unique motto of the Lancashire Constabulary Detective Training School, 'Softly Softly, Catchy Monkey' which inspired the new programme's title, 'Softly, Softly'.

The success of 'Z' Cars was largely due to the excellent way in which the scripts were written. There were a number of script writers but the most familiar and indeed a great friend to us, was Elwyn Jones who was then working full time for the BBC. Later he became a successful writer on his own, and wrote a very good book, *The Last Two to Hang*, a factual account of a murder which occurred in Lancashire while I was there, the two men convicted for the crime being the last two executed in this country.

Because of the size of the Force and the volume of administrative work associated with its management, the Chief Constable of a Force the size of Lancashire was not always able to give close personal attention to operational matters, as in smaller forces. But nevertheless, I did, as far as time allowed, take a personal interest in the way in which operational matters were dealt with and, without interfering with the delegated authority given to John Palfrey, whenever possible attended the scenes of serious crimes.

Although I was in Lancashire for seventeen years and in Durham for less than six, we had more interesting cases of unnatural deaths in Durham. We had, of course, the usual crop of suicide and infanticide cases, but they did not require any particular expenditure of police time or expertise: however, we did have some interesting murder investigations which required good police work before the solution was found.

Within a week of my taking over the Force in October 1950, the body of a man who had been brutally assaulted, was found beside a railway track near Middleton, an ancient mill town on the edge of Manchester. The first detectives called to the scene surmised by the flat shape of his head that the deceased was probably of foreign extraction. It was known that a number of Yugoslavs were living in the Rochdale area and inquiries soon elicited that the dead man was a refugee of that nationality, and that one of his compatriots was unexpectedly missing from his place of residence.

An emergency message, giving the description of this man was sent to all police forces in the country. Of the many hundreds of policemen who received the message, an alert Traffic Patrol officer of the Staffordshire Constabulary remembered that each day an early morning bus from Rochdale to London, passed through Middleton and usually stopped at a café on his beat on the main A6. He went to the café and luck was with him, for there he saw, drinking a cup of coffee, a man whose description tallied with that of the wanted Yugoslav refugee. The constable promptly arrested him and when searched he was found to have on him his passport and all his savings. He admitted the crime and told us that he was about to leave the country. Had it not been for the alertness of the Staffordshire policeman, it is probable that we would never have been able to arrest the murderer. A few days after the arrest, I had to go to London and by arrangement with the Chief Constable of Staffordshire, I personally called at the Police Headquarters in Stafford to congratulate and thank the constable for the great help he had given us in making such a timely arrest.

A Lancashire investigation which was solved internationally with the help of Interpol, arose from the murder of a baby boy at Prestwich, on the outskirts of Manchester, in July 1952.

Imre Kilyen, a 26 year old Hungarian, had come to Britain as a displaced person after the War and in September 1951 he married another displaced person, a Lithuanian girl employed at a large hospital at Prestwich. The couple lived in furnished rooms in Prestwich and Mrs Kilyen continued her work at the hospital until in April, 1952, she gave birth to a son.

In July, Mrs Kilyen was persuaded by her husband, an accomplished money spender, to resume work at the hospital and he told her that he had arranged for a woman to care for the child while she was at work. Later he told her that he had taken the baby to a foster mother in Salford, but he refused to give her the foster mother's address. A few days later, Kilyen changed his story saying that he had given the baby to some people in a motor car whom he did not know. His wife demanded the restoration of her child and threatened to report the matter to the police. That night Imre Kilyen disappeared, taking with him the cash received from National Health benefits given on the birth of a child.

We had plenty of cause for suspicion, but could not find either the baby or the father, so we circulated his description to other forces as being 'Wanted for breach of the Aliens Order', and after a few days we heard from the Folkestone Police that Kilyen had left the country for Boulogne on 19th July, the very day on which Mrs Kilyen had gone to the police. Continental Police Forces were alerted by Interpol, the British link being through New Scotland Yard to Interpol's Headquarters in Paris.

We heard nothing until 13th September, when the Metropolitan Police telephoned to say that Imre Kilyen was detained in Rebsdorf Prison, Eichstatt, Bavaria, on a vagrancy charge and was due for release on 17th September, four days later. After much telephoning, Robert McCartney, then a Chief Inspector and later Chief Constable of Herefordshire flew to Munich with a Detective Sergeant, where they interviewed Kilyen in prison. He confessed to killing his son on the morning his wife went back to work at the hospital and he drew a sketch plan showing where he had buried the body. Then the legal problems began, for as Germany was still an occupied country the Extradition Acts did not apply. After much discussion and many telephone calls it was decided that a Board of the Occupying Powers consisting of British, French, American and Russian representatives must be convened to give their approval before we were authorised to bring the prisoner back to England. Eventually he was convicted and sentenced to death though he was subsequently reprieved and imprisoned for life.

This was the first time that Interpol had been used by a provincial force, and a weakness of communication was revealed, for although our message was circulated on 25th July and Kilyen had been arrested by the Bavarian Police on 14th August, it was not until 13th September that the local police realised he was the person named in the Interpol message, and this left very little time for Lancashire to act. But apart from the failure in the chain of communication, all the police concerned worked together in the utmost harmony. It must be remembered that Interpol is only a communicating and co-ordinating agency, not an investigating force. Police work arising from Interpol messages is necessarily left to the force or forces concerned – and some of these may not be very efficient. International action would be simplified if every member country had just one national force.

In 1952, however the case to hit the headlines was the shooting of Lady Derby, the wife of the Lord Lieutenant, and two of her domestic staff at Knowsley Hall, Prescot, on the evening of 9th October.

Lord Derby was at a Territorial Army dinner that evening and his wife was dining alone. A 19 year old footman, Harold Winstanley, entered the room and immediately fired a gun, the bullet striking her in the neck. Lady Derby fell but remained conscious, and heard her butler Walter Stallard, who must have hurried to the room on hearing the shot, cry out 'Harold.' There was another burst of fire and Stallard fell. Lady Derby heard someone cry, 'No,' and this was followed by two more bursts of firing which no doubt killed Douglas Steward, the under butler. There followed a scene of confusion in the course of which, Winstanley wounded a valet, William Sullivan, in the hand and talked wildly to one or two of the maids although mercifully, he left them unharmed: he then disappeared.

The first that I knew of the tragedy was when, as a result of a message sent from my Headquarters, I was stopped by a traffic control officer on the borders of Cheshire and Staffordshire whilst driving to the Police College at Ryton near Coventry, where I was to stay the night and give a lecture on the following morning. I immediately returned to Lancashire and drove direct to Knowsley Hall. On arrival I found that Lord Derby was still at the hospital where his wife was being treated. The dining room was a horrible sight, with the bodies of the butler and under butler lying in opposite corners, while Lady Derby's dinner lay half eaten on a tray in front of the television set. At that time we were still looking for Winstanley but while I was awaiting the return of Lord Derby, news came in that he had been arrested in Liverpool, where he was found to be in possession of an automatic rifle which he had bought from a friend for £3, and a pair of trousers.

As can be imagined, all the staff in the house were in a state of extreme shock and I decided that it would be better if I stayed the night. Lord Derby returned about midnight, visibly shaken by the events of the evening, though doctors had assured him that Lady Derby would suffer no permanent injury. Indeed she recovered very soon, both physically and mentally, from what must have been a most shocking experience. The bullet passed through her neck within one sixteenth of an inch of the spinal column.

Later Winstanley was tried, and found guilty but insane.

After the tragedy Lord Derby had the rooms in which the shooting had taken place completely re-designed and re-furnished and later it was difficult to remember exactly where the shooting had taken place. Subsequently Lord Derby built a new and very beautiful house in the grounds of the estate and shortly before I left the county, the Hall was leased to the Police Authority for use as single men's quarters and as an operational police headquarters for that part of Lancashire.

The next case of interest began at Ince on the outskirts of Wigan when on Easter Monday 1955 the body of an eleven-year-old boy was found brutally stabbed. A similar murder of a young boy had occurred in August 1954 within the Borough of Wigan, when the late Paul Foster, then Chief Constable of Wigan, had asked for the assistance of Scotland Yard. Two Metropolitan Police Detectives had taken over the investigation and spent some months in Wigan but had not been able to find out who was responsible for the murder.

We thought it probable that the person who had committed the Wigan murder had also committed the one at Ince and naturally we were most anxious to find him before a third boy should die. In the course of our detailed and prolonged inquiries we ascertained that a flaxen haired youth had been seen near the scene of the Wigan murder, and it so happened that such a youth had been stopped and questioned in the vicinity of the Ince murder a month before it occurred. Two policemen on patrol had thought he was acting suspiciously and we later found that he had given them a false name and address.

We therefore felt it imperative to interview every flaxen haired youth within twenty-five miles of the scene of the crime – a very difficult task. By dividing the area into police beats and making copious inquiries in each beat area, we were able to collect the names and addresses of a large number of youths with flaxen hair. They were all individually seen and questioned at length and it was this which eventually led us to a youth named Norman Green, whom we identified as the youth who had been stopped and interrogated by the two constables a month before the murder at Ince.

When Green was interrogated he eventually admitted responsibility for both murders and taking us to his place of employment, he retrieved from a sack of waste corn a large pocket knife which was the murder weapon. There is no doubt that had we not caught him, he would have committed further murders, for he admitted that his whole sexual life centred round stabbing. Green was tried at Manchester Assizes and sentenced to death on 5th July, 1955.

In the minds of all right-thinking people child murders are always the most horrible, and of these we had our share in Lancashire. For this reason it was a matter of concern whenever a child was reported missing, and we always treated it very seriously.

With the very large number of families living in the urban areas in or on the edge of the county, in the holidays and on summer evenings, there were always many children out playing or roaming the streets, for their homes were not big enough to accommodate the whole family, and many parents did not regard it as their responsibility to look after their children all the time.

Small children out playing would often become tired and just go to sleep where they were, or else they would go to relatives, particularly their grandparents' house where they would be put to bed without anyone bothering to tell the parents.

On average in term time we would have twenty children a week reported missing, while the number would increase in the holidays.

Usually the child would be found within a short space of time, asleep in an attic or outhouse, or even under the bed. However insistent the parents were that they had searched their own premises, whenever a child was reported missing we insisted that we should carry out a systematic search of their house, then the houses of relatives living in the vicinity and also the houses of friends of the child and the parents.

We had a strict drill that the search for the child was the responsibility of the local station until 7 pm. If the child had not been found by then, the matter had to be reported to the Divisional Superintendent, and at 10 pm, if the child was still missing, the Chief Superintendent of the CID at Headquarters had to be told, so that a decision could be taken whether to call off the search till daybreak when an organised search on a large scale could begin.

One of the most publicised and most horrible series of murders which has occurred in this country this century was probably the Moors Murders, for which Ian Brady and Myra Hindley were eventually arrested.

Although neither of the murderers lived in the county, the Lancashire Constabulary was much concerned with this investigation, for the first of their victims lived in the county and eventually his body and that of a young girl who lived in the Manchester Police area, were both found buried by Lancashire officers.

Although most children reported missing were found within a short time, when John Kilbride, an eleven-year-old boy who lived in Ashton-under-Lyne was reported missing late one November evening in 1963, intuition told us that we had a murder on our hands.

He was last seen about 5 pm on a Saturday afternoon in the busy open market in the centre of the town, after he had been to the cinema. At daybreak on the following morning a full scale search for him was mounted.

Ashton-under-Lyne is a town of some 50,000 inhabitants situated in the South East corner of Lancashire, very close to Oldham and to the borders of Derbyshire and the City of Manchester. Near to the town there is rising ground and moorland which is a spur of the Pennine chain of hills and is partly in the West Riding of Yorkshire and partly in Cheshire. Thus five police forces had a possible interest in the case.

The intensive search and inquiries which we started were continued throughout the following days and reached massive proportions as time went by. A tremendous amount of publicity was given to the case by the press, radio and television, and over 500 posters asking for information were distributed throughout the surrounding districts. Many extra police were drafted into the area and on the following weekend we asked for volunteers from the public to help us.

Such was the respect that the public had for the police in the area, that on the Sunday some 2,000 people turned up to assist. We divided them into 40 squads of 50, each with some police officers to take charge, and each squad was detailed to search every factory, garden, yard and open space in the area allotted to them, but all to no avail.

Among those that came to the police station that day was Harvey Rhodes, the local MP, who later became Lord Rhodes, KG, DFC, PC, and Lord Lieutenant of Lancashire. At the end of the day he was kind enough to say that he had been so impressed with our police organisation that he intended to write to the Home Secretary to say so.

Shortly after John Kilbride was lost, a young girl, Leslie Ann Downey from Manchester, disappeared in equally mysterious circumstances and despite every effort she was not seen again.

Two years later, Brady and Hindley were arrested for the murder of Edward Evans, a youth aged 17 years, at the house in which they were living in Hattersley, Cheshire. When this house was searched John Kilbride's name was found written on a page of an exercise book and Hindley's brother-in-law, David Smith, who had witnessed the murder of Evans, suggested that Brady and Hindley might well have been concerned in other murders and that the bodies of their victims had been buried on the moors. We therefore re-started our searches with over one hundred officers from the Lancashire, Manchester City and Cheshire Police Forces and on the moors some ten miles from Ashton-under-Lyne, the body of Leslie Ann Downey was eventually discovered, buried in a shallow grave.

Among the articles found in Brady's house was a photograph of Hindley looking at the ground in country similar to that in which the girl's body had been found and by some very clever police work by Detective Chief Inspector J. Mounsey now an Assistant Chief Constable, with enlarged copies of this photograph, the exact spot was discovered, and there the body of John Kilbride was found, buried in the place at which Hindley was looking.

The worst feature of this beastly affair was that the two murderers had tape-recorded the cries of one of the children as they tortured her before killing her. The trial was held at Chester, when both were sentenced to life imprisonment which they are still serving, and there will understandably and rightly so, be a great public outcry if ever they are released, but as they were both young when convicted, as the years go by successive Home Secretaries are undoubtedly going to be pressed to release them and this will cause much discussion and debate in the Home Office and in the Press.

To my mind, however, a more interesting murder investigation began shortly before I left Lancashire, when the body of a man was found in the Manchester Ship Canal near Warrington. He had a bad head wound and there was some doubt as to whether it had been caused before or after death. At first it was thought that after drowning, the body had been hit in the Canal by a passing ship, but the pathologist was satisfied that he had received a blow on the head before he had died, and that this was the cause of death. The body was quickly identified as that of William Morris and inquiries revealed that the dead man had been living with a man called Albert Darbyshire, in a caravan on the outskirts of Warrington. Morris had left a fair amount of money in his bank account, while his companion was known to be in debt and we found that on the day that Morris was last seen, Darbyshire had presented a cheque for a substantial amount, drawn on his friend's account, with which he had settled his debts. Although we were very suspicious of the genuineness of the signature on the cheque, we were unable to prove that it was a forgery.

The dead man had last been seen alive leaving the caravan park with Darbyshire, who told us that they had parted in the town when he went to see his girl friend. The girl corroborated the story and said that she had been in his company the whole afternoon and evening.

Both were brought to the police station and following a fairly intensive interrogation, Darbyshire adjusted his original version of events to disclose that he had borrowed and used for two hours on the day in question, his girl's motor car – a vehicle of distinctive yellow colouring. Further intensive inquiries were made, during which we found a witness who had seen a yellow car similar to the one owned by the girl, near the canal bank sometime during the afternoon. Darbyshire was brought back again to the police station for further interrogation, but we were unable, however, to induce him to confess to the crime. Although everything pointed towards him, we felt that there was insufficient evidence to charge him with murder, especially as we had not found the murder weapon, so once more we let him go.

I had a long conference with the officers in charge of the case and they convinced me that Darbyshire was undoubtedly the murderer, and that we should not get any further in the inquiry unless some form of admission was obtained from him. I therefore agreed that the man should be brought to the police station for the third time at two o'clock the following afternoon and I gave permission for him to be interrogated once again by a series of detectives but instructed them to keep a meticulous record of their treatment of the man at the station. They had to record every time they offered him a cigarette, every time they gave him a cup of tea or offered him something to eat and every time there was a change in the personnel of the interrogating staff. I also said that if they had not obtained a confession from him by ten o'clock that night, they were to inform me by telephone. At ten o'clock they told me that they had so far not been able to get him to change his story in any way whatsoever. I told them that if by midnight he had not confessed, they would probably have to release him but before doing so they should telephone me at that hour. This they did, when they told me that the man still had not changed his story. At the pressing request of the Chief Superintendent in charge of the investigation, I allowed them to hold him a further two hours and shortly before two o'clock in the morning, they telephoned again to report that all was well. The man had admitted the crime, but what was more important, he had told them that the weapon he had used was the starting handle of his girl's car.

A later examination by laboratory technicians of the end of the starting handle revealed the proof we needed, for on it they found human blood of the same category as the dead man's, and hairs which corresponded to those on his head.

When the case came up for trial at the Liverpool Assizes, it was clear that the defence were going to say that the confession had been obtained improperly. If the confession was held to be inadmissible, the evidence against the man, although strong, was entirely circumstantial and it was not at all certain that a conviction would be obtained. Although very busy, I cancelled all my appointments and sat for two days in the court room with my detectives, listening to legal arguments which were made before the Judge, in the absence of the jury, to decide whether the confession was admissible. My men were, I knew, somewhat apprehensive of the outcome of the case, which might easily have led to an inquiry into the alleged ill-treatment of a prisoner whilst in their care. The fact that I went and sat with them greatly sustained their morale and I know that it had its effect amongst those in court. Eventually the Judge did decide in our favour and allowed the confession to be put before the jury, and in due course, we obtained a conviction.

There must, of course, be strict safeguards to ensure that prisoners in the custody of the police are not improperly treated, and particularly that false confessions are not obtained. To ensure this the Judges of the High Court many years ago drew up a set of Rules known as The Judges' Rules, and these, somewhat amended, still apply today. It has to be emphasised, however, that the Rules do not have the force of law and are merely guide lines, albeit strong guide lines. Designed for the protection of the innocent, the Rules can sometimes seem to be a gift to the guilty and a severe hindrance to the investigating officer.

I have always maintained that provided the police behave sensibly and keep a meticulous record of their treatment of a prisoner whilst in custody, the court will usually support the police and allow confessions to be put before the jury, even though the guide lines have in a particular instance been broken.

From time to time there is a public outcry that someone has been wrongly convicted because of a false confession, improperly obtained by the police. Certainly it would be very unsafe to convict someone solely on the evidence of a confession and there must be strong corroborative evidence, as there was in this case. If we had not taken the action we did, we would never have discovered the murder weapon and without the evidence of that, I am quite sure we would not have obtained a conviction, however strong the suspicions were. From time to time, do-gooders and their like press that the police should not be allowed to interrogate any suspect unless his solicitor is present, or that all police questions should be recorded on tape. The police have always strongly resisted this and quite rightly so. In this particular case, if the suspect had been allowed to have his solicitor present during our interrogations, we would never have got him to admit the crime nor to have told us where the murder weapon was to be found.

Some years later at the Anglo-American Centre at Ditchley, Oxfordshire, I attended a weekend conference with twenty American Judges and Attorneys and an equal number of eminent British Jurists. During the weekend I recounted the story of this murder investigation and whilst none of the British Jurists criticised the action we had taken, the American Jurists were of the opinion that had the case occurred in the United States, the courts would not have accepted the confession, nor at that time would they have accepted any evidence which came about as a result of the confession. Thus the American police would not have been able to give evidence of the finding of the murder weapon and the laboratory evidence of the blood stains and human hairs from the dead man. This was known as the doctrine of the 'fruit of the poisoned tree'. The Supreme Court has now overruled that decision and although from time to time confessions may be found inadmissible, evidence obtained as the result of a confession, can now be put before the American Courts.

Every day we read in the daily newspapers of public calamities somewhere in the world, such as floods, fires, rail and air crashes, all of which illustrate the very wide duties of the police. Major disasters demand high professional standards of efficiency, and they emphasise the value of special procedures prepared beforehand to meet such contingencies. At times such as this, there is real co-operation 'in the field' between police and emergency services, and efficient and tactful work by the police has an excellent effect upon police/public relations.

The most serious aircraft disaster during my time in Lancashire occurred about ten o'clock in the morning on 27th February, 1958, when a Bristol 170 commercial 'plane taking a party of motor vehicle salesmen and friends from the Isle of Man to Manchester, owing to a navigational error flew into the summit of Winter Hill, near Horwich, North of Bolton. The hill stands 1,475 feet above sea level and the weather at the time was atrocious with snow and biting east winds.

Luckily there was a manned television station on the Hill and the alarm was quickly raised. At the time I was out visiting police stations nearby and quickly reached the scene to see emergency services assembling in the narrow lanes at the foot of the hill. Large numbers of press men were arriving, their vehicles causing considerable inconvenience and obstruction to the police, ambulance and fire services.

Together we toiled up the hill through snow drifts two or three feet deep, in a bitingly cold wind, to find torn and mangled bodies, personal belongings and debris scattered over a wide area at the top. Had the 'plane been only 100 feet higher, it would have cleared the peak. In all 35 people were killed and seven injured including the crew of three. The injured had to be carried down on stretchers – the bodies being brought down later.

By a stroke of luck, there was a Methodist Chapel near the foot of the hill which was placed at our disposal and used as a mortuary. Cotton sheets were provided by a local mill and three policemen assisted a local undertaker working through the night cleaning and making the bodies presentable in their shrouds for identification by relatives in due course.

It was a hard day's work in difficult and unpleasant weather conditions, and tempers became short. I was particularly angry with the way the Press behaved and I subsequently made a complaint to the Press Council. On the whole, however, we had a very good relationship with the Press in Lancashire, and were the first Force to establish the principle of having a Force Press Liaison Officer – an officer of the rank of Inspector, well known to the press men. He attended the scene of every major incident and helped the Press to get their story. On this occasion, however, things went badly wrong for there were far too many press men there. I discovered that one newspaper had sent four reporters to cover various aspects of the incident, and many present were quite out of control especially those who were, or said they were, freelance reporters. I suspect that some of them were merely inquisitive bystanders who claimed to be reporters.

One matter which gave particular pleasure was the introduction of the Provincial Police Award, given annually to the member of the public who in the opinion of Chief Constables had in the year performed the greatest act of courage in assisting the police in the detection of crime.

Since 1947, there had been such an award for the bravest deed performed in London. This is called the Binney Award, so named because the capital monies of the fund were subscribed by the friends of Captain R. D. Binney CBE a retired Naval Officer who had been fatally injured by a car when attempting to foil a smash and grab raid.

For a long time I had thought it unfortunate that there was no similar award for acts of bravery in the provinces, and in 1965 I recommended to the Association of Chief Police Officers that we should remedy this omission. This was agreed, and with the assistance of three other Chief Constables, I was asked to organise the award.

After consulting officials at the Royal Mint, we appointed a young sculptor to design a gold medal, and since 1966 at the annual conference of the Association of Chief Police Officers, the President has each year presented the award to the person selected.

All the costs of this award are met by members of ACPO, and Chief Constables are glad to do so for it gives them an opportunity to express, in a very small way, their gratitude to members of the public who help the police and without whose assistance we should not be able to serve the public effectively.

By 1961, I felt I had done all I could for the Lancashire Constabulary. The Force was running smoothly, had enough men, a good training schedule and all the equipment we needed, while the building programme had been agreed and some stations had been built. Though we still had some poor stations, provision for their replacement had been made. All we still wanted was a modern Training School, and plans for this had been completed.

I had given evidence to the Royal Commission and even if they accepted my views and recommended that all the smaller forces should be absorbed, I felt sure that because of the slow, creaking progress of the bureaucratic machine in Whitehall and the fierce resistance of Local Government, it would be some years before their recommendations would come into force. How right I was in this forecast, for another ten years were to pass before Lancashire achieved a rational police organisation.

Lancashire II

I was tired of the continued disharmony with my Chairman and in any case I had for many years believed that a Chief Constable should not remain in charge of the same Force for longer than ten years. The Army move officers to a new appointment or command every three years. This may be right for a fighting service which is, or should be, basically mobile, but it is too short a period for a Chief Constable. It takes him some time to get to know his men and for them to get to know him, while he has to become acquainted with the area for which he is responsible and the people in positions of authority who live and work in his police district. But he must remain objective. In time he makes his friends and he makes his enemies, while he becomes too closely associated with some organisations and some people.

Everyone has his blind spots and his prejudices, and however good a Chief may be, the time comes when it will of benefit to all for a fresh eye and a fresh mind to be applied to the police problems of the area. I am quite sure that I was not as good a Chief Constable of Lancashire in 1965, after I had been there fifteen years, as I was in 1955, ten years earlier.

But what was one to do? Not until 1963 did I complete thirty years approved service, when with the consent of the Police Authority, I could take a full pension, and, what was equally important at that time, though the rules have been changed since, I could not commute part of my pension and take a capital sum with which to buy a house, until I had completed thirty years' service.

My chance of being appointed Commissioner of Police of the Metropolis was very remote, for Joe Simpson was Commissioner and there was no reason why he should retire before I would be too old to succeed him. The post of Chief Inspector of Constabulary had not yet been created, so there was nothing left for me but to soldier on. And then suddenly an opening occurred which I was very tempted to accept.

One of my two greatest friends in Lancashire was Henry Spurrier – later knighted – who was at that time Chairman of Leyland Motors, then a very progressive motor manufacturing firm specialising solely in commercial vehicles. Henry and his wife Win had been most kind and hospitable to Joanna and me. In the winter I frequently shot with him on his estate at Sowley on the edge of the New Forest and in the summer I crewed for him on the yacht which he kept in the Solent or on another that he kept on the Clyde.

Henry and I got on very well and he confided in me some of his problems with Leyland and his plans for the future. The firm, which was expanding fast, had an excellent sales and services organisation throughout the world. He was fearful of the competition for the British Motor Industry from Germany and he foresaw the rise of the Japanese car industry. He was very critical, even in those days, of much of the management in our own motor car industry, particularly with regard to our overseas sales and servicing and he felt that the only hope for the industry in this country was to rationalise. He felt that Leyland must break into the motor car industry and he believed that if he bought and made efficient some of the Coventry firms, he could use the Leyland Sales and Servicing organisation throughout the world for all types of vehicles.

I well remember the day he told me in confidence that Leylands purchase of Triumph was about to be announced. I asked him, 'Why are you putting your head into the Coventry noose? You have an efficient company making good profits and with excellent labour relations. You will have nothing but trouble and worry if you to go to Coventry.' He answered, 'Eric, it's our only hope to keep up with the world. Triumph management is bad and when I have sorted them out we shall save over £1,000,000 a year unnecessary expenditure.' I asked him what followed and he told me that he hoped in due course to buy Rover and Jaguar. 'What about the British Motor Corporation?' I inquired. 'Not on your life,' he replied and went on to speak in very critical terms of the troubles of that firm and how in his opinion, the situation was so bad that it could not be put right.

Leyland enjoyed for many years an excellent training scheme, producing all their own senior managers and technicians. After the purchase of Triumph Motors, the scheme had to be enlarged and for this purpose a very fine Training School was built at Leyland, called Spurrier House. I had lunched several times with members of the Board at Leyland and knew them fairly well, particularly Donald Stokes, at that time the Sales Director. I liked him and had a high regard for his abilities, though he was not a close friend like Henry.

About a year after the purchase of Triumph Motors, Henry asked me to see him at his home one Sunday morning. He then told me that he was short of senior management, especially on the personnel side, and inquired whether I would care to join the firm and take charge of the training of the firm's personnel. He explained that the firm had no Personnel Director and whilst he could not offer me a seat on the Board, if all went well, as he was confident it would, he would see that I was elected to the Board in due course. He then told me that the members of the Board were aware of this plan and that he was offering the appointment to me with their knowledge and concurrence.

I was very tempted. Here, at 51, was a chance to start a completely new life with exciting new fields to conquer, and Joanna and I gave the matter careful thought. The snag was that I had at the time served only twenty-eight years and my full pension was still twenty months away. Sadly, I finally decided that I had to refuse the offer, but I told Henry that if he renewed the proposition in eighteen months time, I would accept with alacrity. He told me regretfully that he did not think he could wait that long and so the chance was lost.

The real tragedy for the country was that within twelve months Henry had died of a brain tumour and all his plans went awry. BMC bought Jaguar and Rover, and later Donald Stokes could not withstand the Government pressure to amalgamate with BMC with the disastrous results that have been front page news for so long. The full story is well told in Graham Turner's book, *The Leyland Papers* but the story of my small association in the early days of the amalgamation has not been recorded.

In May, 1962, the Royal Commission published its Second Report making a number of major recommendations, one of which was that the Police Inspectorate at the Home Office should be strengthened and that, without delay, a Chief Inspector should be appointed, who would, in the words of the Commission, be:

> 'regarded as the senior professional advisor to the Secretaries of State on police matters . . . have a general oversight over the Inspectors . . . and . . . a recognised role in the strategic planning of the Police service'.

This recommendation was accepted by the Government and in November, 1962, the Home Secretary, who by then was Henry Brooke, later Lord Brooke of Cumnor, announced that Sir William Johnson, CMG, CBE, then the senior Inspector of Constabulary and a former Chief Constable of Birmingham, was to be the first Chief Inspector of Constabulary. He added that on Johnson's retirement in the following year, he was to be succeeded by Sir Edward Dodd, CBE, QPM, the Chief Constable of Birmingham. This last appointment was not unexpected, for Ted Dodd had been a highly successful Chief Constable of Birmingham since 1945 when he had succeeded Bill Johnson on his appointment to the Home Office. He was a very good public speaker with great charm, and he had been a very popular president of the Association of Chief Police Officers.

Ted and I had been very good friends since our early days in the Police Service. Born and educated in Reading he had joined the

Merchant Navy, receiving his training in T.S. *Conway*, but unable to find a ship during the depression, he had joined the Metropolitan Police as a constable in 1931. Ted was selected to attend the first course at Hendon Police College in 1934 and he passed out high up the list. He was then posted to Vine Street as Second in Command and as I have recorded in an earlier chapter, it was there that he and I first met and became friends in 1937. We were both married in that year and as we both lived in Paddington, the four of us became good friends, playing bridge together alternate Sunday evenings when he and I were both on standby duty.

In 1941, shortly after I had gone to Oxfordshire as Chief Constable, a vacancy occurred for a second Assistant Chief Constable in Birmingham and I suggested to Ted that he should apply for it. His immediate reaction was to ask, 'Where's Birmingham?' However I overcame his prejudices; he applied, was selected, and moving to Birmingham in September, 1941, he and his wife, Eve, lived with my parents for some months until they could find a house of their own. In due course he became the Chief Constable.

As Ted was only three years older than I, his appointment as Chief HM Inspector of Constabulary in September, 1963, would in the ordinary course of events have effectively prevented me from succeeding him, but after only three years in office, he sadly died in Switzerland at the early age of 56 and someone had to be appointed to replace him.

Some time before this, however, when talking with the Prime Minister, at Huyton, one day he said, 'I hope you are helping the Home Secretary, Roy Jenkins.' I replied that I would love to do so but that I had not met him. 'Oh!' said the Prime Minister, 'we'll soon put that right,' and in a very few days I had an invitation to lunch with Roy Jenkins at Brooks, his London Club. Though we had not previously met, I had for some years admired him from afar and I had corresponded with him in connection with a book he had written on the life of Sir Charles Dilke, a 19th century politician, as for some years I had been a trustee of a member of the Dilke family.

When we met, I like to think that we immediately got on to the same wavelength, and I found him very sympathetic to the comments, constructive and destructive, that I had made about the organisation of the Police.

In October, 1966, Dick Taverne, a QC, MP for Lincoln and a close associate of Roy Jenkins, came to Lancashire to spend a day with us. Shortly afterwards Philip Allen asked me to see him at the Home Office where he told me that the Home Secretary had decided to ask me to succeed Ted Dodd. I had anticipated this and I said that while I was delighted to accept, I thought the Home

Secretary should know that if appointed, I should immediately press him to agree to two new appointments – an Inspector of Constabulary (Crime) and an Inspector of Constabulary (Traffic). A few days later Philip Allen telephoned to say that the Home Secretary agreed to the proposal and that my appointment had been recommended to HM The Queen. Until she had given her consent however the whole matter was to be kept secret, as the office of Chief Inspector of Constabulary is a personal appointment of the Queen, given under sign manual – her personal signature.

I did not tell anyone, not even my wife, as I thought it would be a nice surprise for her when it was announced. Shortly afterwards I took a day off to go shooting and at the first stand after lunch, a policeman in uniform arrived to say that Sir Philip Allen wished to speak to me urgently. I telephoned from a nearby farm house to learn that the Royal consent had been given and that the Home Secretary would announce my appointment at three o'clock that afternoon. I returned to the stand just as the birds were coming over rocketing like starlings in a high wind, and I celebrated my appointment by shooting quite the fastest and highest bird I've ever had the luck to hit. It was a good augury.

Originally it was proposed that I should start on the 1st January, 1967, but I had already had a letter from the Prime Minister saying that he was recommending me for a knighthood, and I very much wanted still to be Chief Constable of Lancashire when this was announced in the New Year Honours, for I felt it was an honour for the Constabulary as well as for me. So it was agreed that I should start on the 1st February, 1967.

People were most kind and there were numerous receptions, dinners and presentations, while on the last evening, the Force gave a big farewell party at Headquarters attended by some four hundred policemen, as well as members of the Police Authority, Magistrates, local Chief Constables and friends. There were two notable absentees at the party, the Chairman and the Clerk to the Police Authority, both conspicuous by their absence.

On my last day in the force the Annual Report of the Lancashire Constabulary for 1966 was published over my signature, and in it I said,

> 'As this is the last report I shall write on the work of the Lancashire Constabulary, it would perhaps be of some interest to record the changes that have taken place since I took command of the Constabulary on 1st October, 1950.
>
> No police force can be efficient unless it consists of a happy body of men and woman and I do not believe that police officers will be happy unless their living and working conditions are good.

When I came to Lancashire in 1950, the housing conditions generally were very poor, but with the support of the Police Authority and with the help of the County Architect and his staff, and with determination by the personnel of the Housing and Welfare Branch which was set up in 1951, very great improvements have been made in the houses owned by the Police Authority. The number of houses owned by the Police Authority has increased from 1,012 to 2,501 while we have disposed of 361 houses and quarters which we considered were not suitable for occupation by police officers.

Five divisional headquarters and five sub-divisions, 19 sectional, and 70 detached beat stations have been built during the period of my command. The new buildings are a source of much pride to all who work in them and it has been interesting to see the increased efficiency of all personnel when they move to a new and efficient headquarters. There is still much more to be done, for many police officers today still have to work from old, antiquated, and inefficient buildings.

On 1st January, 1951, the establishment of the Constabulary was 2,789 (male officers) whereas on 1st January, 1967, it was 4,036. In 1951, there were no uniformed policewomen. Such policewomen as there were in the County worked either as matrons or clerks in police stations; they did not have a uniform and had not had any training. Today, we have an establishment of 204 policewomen. The strength is 128 and they are a very efficient, well-trained body of women.

In 1951, we had 67 cadet clerks – boys under the age of 19, who were used as clerks in police stations and whom it was hoped would become police officers when they reached the requisite minimum age. Today, we have a uniformed body of 300 boy police cadets and 30 girl cadets. In addition, we have more than trebled the number of civilians employed.

Since the War, all recruits to the police service have been trained at a regional training school, but the amount of in-service training in the Lancashire Constabulary has been very greatly increased. Most traffic patrol officers have now passed the Advanced Driving Course at the Motor Driving School; most detectives have been on a detective training course; and most members of the Force attend each five years, one of the two week refresher courses organised at Pontin's Camp each winter.

In equipment, we have increased our vehicle fleet from 400 to 698, while traffic patrol vehicles are organised, particularly on the motorway, on most efficient lines, and are equipped with sophisticated equipment. We are the only Force which has our police cars painted in day-glow colours which make them very conspicuous in times of bad visibility.

Since 1951, a total of 10 members of the Constabulary have been appointed to posts of Chief Constable and Assistant Chief Constable of other forces, thus spreading to other parts of Great Britain and overseas, the knowledge and experience gained whilst serving in the Lancashire Constabulary. A former member of the Constabulary Mr N. Galbraith, is one of Her Majesty's Inspectors of Constabulary.

During this period, we have pioneered in the Police Service, radar, police frogmen, white police cars, day-glow coloured police cars, and

Lancashire II

women police motor patrols. Undoubtedly the greatest contribution we have made to the police service has been the innovation and adoption of personal radio. This has revolutionised the work of the man on the beat. It has made his daily tour much more interesting and efficient. Now, as a result of the Kirkby Mobile Scheme, the unit beat policing scheme has been developed and this, too, will revolutionise the organisation of police work in the next few years.

All this has been possible in the first place because the Police Authority has had confidence in our efforts and given us the money with which we can purchase the equipment, but mainly it has been due to the initiative, enthusiasm, and hard work of members of the Force of all ranks. It has been a great privilege to have served as a member of this great Force, and I lay down my command with regret, but with a feeling of gratitude for having had the opportunity to work alongside such a very fine body of men and women'.

And so with very mixed feelings for I had many regrets at leaving on the one hand of a Police Force of which I was very proud, and friends and a lovely house, while on the other relief at the end after so long of the unhappy relations I had had with County Hall, we went South to a new and very different life.

Chapter Eight

ROYAL OCCASIONS

One of the great privileges of being a Chief of Police is the opportunity it presents to meet members of the Royal family, and to be able to be of some assistance to them in helping them carry out their arduous duties. My diaries record that while a Chief Constable I had to look after members of the Royal family on fifty-five occasions.

I have already recounted how lucky I was to be a member of the staff of the King's camp and there had met His Majesty King George VI and on several occasions Her Majesty the Queen Mother and the two little Princesses at Balmoral in 1939.

While Chief Constable of Oxfordshire I met the King and Queen again on several occasions, and I had the opportunity to meet Queen Mary but unfortunately did not do so. During the War Queen Mary lived at Badminton with the Duke and Duchess of Beaufort, and on one occasion the Duchess of Marlborough telephoned to tell me that Queen Mary was coming to luncheon at Blenheim and asked my wife and me to lunch too. Unfortunately the date clashed with a meeting at the Home Office arranged to discuss some subject to do with the prosecution of the War. So I asked to be excused and I have always since regretted it for I would very much have liked to have met that formidable person. As so often in life it is not the things one has done in life that one regrets, but the things that one had the opportunity to do, but did not do for one reason or another.

Durham, alas, sees Royalty all too seldom and during my five years in that county we only had two such visits. In October, 1947 Princess Elizabeth came up to lay the foundation stone of St. Mary's college at Durham University, while on the second occasion Her Royal Highness Princess Marie Louise came up to some YMCA function in Sunderland.

The visit of Princess Elizabeth was one of the first functions she had attended since the announcement of her engagement to Prince

Philip, whose face at the time was unfamilar to the British public. I was wearing for the first time the full dress regalia of a Chief Constable which consists of a very smart navy blue tunic covered with a great deal of silver braid at the neck, cuffs, and skirt, and wearing a naval type cockade hat. When we arrived at the first stop where a fair sized crowd mostly of women were waiting to see the Princess, the cry went up 'Look, she's brought her fiance with her!' I beat a hasty retreat to the rear.

The visit of Her Royal Highness Princess Louise was a hilarious affair. She stayed the night with Sir Robert and Lady Chapman at their house at Cleadon and some twelve of us were bidden to dine to meet her. The Princess, a very spritely old lady, stood only some five feet high and she looked – and to some extent behaved – just like Nellie Wallace, the well known music hall comedienne. Before we went into dinner with another man I was talking to her when a maid brought round a tray of canapes which included, rather foolishly, some small white onions. The other man took one of these, whereupon the Princess said 'Mr X, did you take an onion?' When he admitted he had she immediately said 'Well please don't come near me for the rest of the evening,' and she moved away to join another group.

At dinner I sat fairly close to the Princess on the opposite side of the table. The lady on my left was deaf and although I have a very clear voice I was speaking louder than usual, when the butler came to me and said quietly 'Excuse me Sir, the Princess says that you are talking too loudly: she can't hear herself speak.' Rebuke No. 2.

Next to the Princess was sitting Cyril Alington the Dean of Durham, and behind him was the dining room fire. After the ladies had retired, Sir Robert said to the Dean that he hoped he had not been too hot with the fire. 'No,' replied the Dean, 'but I've been roasted about the Apostolic Succession.' Sir Robert had given us some very good cigars which we had just lit when Lady Chapman came into the room to say that the Princess has just announced that she hoped the men were not going to come in smoking cigars as she could not abide the smell of them. 'In that case,' said Sir Robert imperturbably, 'you'll have to keep her amused for some time. We've just lit these cigars and they are too good to throw away.'

My wife afterwards told me that the Princess spent the next hour tapping her fingers on her knee saying, 'I wish these men would come soon. I don't like talking to women all the time, and in any case I am going to bed soon.' And she did. She was, indeed, a real character, with a very strong personality.

But it was while I was in Lancashire that I had most to do with members of the Royal family. For apart from the fact that I was in that county longer than anywhere else, Royalty came to the county frequently.

Such visits had to be carefully planned beforehand. The preparations were the responsibilites of the Lord Lieutenant, and Lord Derby was most efficient in his approach. As soon as he knew of a projected visit, he would ask me to discuss with him the main points of the programme and we would consider alternative places to visit and the routes that should be taken. I would then arrange for a dummy run by police officers in plain clothes in unmarked cars to test the timing required. When alternatives were being considered, it was most important that nothing should leak out at that stage because there was always a great deal of in-fighting between Mayors and Chairmen of Local Authorities to ensure that their area was included in the visit.

I would then put up a draft timed programme to Lord Derby which as approved or amended by him was sent to the Palace – or to the secretary of the person concerned. When the programme had been approved Lord Derby would call a meeting of everyone concerned when detailed arrangements would be discussed and the Clerk of the County Council or Clerk to the Lieutenancy would then issue a printed programme and a press notice.

At Police Headquarters a special staff prepared a detailed police order to cover all the arrangements that had to be made to man the route – using the same policemen several times by a series of leap frogs if the route was a long one. Police escorts not only for the Royal Procession but also to look after the Lord Lieutenant, Mayors and other officials, had to be detailed and briefed. Personnel had to be taken to and from their stations and moved from post to post throughout the day. The CID and Special Branch Officers had to be briefed and posted for their special responsibilities while all the personnel on duty had to be fed.

A police operation order for a whole day ran to some fifty pages of pages of print, and we had our own printing shop at Police Headquarters so that we could ensure the necessary secrecy.

On the day before a major visit, we had a rehearsal and I went over the whole route and discussed with the local officers on the spot any difficulties that might occur. At the same time this gave me an opportunity to attempt to put at ease those people, other than police, who would be in any way concerned with the morrow's programme.

Although he took a great interest in points of detail Lord Derby always left the rehearsal to me, and I do not think I ever let him down. Provided we had planned carefully beforehand, events on the day usually went smoothly, and if any snags did occur, because everyone had been briefed, we were usually able to put things right without difficulty.

In arranging a Royal Visit we had to cope with two conflicting interests. In the first place one must ensure the safety and comfort of the Royal, and at the same time one had to ensure that as many people saw them and met them as could properly be arranged.

At the end of each visit when we were bidding farewell I always had those officers who had prepared the plans and those who had carried the main operational responsibilities to be at hand and present them to our guest, who invariably had a happy knack of making them feel that all the extra work was much appreciated, and this was invariably confirmed by the letters we afterwards received from the Equerry or Secretary.

Many of the visits especially by lesser members of the Royal family were comparatively minor affairs and only took one day, but during my time in Lancashire I had three major visits of the Monarch each taking two full days.

Before recounting the details of these visits, however, I feel I must interject one Lancashire story of a royal visit that took place during the War, though, as this was before I went to the county, I cannot vouch for the truth of it. The story is told that on one occasion during the War, the King and Queen came to the county on one of their visits that did so much to sustain the morale of the people when things were going so badly for us. Food was very short at the time and when they went into luncheon which was being given by the Mayor of one of the County Boroughs, they were somewhat taken aback to see that a really good Lancashire spread (as this is called in the vernacular) had been arranged for them. Somewhat as a rebuke to the Mayor, the Queen is reputed to have said 'You know Mr Mayor, while food is so short in this country, we don't have any more food on the table at Buckingham Palace than is allowed to the ordinary householder according to the rations for the week.'

'Ah well,' said the Mayor not at all abashed, 'then thou'll be glad of a bit of a do like this.'

In 1951, His Majesty King George VI accompanied by Her Majesty the Queen and Her Royal Highness Princess Margaret came to Lancashire on the occasion of the five hundredth anniversary of the Duchy of Lancaster becoming part of the Royal possession. This had become about because the only son of John of Gaunt who lived in Lancaster Castle came to the throne of England as Henry IV. The Duchy estates in Lancashire consists mostly of farms in the County, North of the River Ribble in beautiful country close to the River Lune.

Apart from a civic luncheon on the first day in Lancaster Town Hall – a magnificent building, presented to the city by Lord Ashton, and much too good in many ways for a town the size of Lancaster, and a civic luncheon in County Hall, Preston, on the second day, the time was spent visiting some of these farms.

It was a delightfully informal occasion with the King as a country man in his element. The occupants of the farms selected were especially delighted not only because of the opportunity to meet the King and Queen but also because for the occasion each farm visited was given a new bathroom and lavatory.

I had been round all the farms the day before to rehearse what should happen and told each farmer and his wife where to stand and suggested what they should show their guests.

The occupier of one small farm, a very rough, uneducated man, whom we were to visit was most apprehensive, and I told him that after the Lord Lieutenant had introduced him, he should introduce his wife, and that as it would be about four o'clock his cows would be in for milking, I suggested that he should ask the King to have a look at them. I also warned the King before we arrived at the farm that I could not tell what might happen.

On the day, when we arrived and the farmer had been presented, he took off the cloth cap he was wearing, and in one breath said, 'Good afternoon, your Majesty this is the Missus.' There was some conversation and having caught my eye, he interjected, 'Like to come and have a look at t'coos?'

We entered a cow byre where some twelve Ayrshires were tied up. The King stopped at the sixth cow and pointing to her said to the farmer, 'That cow's got a remarkably fine head.' The farmer looked at the cow and then looked at the King; then he slapped the backside of the cow, and said, 'Aye, King, but this is business end.' The King was much amused and for me it epitomised completely the Lancashire attitude towards life.

As we said farewell to the King on Preston Railway station that afternoon, little did any of us think that it would be the last time we should see him for he died in the following year.

I went to London for the Lying in State in Westminster Hall and for the funeral – a poignant and most impressive occasion.

It is customary for the Monarch, as Duke of Lancaster, to pay a ceremonial visit to Lancashire soon after his or her coronation. In 1937 King George VI came on a visit lasting four days, but on this occasion the Queen decided she could not spend that length of time on one visit so she agreed to come for two days in 1954 and two in 1955. These visits required a great deal of organisation for the visit was to cover the whole geographical county which meant that most of the seventeen mayors and one hundred and twenty-six Chairmen of local authorities were involved.

At first, until the programme had been agreed by the Queen, there had to be the utmost secrecy for had there been any leak of the suggestions we were considering, not only would Lord Derby have been the recipient of appeals and demands from all the local authorities not included but there would have been the inevitable bitterness and jealousies.

Lord Derby told me that in addition to the traditional civic welcome at the Town Hall in each town he proposed to suggest to the Queen that we should show her Lancashire life as lived by the people, and he would like us to include in the programme one visit each morning and afternoon to a place of interest. He told me in outline which towns he wanted us to visit each day and asked me to prepare an outline programme with timings, and to suggest places of interest that I thought the Queen would like to visit.

I put up a provisional list of suggestions and with some hesitation included a visit to Police Headquarters at Hutton. To this Lord Derby agreed, and we were delighted when we heard that the Queen had agreed to its inclusion, only that she had cut the time allowed from one hour to forty minutes.

It was impossible to have many policemen there as all were required to be on operational duties outside, but we invited all policemen's wives and children to be in the grounds, and we arranged an exhibition of every aspect of police work placing as many exhibits as possible outside so that all could see the Queen and Prince Philip, who was also there. This, as far as I have been able to ascertain, was the first occasion that a reigning Monarch had visited a provincial Police Headquarters though there have been other similar visits since.

The best compliment we were paid was that after she left Lord Derby told me that she had said that she was sorry that she had cut the time at Hutton.

That evening after a long and tiring day she attended a reception at Knowsley Hall given by Lord and Lady Derby and as they felt that they should be at their home to receive the Royal Party he asked me to go to the railway siding where the Royal Train was stationed for the night, to escort the Queen to Knowsley.

Whenever King George VI or the Queen came to Lancashire for more than one day, they stopped the night in the Royal Train at one of three quiet sidings where there was privacy so that we could mount a discreet but strict surveillance and where any of the Royal Party who wished could go for a country walk in the morning without prying eyes.

The siding nearest to Knowsley was very close to the spot at which the first passenger railway in the world between Liverpool and Manchester was officially opened, an occasion when the local Member of Parliament was fatally injured.

The reception of some five hundred people included all the Lord Mayors, Mayors, and Chairmen of Local Councils in the County, all of them and their wives wore the chains of office which prompted Prince Philip to remark that the chain gang were there in force.

When it came to the time to plan the following year's programme in 1955, Lord Derby suggested that we should have a Royal Variety Performance in Blackpool – an occasion so far confined to London. As I knew Jack Hylton, a Bolton man, and at that time England's top impresario, Lord Derby asked me to put the idea to him. Jack readily agreed to be responsible for its production, and when the time came we had a most wonderful evening with all the best music hall stars lead by the Crazy Gang in their best form.

A special Royal Box was built beside the dress circle, and for security reasons Lord Derby gave me the nearest ten seats in the front row for the five most senior officers and their wives. This was more than sufficient reward for all the hard work we had put in to make the two visits the success that they undoubtedly were.

Of course others too made their contributions to the planning, for the Clerk of the County Council, and the Town Clerks and Chief Constables of the seventeen Cities and County Boroughs in the county all had their own detailed planning to make, but the County Police had by far the most to do, and in this I was served well and efficiently by a loyal team of staff officers.

The next big occasion that the Queen came to Lancashire was to see her mother's horse, Devon Loch, run in the Grand National in 1956.

I said in the prologue to this book that I did not keep a day to day diary but that I did record details of special occasions immediately after they occurred.

After that momentous and in some ways tragic day I did dictate a long note, and although much of the first part does not affect the Royal family I have included the whole of the account for it portrays a little of the work and responsibilities of a Chief Constable.

Monday, 19th March, 1956
This was a normal day at the office with interviews, many problems to discuss relating to promotions, transfers and housing of police officers. I had been away for the weekend and when I read my weekend summary on my return home on Sunday night I had noticed that there had been two fires in the Seaforth district on the Friday night and one fire on the

Royal Occasions

Saturday night. We had, for some time, been worried about the activities of a fire-raiser in that district and I felt that the time had come that I personally should look into the whole matter. I, therefore, decided to call a conference at Seaforth and as a number of fires had also occurred in the adjoining police district of Bootle Borough, I felt that it would be useful to have a number of Bootle Borough police present as well. I, therefore, spent some time during this day discussing with the Detective Chief Superintendent, the calling of this conference which we arranged should take place on Tuesday at Waterloo. I had to explain on the telephone the whole situation to the Chief Constable of Bootle Borough to gain his co-operation.

Also on this day, I was very busy making the final arrangements for the printing and distribution of a pamphlet relating to the setting up of the three Regional Criminal Record Offices at the Headquarters of the Lancashire Constabulary, Manchester City Police and the Liverpool City Police. As a result of a Working Party set up by the Home Office in 1950, there had been a Recommendation that there should be a number of Regional Criminal Record Offices in the country of which one for the North East should be at the Headquarters of this Force.

As this proposal was very severely criticised by the Chief Constables of Liverpool and Manchester and as I had some sympathy with their point of view, I had recommended, two years ago, that we should proceed to set up three Regional Criminal Record Offices in this District instead of one. I had taken a leading part in the negotiations to achieve this because not only had we to obtain the approval of all the Chief Constables in the District but we also had to have the blessing of our Police Authorities and of the Home Office.

All this, after many negotiations had been achieved and the only thing left was for a pamphlet to be printed which would tell all police officers in the District how to use these Criminal Record Offices. After some deliberation, I eventually achieved agreement between all three Chief Constables as to the wording of this pamphlet and I spent some time during the day dealing with this important matter.

At six o'clock, I hastily changed and drove to Morecambe where I dined with two Divisional Chief Superintendents, the Commandant of the Special Constabulary and his Chief Staff Officer.

Following the dinner, I went to the Floral Hall where I inspected a joint parade of the 'B' and 'C' Divisions of the Special Constabulary and after presenting medals to some ten of them, I spoke for three-quarters of an hour on the work of the Special Constabulary. This parade finished at approximately quarter to ten and I was home by eleven o'clock.

Tuesday, 20th March, 1956

I was at the office by 9.00 a.m., and having completed a lot of work within the hour, I left at 10.00 a.m., with John Palfrey and the Detective Chief Superintendent for a meeting with Mrs Topham at Aintree to discuss the final arrangements for the Grand National Meeting later in the week.

ONE POLICEMAN'S STORY

With Mrs. Topham and Mr. Bidwell, her co-director and nephew, John Palfrey, the Chief Superintendent in charge of the CID, and the Chief Superintendent in charge of the Traffic Department, we discussed the various detailed arrangements for the policing of the Aintree Meeting which we were expecting some 80,000 people to attend.

Most of the time was spent in discussing the arrangements for Mr. Malenkov and the party of Russian engineers who were being entertained at Aintree by the Central Electricity Authority.

Mrs Topham told me that the Russian visit had come about because the official who was in charge of the Electricity Board in the Liverpool area and who was well known to her, had telephoned some three weeks before to say that a party of Russians was visiting this country to visit power stations and as they would be in Lancashire during the weekend on which the Grand National was run, he would like to bring them to see the big race. He, therefore, asked Mrs. Topham to arrange that a 'bus should be placed in the Central Enclosure in a good position and undertook to pay for the cost of this.

A week or so later he had telephoned to Mrs. Topham to say that he now gathered that Mr. Malenkov was coming with the visitors and, because of his importance, it would be necessary for him to be in the County Stand rather than in a 'bus in the Central Enclosure.

Mrs. Topham had thereupon said that she would be pleased to entertain Mr. Malenkov and the other senior Russians who would be with him and that she would give lunch in her box to Mr. Malenkov, Mr. Malik, the Soviet Ambassador in London, and his wife, and to Lord and Lady Citrine who were their official hosts in this country. She said that the Central Electricity Authority had told her that there would be some twenty-four Russians in all and she had, therefore, arranged two luncheon rooms for them in the County Stand and she had also sent them twenty-four badges.

I also discussed with Mrs. Topham the arrangements for the Queen's visit and I said it would be important to see that the Russians did not put themselves in such a position that they made it necessary for the Queen to recognise and meet Mr. Malenkov.

The more I talked to Mrs. Topham the more I foresaw difficulties with regard to this and I told her that I had better discuss the matter with Lord Derby.

I left Mrs. Topham at 12.30 p.m., and drove to Seaforth Railway Station where I was met by the Chief Superintendent in charge of the Division, and he showed me, from the elevated Railway Station, the position where a number of the incendiary fires had occurred.

We then went to lunch at a hotel in Blundellsands and, at two o'clock, in the Waterloo Council Chamber, I met those who had been summoned to the Conference.

At the meeting, at which senior members of the Lancashire and Bootle Fire Service were present, as well as senior police officers from the Seaforth Division, Bootle Borough Force, and our Headquarters and Liverpool City, we discussed the facts known about each of the thirteen fires which we thought had been caused, since last October, by malicious action on someone's part and we then considered plans to catch the person responsible.

Generally speaking, all the fires had occurred on either a Thurdsay, a Friday or a Saturday night and we, therefore, decided that there should be a joint and comprehensive plan of observations on those evenings with one officer, namely, Detective Chief Inspector Roberts, in charge to co-ordinate all the police activities both in Bootle Borough and in the Seaforth Division. I also said that we would provide sixty men from other Divisions to assist in this operation.

It was agreed that these people should all be hidden in places that were likely to be set on fire each Thursday, Friday and Saturday nights in future, the first night being Thursday, 22nd March, 1956. I also arranged that Liverpool City should lend us some of their dogs and that we should send eight or nine of our own dogs with handlers to assist.

The Conference finished at 4.15 p.m., and it was agreed that nothing should be said to the Press with regard to it.

On leaving the building I found that there was a Press man outside. He asked me to make a statement. I told him that while, as a general rule, the Police were prepared to assist the Press, in this particular instance, I had no statement to make and I told the reporter that it would be in the public interest that nothing should appear in the papers about the Conference that had taken place.

I was much annoyed, therefore, to find in all the newspapers on the following day, including *The Times*, a full account of our Conference. This clearly must have been given to a Press Association by one of the eighteen of us who was present at the Conference.

I then drove from Waterloo to Manchester to attend a meeting of the Match Sub Committee of the Lancashire R.F.C. Committee to discuss the arrangements for the game between Lancashire and the Police Athletic Association R.U.F.C. which had been fixed to take place at Waterloo on the 16th April, 1956.

I left this meeting at 6.30 p.m., and went straight to the Opera House at Manchester where I met Joanna who was having a drink in the Manager's Room with Sir Laurence Olivier.

It was the first performance of Noel Coward's latest play 'South Sea Bubble' in which Vivien Leigh was taking the leading part.

We enjoyed the evening and were home by midnight.

Wednesday, 21st March, 1956

On my arrival at the office at 9 a.m., I discovered that Lord Derby had telephoned and spoken to Waddington on the Tuesday evening to say that he had had instructions from the Palace that on no account was the Queen to meet Malenkov while they were both at Aintree and he told me that he wanted special arrangements made to ensure that this could not happen. I thought I ought to discuss the matter with Lord Derby as soon as possible and I tried, during the morning, to speak to him by telephone but was not successful.

At 11.30 a.m., I left to go to Lytham St. Annes where the Superintendents of the District were having a meeting. I had lunch with some 40–50 Superintendents from the North of England and had a pleasant time chatting with old friends.

After luncheon, I was expected to make a speech and just as I was getting to my feet, I had a telephone message that Lord Derby wished to speak to me urgently. I cut short my speech in which I took the line that I thought that although we were in a disciplined Service, relations between employer and employee in industry and between officers and other ranks in the Armed Services and in the Police were altering so much at present that we would have to re-think attitudes in our own profession if we were to maintain a happy, contented and efficient Service.

I instanced the difficulties we had these days in making young policemen move from one place to another because of the resistance of their wives – something with which we were not troubled before the War.

Immediately after I had finished, I spoke to Lord Derby and told him of my conversation with Mrs. Topham and of the difficulties I foresaw. He seemed impressed with what I had said and thought that we ought to have more guidance from the Home Office than we had had so far, asking me to telephone to Sir Frank Newsam to inquire from him what we should do. I told him that I thought that as the policy had been settled by the Palace there was no help that Sir Frank Newsam could give us and that it was for Lord Derby and me to work out some plan so that the danger of a meeting would be reduced to a minimum.

I arranged with him, therefore, that we should have a meeting at Aintree after the first race on the Thursday.

I returned to the office where I spent a busy afternoon and evening getting home at 9 p.m., in time for a late dinner.

Thursday, 22nd March, 1956
Because of my many pre-occupations at this time and because of the varying times of arrival of my own guests (there were eight of them), I had prepared an operation order so that my staff at home and at the office knew exactly what to do when the guests arrived, what cars were required, where they were staying, and so forth. It was as well that I did do this because it left me free to attend to other matters.

I went to the office where, after the usual morning's work, I left for Aintree with some of my party at 11.30 a.m.

After luncheon, the Clerk of the Course told me that Lord Sefton and Lord Derby were meeting in the Stewards' Room after the second race and that they would like Mrs. Topham and me to be present.

When the time came, I went there and we discussed the arrangements for the Saturday. Mrs. Topham outlined what she had arranged and it was agreed that she would keep the Russians engaged in conversation the whole time.

I said that I thought the only danger was that the Queen would be moving from Lord Derby's box to the parade ring to see the horses at the same time that Malenkov would be leaving Mrs. Topham's box also to go to the paddock and that if the Russians attempted to engineer it, that would be the best opportunity for the Queen to be confronted with Mr. Malenkov.

It was, therefore, arranged that we would have a car on the course at the County Stand gate and that Mrs. Topham would ask Mr. Malenkov if he would like to go to see Beecher's Brook. He would then be taken there and brought back again just before the Grand National started.

In the course of our conversation, I said that I thought this was all very well but Malenkov might have other ideas. So many incidents had already occurred in connection with their visit where the Russians had changed their plans at the last minute and I was concerned that something similar might occur on this occasion. If that happened, we might find ourselves in difficulties whereupon Mrs. Topham said that if Malenkov started to make any move in the direction in which the Queen was she would promptly faint into his arms. Lord Derby replied that that might be all very well but Mr. Malenkov might just put her on the ground and leave her there en route for seeing the Queen. 'Ah, not with my weight', Mrs. Topham replied, 'I would flatten him'.

Following the meeting in the Stewards' Room, I had a meeting with several of my senior officers when two of them expressed strong disapproval of the proposed arrangements. They said that it would be quite impossible for a car to come back after visiting Beecher's Brook so shortly before the Grand National without becoming involved with all the various horses. They proposed, instead, that Mr. Malenkov should be taken down the County Stand, through Tattersalls, around the back of Tattersalls and between the Totes to arrive at the parade ring outside Mrs. Topham's house and on the far side of the parade ring from the Queen.

After the meeting, I told Lord Derby the views of my men and he agreed that the car should be cancelled and that we should adopt the alternative plan.

I saw Mrs. Topham again and agreed this with her and arranged with her that we should have a rehearsal of these arrangements on the Friday after the second race.

Friday, 22nd March, 1956

I again went to the office in the morning and after spending an hour there, went on to Aintree where, after luncheon, I met Mrs. Topham and we had a rehearsal on the lines that had been suggested.

It was now arranged that we should take Malenkov not through Tattersalls but right along the course round to the gate where the horses go on to the racecourse and thence to the parade ring to a point opposite her house.

I asked my Deputy to be responsible for all the arrangements at the entrance to the racecourse, to receive the Russians and to separate the two parties; also to receive the Princess Royal and to take her to Lord

Sefton's box and also to see that everything was in order for the arrival of the Queen at one o'clock.

I also agreed with Waddington and Palfrey that all three of us would wear uniform.

I also saw the Chief Constable of Liverpool on the course, and as he was to take the Russians with him from Aintree to Liverpool, I agreed with him that he, also, should be in uniform on the course and that he should go to Mrs. Topham's box immediately after the Grand National to take the Russians with him to their cars and ensure they left the course before the Queen wanted to go.

I also arranged that in the event of the Queen Mother's horse winning the race, two parties of police should be at the rear of Lord Derby's box – one party to take the Queen, Princess Margaret and the Princess Royal to the unsaddling enclosure.

Before leaving the course I also had a conference at Aintree with the Detective Chief Inspector about the arrangements that he had made to catch the man responsible for the fires at Seaforth.

He told me that he had arranged for all the men, as agreed, to be in position on the Thursday, Friday and Saturday evenings but that they had not had any luck on the Thursday night. He also told me that he had a squad of nine experienced detectives following up a great number of inquiries which had come as a result of information received.

After racing had finished, we returned to Longridge where we changed and then, that evening, my whole party went to a very good private party which did not end until 1.0 a.m.

Saturday, 24th March, 1956

The weather forecast for the day was not particularly good. We started off in the morning from home at 8.30 a.m. It was cloudy, with a fairly strong easterly wind blowing. I went first to the office and then left in order to be at Town Green Railway Station at 10 o'clock to meet the Queen. When I got there, I found Palfrey and Wren already there and at 10.15 a.m., Lord Derby arrived.

The Royal cars were, of course, already there. Chivers, the Queen's chauffeur, and the second chauffeur, were polishing them up and also making sure that their own uniform, shoes, etc., were clean.

At 10.25 a.m., exactly, the Royal train came into the special siding that had been built for the Queen. I should explain that it is quite a performance getting the Royal train into the siding as they have to come in on the main line, be pulled in reverse by an engine which is waiting there for that purpose and then pulled forward again by a third engine into the siding, the two engines that originally brought the train having gone off for cleaning, overhaul, etc.

As soon as the train came in, Squadron Leader Christopher Blunt, the Equerry whom I know, came along to greet Lord Derby and me, and introduced Sir Michael Adeane, the Queen's Private Secretary, whom I had not met before.

Royal Occasions

There was also Martin Gilliat who looks after the Queen Mother and also a Mr. Seymour who came with the Queen last year.

The Queen came out of the train with the Queen Mother and Princess Margaret and were greeted by Lord Derby and me. The Queen walked with Lord Derby and I looked after the Queen Mother and Princess Margaret until we put them in the Royal car. On the way to the car the Queen Mother said that she understood Mr. Malenkov would be there and that she would like to see him. I asked her whether she knew that my head would be chopped off if Mr. Malenkov met any of the Royal Family. She replied with a smile, 'I only want to see him, I didn't say "meet him".'

We then went to Knowsley arriving there at 10.45 a.m. I am always very proud to see the way in which the Lancashire Police man the Royal route and, on this occasion, they looked smart and were doing their job well and happily.

At Knowsley, Lady Derby was ready to receive the Queen and immediately the party went off with Lord Derby in a Landrover to see his yearlings.

We eventually left Knowsley at 12.10 p.m., which was half an hour later than we had meant to leave. We got back to the train at 12.30 p.m. The Queen was due to leave the train at 12.45 p.m., for Aintree but she did not reappear until 12.50 p.m., which was just as well as we had to get all the men who were on the Knowsley/Town Green route on to the Town Green/Aintree route. As it was, there were not enough policemen on the route although it did not really matter.

In the meantime, the Queen had changed into a delightful cherry coloured dress and the Queen Mother was in her usual ice-blue while Princess Margaret was in a rather warm beige with a very amusing little fur hat. Everything went well on the way to Aintree and we arrived there at 1.5 p.m.

In the meantime, I had heard over the police wireless that the Russians had arrived at 12.5 p.m., which was ten minutes earlier than they had been expected and that the Princess Royal had arrived at 12.30 p.m., so the first part of all our arrangements had gone well.

I then went to my room for luncheon where I found that most of my party were just preparing to leave to drive round the Course.

After I had lunch, I went along to Mrs. Topham's box to see Mr. Malenkov and Mr. Gromyko, who had also come with Mr. Malik. I did not go forward to be introduced to them and I was interested to see that immediately behind them were sitting there five members of their strong-armed body guard – a very tough looking lot of gentlemen.

After the first race I went back to Lord Derby's box to see whether anything further was required and found Lord Derby looking for me. He then told me that the Queen Mother had repeated she wanted to have a look at Mr. Malenkov and Lord Derby asked me how this could be arranged. I suggested that we had better take the Queen Mother down through the County Stand on to the course to have a look at the Chair Jump. On the way she would be able to look up at the Grandstand and see Mr. Malenkov sitting there in Mrs. Topham's box in the front row of seats.

Lord Derby said that he would tell the Queen Mother of this proposal but I emphasised that they would have to be very quick or they would get mixed up with the second race. In the event, the Queen Mother decided happily, I am glad to say, that there was not time for this.

Immediately after the second race, people started to collect outside Lord Derby's box to see the Queen cross to the parade ring. I had a number of plain clothes men present as well as uniformed officers and we were able to make a lane to the paddock. The Queen came out at 2.45 p.m., with the Queen Mother and Princess Margaret. All three were looking radiantly happy and were obviously very excited. With Lord Sefton, Lord Derby, and their trainer, I walked across with them into the parade ring where we watched the horses parade and eventually saw Devon Loch being saddled up and mounted.

I looked around to see whether the Russians had got there but did not see them. I afterwards learned, however, that they had, in fact, gone along the course with Mrs. Topham, around Tattersalls and had gone to the parade ring outside her house. In fact, our plans worked excellently and at no time was there any danger of the two parties meeting.

After the horses were mounted, the Queen and the rest of us went back along the same lane with everybody smiling happily and full of expectancy in the hopes that the Queen Mother would have the success that we all so badly wanted her to have.

We returned to Lord Derby's box where they picked up their glasses and portable radio, and we went through to Lord Sefton's box and up on to the roof. In the front row standing there were the Queen, Queen Mother and Princess Margaret with Lord Sefton and Lord Derby and behind them in the second row was Lady Sefton, and one or two friends of Lady Sefton. I stood in the corner with Lord and Lady Harewood.

Eventually, after the usual parade and difficulties at the start, the tape went up and the race began. Devon Loch went really well and when the leaders were some way from the finish it was clear he had a winning chance.

When Devon Loch jumped the last fence ahead of E.S.B. and was obviously going away from him, the crowd on the stands were cheering, and the Queen and her Mother and sister were jumping in the air with excitement and shouting as all the rest of us were too. It was a most magnificent sight. I felt then the time had come when I should go down from the stand to make sure that I had the police properly organised for the Queen Mother to lead her horse in. I had just got to the top of the steps when I heard a great groan I turned round and saw Devon Loch lying spread-eagled on the ground.

It was a sickening sight and the quietness that came over the crowd was something that was quite amazing and a sight and sound I shall always remember. I then felt there was nothing further for me to do there and that I would go down to see what happened in the unsaddling enclosure. I went across and just got there as E.S.B. was led in by the owners, Mr. and Mrs. Carver whom I recognised as people that I had known years before in Birmingham.

Usually there is great excitement in the unsaddling enclosure with everyone cheering and clapping but on this occasion there was absolute silence except for the one or two rather forced cheers for Mr. and Mrs. Carver, their trainer and jockey which in the circumstances seemed almost to be in very bad taste.

As soon as I saw what the situation was there I then went back from the unsaddling enclosure to Lord Derby's box. As I arrived at the box, the door opened and out came the Queen Mother and Lord Derby. Lord Derby said to me, 'The Queen Mother wishes to see her horse', so with Lord Derby, I led her up towards the stables. There were just the three of us – no other police – and hardly anyone at first recognised her. It was extremely difficult to know what to say. I just said, 'Ma'am, there is really nothing one can say on an occasion like this. This is something that I am sure has never happened before in the race and will never happen again, and it is just too terrible that it should have happened to you.' The Queen Mother said, 'It is really very difficult to understand what has happened', and I could see that she was quite stunned. My admiration for her, which has always been enormous, was immeasurably increased by the magnificent way in which she was taking this terrible disappointment. I said, 'Well, this shows that your horse can do it and you must bring him again next year and show all of us that Devon Loch can win the Grand National'. She said, 'Yes, I think he must come back and race here again'.

In the meantime, I had caught sight of one of my detectives and I sent him along to find out in which stables the horse was to be found.

By this time a number of people, mostly stable boys and their families, had recognised the Queen Mother and were walking along beside us.

As we were walking along Princess Margaret, the Princess Royal with Martin Gilliat came along behind and caught up with us.

Luckily, the Detective very quickly discovered where the horse was and we eventually arrived at an enclosed stable yard where the stable boy was walking Devon Loch around. Except for a few superficial cuts where he had hit the top of some fences he seemed perfectly well. The jockey and trainer was there and they, too, said that they thought that there was nothing wrong with the horse.

Princess Margaret looked very glum but the Queen Mother was just wonderful saying both to the stable boy and to the trainer how sorry she was for them after all the work they had put in to have this great disappointment.

When the Queen Mother had satisfied herself that there was nothing wrong with the horse, we started to walk back but by this time the crowd was immeasurably thicker and people started to come up and shake hands with the Queen Mother. Normally one prevents people doing this but on that occasion I felt it was best to allow people to do so, and the Queen Mother seemed to appreciate it. All the time there were cries of 'Bad luck, Ma'am, what bad luck – we are so sorry for you. Come back and win it next year'! It was all most moving.

We walked slowly back to Lord Derby's box and by this time Mr. and Mrs. Carver, the owners of E.S.B., and the jockey were talking to the Queen. The Queen Mother went up to them and congratulated them and I thought that this was quite the most bitter moment but she did it superbly.

The Carvers then left and there was a most miserable and glum atmosphere in the room. Altogether, there must have been some fifteen of us there and there was nothing that anyone could say. Lord Sefton came in and said that he had been talking to his trainer and that he thought that probably what happened was that Devon Loch saw the water jump the other side of the rail and had tried to jump it, slipped, and then, being so tired, he had not been able to pull himself together in time.

The fourth race started but nobody bothered to look out of the window to see what horse was winning.

The Queen Mother then went into Lord Derby's other room to have a private talk to the trainer and jockey. The Queen and Princess Margaret went with her and they were away for some five minutes. They then came back again and the Queen just said, 'The jockey is simply wonderful about it – it is all so sad'.

They were due to leave at 4 o'clock but it was now five minutes past four and I went downstairs to ensure that all was ready for their departure. We eventually left at ten minutes past four and we were back at the train at 4.25 pm. As soon as they got out of the car, Lord Derby and I went on to the platform where the Queen and Princess Margaret said 'Goodbye'. The Queen Mother came forward and I then said once again how terribly sorry we all were for her and I said she might like to know that I had gone down to the unsaddling enclosure and that whereas generally, there was the most tremendous rejoicing on this occasion, there was almost complete silence. I said to her, 'Everyone felt, Ma'am, that the wrong horse was in the unsaddling enclosure and that yours ought to have been there instead'. I repeated what I had said earlier that she must come back next year and show us all that she could win the National. She said, 'It is very kind of you to speak as you do, Chief Constable, thank you very much', and she then went into the train.

It was a most moving and melancholy experience and although if you do look at it in its proper context, the losing of a horse race does not really mean anything important, because we all knew it was the Queen Mother's great and absorbing interest and pastime, it did seem a very great tragedy that afternoon.

The day for me was not yet over for that evening we had a dinner party for fourteen people, most of the people being my own private guests at the races.

Just as we were going into dinner, I received a message that a young traffic patrol of ours had been killed on the A.6 road.

After dinner, we went back to Longridge and I had no sooner arrived there than I had a telephone message from the Information Room to the effect that there had been a train crash at Old Trafford but that judging from the first information they had received, it was not a serious matter.

I decided not to turn out and they later telephoned to say that twenty-four people had been slightly injured but everything was under control and there was no necessity for Headquarters people to go to the scene of the crash.

Such was my account written at the time of an unusual week in my life as a Chief Constable. This was not typical, but it does give some indication of the pace at which the Chief Constable has to work, especially when one remembers that in addition to all these outside activities the routine paper work is piling up on one's desk and has to be coped with in the evenings or in the very early morning at home, or at the office.

We had during the next ten years numerous other visits from the Queen Mother, Princess Margaret, Prince Philip, Princess Marina and the Princess Royal.

We saw a good deal of Princess Alexandra after she became Chancellor of Lancaster University and indeed shortly after I arrived in the county she made her first public appearance when in 1951 she accompanied her mother on a visit to a number of cotton mills in North East Lancashire. This was the only occasion when our timing went badly wrong, but I had not realised how many people would turn out to see them, and since Royalty insist on travelling slowly when people have been waiting to see them, we were an hour and a half late at the end of the day.

Princess Marina took a great interest in the problem of mental health and one of the last occasions on which I had to look after a member of the Royal family on a visit to Lancashire was when she came up to visit one of our mental institutions.

At that time her son, the Duke of Kent, who was then unmarried, was a soldier at Catterick in Yorkshire, and all his activities were being closely monitored by the press. He was behaving perfectly properly as any young man of spirit would do, but he had only to put his car in the ditch or return late from some party for the whole incident, no doubt greatly exaggerated and embellished, to be fully reported in some sections of the press on the following day.

On the day before the Princess's visit while the premises and grounds of the institution were being cleaned up, with paint applied here and there, an inmate, a lugubrious woman, asked one of the staff what all the fuss was about and when the nurse said, 'Haven't you heard, the Princess Marina is coming here tomorrow.' The woman replied, 'I'm not at all surprised, too, after all the worry her son must be causing her.'

When the Princess arrived on the following day I told this story to

Sir Philip Hay who was accompanying her, but whether he ever passed on the story to the Princess I do not know.

After I left Lancashire my job did not entail any responsibility for looking after Royalty but I did have the pleasure of meeting the Queen on several occasions for besides the annual Garden Parties, I went to the Palace to receive my knighthood, and also because of two occasions I represented the Police Service at the Cenotaph on Remembrance Sunday, when I met the Queen briefly inside the Home Office. The second occasion that I was involved in the Cenotaph service was a most horrible one for me as suddenly, during the Service I felt faint and I had to summon up all my concentration and determination to stay upright, while all the time trying to decide whether I would withdraw from the parade which would have been most difficult as I was next to the Queen and on the opposite side of the Cenotaph to the Home Office, with all the TV cameras on us or, whether I would allow myself to faint and be carried off. Luckily in the end I just managed to hold on but it was a very near thing.

One pleasant side line for the Chief Inspector of the Constabulary is that he is invited to be the President of the Police Mutual Assurance Society – a Registered Friendly Society which was started in 1921 by a group of Birmingham Policemen. Originally it had assets of £7,800. These have grown through the years and today total thirty-four million pounds. Officers and their wives in Great Britain have at the present moment a total of over two hundred thousand policies with the Society.

Because of the growth of the Society, in 1968 while I was President, the Headquarters were moved from very inadequate premises in Birmingham to a fine purpose built office block in Lichfield, Staffordshire.

Princess Alexandra very kindly agreed to open the building and in her honour it is named Alexandra House.

We had a very happy day entertaining her and as we showed her around the premises she spoke to everyone of our employees. Indeed because we thought it would be too exhausting for her we had planned to leave out one floor, but when the Princess arrived and learned of this, she insisted that we changed the programme so that she would meet everyone, even though it meant she left later than intended. This thoroughness, with her charm and ability to make everyone presented to her feel that he or she was the one person the Princess had been waiting the whole day to meet, greatly endeared her to us all.

The last occasion that I met the Queen was a most happy and

pleasant one when Joanna and I had the great honour of being invited to a small and intimate evening reception at the Palace when only some thirty people were present. It was all most informal with the Queen chatting happily with all her guests several of whom I knew.

The occasion had its amusing and, for me, slightly dramatic side. My wife and I arrived first, Joanna wearing a very smart two piece sky blue dress bought specially for the occasion, to be followed immediately by the Indian High Commissioner and his wife, and as we were talking at the entrance a third car drew up and out got an old friend, Adrian Cadbury, and his wife Jill when we saw that she was wearing exactly the same dress as Joanna! To some women this would have been the end of the world, but luckily both of our wives were sensible girls and we all laughed and each congratulated the other on her good taste. It would not have mattered so much had it been a very large reception, but with only some fifteen women present there was no disguising the matter, and we often wondered afterwards what the Queen thought.

As one who has been able for some years closely to observe the effect that a Royal Visit to a provincial town or village has on all concerned, I can vouch for the general good that is generated on these occasions.

Apart from the fact that every place to be visited is spring cleaned and given a touch of paint[1] a Royal Visit inspires most who live in the district to realise that they are citizens who have every right to be proud of the country in which they live, while for weeks before and weeks afterwards the great majority of older and middle aged people who live everyday commonplace and somewhat drab lives have something glamorous to talk about.

I like to think that there is something very solid and worthwhile to remember that with a monarchy we are carrying on the tradition of a thousand years in having someone at our head who is a symbol of all that is good in our country and who gives active encouragement to the many who work voluntarily in local politics or social organisations to improve the conditions in which people live.

It is a matter of regret to me that school children are not brought up at school to revere the Queen as they should. In US schools each day school children dedicate themselves to their flag. We should do the same every day before a portrait of the Queen, and thank God for her example and leadership.

[1] However, sometimes as little as possible is done. During the Coronation Tours of 1954 and 1955 the Royal Train arrived at several stations in Lancashire. When the Queen had to walk up a wide staircase, British Rail painted half the staircase, and put a canvas screen down the middle to hide the unpainted part.

ENTR'ACTE

So far my story has been told in chronological order, but there are some facts that are perhaps better told out of place and in a collected form. In the following chapters therefore, there is, as it were, a halt in the story, to tell of my travels overseas and in it are recorded experiences which do not often come to policemen, and which have helped to provide a very full and rounded life.

Police work tends to make one narrow minded and I have observed that, generally speaking, men who are policemen and nothing more, however worthy they may be, are often dull dogs. I do not believe that such people either enjoy life to the full, nor do they have a sparkle which endears them to others, nor are they such good leaders of men as those who do have outside interests and who take part in activities away from their professional life, while after they retire they do not live so long.

For these reasons I have endeavoured throughout my life to have hobbies, pastimes, recreations, interests, call them what you will which have provided a lot of fun, and which I really believe have helped me be a better policeman because of them.

At first it was the Territorial Army and Youth Club work but after the War I was introduced to ocean racing and cruising off the coast of France, while shooting became my main winter recreation.

Deep water sailing tests one's physical and mental stamina and there is no time to think of problems at the office, while shooting gives one an opportunity not only for exercise, but it enables one to meet and talk with men of all classes who live in the county, and rarely did I return home without some useful snippet of information about police problems and policemen working in the county. Keepers, loaders and beaters as well as the other guns were all men who had a keen interest in the countryside, and I had much in common with them. Though I did spend at least one day a week shooting, I don't think I neglected the job, though someone at

Entre'act

Headquarters was heard to remark that 'in the shooting season, the Chief Constable doesn't work, he only functions'.

But of all interests outside my work which gave me the greatest stimulus and recharged the mental batteries has always been the opportunity to travel overseas to learn how people in other countries live their lives, to look at different styles of architecture, to visit archaeological sites, museums and particularly art galleries.

There is no room in the book to recount all the journeys I have made and to describe the places visited and the amusing and interesting incidents that occurred, but the following chapter gives some indication of the parts of the world that I have visited and of the experiences I have had.

Chapter Nine

TRAVELLING OVERSEAS

Like so many of my forebears, travelling overseas to see how other people live their lives in different conditions of climate, economic growth, and culture, had for long been an obsession with me, but through lack of finance and time until I was well established in my police career, opportunities to do so had been few and far between.

As a child my parents had taken me on short holidays to Europe, the first occasion being when we went to Germany in 1920 to see friends who had lived in England before the War. I remember seeing the Union Jack flying at one end of the bridge over the Rhine at Dusseldorf denoting the area of our army of occupation and the Belgian flag flying over the other end at Crefeld to denote the extremity of their area of responsibility.

I had been to see the battlefields in Belgium with my grandfather and I had ski'ed at Pontresina and in the Arlberg, as well as spending two dull months buried in a small village in the forests of the Loire trying, not very successfully, to learn French.

In 1931, while at Cambridge, with my great friend Richard Marriott, who later achieved a high post in the BBC, collecting on the way two good DFCs for gallantry, and a CBE, I joined a party organised by the National Union of Students – not so left wing as it is now – and paddled in rubber canoes some 350 miles down the Danube to Vienna, sleeping in hay barns and cooking our own meals. There were twelve of us in the party of five different nationalities, six boys and six girls. We were all very innocent at the time and although it was all good fun it is a commentary on the different *mores* that prevailed in those days that everyone behaved most correctly and as far as I am aware, no one slept with anyone else.

The first time that I went overseas under police auspices was during our summer holidays at the Police College. I had tried to find a ship going to Leningrad for I wanted to see something of Russia and was especially keen to see the pictures in the Hermitage, but not being too successful in this, through a contact in a shipping company, with George Wilkinson, a fellow student who eventually became Assistant Chief Constable of Buckinghamshire, I signed on a ship at Hull as supernumerary crew. The ship, a coal burning one of some 7,000 tons was due to go to three ports in Finland to pick up timber for transport to South Africa, but was to stop at Newcastle-upon-Tyne to re-coal and there we were to leave the ship. We spent most of our time on board chipping and painting and we learnt a little of the tough and poorly paid life of a merchant seaman before the war.

We had gone armed with letters of introduction to the Finnish Police and they gave us a real royal reception for they told us that we were 'the first gentlemen from Scotland Yard' who had visited them.

The Finns are hard drinkers and they did their best to convert us to their way of life, whilst showing us around Helsinki with its beautiful modern buildings, and the surrounding countryside. We visited Kotka and rejoined the ship at Vipuri, a beautiful little town, now part of Russia.

The hospitality at this last place was overwhelming and when at about midnight I noticed that the Chief of Police was no longer with us, I was told, 'The Chief of Police – he has gone home: it is not so good that he is so drunk in uniform in public.'

In 1949 while in Durham, the opportunity arose for my wife and me to travel to Lisbon on a cargo ship being built at Sunderland for a Portuguese firm. The owner was Mr de Mello, one of the wealthiest men in Portugal and he and his wife came over to accept the vessel, the four of us travelling back together. Although it was only a cargo boat the passenger accommodation was quite luxurious and with the owner on board it was as if we had our own 4,000 ton private yacht.

When we arrived in Lisbon where all the de Mello family met us, the crane hoisted aloft our car, which we had taken with us. When the vehicle was some thirty feet above the ground the crane stopped and the foreman of the stevedores in charge of the operation came over and spoke to me in Portuguese. I asked one of the family what he was saying. 'He's asking you for a tip.' 'How much do I give him?' I asked, and received the reply that it all depended how fast I wanted the car to come down the last thirty feet. As we had a five week tour of Portugal, Spain and France in front of us, I paid enough to ensure the car had a safe landing. It was as nice a form of blackmail as I've known.

To help pay expenses on this trip I had arranged with the British Council that I would give lectures in Lisbon and in four cities in Spain. This not only paid the hotel bill for one night in each of these towns but it gave us an introduction to local residents of a pleasant and intelligent type. I had taken with me a collection of coloured slides so that I could talk not only about the British Police but also about the British way of life. These lectures seemed to go down very well and indeed, were rather more popular than those given by an eminent literary critic who was on the same milk-round, talking on Contemporary British Writers. I attended one of his talks and all I remember of it was his firm assertion that Christopher Fry's *The Lady's not for burning* was the best thing out of Great Britain this century. What irritated me was that I learnt that, unlike me, this gentleman was getting a fat fee for his opinions as well as being paid all his expenses.

We spent a wonderful four weeks touring Spain, for it had not yet been discovered by the package tour operators, and there was no concrete jungle, nor indeed were there many paved roads, usually just one strip of tarmacadam down the middle. There was very little traffic and when one met another car, one swung on to the gravel at the side and proceeded for the next few hundred yards through an opaque sandstorm caused by the approaching vehicle also travelling on the gravel.

Thus we visited Seville and after I had given my lecture we spent a happy few days looking at the architecture, seeing some very good Zuberan paintings and spending the evenings drinking and eating in the Sierpes. Frustrated because neither of us spoke Spanish, and therefore could not take part in the animated conversations around us, we made a resolution that whatever education our children might or might not have, we would ensure that they spoke at least two other languages besides English.

It was at Seville that we saw our first bull fight and were as excited and thrilled by the first ten minutes of each fight as we were nauseated by the last five. It was ballet with death as the climax.

From Seville we drove on to Cadiz where we were very hospitably entertained by Mr and Mrs Williams of the well known sherry firm Humbert and Williams Ltd, and were introduced to the intricacies of making sherry at their bodega.

We returned to Cadiz three years later, but on that occasion went by sea on a cruise where the next stop was Algiers, where for two days the French police looked after us.

On the first day the Chief of Staff of the Police commander entertained us and showed us round the main part of the City. While he took me out to lunch, his wife entertained Joanna. When we met again at our hotel in the evening and compared notes we discovered that while he had been suggesting to me that on the next occasion

I should come without my wife when he would take me into the Southern Sahara where the Arab girls were not only beautiful but very obliging, the policeman's wife was quizzing my wife about her lovers and commiserating with her on how dull life must be without one.

On the following day we were shown by the Arab Chief of Police round the Casbah, the Arab quarters, where we were taken into some of the houses, shown the shops, the schools, the scribes writing letters for the illiterates and introduced to some of the Arab worthies when we sat making stilted conversation in bad French which was translated for us into Arabic and the replies translated into French for our benefit. We were then asked whether we would care to visit 'une maison des jeune filles' and were taken to a small very clean Arab house gay with flowers and cooing doves in cages. Here the madam greeted us literally with a flashing smile for every one of her teeth was completely capped with gold. There were some six or seven plump young girls somewhat flimsily dressed in the room feeding the birds. Madam explained to us that they were all the daughters of poor farmers from villages in the Southern Sahara, that they came to her at the age of sixteen, stayed two years and that they were then able to return home with all their savings which she had kept for them, when their parents would be able to contract a satisfactory marriage for them because of the size of their marriage dot. One of the girls brought in a drink and while the Inspector and I were talking, my wife was much amused to find herself sympathising with the Madam over the problems of satisfying the virility of the American Sixth fleet which was due to arrive in Algiers in the following week and agreeing that it must be very tiring for the girls.

Following our first visit to Cadiz we drove to Grenada to visit the Alhambra with its glorious views and exquisite architecture and we spent an evening watching the gypsies dancing 'Flamenco' in their caves. Then driving North through Cordoba with its wonderful mosque Cathedral and on to Aranajuez we reached Madrid.

Here after I had given my lecture and attended a reception at the British Embassy given more for the members of the Fulham football team than for us, we spent two happy days with the Velasquez and the Goyas at the Prado, and eating sucking pig in the small restaurants off the Plazo Maior.

We were lucky enough to see Dominguin – then at his peak - fight the bulls one afternoon and then on another we saw, Conchita, a beautiful and dignified Mexican – fight the bulls on horseback – and what magnificent horses she rode.

Then after stopping at Toledo to see the El Grecos we went on to Burgos to see the great Cathedral with cobwebs festooned from the chandeliers and we visited the exquisite little monastery of Mira Flores, luckily found by so few tourists, where the Chapel is beautifully kept with its exquisitely carved angels with their skirts and flounces looking for all the world like the milkmaids out of Gilbert and Sullivan's *Patience*.

When we had entered Spain from Portugal at Elvas, the customs subjected us to a minute search of our possessions, and even entered into our immigration papers the numbers of the tyres on the car and we were warned that these would be checked when we left.

We left Spain at Hendaye four weeks later arriving at the customs post in the afternoon on a very hot day after an excellent large luncheon. There was no sign of life and no answer to the sound of our horn. A car containing a French couple arrived at the same time. After some minutes the Frenchman who was clearly in the same somnolent conditions as myself, accompanied me into the Customs house. There on either side of the customs bench were sitting two customs officials with a chess board between them, oblivious to the world and their own responsibilities in it. White was in a difficult position. He was likely to lose a Bishop or a Knight and much depended on the next move. The Frenchman played chess and so did our wives. Both were summonsed from their cars and in a mixture of English, French and Spanish we argued the best move for White to make. Eventually a decision was reached: the move was made: there were smiles all round and much hand-shaking, our passports were stamped, the barrier raised and on we went. We could have been carrying the Spanish Crown jewels for all anyone cared.

And so we drove up through France drinking the red and white Bordeaux and failing to resist our firm determination not to go to Paris where we stayed for two days and when we spent, I seem to remember, as much as we had done in the whole of the previous four weeks.

During my time at SHAEF I had become friendly with a number of American officers and I had received a number of pressing invitations to visit the United States. I was firmly resolved to go when time, money and opportunity arose and in 1949, it arose in an unusual way.

I was driving from Henley-on-Thames to Oxford when I picked up a well dressed Negro hitch hiker, who proved to be a Professor of Economics at Chicago University. He told me he was here in England on a Fulbright Scholarship about which I had not heard. When the war ended, there were many millions of dollars worth of

American equipment lying in various countries in Europe. Much of it, vehicles, clothing – albeit of a military type – food and oil, were badly needed by the people of the countries in which it lay. The Americans had to decide what to do with it. They could take it back to the USA, which would cost much money, and unload it on the US economy which did not need it, while it had already been paid for by the US War Budget. Senator Fulbright persuaded Congress to sell it to the countries in which it lay and to use the income from the money obtained to pay the costs of American students to visit that country or for inhabitants of that country to visit the USA. 'We have got to give a lead to the Western world: to do so our people must get to know more about them, and they must get to know us'. This imaginative piece of legislation had brought my passenger to England, and in due course after I had made the necessary inquiries, I too was offered a Fulbright Scholarship to visit the USA in 1951 for three months.

Then in 1950 I moved to Lancashire and realising that I couldn't ask for three months leave in my first year I very reluctantly withdrew, but added that I hoped I might be offered a similar opportunity in a few years' time.

In 1952 I met by chance Julius Holmes with whom I had become friendly when he had been the US political adviser to Eisenhower at SHAEF and who was now the US Minister at the Embassy in London. I told him of my desire to get to the USA and as a result I then received an invitation to go to the USA for three months in 1953, but in a more elevated status. Apparently some ten Englishmen a year were at that time invited to the USA on what was called a Smith-Mundt Leader programme, the Fellowship being awarded to people who were somewhat pompously described as being 'potential leaders of thought'.

The Police Authority agreed that I could go and I set off in May, 1953, travelling first class by stratocruiser bound for New York. It seems incredible that only twenty-five years ago the journey was such a long one. We left at 7.30 pm and after a very good dinner were asked by the stewards to go below to the bar for coffee and liqueurs. When we returned we found that the whole of the first class seats had been converted into double decker sleeping berths. We undressed discreetly in our berths, and slept through the night in pyjamas and in a bed with sheets.

In the morning we were at Gander, where we shaved, had baths and breakfast and returned to the plane, to find the sleeping berths had disappeared and the seats in place again. After a delay due to fog we arrived eventually at New York at 4.30 pm – a journey – allowing for time changes – of 24 hours.

I went on immediately to Washington where an official of the State Department, and Philip Mettger, then Director of the Governmental Affairs Institute looked after me. 'You are our guest for three months. Where would you like to go: who would you like to meet: we will arrange it for you.' Somewhat to their surprise I knew exactly where I wanted to go and when and who I wanted to meet for I had, before leaving England prepared for myself a full programme. Within twenty-four hours with great efficiency the air and rail tickets had been obtained, the hotel bookings made and copies of the letters of introduction handed to me.

While this was all being arranged I spent a day with the FBI though I did not meet Edgar J. Hoover as I had hoped, because he was out of town.

My first stop was at Columbus, Ohio, to meet Bill Warner who was with me at SHAEF and who was then Director of Education at Columbus University. I found the local police to be well organised and provided with equipment to make a Britisher envious. For the first time I saw in use an observation mirror, which has become popular as a one way mirror for more erotic purposes, and was able to watch unseen a murder suspect under interrogation. Here for the first time I saw speed checking by radar, one equipment I introduced to Lancashire and England in due course.

Before I left England, Bill had asked me to lecture to the Patriotic Leaders of the State of Ohio, an organisation of which he was Secretary. I had assumed that my audience would consist of Mayors, Town Clerks, responsible business people and the like, instead of which I found them to be a bunch of Taft, Isolationist, Anti-British, pro-McCarthyite screwballs.

I gave my talk on the importance of Anglo-American Unity, after which I was subjected to an almost offensive interrogation about England's complacency on communism. The first question by a fanatic with flashing eyes was, 'Why do you allow a communist like Aneurin Bevan to be a Member of your Government.' No one can have given a more impassioned defence of Nye than I did and there were the cold stares of hatred when I added 'I know the man and I like him.'

Socialism I was told was the same as communism 'only different in timing and degree.' While in Columbus I was shown private indices of so called communists and fellow travellers being maintained by people who could make no proper evaluation of the information acquired. Those unfortunate enough to get into these indices were likely to lose both jobs and friends. At that point in time I could not help feeling that freedom in America was in very great peril. Excessive emotion at one extreme of the political spectrum calls forth excessive responses from the opposite end. Lack of moderation is political dynamite in any country especially one which at that time was still short of experience as a great power.

I then flew on to Chicago. The American police seemed to think that every visiting policeman wished immediately to tour the night life of the city, and I generally found on arrival that on the first evening it was arranged that the officer in charge of the vice squad would take me to a selection of the strip clubs in the town, and they thought it odd – I would almost say queer – when I expressed a wish to see the French Impressionists or the Blue period Picassos in the Art Museum in Chicago, or the New York ballet in San Francisco or Forest Lawn in Los Angeles. Indeed when I arrived in Chicago I was met literally off the 'plane by a Police Sergeant who told me that he had been detailed to look after me for the week that I was to be there and he added, 'I hope you are a good lover, because I am and if so we can have a great week together.' I made some non-committal reply but was placed in a dilemma for I felt that in some way the honour of the virility of the English Police was in question. Luckily in Chicago I had an introduction to a prominent banker, Tom Beacom, now alas dead, and he looked after me most evenings though as he lived at Winnetka some distance out of town he had arranged for me to stay as his guest at the University Club. 'You will be comfortable there' he said 'but I warn you it's not very exciting. The only noise in the Club you will hear is the noise of the hardening of the arteries of the members.' It was not like that at all, but it was very respectable and the members most hospitable and kind to a stranger.

I was not at all impressed with what I saw of the Chicago Police at that time. The men – mostly overweight – wore their uniform badly: they were officious or indifferent: they gave the appearance of being in the job for what they could get out of it and not for what service they could give to the community, I am sure that there were some good men in the force but I didn't meet any. The police stations were old, untidy and unclean, and I was appalled at the conditions in which the overnight prisoners were kept – one great big iron cage called the 'Calaboosh' in which some fifty or sixty dirty, drunken, smelly rejects from humanity were huddled in most primitive conditions.

On the other hand, through the introduction of Tom Beacom I was taken for a day to Joliet State Penitentiary where some 3,000 of Chicago's worst criminals were incarcerated. This was – and still is – the finest top security prison I have ever visited. The place was light and airy, clean as a new pin, and although institutional, it gave the appearance more of a hospital than a prison. The grounds were a garden of flowers. Adams, the Warden, who had been in charge for some years told me that when he arrived there were only concrete yards within the prison, and that he had had the prisoners dig up all the concrete and make the gardens. The men who kept the gardens were all volunteers and each was proud of the patch for which he was responsible, though the whole had to conform to a plan. The inmates could learn and practise any one of some forty trades and crafts. Tobacco was unlimited, and except there was no alcohol and no women, men were allowed to live as normal a life as was possible.

Among the prisoners there that I met and talked with was Leopold who was the prison radiographer. Some twenty years before Leopold and his friend Loeb, the educated sons of wealthy people, had killed a small boy just to see if they could get away with it. They didn't and their trial was widely reported in the world's press. Loeb had been murdered while in prison in a quarrel with a homosexual and Leopold was still inside though he was in fact released on parole a few years after I met him.

While in Chicago I also spent a morning at the stock yards where at that time some 10,000 animals per day were sold and slaughtered in the neighbouring abattoirs. I visited a hog factory and saw the hogs being urged up the circular ramp outside a four storey building by the simple means of a steel rod which gave them an electric shock when applied to their backside. When they reached the top they were seized by a hind leg, hooked up on an endless belt, had their throats cut, and on a gravity system by the time the ground floor was reached the neatly packeted rashers of bacon and hams were being loaded into trucks for consignment throughout the country.

I am glad I've seen it once but I don't want to see it again, and in any case the Chicago stock yards have now disappeared.

Then on the advice of friends I travelled from Chicago to California by train. The Zephyr, an almost silent air-conditioned beautifully appointed train takes two days to make the journey, the first day over the flat plains of the Middle West to Salt Lake City and Denver and then on the second day the route winds leisurely up and over the Rocky Mountains, with their rugged beauty and breath-taking panorama of wild scenery.

This was an experience I would not have missed. Each passenger had a roomette, complete with WC, washbowl, cupboards, arm-chair and bed and there were common rooms where friendships were readily made. Crossing the great divide into California still raises a thrill of anticipation. How much greater it must have been for those who in pioneering days braved so many dangers to 'Go West, young man'. The train stops at Oakland for the line does not run over the Bay to San Francisco, and there I was met by O. W. Wilson, whom I had not seen for four years and who was Dean of Criminology at the University of California.

I had, of course, written to tell O. W. as he was always known, that I was going to the United States, and he had immediately offered me a visiting lecturer's appointment for the summer semester at the University at a fee of $1500 for six weeks' work. This I had accepted for the $24 per diem. allowance given me by the US Government did not meet all one's costs. O. W. had arranged that I should have a small two roomed apartment on the campus and I ate my meals at the Professors' Club. While all were friendly, conversation was stilted and I later discovered that the menace of McCarthyism was such that no one would speak freely on any subject unless later he should be accused of being 'soft on communism'.

Of the fifteen students in my class three were obviously first class, two were moderately good, while the remaining ten would never have gained admittance to an English University.

Degree courses in American Universities normally last four years during which an undergraduate may make as many switches of subject as he chooses. Degrees are awarded by a points system, an 'A' marking earning three points, 'B' two points and 'C' one point. Subjects are graded according to depth and length of course and my subject was worth two points so that a top mark was $3 \times 2 = 6$, which would go towards the total number of points required – ninety as I recall – for a pass degree.

I had contracted to work for seventy two hours but this included examinations and time spent on revision, while I had taken with me some films on police work so that my task was not too arduous.

I had rented a car and at weekends went to Carmel, or to Yosemite, one of America's Nature Parks or up to Napa Valley to drink the wines which were then little known but which have now become famous.

At that time there were $3 to the pound sterling and I was horrified to find that a hair cut cost $2 whereas in England it was only 2/-. On the other hand one could buy a bottle of French champagne for $3, the same price as in England. So whenever anyone asked me to have a drink I would say 'Let us have a bottle of French champagne. It only costs one and a half haircuts.'

I fell in love with San Francisco and have remained so ever since. It has to my mind got everything and if an English policeman's pension would allow, that is where I would be living today.

The people I met, many of whom have remained firm permanent friends, are intelligent, cultured, broad-minded, amusing, and enthusiastic. I've been back many times since and hope to go many times more.

It was while there, however, that I was arrested by the police. I was driving back up Highway 101 from Carmel to Berkeley in the early hours of the morning after a relaxed weekend and was listening to an opera on the radio, when there were flashing red lights and sirens. I stopped and a patrol man said to me in a belligerent tone, 'Do you know what speed you were doing through our city?' Luckily I didn't say what I was afterwards told particularly irked them that I had not noticed their city, which consisted in some twenty houses and shops on either side of the highway. I confessed ignorance of my speed and was told that the speed limit was 30 m.p.h. and that I was doing 65. 'I'm going to arrest you. Follow me to the station'. The policeman then asked to see my driving licence which I produced. He looked at it, turned it over, and remarked that he had never seen one like that. 'Perhaps you have never seen an English one before.' He put his head in the window and said 'Are you a Limey? What are you doing driving over here?' I then told him that I was having a look at American police methods. 'Don't you take the mickey out of me,' he shouted. I said, 'Well, look at the address on the driving licence,' for it had my police address on it. His tone then completely altered and for the first time he spoke politely to me. 'Well, Sir,' he said, 'You were driving a bit fast. But carry on, have a good time.' 'Wait a minute,' I said, 'you've arrested me. Carry on. I want to see what happens next.' 'Oh no I haven't,' he replied. 'You get out of this city. You're dynamite' and he got in his car and drove away.

While at Berkeley I was taken over to the island of Alcatraz, In the Bay, then a Federal prison, and shown around by the Warden. This was somewhat depressing and more the standard of an English prison. While there I saw in a separate room in the prison hospital a man in bed and I was told he was quite mental. 'He used to keep birds but went mad when they were taken away from him.' I was told the story of the life of this double murderer, who died in gaol and subsequently the book and the film *The Bird Man of Alcatraz* became best sellers, and rightly so for it is a sad and gripping story.

I was also invited to address the members of the Commonwealth Society and there found the same sort of audience that I had met in Columbus, and again after the meeting with the same mumbo-jumbo type of secrecy such as shutting the door and then a moment or so opening it quickly to see if any one was listening, I was shown a whole filing cabinet full of documents purporting to show how many members of the University and citizens of San Francisco were associated with the Communist Party.

Travelling Abroad

From Berkeley I went on to Los Angeles where I was very well looked after by Bill Parker, the Chief of Police – a real professional. He ran a most efficient force and was very proud of it, but he was an abrasive character and strong minded and he quarrelled with most people. Usually American Chiefs of Police are careful not to upset the Mayor on whom they were dependent for their appointment. But not so Bill Parker. If he thought the Mayor wrong he told him so in plain terms and the surprising thing was that Mayors took it, for they knew his worth and he was re-appointed for several terms by different Mayors. It was a sad day for the US Police when he died.

On the first night, as usual, I was sent out with the Vice Squad, and after visiting one somewhat lurid performance I mentioned how the standards of what was allowed differed so much from city to city. I was then told with admiration that in Los Angeles everyone – the police, the owners of the clubs and the girls, knew exactly where they were, for the Chief had laid down in writing what was permissible. As far as I remember the rules were:—

(1) there may only be one person on the stage at any one time;
(2) at all times the vagina must be covered with a non-transparent material;
(3) the performer may not touch the breasts or the vagina during her performance;
(4) the performer's shoulders and bottom may not be in contact with the floor at the same time;
(5) the only equipment allowed on the stage may be the microphone and stand;
(6) the performer may not go through the motions of sexual intercourse with the microphone or stand.

Explicit, graphic and comprehensive, I thought, but there were other and more important sides of police work in the Los Angeles Police Department that Parker had organised and about which there were written orders and I was very impressed with what I saw. The police situation is complicated by the fact that in addition to the Los Angeles Police Department there are some other forty separate law enforcement agencies in the conurbation.

While in Los Angeles I spent a day in Hollywood with the Chief of Police of the MGM Studios. He introduced me to William Holden and Barbara Stanwyck who were making a film together and I had my photograph taken with Anne Blyth on the set of the film she was taking.

We lunched in the main dining room with directors and film actors and actresses all around us and in a conversation about film actresses the Chief of Police shook his head and said sadly and wisely, 'I've been here for twenty two years and I've seen them all come and I've seen them all go. You can take it from me, they're all the same. They are tramps when they arrive and success does not change them.'

Much as I enjoyed seeing the organisation and work of the Los Angeles Police I was glad to leave for I did not like the area at all. It is hot and humid and the air laden with oil fumes to such an extent that it is difficult to breathe and one's eyes smart.

After leaving Los Angeles I went by train to the Grand Canyon en route for New Mexico. The train arrived in the morning and waited all day while we visited the Canyon, moving on again in the evening. When I returned to the train the Negro attendant greeted me 'Have you had a good day, Sir?' I replied that I had but I thought that I had made a mistake and I explained that one had the choice of remaining on the top and looking down at the awe inspiring sight of the Canyon with the Colorado river a mile below or alternatively going on a mule down the narrow winding path to the bottom, I had stayed at the top and on reflection felt I ought to have gone on the mule trek. He looked me up and down and remarked, 'Well, Sir, you are a bit heavy for one of the mules.' 'I know', I said, 'that there is a notice that no one who weighs more than 200 lbs could go on a mule but I would have told the man that I weighed 200 lbs and it would have been all right,' whereupon the man replied, 'Sure, Sir, the man might have believed you but the mule wouldn't have.' I like that sort of humour.

From Grand Canyon, after a short stop at Carlsbad in New Mexico to see an old war time friend, I went on to Texas.

When at the beginning of the tour I discussed with Philip Mettger where I should go in Texas he had promptly said that I must go to Dallas. When I inquired whether they had the best police department in the State there, he had replied, 'I know nothing of the Police department, but Dallas has the prettiest girls in the whole of the USA.'

So I went to Dallas for two days and then on to Austin, the capital of the State where the Headquarters of the famed Texas Rangers is situated, and where Homer Garrison, their Chief, was most hospitable. The Texas Rangers are in fact the State Police, but they stick to their traditional uniform of a Stetson, two guns at the hips and high heeled boots and spurs. I was presented with a Stetson and a pair of boots which I found most uncomfortable to wear and I was made an Honorary Sheriff of the county.

Then on to Houston to spend two days in the famous Shamrock Hotel, where I was surprised to find one could not buy a drink though one could buy a bottle in a State liquor store and consume it in one's room.

At the time Stevie Morrison was the Chief of Police – an old tough professional. Here for the first time I saw closed circuit television in a police station. He had a monitor on the desk in his office with four buttons each connected with a camera, one of which was at the reception desk: one in the charge room, and one in each of the male and female cell corridors: As Stevie remarked to me 'This keeps them in order: the cameras are there all the time, but the men don't know when and which button I'm pressing.'

In the course of a conversation with the Chief about police problems in Houston he told me that he had run all the prostitutes out of town and when I expressed disbelief, he sent for his Chief of Detectives and telling him of my doubts said, 'Take him to talk to Sadie.' So I was taken in a police car to a large neo-Georgian house standing in its own grounds on the edge of the town. A maid answered the door and we were shown into a very well appointed drawing room where we were received by a smartly groomed woman some sixty years of age. She confirmed that there were no girls in Houston. 'I have two houses at Galvaston some sixty miles away and there are plenty of girls there, but none nearer.' I then asked why she was keeping on this large house if she was not doing any business and she replied, 'There's an election for a new Mayor next year and when he is appointed, Stevie Morrison won't be Chief of Police any longer. I've seen to that. And I'll then be able to open up again.' When I repeated this story to Stevie the next day, he shook his head sadly and said, 'She's probably right' and next year I heard that she was.

From Houston I went on to New Orleans where I did not like the police atmosphere at all. I had been told about the Chief of Police and while I was there I learnt that the State Police had come into the city to raid a gambling saloon that was under the protection of the City Police.

Then I returned to Washington and while there met and spent two days with Ted Heath, who was then Chief Whip of the Conservative Party and who had also been invited to the United States on the same programme as me. We did the sights together and I learned much of the problems of the Conservative Party at that time. It was not until twenty years later that I discovered that in Washington at the same time also a guest of the US Government under the same programme was a Labour back bencher MP who was later to influence my life greatly. His name was Roy Jenkins.

Ted Heath and I were both invited to see the President on the same morning. I had a pleasant talk with Ike partly reminiscing about the time at SHAEF but he was particularly interested in what I had discovered about the activities of McCarthy's supporters and called in one of his aides to listen. He said, 'I tell you this, Chief, I'm having as much trouble with that man as Clem Attlee is having with Nye Bevan.'

I was scheduled to have twenty minutes with the President but he kept me some three-quarters of an hour and when I returned home I was shown a copy of a report in the *Daily Telegraph* headed, 'Chief Constable makes an Ambassador wait' for the President's next visitor was the Italian Ambassador.

After my meeting with Ike I had a talk with the Head of the White House Secret Service detail. When I asked him his responsibilities he replied, 'I protect the President. It means that I'm the guy who shoots the guy who shoots the President.'

I also had an appointment to see Senator McCarthy but this was cancelled at the last minute because he had decided suddenly to get married, and I was told an interesting reason for it. His attack on those he disliked usually took the form 'You are a communist. Prove you are not'. One newspaper editor who disliked this form of allegation wrote a leader criticising McCarthy and ended, 'You are a homosexual: prove you are not'. So McCarthy hurried off and got married to his secretary. Not that that in itself disproved the allegation.

My last stop on this tour was to be New York but I arrived just as the World Game Series was starting, and no one that week had any thoughts of anything but baseball and certainly they didn't want to bother with a visiting policeman, so having been to the first game with the Chief of Police I cut short my visit, flew into Bermuda for a delightful few days with friends and then flew home with my mental batteries recharged and full of new ideas to introduce directly into the Lancashire Constabulary and indirectly into the British Police Service as a whole.

My next interesting trip abroad was two years later when in 1955 I went to Greece, Israel and Cyprus.

I had for some time been interested in the problems of Israel as a result of conversations I had had with Sam Watson who was a great friend of Amos Ben Gurion, and with Marcus Sieff, my friend from Cambridge days.

Early in 1955 the Israeli Ambassador asked me to call to see him in London, when he told me that his Government had heard of my interest in their country, and that he was instructed to invite my wife and me to visit Israel as their guests for two weeks.

In Israel we were shown real hospitality and great friendliness.

Moses Sahar, the Inspector General of Police was a magnificent host and arranged that we should see as much of the country as possible and we were accompanied throughout by a very intelligent and young Police Inspector, Saul Rosolio, who has become one of my closest friends. He has since been a most successful Inspector General and is now Israeli's Ambassador in Mexico. He and his wife have several times stayed with me in England and my daughter has been his guest in Israel.

In the fourteen days that we were there we saw something of the way in which the infant state – then only seven years old – was building itself up with hard work, intelligence, and enthusiasm. We visited several kibbutzim, the Hula River drainage scheme, Jordan river hydroelectric plant, the sodium chlorate works on the Dead Sea and the phosphate works in the Negev desert. I went to many police stations and lectured at the Police Training School. We were entertained in a Bedouin camp by Sheikh Sulaman and went to a Druse feast specially put on for us on Mount Haifa. We swam in the Mediterranean, the Sea of Galilee, and the Dead Sea on consecutive days and only failed to bag the fourth – the Red Sea at Eilat because the aeroplane broke down. We made many friends and had a lot of fun.

When one saw what wonderful farms and orchards the Israelis had created, it made one feel sad that the Jew and the Arab seem unable to reach a modus vivendi. There is room for both in all that country and with the technical know how of the Jew and the manpower of the Arab the whole desert could be made to flourish like a Garden of Eden, for the natural salts in the ground require only water to turn the desert into a garden.

On our last night at a party that the Inspector General gave for us, in a speech of thanks I said that I doubted whether any other two foreigners had seen so much of their country in so short a time. In his reply Sahar remarked that he was quite sure that was correct and he added, 'And we are very glad you are going. We are all tired out and can't stand your pace any more.'

We then flew off to Cyprus where we spent two weeks. At that time George Robins, an old school friend was Commissioner of Police, while Sir Robert Armitage was Governor. Trouble was only just starting to appear on the surface. The police had recently caught a Greek caique landing arms secretly at night and while we were there a bomb was placed in a cinema to which the Governor was going. School children in gangs were parading aggressively along the street singing patriotic songs, while the police were obviously understrength and owing to lack of funds badly equipped and in a low state of morale.

We stayed the first three days with George and his wife, Lou, and on the first night out hosts gave a reception for us, on the second night the Chief Justice gave a dinner party for some ten people to meet us, and on the third night we were bidden to dine at Government House with some sixteen others. At the end of the three days we had met socially only one Cypriot. This to my mind in many ways explains much of the beginnings of the Cyprus tragedy.

After dinner I walked on the lawn with the Governor and asked him about Makarios and inquired whether he was a man with whom one could have a drink and get on some personal terms of friendship. 'I don't know', replied the Governor, 'I've never met him'. I was aghast at this for he had been in charge of the Island for eighteen months.

After three days in Nicosia we moved to Kyrenia to stay in a very pretty house with Marjorie Jeeves, my landlady from batchelor days, who had emigrated to Cyprus and later was to give much welfare help and support to the British police officers sent to Cyprus. While with her we at last met some charming, intelligent and cultured Cypriots, both of Greek and Turkish origin and we found them very critical of the British Government's policy. 'They only send here civil servants who have governed blacks in Africa', they said, and at that time all the leading officials in the island had come from our colonies in that continent.

Cyprus is a lovely island which in her history has experienced five layers of civilisation. Someone we met told me that our basic and fundamental mistake was not to make English the universal language when we accepted responsibility for the Island in 1878, and the reason we did not was because Lord Salisbury, who was the British Plenipotentiary at that time, was a classical scholar who loved his Greek.

As it was I came home with the firm impression that the Commissioner of Police was not supported adequately from above by the Governor nor from below by some of his senior officers, who lacked drive, while the rank and file lacked a sense of purpose and it was clear that the loyalty of many of the Greek Cypriot policemen was suspect.

Before I left I suggested to George that on my return to England I should ask the Police Authority and the Home Office to allow me to send out fifty Lancashire Police Sergeants to give his force the stiffening that they so obviously needed. This was not entirely philanthropic for the opportunity to serve for a year or so in Cyprus would be of great benefit to the men who went there.

George was non-committal, and when I told Sir Frank Newsam, who was then Permanent Under Secretary of State at the Home

Travelling Abroad

Office of my views and of the suggestion I had made, he said that while he agreed with me in principle there was nothing that he could do unless and until the Colonial Office asked for help.

I also told him that in my opinion in due course before matters were put right there would have to be a new Governor and that probably there would have to be a change in command of the police and that if this came about, I would welcome the opportunity to go to Cyprus to take charge of the police.

Matters moved with speed in the next few months. Violence became worse, the British Institute was burned down, and, as I anticipated, both the Governor and the Commissioner of Police were replaced. General Harding[1] was made Governor with almost plenary powers and with authority to choose his own staff. He took with him as Commissioner of Police, Geoffrey White the Chief Constable of Kent, who had been Provost Marshal of the Military Police in General Harding's Army in Italy at the end of the war.

Eventually instead of the fifty Lancashire policemen I had proposed giving to Cyprus almost one thousand men and women drawn from police forces throughout the country went to that unhappy island during the next few years.

---

[1] Now Field Marshal Lord Harding of Petherton GCB, CBE, DSO, MC.

Chapter Ten

THE IMPERIAL DEFENCE COLLEGE[1]

I was naturally disappointed not to be chosen to take charge of the Police in Cyprus but there were compensations for when Sir Frank Newsam explained to me why another had been chosen, I was emboldened to ask him whether instead he would nominate me for the Imperial Defence College. No Chief Constable had ever been to the IDC and indeed only once had an English policeman – a senior Metropolitan Police Officer – been selected and I knew from friends that it had not been a success. I felt that not only would I learn a great deal but also that I would also be able to make a contribution for it was clear that the Army and the Police would have to work much more closely in the future, and the more we knew each other and understood each other's work, organisation and responsibilities, the better it would be.

Sir Frank agreed with my views and promised to discuss the matter with Sir Richard Powell, the Permanent Under Secretary of the Ministry of Defence. Shortly afterwards I was called up for interview and subsequently learnt that I had been selected for the course starting in January 1957 and that the Police Authority had agreed to allow me to attend.

The year at the IDC is a fascinating experience and very worth while for anyone who has the good luck to be selected for it. The course, which is non-residential, is held at Seaford House, Belgrave Square. This was a large 19th-century house containing one of the most beautiful staircases in London. There are large reception rooms on the ground and first floor, but no decent sized rooms which could be used as bedrooms. Lord Sefton told me that the house was built by his grandfather solely for the puspose of entertaining, as he did not like having guests at his home.

On the 1957 course, there were sixty-four students – ten from

[1] Now called the Royal College of Defence Studies.

The Imperial Defence College

each of the three British fighting services, in the rank of Captain RN, Brigadier or Group Captain, and ten from the Civil Service. There were a further twenty from the equivalent services in the British Commonwealth countries and four from the United States.

The commandant of the course was Admiral Sir Guy Russell, CBE, KCB, DSO, while the four Directors of Studies, all of whom later received knighthoods, were Bill Crawford,[1] Roddy McLeod,[2] Teddie Hudleston[3] and Evelyn Shuckburgh.[4]

The object of the course, which was divided into three school terms, was to study the political, economic and strategic problems of the world's major countries with, of course, particular emphasis on Great Britain.

During the first term we studied the problems of each country in the Commonwealth and had lectures from each High Commissioner in London, while politicians and economists spoke of England's special problems.

During the summer term we studied the world by continents, with special reference to the problems of nuclear warfare, while in the third term we looked in more detail into the strategic military problems that faced us at that time.

During the year we had the opportunity to meet and listen to all the Chiefs of Staff and most members of the Cabinet as well as senior civil servants and many highly intelligent men who had special knowledge of the problems facing the United Kingdom at that time. At the end of the year, my diary records that 'undoubtedly the two best lectures of the year were given by a young Labour backbencher called Denis Healey, of whom much more will be heard'.

During the Easter holidays the students split into parties and went on a tour of industrial plants in Great Britain, and the high note of the year was undoubtedly the summer tour when we went off in four separate parties to different parts of the world.

There was one marked difference between everyone else on the course and myself. All the others were taking a year off from their ordinary work and responsibilities and in many ways it was for them a year's breathing space when they could step back mentally and look objectively, not only at the problems we were studying, but also at their own career. Not so for me: I was still Chief Constable of Lancashire returning North each Friday evening to spend the weekends at the Police Headquarters. I had, of course, to leave

[1] later Vice Admiral Sir William Crawford KBE, CB, DSC.
[2] later General Sir Roderick McLeod GBE, KCB, DL.
[3] later Air Chief Marshal Sir Edmund Hudleston GCB, CBE.
[4] later Sir Evelyn Shuckburgh GCMG, CB, Ambassador to Italy 1966–69.

much of the day-to-day running of the force to my Deputy and Assistants, but each Saturday morning, I dealt with any disciplinary cases, and major matters of policy, while once a month we had a Superintendents' Conference. On Sunday mornings I dealt with correspondence which required my personal attention and saw any member of the Force who asked for an interview. In the whole year I missed only two days of the course and this was to attend meetings of the Police Committee which occurred during term time.

For my overseas tour I selected Africa, for it was the year after Suez, and following Macmillan's famous 'wind of change' speech, I was sure that the problems of Africa would mostly engage our attention in the decade to come.

Roddy McLeod was in charge of the party, and I was appointed student leader. We flew off from Northolt in our own RAF plane which carried us on the whole tour and we stopped the first night at the RAF base at El Adem in Libya, before going on to Entebbe. We spent five days in Uganda and we were all as much disturbed to find the narrow-minded colonial view of those Europeans to whom we talked as they were to learn our views. The attitude of our administrators was that the Ugandans would not be fit to govern themselves for at least another thirty years and they were aghast when we suggested that none of the English would be there in five years' time. In the light of subsequent events, perhaps they had the balance of arguments on their side, but they could not see that it was impossible to hold back the strong tides of nationalism.

I was somewhat annoyed to be refused permission to meet the Kabaka of Buganda for, not only did we have mutual friends, but also it was my view at that time that, properly supported, he could be the future ruler of the country. 'What do you want to see him for? He is conceited enough as it is, and he'll be worse if he's invited to meet you people' was the reaction of one senior official.

We then flew on to Nairobi and spent a week seeing something of a country which was settling down after the horrors of the Mau Mau emergency. This was in some ways a disappointing week for Kenyatta was still locked up and there was no question of seeing him, while both Tom M'boya and Sir Michael Blundell, whom I particularly wanted to meet as I felt that they above all others could save the country, were that week in England.

We spent the day at the Police Headquarters; we were all very impressed with Dick Catling, later Sir Richard Catling, CMG, OBE, KPM, the intelligent and strong minded Commissioner of Police. We also went to Nanyuki and Nyeri to see something of the work of the Army.

At Nanyuki we met some of the African police in the field. They were all very smart in navy blue jerseys and shorts, blue puttees and red tin helmet or tarboosh: all seemed cheerful, a strong African characteristic and there was an atmosphere of efficiency. Whilst I was there, Inspector MacLoughlin came in with some of his team. This remarkable young man had performed marvellously during the Mau Mau troubles and he was currently attached to the Special Branch working in the forest with pseudo gangsters. His task was to capture important terrorists still wanted and he was using gangs of ex-Mau Mau living in the forest as informants. MacLoughlin was short, wore glasses and sported a large moustache, altogether an improbable looking leader of security forces. Later in the day he whistled some of his men out of the forest and to European eyes they looked even more improbable – a most fearsome crowd of gangsters. Mau Mau presented a great psychological puzzle. Participants were capable of the utmost ferocity and cruelty but, having confessed and purged their Mau oath, they reverted to a simple cheerfulness with apparent sincerity. Few Europeans could undergo conversion to devil worship and then re-conversion to Christianity apparently unaffected by the evil interlude. I was taken to see the camp at Athi River, near Nairobi, where 1100 hard-core Mau Mau were detained. It was August Bank Holiday and a Sports Day, when men, women, children, staff and prisoners, Africans and Europeans, were mingling in an atmosphere of friendship and gaiety which was quite extraordinary. Jomo Kenyatta's son was anchor man in a tug-o-war team. This capacity for forgetting and presumably forgiving must have played a great part in the change from colonial rule to Kenyan national independence. Tribalism still militates against nationhood but Kenya has done better than most African nations in reconciling tribal traditions with national aspirations. How typical of the change from Empire to Commonwealth is Kenyatta's emergence as statesman and father figure. To have been a rebel, to have been imprisoned as a rebel, and then President is an experience Kenyatta has shared with many other leaders of Commonwealth countries with newly acquired independence. One can only hope that much the same thing will happen in Rhodesia and South Africa in the fullness of time despite the firmly entrenched white dominance.

We visited Government House where Sir Evelyn Baring, the then Governor, gave us his analysis of the situation in Africa. He contrasted those parts of Africa in the West where white people only came to trade with those in the East and South where they came not only to trade but to live and own land and he hoped for a middle political party which would attract the best of African, Asian and European people.

But it seems to me that politics is too much about power to make such unity possible and since the Africans are in the majority, it is difficult to blame them if they feel that the needs of the majority should come before those of minorities, however talented and useful those minorities might be.

When we went on to Salisbury we met Sir Roy Welensky and his view was that the problem of Africa is not black versus white, but the poverty of the Africans. This is basically true but over-simplifies the political situation. Ambitious Africans may well feel it better to be independent and very poor, than to be a subject race with moderate standards of living. Nevertheless Welensky gave an impression of wisdom and reasonableness. He is a big man in every way. The son of emigre Poles, he had been a heavyweight boxer and a train driver. I liked him enormously for he reminded me forcibly of many of the best of the Durham pitmen's leaders. Self educated, rugged, direct and well read, he told us that he was in favour of having Africans in his government but could not find any with sufficient education to play their part. This, it seemed to me, was an indictment of past British policies.

On the whole we were favourably impressed by the reasonable attitude of the white leaders that we met in Southern Rhodesia; we liked the people and the country and, though we saw great problems ahead, we were not clear-sighted enough to see UDI not many years away.

After a visit to the Kariba Dam then being constructed, alas by Italian not British engineers, we flew to Pretoria and found it very cold after the warm summer weather of Rhodesia. The Minister for Native Affairs lectured on government policy and we were given the full treatment to persuade us of the advantages of apartheid. Unfortunately, the atmosphere was tainted with suspicion. We were warned by some friendly residents to be careful to whom we talked, and voices were lowered when imparting information. An officer of British stock was pointed out as one whose army career had been checked by his British loyalties; another had been a member of the local Nazi party who resigned his commission when South Africa entered the war against Germany and then, in 1945, was given back his commission and his seniority.

I made contact with General Rademayer, Chief of Police for South Africa. He was very hospitable and, among other things at my request took me to see the mass treason trial of 156 defendants which was then in progress. Among them Helen Joseph stood out in dock as clearly as Goering had at Nuremburg. Elegant, alert and disdainful, her powers of leadership were obvious to all.

Rademayer talked to me at length about the communist problem.

The Imperial Defence College

According to him the Communist Party became firmly established in South Africa in the period of the 1939–45 War when Russia was an ally, and communists started to infiltrate a number of important organisations, even the armed services. In 1948 there was a communist inspired strike in East London promoted by a non-European trade union. Riots broke out and there were deaths and injuries. A prosecution against ten leading Communists broke down, and Field Marshal Smuts tightened up the law with the first Supression of Communism Act, an Act which has since been considerably strengthened. Rademayer claimed that the South African definition of communism in no way differed from that of the United Kingdom or USA, but under the South African law a Magistrate could label someone a communist, and those so labelled were subject to surveillance, had to register with the police, and might have their movements and activities restricted. As a result of mass raids, the names of all party members at the time were known and, according to Rademayer, the African National Congress was under Communist control with leading members trained in Moscow. He displayed a somewhat pathetic faith that the mass treason trial was likely to prove an example that other Westernised countries could follow, and he could see no difference in the South African methods of dealing with Communism than those of the United States. The United Kingdom he thought was much too liberal towards Communism but believed that events would force other nations, especially Australia and Great Britain, to support South Africa.

On the racial problem, which General Rademayer sought to separate from the Communist menace, he claimed that native Africans were not yet fit to govern. He had no doubt they must and will take a larger part in government as time goes by and that, left alone, South Africa could work out a destiny fair to all races. Europeans living in the areas set aside for Africans (and there were more Europeans there than I thought) would no doubt leave in the long run as separate development took greater hold. Finally General Rademayer pointed out, rather like a man playing a trump card, that nearly all the Europeans in the White areas had no country save South Africa in which to live. They could not be driven out as they had no country to return to and therefore in their own selfish interests they must ensure white dominance for all time.

While in South Africa, besides staying in Pretoria and in Johannesburg, we were taken to Durban, Umtata, a tribal area, Port Elizabeth and Cape Town. We left with a feeling of sadness. No solution seems possible to make the inhabitants of that beautiful country live together in peace, harmony and mutual trust, for all of them, black, coloured, Boer or British are natives in the best sense of the word and at some time there must be equal opportunity for all.

From South Africa, after a visit to Victoria Falls and a copper mine at N'dola, we went on to Nigeria, where I soon felt that it was a country that could in time be the most influential nation in the African continent.

The Governor, Sir James Robertson, gave a reception for us, and I was delighted to find that his chief civil servant was Peter Stallard who was at school with me. He later became Sir Peter Stallard, KCMG, Governor of British Guiana and finally Governor of the Isle of Man. At the reception, Sir James introduced to us Abu Bakr – who was at this time the Minister of Communications and whom, we were afterwards told in confidence, would shortly be appointed Prime Minister as a further step in Nigeria's path to independence.

Abu Bakr was a tall courtly man who spoke very good English and who had been knighted in 1956. I liked him very much and was delighted to meet him again two years later in Lancashire when he came up as the guest of Lord Nelson, and we also met that summer at a garden party at Buckingham Palace. In 1965 he was kidnapped and murdered in a successful political coup.

Soon after Abu Bakr was murdered, I happened to be with the Prime Minister one evening and when I mentioned my acquaintance with the dead man, Mr Wilson told me a somewhat macabre story. After the failure of the talks on HMS Tiger with Ian Smith on the problems of Rhodesia, the African Heads of State in the Commonwealth called a meeting at Lagos to which they invited Mr Wilson, and most of them pressed him to agree to take military action. In the end, with the assistance of Abu Bakr he persuaded them not to take any firm decision for six months, and on the way to the airport, he asked Abu Bakr how they could best use the six months. Abu Bakr put his hand on Mr Wilson's knee, looked him straight in the face and said 'Kidnap Smith next week'. One can imagine the Prime Minister's feelings when a week later he heard that Abu Bakr had himself been kidnapped by his political opponents. From Lagos we went to Abadan, the capital of the Western Region and then up North to Kano, where I stayed in a mediaeval fortress-like house, the guest of the administrative officer for the area.

In Kano the Emir ruled in almost feudal style. When Lugard entered Kano in the early years of this century, the first white man to do so, he describes seeing the heads and hands of criminals sitting on spikes beside the gates of the city, and I had the feeling that as soon as the British left, the same grisly relics would reappear.

The Imperial Defence College

We were received in audience by the Emir in his mud fortress. He was an unattractive looking man wearing small gold rimmed glasses with thick lenses. He sat on a golden throne while we sat on little chairs in a semicircle around him. The members of his cabinet sat at his feet. They were all Hausas and as such wore turbans made of muslin in beautiful pastel shades, looking for all the world like the candy floss one buys on Blackpool promenade. While we seriously discussed, through an interpreter, the economic state of the country, and the need for better medical provision for his people, I glanced behind the throne and there saw, amongst his mediaeval splendour, a juke box complete with records in place just waiting for the buttons to be pressed.

We were told that he had a harem of dusky beauties all of them kept enfermé, and that, from time to time, when he wanted some new recruits, his agents were sent to the Falali villages to select a number of likely candidates. These were brought to the throne room for his inspection whereupon the girls were stripped naked and made to face the wall with their toes, knees, nipples and noses touching the wall. Those whose bottoms stuck out the furthest he chose.

From Kano we flew to Accra to spend several days in Ghana which had already achieved independence. We were received by the President Nkrumah who was then in charge of the country, in his mediaeval castle which was a relic of the slave running days. He seemed apprehensive and tired and not at all of the strong extrovert type, but in discussing his political problems with us, he told us that tribalism as such must go for 'we cannot have our type of democracy without discipline'.

I was asked to inspect the police recruits under training at Cape Castle, another prison fortress on the sea coast, and here one still felt the sinister influence of those days when herds of captured slaves were driven in on the land side, men and women separated on opposite sides of the prison, awaiting the arrival of the slave ships when the human cargoes would be loaded on the slaving vessels and none of them ever saw their homeland again.

We flew back via Gibraltar more knowledgeable and I hope, wiser men, and after a short holiday returned to Seaford House for the final term.

Every year at the IDC tends to be a vintage year, for attempts are made to select as students those who were likely to be future leaders in their respective professions. Our year did not do so badly for, of the forty students from the British Isles, we produced three Admirals (John Frewin, Patrick Bayly and Hugh Martell), a Field Marshal (Mike Carver and now a Peer), a General (Charles

Harrington), a Chief of the Air Staff and subsequent Governor of Gibraltar (John Grandy), one Air Chief Marshal (Fred Rosier), two Air Marshals (Bill Coles and Chris Hartley), one Ambassador and High Commissioner (Colin Crowe), besides a Chief Inspector of Constabulary. In all eleven gained knighthoods. Of those who came from overseas Sam Manekshaw is the only Indian to have reached the rank of Field Marshal.

So ended a wonderful year in which much was learnt and the mind broadened, but above all when new and permanent friendships had been formed.

Chapter Eleven

OVERSEAS AGAIN

In the following years I was able to make other equally interesting visits overseas.

In 1961 I was invited to speak at a luncheon of the Executive Committee in Chicago at which over 900 businessmen were present when I was told I was only the second Englishman to have done so since the War, the other one being Clem Attlee when as Prime Minister he had visited Chicago.

As the Executive Club in Chicago were not only paying for my journey from England and also the hotel bill for my wife and me for a week, I had taken a great deal of trouble to prepare what I should say and I had let the British press have copies in advance. At the end of my talk there was time for a few questions – all of them pretty superficial. One man asked me my opinion of the use of police dogs, as it had been published that Chicago was thinking of introducing them. I told them how useful we found them in England and added in jocular way 'There's only one snag and that is that the handlers are as difficult to handle as the dogs: they are all prima donnas.' When I returned to England I discovered that the only coverage that the press and given to my talk was 'Chief Constable tells the Americans that all dog handlers are prima donnas'.

I was glad to be able to visit Chicago once again for I was able to spend a happy and interesting week with my old war time friend, O. W. Wilson. He had been in charge of the Chicago Police for the three years after a very successful tenure of office as Dean of the School of Criminology at Berkeley, California. Originally while at Berkeley, he and two others had been invited by Mayor Daley to recommend the best man in the United States to take charge, modernise and re-organise the Chicago Police. After some months' fruitless search, the other two members of the committee advised Mayor Daley privately that the only man who could do the job really well was O. W. Wilson. At first O. W. refused to move from

253

Berkeley because of his pension problems and only accepted the appointment when these had been satisfactorily settled.

O. W. had been in Chicago for three years by then and I was delighted to see the great changes that had taken place in the police since I had last been there eight years before. The men looked smarter: the stations cleaner: and there was everywhere an atmosphere of efficiency and enthusiasm. Mayor Daley was obviously very pleased and when I saw him he told me 'When I came into office Chicago was known throughout the world as a city of hoodlums. By the time I leave I want it to be known as the most honest city in the world.' He didn't achieve this ideal, but O. W. Wilson certainly helped him to get some way along the road.

In 1966, however, an even more interesting invitation came my way when the British Council asked me to give a series of lectures to Police Forces in Australia and New Zealand.

As the cost of a return fare to New Zealand from England is the same as a round trip I arranged to fly out the Asian route and to return via the United States, thus achieving the object of anyone who enjoys travelling by making a circumnavigation of the globe.

The Police Authority gave me six weeks' special leave to which I added my annual leave and in March I left England on a tour which lasted ninety days and during which I travelled 35,000 miles.

Before leaving I wrote to the Chiefs of Police in all the places that I proposed to visit and not only asked to be allowed to see something of their police forces, but also offered to give lectures to their men on the way in which the British Police were organised and carried out their responsibilities.

There is an international freemasonry among policemen, and when visiting another country, one is received and looked after extremely well and with great generosity, and I am glad to say that this continues even after one has retired.

Thus I visited Thailand, Malaysia, Singapore, Borneo, Hong Kong and the Philippines before arriving in Australia and in each place I had the opportunity to see something of the country and of the organisation of the police and everywhere I was very well entertained. In Malaya I found the police to be very much still a paramilitary organisation since the communist menace was still very much in their minds and I was flown by helicopter deep into the jungle to visit one of their forts manned entirely by policemen, while at Ipoh they put on for me a demonstration of a police unit advancing in a most realistic fashion under real mortar and rifle fire.

The visit to Borneo, now part of the New Federation of Malaysia, was particularly interesting because at that time it was much coveted

Overseas Again

by Indonesia and under out treaty with Malaysia we had a strong military presence in Sarawak, Borneo and Sabah.

After visiting Kuching where I was able to sense the atmosphere of that exciting country, so long the personal possession of the Brook family, and sat drinking in the market square as did Rajah Brook so often when he was living there 'across river'.

I went on to Sibu where I was taken some sixty miles up river by canoe (with an outboard motor) to spend the night in a longhouse. Alas, what an anti-climax: instead of the semi naked beauties whose photographs appear in Western geographical magazines, all that I saw were toothless and not over clean old crones and I was toasted in and made to drink some foul tasting brew from fermented coconut.

Imagine my surprise, however, when on the wall of a police station I found the helmet of the Durham City Police – a force which ceased to exist in the 1920's. How it got there and why it was there no-one knew.

From Sibu I was taken deep into the jungle to see how a forward unit of the Border scouts operated. I was first flown in a short take-off aircraft to Sepulet where we landed beside a stream on the smallest airstrip I have ever encountered completely surrounded by barbed wire, booby traps, and slit trenches, permanently manned. From there by helicopter I flew over what appeared to be impenetrable jungle with high trees to a place close to the Indonesian border where a clearing had been made, and we dropped down almost vertically through the trees on to the ground. I was told by my escort to alight and to stand quite still. It was an eerie feeling standing defenceless against the helicopter knowing that armed men whom we could not see were peering at us from the jungle. When we had been identified, out from different directions came eight Murat scouts – small men in jungle green combat clothing armed to the teeth.

They escorted us to their camp – some thirty yards inside the jungle where each man had built himself a hammock with the branches of trees. We had brought with us food, drink and cigarettes for the men do two months on patrol before returning to their base and their wives, their job being to be the eyes and ears of the security forces in the jungle area. I was told that our arrival and departure would have been seen by the Indonesians and that a patrol would start immediately to try to find our landing site so that as soon as we left those we had met would break camp and move elsewhere.

Scouting in the jungle was a deadly game of hide and seek to be played only by the brave and the skilled. Within a yard or so a man simply disappeared into the jungle background. One could ambush or be ambushed. He who was most alert survived longest. For me the experience was stimulating and exciting and no other part of my trip, as it seemed to me, could bring me so close to history in the making.

After an interesting week in Hong Kong I flew on to Manila where during the course of my stay I received a message that the President of the Philippines, Eduardo Marcos, wished to see me.

I was taken up to Baguio, a beautiful small town in the mountains where the President has his summer palace. Apparently he plays a round of golf every morning stopping for breakfast after playing the 9th hole. I was bidden to have breakfast with him at the club house, during which he told me of his concern about the crime situation – which was undoubtedly very bad, and he asked me to advise him what he should do. I told him that without spending some time in the country and looking in detail at the organisation of the police force, I really could not make any constructive suggestions. He replied 'I am sure you have got some good ideas, please write me a memorandum and send it to me' and off he went to the 10th tee. This I did a week or so later, and I was later told that as a result of it, some of the laws relating to the police were altered.

From Manila, I flew to Sydney to start my first visit to Australia, arriving on Easter Sunday. Truth to tell I was not greatly looking forward to this part of my tour. It was the Asian part which I had thought would be the most enjoyable and interesting, but how wrong I was.

Within a very few days I found myself completely in love with the country – a love that I have never lost. I liked the climate, I liked the people, I liked their way of life. I found everyone so very extrovert, so very hospitable, and so very full of enthusiasm and determined to enjoy life and get the most out of it. Everyone I met seemed to be beating their chests and saying 'We are good today – but we will be better tomorrow.'

I was fortunate to step off on the right foot for on arrival I found an invitation from the Australian Jockey Club to go to the races at Randwick on the Easter Monday – one of the big meetings of the year.

Racing in Australia is much more comfortable than in England and if one is lucky enough to be invited as a guest of the Committee one is entertained extremely well. On this occasion apart from leading politicians, the chairmen of all the Jockey Clubs in Australia were there – and there is one in each State.

I was introduced to the Prime Minister, Henry Holt, who afterwards so tragically lost his life when swimming, and he introduced me to each of the chairmen who when they learnt that I was to visit their State, invited me to race with them. Thus I visited in great comfort race courses every Saturday during the next six weeks.

It is usual for the committee to have an excellent sit-down lunch for some sixty people after the first race, at which it is almost 'de rigeur' to start with a plate of oysters, while there is always plenty of very good Australian wine.

I spent a week in each State being entertained and looked after by the police. Though I found myself very critical of many detailed aspects of police organisation and police work in Australia, in principle they have to my mind the best organisation of any country that I have visited. That is to say, they have one police force and one police force only in each State, while to deal with Commonwealth or Federal matters, there is a Commonwealth Police with its Headquarters in Canberra, and with detachments in each State capital.

As this book is not a treatise on police organisations throughout the world I will not expand on my criticisms of the police that I had, and indeed it would perhaps be churlish to do so, for everywhere I found courtesy, kindness, hospitality and generosity.

Travel in Australia is very time consuming for distances are vast. It is as far from Sydney to Perth as it is from London to New York and an Englishman needs time to adjust his mind to what this means in terms of governmental organisation.

I seemed to spend much time in an aeroplane for I flew from Sydney to Brisbane: then to Canberra, Melbourne, Hobart, Adelaide and Perth, spending a week in each place except Canberra.

In Melbourne I met the Chief Secretary, Sir Arthur Rylah, and his senior civil servant, John Dillon, and had several discussions with them about police organisation in England. They were particularly interested in the work of the Inspectorate and although I was at that time only a Chief Constable they invited me to return in the following year to inspect the Victoria Police, but when I said that I would not be able to return to Australia until I retired from the police in five years' time, they said that they were prepared to wait and would expect me then.

In Perth at Government House, I once again met Mrs Pandit who was then a very influential world political figure. I had met her first in Lancashire when she was staying with Henry Spurrier and on this later occasion we flew together from Perth to Sydney when we had plenty of time to talk.

I said that I found it very surprising that India could have produced two such eminent international figures as Mrs Gandhi and her in the 20th century when the high caste women of India had been emancipated for such a very short time, most of them for centuries having been kept enfermé after marriage. Her reply was that since they were enfermé they had the time to read and that generally speaking Indian women of that type who were intelligent were probably better read and better informed than their counterparts in the Western world, and that their husbands always consulted them about their business and governmental affairs. When I remarked that it must have been difficult for wives to advise since they would not have met the men with whom their husbands were negotiating, she replied, 'You must remember that the harems of India probably had one of the best intelligence services the world has ever known.'

All too soon, alas, it was time for me to leave Australia, and I flew on to New Zealand with great regret, determined I would return as soon as possible to this wonderful and exciting country which has so much to offer in the future for those who are lucky enough or sensible enough to be living there. As an Australian friend said to me, 'This country is a wonderful place for the young, and its no bad place for the old.'

After completing my lectures in New Zealand I spent three days with the police in Fiji and then flew on to Honolulu.

The day before I was to leave, Thursday, 24th May, 1966, I lay on the beach at Nandi in the sunshine relaxing with a very pretty air hostess to whom the police had introduced me.

At 9 pm that evening we bid each other a fond farewell and I flew through the night across the International Date Line arriving at Honolulu on the morning of the 24th May, 1966, Owing to the change of date, there had been a mix up over the day of my arrival and the Police Chief was not expecting me until the 25th and he was too busy to see me that day. The police however, efficient as always, soon provided an alternate diversion and I spent a happy day relaxing on the beach with an even prettier girl than the one at Nandi. So I spent 24th May, 1966, twice on two separate beaches with two separate girls 1,500 miles apart. I will never know whether I am a day older than I ought to be or a day younger, but I do know I am a day better off.

This was really the end of the tour for after three days I flew on to Los Angeles, Chicago and Washington, merely spending a night at each place to see old friends, before returning to England.

And so the tour ended ninety days after it began, and though I took ten days longer than Phineas Fogg, Jules Verne's hero, I feel I had as many interesting experiences as he had, and made many friends.

It had been a most stimulating three months, but apart from the travelling it had been hard work for at each new stopping place I was met by strangers, and one had to overcome the natural suspicions and doubts as to what sort of a fellow this Englishman was. I am glad to say that everywhere we parted as friends and many of those who entertained me so very hospitably have visited me in England or I have seen them again on later visits.

There were other police visits to the United States and to Canada in the ensuing years and my last visit under official police auspices was in 1969, when I visited a number of American Universities to lecture to the Law Schools there and at the same time had an opportunity of ascertaining something of the problems of student unrest which had for some time been plaguing the authorities in America and were starting to cause difficulties in this country.

I returned via Washington and while there I had a long talk with John Mitchell, the Federal Attorney General, who was then at the height of his power and who since has been sent to prison for his part in the Watergate scandal. I must say that at that time I was impressed with him and I noted in my diary that 'he seemed wise, relaxed and competent'. We talked mainly about the problems of student unrest and I told him of the discussions I had had with Vice Presidents of the various Universities that I had visited.

The problems of student unrest were much more serious in the United States than in the United Kingdom for undoubtedly there was at each University a much more militant faction than at any university in this country. The main trouble however was and is that because of the size of the universities, (most of them being of the order of 20,000–30,000) there is no communication from the top to the bottom. Furthermore, the police, by their aggressive look and by their aggressive actions, had undoubtedly alienated the moderate students and as a consequence there was far greater opposition to the police in any American university than there was in any British university. I talked at length with the President of the University of Minnesota and the Vice President of the Californian State College on this subject and when I suggested that universities ought to expel more quickly people who demonstrated violently against the establishment, they pointed out that once a person was suspended, he was at that time eligible for draft into the armed service and that they were therefore reluctant to adopt this policy. Furthermore because of the size of the problem it was difficult, if not impossible, to set up a series of disciplinary courts. The Vice President of the Californian State College told me that if they took disciplinary action against militant students, they might at any time have 200 cases waiting to be heard and with the American judicial system as it is, a student might well finish his University career before his case was heard. He also added he could not persuade University staff to sit on any disciplinary tribunals he might set up. 'We came here to teach and to do research, not to be judges' was the usual comment.

When I discussed the matter with John Mitchell I said that from what I had heard and from what I had read I took the view that the fact that there had not been so much civil disorder in England was greatly due to the fact that the Police had done everything they could to keep the temperature down. They had not been at all aggressive and had only taken physical action when necessary to defend themselves. I told the Attorney General that we had not called in the military, while neither steel helmets nor firearms had been seen on the streets carried by the police. I could not help but feel that the aggressive looks of the police and military as well as their actions had escalated the trouble in the United States, and that many moderates had supported the militants because of this.

I also said that in England the Courts supported the police better than they did in the United States by dealing with cases much more expeditiously. The Attorney General agreed with this assessment of the position.

I returned home with a strong feeling that although on many occasions we have much to learn from the Americans in the way they handle their problems, in this instance we were acting much more sensibly than they were, and indeed the police can at least be thankful that students at our Universities and Polytechnics are now behaving in a much more responsible manner.

FINALE

Chapter 12

THE HOME OFFICE

The office of HM Inspector of Constabulary is a hundred and twenty-two years old. Until 1856 individual counties, cities and boroughs could if they so desired, set up their own police forces, but if they did so all the finance had to be found from local funds.

Most local government areas had police forces of a kind but they varied greatly in standards of efficiency and most were very poor, while some county areas had nothing at all.

Because of the increase in population in the middle of the 19th century, and with the coming of railways and the improvement in roads as a result of the invention of tarmacadam, criminals were increasing in number and mobility. The government of the day, therefore, passed an Act requiring every county and every town above a certain population to establish a police force, and for the first time the central government agreed to pay a proportion of the costs. At first this was 25 per cent but it was later increased to 50 per cent, a proportion which still obtains today.

To ensure that the Government's share of the money was properly spent, the Act provided that two people, to be known as HM Inspectors of Constabulary, should be appointed and required to report annually whether the forces for which they were responsible were adequately efficient. The number of Inspectors authorised to be appointed has been increased from time to time and by an Act of 1945, the Home Secretary may now appoint whatever number of Inspectors he thinks necessary, and may also appoint one of them to be the Chief Inspector of Constabulary.

Since they were first introduced, successive Inspectors of Constabulary have had a profound influence for good on the Police Service in this country. Almost from the start the men appointed have been chosen from the ranks of Chief Constables and their selection has been good.

Although possessed of no authority of command, and with only the ultimate threat of the withdrawal of the Government grant in the background, the HMIs as they are always known, by the very influence of their character and experience, have been able to ensure that the individual police forces of this country are well organised to cope with the problems facing them, and have a standard of efficiency which is the envy of the world.

Most people believe that in some way the Metropolitan Police controls the various provincial police forces and that New Scotland Yard is the Headquarters of the nation's police. This is not so. The Metropolitan Police are solely the police for London – and not even for the whole of that for the square mile in the centre, the City of London, has its own quite separate force.

Of course all the various forces work closely together, but legally and practically, they are quite separate entities, and until 1919, each Police Authority decided the rates of pay and the conditions of service for its police officers. Since then the Home Office has been able to ensure standard pay and conditions of service for all the officers in all the forces and it is to ensure this uniformity and efficiency that the Inspectorate directs its attentions.

When I submitted my written evidence to the Royal Commission in 1960, I had said:

'The Memorandum of the Association of Chief Police Officers submitted to the Royal Commission paid a tribute to Her Majesty's Inspectors of Constabulary for the way in which they carry out their duties. I would like very much to be associated with those remarks. A Chief Constable is officially a lonely person. He has often to make decisions which greatly affect the life and activities of other people. In deciding on prosecutions for criminal offences, he can consult the Director of Public Prosecutions but in making administrative decisions within the Force he has no-one of equal standing to whom he can turn to discuss the matter. There are often grave decisions to be made and he would often greatly like to discuss the course of action he should take with someone who has the necessary technical background and local knowledge.

In such circumstances it is to one's Inspector of Constabulary that one turns, and never turns in vain. With their wide experience and their wise understanding of the difficulties which from time to time beset a Chief Constable, H.M. Inspectors of Constabulary can and do give inestimable help and assistance to the Chief Constables of those Forces for which they are responsible.

Whatever the future structure of the Police Service, the importance of an effective Inspectorate cannot be overstated. H.M. Inspectors of Constabulary are linch-pins in the Service.

Consideration should also be given, I suggest, to the conditions of service of the Inspectors of Constabulary. At present their pay is inadequate for the responsibilities of their appointment. It should be the objective of all enthusiastic and ambitious Chief Constables to be invited to become an Inspector of Constabulary. At present the post is only financially attractive to the Chief Constable of a small or medium sized Force or to a man with a strong sense of vocation. The Chief Constables of the larger forces would lose financially if they became Inspectors of Constabulary.

Not only would many a Chief Constable lose financially if he becomes an Inspector of Constabulary, but he has to work in conditions which are not so comfortable as those of a Chief Constable. Each Chief Constable has a secretary and Chief Constables of larger forces usually have also a personal assistant of the rank of Inspector. Not only do they have this assistance with their secretarial and detailed work but also, in addition, they have at their Headquarters a number of staff officers who are able to undertake for them at a moment's notice, detailed staff studies or research into any matter which might affect the efficiency of their force, or indeed of the Police Service.

An Inspector of Constabulary has the part-time services of a secretary but has no office in his territory and no personal assistant. At the Home Office all five share one room, and, I believe, the services of one secretary, though they are not, of course, often all at the Home Office at the same time. If an Inspector wishes to undertake any research work, he has either to do it himself or he may, on rare occasions, ask a local Chief Constable to do it on his behalf.

If the number of H.M. Inspectors of Constabulary is increased to one for every police district, as I suggest, I am of the opinion that each Inspector should live within his police district and that he should be allowed to have the use of a full-time secretary and staff officer. He should base his Headquarters either on the recruit training centre of the district or at the Regional Civil Defence Headquarters within the district. He would then have adequate staff at his disposal to help him with his work and he would be "tied in" to the police or Home Office communications system.'

I am glad to say that the Commission accepted these suggestions and most of them have been implemented by the Home Office.

Although the office of Chief Inspector of Constabulary was created in 1945, it was not until 1962, after the Royal Commission on the Police had issued its main Report, that the first Chief Inspector was in fact appointed.

The first Chief Inspector was Sir William Johnson, CMG, CBE, the senior Inspector, but his was only a caretaker appointment for he was due to retire within a year, and the first real incumbent of the office was my predecessor, Ted Dodd. He had set the tone and established the parameters under which I was supposed to work. Ted was my closest friend in the Police and I much admired him, for he was a strong minded man of great integrity and he had run a very efficient force in Birmingham. But he was conservative by nature and I never felt that he wished to initiate new ideas. He was, however, very popular in the Police Service, an advantage that I did not have, and thus I knew that he would not be an easy man to succeed, particularly as there were a number of major changes that I wanted to make, changes which some Chief Constables would not like.

Soon after my appointment had been announced, Roy Jenkins asked me to see him at the House of Commons. The interview was a short one for he was very preoccupied with parliamentary business. After saying how pleased he was that I was coming to the Home Office he counselled me to be rather more tactful, saying that I had a reputation for rubbing people up the wrong way by speaking my mind too plainly. I acknowledged the fault and promised to see that things ran smoothly. At the end of the meeting he added, 'And I want you to know that if all goes well, I shall not consider you too old to go to the Metropolitan Police when Simpson retires.' I left the House walking on air for it looked as if my life's ambition was likely to be realised.

In January 1967 the *Police Journal* in its editorial leader commented:

'The New Year brings with it a new leader for the Police Service. The appointment of H.M. Chief Inspector of Constabulary is one which has already been established as being of capital significance during its brief tenure by Sir William Johnson, and by the longer but still tragically short period in office of Sir Edward Dodd. No-one is in any doubt that their successor will carry on their work in other than the most constructive and forceful spirit.

Colonel St. Johnston has long been known for his vision and his initiative. His career has been one of quite exceptional distinction and scope. His quarter of a century of Chief Constableships, one with the largest police force outside the Metropolis, has been distinguished by bold and productive experiment and by the international status his travels to police forces all over the world have given him.

Colonel St. Johnston is a hard taskmaster, trenchant and demanding. He comes to his high office at a time of unprecedented and far-reaching change. Everyone who knows him respects his great abilities and his superb confidence. We may be sure that he will not falter, however fell the clutch of circumstance may be, in giving the Service the lead to the greater effectiveness our troubled days demand.'

I started work on the 1st of February 1967, the offices of the Inspectorate being in Horseferry House, a gloomy characterless

The Home Office

building, one of a number housing branches of the Home Office which could not be accommodated in Whitehall.

My direct staff consisted of a driver, a secretary and a staff officer, though there were in addition six Regional HMIs with their small staffs situated at strategic centres in the provinces.

The Chief Inspector's primary official responsibility is to act as Chief Police Adviser to the Home Secretary and to the civil servants in the Home Office. He is Chairman of the Police College Advisory Committee and he is responsible for the work of the Police Research Department. The Chief Inspector is not in any way responsible for the organisation or operations of the Metropolitan Police, whose Comissioner is directly responsible to the Home Secretary.

He is also responsible for co-ordinating the work of the six regional HMIs. Each of these is responsible for a certain number of Forces and they not only carry out the statutory annual inspections but they also keep an eye on the Home Office Regional Recruit Training Centres in their areas. They also act as father confessors to the Chief Constables in their region and are readily available to give advice to the chairmen and clerks of the Police Authorities of the Forces in their area.

When I went to the Home Office, my colleagues were John McKay, who had been Chief Constable of Manchester and who eventually succeeded me; Neil Galbraith, formerly Chief Constable of Monmouthshire; Sydney Lawrence, who had been Chief Constable of Hull; Stanley Peck who had been Chief Constable of Staffordshire; Alan Scroggie who had been Chief Constable of Northumberland, and Joe Manuel who had been a Deputy Assistant Commissioner in the Metropolitan Police. There was also Nick Bebbington, sometime Chief Constable of Cambridge, who was in charge of the Police Research Department. Besides myself, McKay, Peck and Bebbington had all received their early police training at the Hendon Police College.

My colleagues in the Inspectorate came to London once a month when we discussed amongst ourselves and with the civil servants in the Police Division, the current common problems facing the Police Service and we decided what advice should be given to the Home Secretary verbally or in writing.

Except for these collective discussions and private conversations with individual HMIs on problems peculiar to their Region, I left them to run their own show. It was not a question of a commanding officer with seven deputies. I regarded us all as equals, with myself as *primus inter pares*. Indeed, when the Police Act of 1945 first allowed the appointment of a Chief Inspector, Sir Frank Brook, the senior and quite outstanding HMI, refused to be considered for appointment to that office for he felt strongly that if such an appointment was made it would lower in status the position of his colleagues and it was not until after he had retired and the Royal Commission had issued its report recommending such an appointment forthwith that the first Chief Inspector was appointed.

The annual inspection of a provincial force is a very detailed affair, the HMI not only taking one or two formal parades, but examining books, records and procedures at police stations, ensuring that complaints against the police are properly recorded and investigated, that prisoners have been properly dealt with, that buildings and equipment are adequate and properly used and by detailed questioning of the men, he ensures that training is adequate and that everyone knows his job and has the right attitude towards his work. Finally the HMI will discuss his findings with the Chief Constable, who usually accompanies the Inspector the whole time, and with the chairman and members of the police authority. Any man in the force may apply to see the HMI in private to voice any grievance he may have and though this right is rarely used it has at times lead to later investigations into the actions of the Chief Constable.

In a large force the inspections will take several days, or even weeks spread over the year, and they are a very valuable way of ensuring the efficiency of the force. It puts everyone on his toes, and apart from anything else ensures that all records are correct and up-to-date and that every police station is spring cleaned and tidied up. The days preceding an inspection are indeed hectic. At the end of the inspection, the Inspector writes a full report on his findings and this is filed at the Home Office.

If I have a criticism of this system it is that there is no inspection of the financial side; not to see whether the books are kept correctly, for that is the responsibility of the County or City Treasurer and of the Government Auditor, but to see whether the money required for the police is wisely allotted and wisely spent.

But on the whole this system of inspections has not only stood the test of time but is, I believe, one of the many reasons why the British Police have the deserved reputation for being the best in the world.

The only Force that the Chief HMI inspected formally was the City of London Police, and this had in the past been a very perfunctory affair – a talk with the Commissioner, a visit to one or two of the police stations and then lunch with the chairman of the police committee. Although, in fact, on the three occasions I inspected the City I dug a little deeper, particularly into the work of the Fraud Squad which was a joint affair with the Metropolitan Police and in which there was, I knew, an uneasy alliance. But I do

The Home Office

not pretend that I went into matters as fully as the HMIs did when inspecting a provincial force.

Curiously enough, however, until 1967 there was no similar system of inspections in the Metropolitan Police. An internal inspectorate was set up by Joe Simpson under pressure from Roy Jenkins, but I believe that it would be better if the Home Office Inspectorate, suitably augmented in staff, was responsible for inspections of all forces throughout the country, including the Metropolitan Police.

As soon as I arrived at the Home Office the Home Secretary agreed to my suggestion that he should appoint two additional Inspectors, one to be responsible for the co-ordination of crime investigation and one to be responsible for traffic matters. I asked Joe Manuel to look after traffic and recommended that Frank Williamson, who was at that time Chief Constable of Cumberland and Westmorland, should be appointed HMI Crime. I had known Frank Williamson since I first went to Lancashire, when he was a Detective Inspector in Manchester, which was suffering at that time under a Chief Constable of poor calibre. I had the highest regard for his integrity and for the pertinacity which he showed when working in very difficult circumstances. His father John Williamson was for thirty-one years a much loved Chief Constable of Northampton.

To fill Joe Manuel's vacancy as a Regional Inspector, I recommended in the first place that Douglas Osmond, at the time Chief Constable of Hampshire, and who was later knighted, should be appointed, for I regarded him as having the best intellect in the Police Service. He, however, refused to be drafted and instead the Home Secretary appointed Robert Fenwick, a Metropolitan police officer with a background of CID experience who had been Chief Constable of Shropshire and who had recently lost his appointment when Shropshire had been amalgamated for police purposes with Worcestershire and Herefordshire to form the West Mercia Constabulary. This was a happy choice for Bob, who is a barrister of Gray's Inn, is lucid of expression and applies his mind objectively and with sound judgement to any problems put to him. We became good friends and close colleagues.

Before I arrived at the Home Office there had recently been set up throughout the country, a series of Regional Crime Squads to combat the activities of gangs of sophisticated criminals who were carrying out their activities in various parts of the country, regardless of police boundaries. We had anticipated this in Lancashire two years previously by setting up three district crime squads superimposed on the divisional detectives, and they had proved a spectacular success. The work of the Regional Squads was co-ordinated by a senior London detective working from the Home Office but I felt that we should have someone of higher rank to give weight to his command when dealing with Chief Constables, some of whom disliked the Regional Crime Squads because they felt they were impinging on their independence, and it was this that I asked Frank Williamson to do. Roy Jenkins had also set up a Crime Prevention Committee of Industrialists with which Frank Williamson worked closely.

I had been concerned with the increase in the number of drug offences coming to the notice of the police and asked Frank Williamson to ensure that this aspect of police work was adequately covered. In 1967 only a few police forces had drug squads and I made it my business on every possible occasion to impress on Chief Constables the importance of having men specially trained and detailed for this work. Many Chief Constables were apathetic and a number told me that it was not necessary. 'We don't have a drug problem in my area,' I was often told and my reply was always that they didn't know whether they had such a problem until they detailed trained men specially for the work. In due course, I'm glad to say, all Chief Constables were persuaded to have a special squad, but it was hard going. One sequel, of course, was that in the following year the number of drug offences recorded in the annual statistics of crime showed a very great increase, and this probably greatly exaggerated the apparent increase in actual drug taking in that period.

This is the basic trouble with criminal statistics. Increased police activity tends to inflate crime statistics, and while only 50 per cent of all crime reported to the police is detected, it is dangerous to theorise about the age and type of criminals in this country. The young, the inept, and the inadequates are more likely to be caught. Until and unless we know who commits the other 50 per cent of crime that we don't detect, we cannot pontificate with accuracy on the types of people who commit crime.

Similarly, in my predecessor's time consideration was being given to the co-ordination of traffic patrols, and an experiment had been carried out in the West country to link up the work of the Traffic Patrols of several forces. Indeed, we had done much the same in the North West, for when the M6 was built as the Chief Constable of Lancashire I had agreed to work on uniform lines with my colleagues in Staffordshire and Cheshire while the Chief Constables through whose areas the first stretch of the M1 ran had made similar arrangements.

With the increase in the number of motorways and with the great increase in the number of vehicles on all the roads throughout the country even greater efforts to ensure uniformity of patrol procedures and enforcement policies were needed, it was to this problem I asked Joe Manuel to direct his attention, which he did in full measure.

I took the view that it would not be extravagant to arrange that a motorist would see and be seen by a police car every 15 miles he travelled on a motorway or a trunk road in this country, but with 9,730 miles of such roads the number of additional cars required, and especially the extra men, – would be astronomical and quite beyond our financial capacity. But in 1968, at my request, Roy Jenkins did persuade the Treasury to let us have an additional £2,000,000 to be spent by police authorities on motor vehicles, and as a result there was a considerable improvement.

In all these matters Chief Constables had to be persuaded to co-operate, for we had no power to order them to do so, and I regard it as a retrograde step that as soon as I left the Home Office, advantage was taken of the fact that Frank Williamson resigned, to move Joe Manuel back to Regional work, and responsibility for crime and traffic was given to officers of lower rank who could not carry so much weight when discussing matters with Chief Constables.

Beside the small police staff at the Home Office, there was also a plethora of civil servants. The Police Division was divided into five separate sections – it has since become increased to eight – and we worked closely with them. The work of the sections was co-ordinated by Jimmy Waddell, later Sir James Waddell, CB, a Deputy Under Secretary, who in turn was answerable to Sir Philip Allen, the Permanent Under Secretary. Technically I had the right to see Philip at any time but he was quite the most overworked man I have ever met, and I marvelled at the way in which day after day, week after week for three years he coped with his responsibilities. Apart from being the Home Secretary's right-hand man and at his beck and call all the time, no less than fifteen people had a right to knock on Philip's door, and many of them did so, while many outside the Home Office were continually asking to see him.

I therefore dealt mainly with Jimmy Waddell – though he too was a busy man, but whenever I did go to see Philip I was treated with courtesy and kindness and I always received wise and sensible advice. I had known him since 1945 when he was head of the Police Division and I had from the first the highest possible regard and affection for him. Born of strict non-conformist parents, he has always been a teetotaller and a non-smoker, but he has one vice which I find quite out of keeping with his character – a love of fast motor cars – and his Bristol was for years second in his affections only to his wife, Marjorie.

He has been responsible for much important work in many Government fields and all his many friends were delighted when he was included in the list of peers appointed by the Queen in Jim Callaghan's first Honours List – a worthy recognition of all he has done for this country.

But the Home Office is not an easy place in which to work, especially for someone of my temperament. When friends wrote to congratulate me on my appointment many of the letters contained such remarks as, 'I wonder how long you will stick it?', 'I can't imagine you working with those civil servants', 'The frustration will get you down sooner or later'. The trouble is that all those I worked with were such pleasant and courteous people that it was impossible to quarrel with them. You would argue your case, they would put their point of view and in the end say that they would think about it, but that so often was the end of the matter. Most of them were frightened to initiate policy and merely wanted to pick holes in ideas presented to them by someone else. It was like pushing against a feather bed rather than a brick wall. 'Don't do anything unless we are pushed and then do as little as possible', was the motto I read in one newspaper article criticising some action – or the lack of it – that the Home Office had taken.

On one occasion when R. A. Butler was Home Secretary I complained of the dilatory way some matter was being dealt with. 'The trouble is', he replied, 'that civil servants live their lives inside files. They don't understand life or people.' While not subscribing entirely to that view – for there are many lively civil servants who do have worldly interests – there is some truth in it.

An example – extreme perhaps – of the way the Home Office looks at matters, occurred while I was still a Chief Constable. Each year we had a three day conference of Chief Constables at some seaside resort. We were accompanied by representatives of police authorities and although quite frankly, I thought the conference a waste of time, I usually went if only to see my friends. At the end of each conference the President announced where the Executive Committee had decided that the conference would be held in two years time. On this occasion the President announced that two years hence the conference would be held in Jersey. Normally there is no discussion on this item, but on this occasion I, who was at that time not on the executive Committee, pointing out that the country was in a state of financial stringency, said that it was a great waste of public money and that I thought we should place the Home Secretary in an impossible position if questions were asked about it in the House.

The President replied that he had approached the Home Office Office who had not raised any objections and as I gained no support for my opposition, the proposal was agreed.

However, the Executive Committee had second thoughts and when we next met, we learnt that they had changed the venue to somewhere more central, and had so informed the Home Office. The Secretary then read out the classic reply from the Home Office, signed by an Assistant Secretary, that 'if the Chief Constables decided not to hold their conference in Jersey, the Home Office would not object.'

Philip Allen had only three deputies to assist him, while the present Permanent Under Secretary has five but in my view the Home Office has responsibility for too many subjects, many of them of an entirely different nature. They have on the one hand responsibility in one form or another for the manned services such as police, fire, prisons, immigration, children's officers and probation officers, while on the other hand they are responsible for policy matters relating to the Government of the Isle of Man and the Channel Islands, the Royal prerogative, the relationship between the Crown and the people, the Wild Birds Protection Acts, the Gaming Board, the Tote Board and so on, to name but a selection.

During the War, under the general control of the Home Secretary, we had two departments each with its own Permanent Under Secretary of State – the Home Office and the Department of Home Security. In peace time too I feel that we need a Department of Public Safety-or call it what you will – to look after the manned services, in addition to the Home Office proper to look after the more esoteric matters where policy decisions are required.

Although the Royal Commission had in its report of 1962 recommended the re-organisation of the Police Service into a smaller number of larger forces, successive Home Secretaries had avoided the issue and it was not until May, 1966, while I was in New Zealand, that I heard over the radio that Roy Jenkins had announced the Government's intentions to implement this part of the report, namely to reduce the number of separate police forces in England and Wales from 117 to 49. There was a great resistance to these proposals from local authorities and very few of the proposed amalgamations were accepted without a fight. The Act allowed for a public hearing to hear objections and much time and public money was expended in preparing for these hearings. The whole process had already started when I arrived at the Home Office and my colleagues were much occupied in preparing the evidence that they had to give to support the proposals. I did not, myself have to give evidence at any inquiry, but, of course, I was much consulted and read all the documents. Of all the inquiries held, the proposal to amalgamate almost all the County Borough Forces in Lancashire with the Lancashire Constabulary was much the biggest and took the longest time. While greatly in favour of this, I felt at the same time that much of the work of police re-organisation would be undone after a few years when Local Government was re-organised, and this I pointed out to the Home Secretary. We agreed, however, that the police re-organisation could not wait and so it happened that Lancashire suffered two police re-shuffles in the space of three years.

On the whole, however, the amalgamations went ahead successfully. When I went to the Home Office in 1967, there were 125 provincial police forces in England and Wales. When I left there were only 41. In 1967 only 4 forces had more than 2,000 men, while 68 had less than 500. Today no force has less than 800 men, all but 7 have over 1,000 and 18 have over 2,000 men.

There was no doubt in my mind that the Lancashire Constabulary was too big a unit to be really efficient. Apart from the complication caused by having sixteen separate independent urban police forces in the County, having an organisation comprised of over four thousand people makes it very difficult, if not impossible, for one person really to know or be known by his men. On average I dictated no less then 5,000 letters and memoranda a year and was in London several days a month and all this prevented me from visiting the stations and the men as much as I should have done.

When I gave evidence before the Royal Commission, I said that I believed Durham, with its 1,500 men, was the ideal command. It was a large enough unit to be able to afford the sophisticated equipment required by any Force, while the base of the pyramid was wide enough to give satisfactory promotion prospects to ambitious men, and in a Force of that size one could pick young men of potential for accelerated promotion without causing too much apprehension or jealousy among the older men.

Although I have long been an advocate of the nationalisation of the Police, I always envisaged that one would break up the whole into manageable commands, ideally with some 1,500 men in each unit, giving the unit commander virtually independent control within certain defined parameters: but with the spread of population being what it is, however, one cannot always realise this, for such urban areas as Birmingham and Manchester must be treated as a whole. I would not, however, have gone so far as to make the whole of the West Midlands or the Greater Manchester area one police unit. In my view by so doing the pendulum has swung too far.

The Home Office

One of the main responsibilities of the Chief Inspector of Constabulary is to keep an eye on the Police College. The College is administered by a Board of Governors under the Chairmanship of the Permanent Under-Secretary of State and on the Board sit representatives of local authoritities and of the three constituent negotiating bodies of the Police Service, the Association of Chief Police Officers, the Superintendents' Association and the Police Federation representing the lower ranks, in addition to the Commissioner of Police of the Metropolis and the Chief Inspector of Constabulary. This body is responsible for the general policy, for the provision of funds and for the appointment of the Commandant and his Deputy.

The day-to-day running of the College is in the hands of the Commandant who is responsible to an Advisory Committee of which the Chief Inspector is Chairman, the members all being policemen of various ranks.

The College was started in June 1948 almost ten years after the demise of the Metropolitan Police College, and its first home was a series of converted workers' hostels at Ryton-on-Dunsmore, near Coventry. In 1953 the Home Office bought Bramshill, a fine Jacobean mansion made into a Royal Palace in 1611 by James the 1st for his ill-fated son, Henry, Prince of Wales, elder brother of Charles the 1st. After certain new buildings had been constructed, the College moved there in October 1960.

Although most people in the Police Service thought this to be a wonderful move, I was and still am, critical of it. In the first place the adaptation of old houses for institutional use is never entirely satisfactory: there is much wasted space and the upkeep of old buildings is very expensive. Secondly, it is in the wrong place, for it is difficult to reach except by car as it is in an isolated area some distance from a railway station, while it is in the southern part of the country, whereas most provincial policemen come from the North or the Midlands. In consequence this means a long journey for men to get home for weekends, and because of the ages of the men at the College most are married and want to see their wives. My third objection is that the new buildings were not well sited. For example, I consider it unfortunate that the residential block for the female domestic staff lies between the classroom block and the students' residential block.

It would have been much better to have struggled on in the temporary accommodation of the college's first home until purpose-built accommodation, such as the Fire Service now have at Moreton-in-Marsh, could have been constructed in the West Midlands close to a good railway station and near to the main motorways.

However, there it is and there it will remain, and the Police Service is proud of it.

When I went to the Home Office we wanted a number of additional buildings to accommodate all the additional courses that it was decided to hold at the college, but the most serious problem that the Commandant and his staff had to cope with was the lack of indoor accommodation for recreational purposes. I was determined to ensure that something was provided to remedy this, and I badgered everyone concerned until the money was allocated, the plans drawn up, and a really good sports hall built. This was completed soon after I left the Service and I shall always feel that it is the one major permanent constructive contribution I made to the College, though the swimming pool which was designed to join on to the sports hall is still, alas, only on the drawing board.

The original idea of the College was to ensure that every Sergeant to be promoted to the rank of Inspector should have a six months' course to fit him for his responsibilites as an officer in the police service with all that means, not only in technical knowledge but, just as important, in responsbility for looking after the men serving under him. The trouble at Ryton-on-Dunsmore and at Bramshill has always been the inadequacy of accommodation for all Inspectors, to attend the college either on or shortly after promotion. In 1966 it was calculated that some 650 Inspectors were made each year a number which was likely to increase and did so formidably each year as forces filled their new establishments. A recent Working Party Report of the Association of Chief Police Officers revealed how the situation has since worsened. It said in the starkest terms:

> 'More recently, attempts have been made to provide Police College training for Inspectors on a universal basis, initially through the opening of a detached training wing of the College and later by reducing the duration of the College course from six to four and then to three months, so as to obtain a higher through-put of students at the College. In spite of these measures and of the building of additional accommodation it has never been possible to provide College training for all Inspectors and the present situation is that there are, throughout the country, a total of 977 Inspectors who have had no training in relation to their rank.
>
> The situation in future years is certain to be very much worse. The Police College, providing four courses for 140 Inspectors each during 1977, can provide training for 560 officers. Requests for places on the Inspectors' Courses during the year already total 930 so that in addition to the 977 untrained Inspectors currently serving, another 370 may take up their duties without training for the responsibilities of their rank'.

The selection of those to go was left in the hands of individual Chief Constables and those not selected felt aggrieved, for they considered that their chances of further promotion were prejudiced.

It was soon realised that men selected for College training were going there too late in life, for the average age was in the middle thirties, so a Special Course of one year's duration for bright young men who had passed the examinations for promotion to Inspector was introduced, while additional shorter courses, then known as Junior and Senior Command Courses, were started. All this is to the good, but I personally have felt it wrong that all these courses should take place in the same series of buildings, and not only has it added greatly to the burden of the Commandant, but it has considerably reduced the accommodation available for Sergeants about to be promoted to the rank of Inspector.

I therefore proposed that we should start a subsidiary College in spare accommodation at a Recruit Training Centre at Dishforth in Yorkshire, and this was agreed. It was not ideal but it was better than nothing, and would, I hoped, fill a gap until enough accommodation could be found for all Sergeants to be trained together. Alas, after I left, Dishforth was closed down and no other solution to the problem has yet been found.

The Advisory committee, of which I was Chairman, is responsible for choosing all the Instructional staff except the Commandant and his Deputy. Over this, we took great trouble for the whole atmosphere depended on having the right staff, not only technically good, but men of sound integrity, inquiring minds and the ability to impart qualities of leadership.

The same considerations apply in selecting the Commandant, but the Board of Governors has to select the best man who applies and, as many regard it as a dead-end job, the selection is usually limited. The Commandant of the Police College should be a man of the best potential in the Police Service: he should be selected from among those that are likely to be Commissioner of Police or the Chief Inspector of Constabulary in a few years' time. If we had a national police force such a man could be selected and nominated, but in the circumstances this is not possible. As a consequence some Commandants have been mediocre, but this is a generalization of which there are important exceptions. For example, both John Alderson, the present Chief Constable of Devon and Cornwall, and Colin Woods, the present Chief Inspector of Constabulary, were highly successful commandants before they achieved their present positions.

But in-service training for the potential top rankers is not enough, and knowing how much I benefited from my year at the Imperial Defence College, I persuaded the Home Office to arrange that another Chief Constable should go there in 1968, and now a regular scheme of nomination has been agreed. Furthermore, I also arranged for officers of ranks below that of Chief Constable to go to the Joint Services Staff College.

Knowing too what value it had been to me to visit police forces overseas, and being unable to get the money from the Treasury, I approached my Cambridge friend, Marcus Sieff, as a result of which the firm of Marks and Spencers provided a sum of £1,000 a year for seven years to allow a police officer of potential to go on an extended visit abroad. It is good to know that the firm has recently undertaken to provide the same amount for a further seven years.

Policemen tend to come from narrow and circumscribed backgrounds, and if they are to be good leaders in the future, the more they are able to mix with others outside the Service, the better for them and the better for the men they lead.

Though I was careful not to interfere with my colleagues in the field, I did make it my business during the three years I was at the Home Office to visit at least once every police headquarters and training school in England and Wales. This gave me an opportunity to know not only Chief Constables but also their senior officers, for it is an important part of the Chief Inspector's duties to advise the Home Secretary on the future leaders of the Service.

The appointment of a Chief Constable is a matter for the local Police Committee, but the Home Secretary has to confirm the appointment and he has the right to refuse. To my knowledge only once this century has the Home Secretary taken such a course.

When a vacancy occurs, the local Police Authority advertises the appointment and the Home Office tries to persuade the Authority to send them a full list of those that apply and those that they propose to interview. The Home Office then lets it be known whether there is anyone on the short list that would be unacceptable to the Home Secretary. The trouble in the old days was that Police Authorities, particularly in small Borough Forces, tended to appoint the Deputy, for he was someone they knew and someone they could control. This was bad for the Force and bad for the men. As someone once said, 'If you appoint the Deputy, he only carries on the bad habits of his predecessor, and introduces his own bad habits on top.' This criticism does not apply, of course, where someone is brought in from outside as Deputy to give him a chance to become acquainted with the problems before he takes command.

The Home Office has now, I'm glad to say, introduced a rule that no-one can be appointed Chief Constable of any Force in which he has spent the whole of his service. But to my mind even this is not enough, and we shall not have a really efficient service until the appointment of Chief Constables is entirely in the hands of the

The Home Office

Home Secretary, who should act to a great extent on the advice of the Inspectors of Constabulary. If this ever becomes so, then one will be able properly to groom potential leaders, and by moving them around, test their capabilities and ensure that those at the top are the best we have. As it is, I can think of at least two Chief Constables who are not as good as men who were on the short list with them. It is often a matter of luck and how the interviews go on the day which man is selected.

When visiting Training Schools, apart from formal occasions when as Chief Inspector I was invited to take passing-out parades, I tried as often as I could to lecture to recruits on the responsibilities of their office. When doing so, I always used to emphasise that a policeman could always be honest, he could always be courteous, he could always be fair, but he could not always be right, and that if he had made a mistake he must realise that it is in his own interest as well as that of the Service that he should admit it. If a a man owns up immediately to having made a mistake, everyone will help him remedy the affair, but so often for a variety of reasons, a man knowing he has made a mistake will try to lie his way out of it. Nothing is more annoying to a Chief Constable than to be faced with a situation where it is clear that the policeman is lying, and it is my experience that policemen are usually bad liars.

In addition to lecturing to police officers, I received many invitations to speak to organisations or bodies of citizens who wished to know more about policemen and the service they were giving to the community. When I did, the general theme I sang may be summed up in the precepts that I included in the first chapter of the report written in 1971 for the Government of Victoria, Australia after my inspection of the Force.

'The Community has the right to demand a Police Force which is comprised of men and women:
  (a) Who are of complete integrity and who conduct themselves as good citizens when off as well as on duty.
  (b) Who are at all times courteous in their dealings with the public. Courtesy and firmness are not incompatible.
  (c) Who are enthusiastic and hardworking and who devote the whole of their energies to police work.
  (d) Who are properly trained in the techniques of their job.
  (e) Who are aware that their work is a vocation in which service to the community gives satisfaction in itself.

In return, each member of the Police Service has the right to expect from the community:
  (a) Adequate remuneration so that he and his family can live comfortably,

in that section of society to which they belong, without getting into debt and without having to take other work.
(b) Adequate training facilities.
(c) Adequate buildings and equipment.
(d) Well maintained houses in which to live when required to occupy police premises.
(e) Sensible laws to administer.
(f) The support of the courts, and judicial procedures that do not hinder the course of justice.
(g) Full support from those in authority, from the Press, Radio and T.V., and from all honest members of the community in those difficult and often dangerous tasks that it is the duty of the Police to carry out.

As part of man-management and especially for those being considered for promotion, it is desirable that a written annual report on each officer should be prepared and submitted to headquarters by the man's immediate superior officers. They are the ones who know him best and who have seen him throughout the year dealing not only with the routine work but operating in an emergency and working under conditions of tension and stress. From time to time there is discussion whether these reports should be seen by the man concerned or whether their confidentiality should be preserved. I personally have always been of the opinion that they should not be shown to the man himself. Defects in character are of two kinds; those that an individual can remedy and those that he cannot.

If you think that a man is lazy or tactless, does not always tell the truth, or is brash and conceited, you can point this out and he can, if he so desires, mend his ways. If on the other hand he has no sense of humour or is a bore, or has unfortunately married the wrong girl who would be a hindrance to him if he was promoted to a position of command, it is no good telling the man, because he cannot do anything about it, and the fact that this has prevented his promotion would embitter him for all time.

The problem of the person with no sense of humour is, to my mind, the most difficult, because if you tell a man of that defect, he just does not understand what you mean, and you cannot explain. It is, of course, arguable that even without a sense of humour one can still command men – and I suspect that one very eminent senior officer in World War II suffered from that defect of character - but generally speaking it has been my experience that men who have no sense of humour do not run a happy ship.

Assessment of another man's character should always be as objective as possible, but human nature being what it is, subjective judgements inevitably creep in and from time to time there is a clamour for men to be allowed to see their reports.

'My Superintendent has got a down on me,' was the usual cry. My answer to this was always to offer the man a move to a new division where he would have fresh officers to observe his work and to report on him in the following year. Sometimes, but only rarely, was the offer accepted.

Whenever a report was submitted which was critical of some characteristic that the man could remedy, I refused to accept it unless the person making the criticism stated that he had told the officer of his opinion; so often supervisory officers hoping to gain popularity, do not have the mental strength to criticise men to their faces.

It is an important part of a Chief Constable's duties not only to select the right men for promotion but also to ensure that they receive the right training for their new responsibilities. This is especially important in the case of men promoted to the rank of Sergeant, for this would be their first experience of man management.

The whole tenor of my talks with them used to be that they must not only keep themselves technically competent, but, as we had been taught at Hendon, they must also at all times look after their men. I used to remind them that when a man was selected for the Police Service he was almost certainly a good man for great care was taken in our selections, and that if we made a mistake, then poor material could be weeded out in the probationary stage. So if things went wrong early in a man's service, it was probably due to bad leadership or at any rate lack of good leadership. But as men grow older life does not treat everyone equally or necessarily fairly. For some men, their health deteriorate, others marry the wrong girl, some have mentally or physically disabled children, some start to drink and some become infatuated with the girl in the shop on the corner. A good leader must get to know his men and appreciate their strengths and weaknesses. He must be ready to praise, to advise, to encourage, to cajole, to warn and if necessary, to bite. I used to advise them not to try to be popular, but to try to be respected and to be fair. If they were that, then with a bit of luck, popularity would come.

In my own dealings with my men, I used to try at all times to carry out these ideals. I have never tried to be popular, but always to be fair. There is a story that Thomas Arnold, the great Headmaster of Rugby, said that the greatest compliment ever paid him was when a boy said of him, 'He's a beast – but he is a just beast.'

In his dealings with the men under his command a Chief Constable has in the last resort to exercise his disciplinary authority, and in the twenty seven years I was Chief Constable I suppose I've sat in judgement in some two hundred cases where allegations were made of misconduct not amounting to criminal conduct. These cases take a great deal of time and cause a great deal of hard thinking, first to decide whether the man is guilty of the offence – and he usually is, though sometimes the evidence is too thin – and when convicted, to decide what the punishment should be. One can at the worst dismiss the man from the Service, or at the other end of the scale, merely caution him. In between one can reduce in rank, reduce in pay for a stipulated period, fine or reprimand. I always took the line that one had either to be very tough or very lenient. Sometimes the offence was such that the man had either to leave the Service or be reduced in rank, but generally if it was the first time the man had appeared before me, I would let him off with a warning that if he offended again he would be for the high jump. For most men this was enough. It was, I feel, important that a man should not go through life feeling that he had been unfairly or too harshly dealt with.

Every man who has been punished has the right to appeal to the Home Secretary if he so desires, and the Chief Inspector has to advise whether the appeal should be allowed or dismissed, or, in particularly difficult cases, whether an appeal tribunal should be set up to rehear the whole case. Such cases always present problems for on the one hand one has to be fair to the man, but on the other one wants to support Chief Constables in the difficult and lonely decisions that they have to take.

All the way through this book I have spoken of men, but of course, that includes women, for they have in the past twenty years played an increasingly important part in our police work. I had only two elderly women police in Oxfordshire and there were none in Durham when I arrived, but twenty when I left. Although there were a few in Lancashire in 1950 they were all in plain clothes and mostly used only as clerks in offices, but by the time I left we had one of the largest and most efficient units in the country outside London.

The great contribution made by women was due mainly to the enthusiasm and drive of Miss Barbara M. Denis de Vitre, OBE, who in May 1948 was appointed an Assistant Inspector of Constabulary at the Home Office. Her pioneering work was carried on after her early and untimely death in 1960 by Miss K. M. Hill, OBE, and later by a Scotswoman, Miss Jessie Law, MBE, who was a most efficient and popular member of the Inspectorate staff throughout the time that I was at the Home Office.

I have always been a strong supporter of the women police, and from the start I encouraged them to play as full a part in our work as possible, but in recruiting girls, however, I insisted that we should select feminine girls rather than 'collar and tie' types. What one wants from a woman is the feminine point of view and intuition. The disadvantage of selecting the feminine type of woman is that they usually get married after a short while, so there is a big turn-over and this is expensive in terms of one's training budget; but all is not lost for they usually marry policemen, and make good wives, for they understand the difficulties of a policeman's life with its unsocial and often uncertain hours of duty.

No account of the work of a Chief of Police would be complete without mention of his association with the Police Federation. Following the police strike of 1918 and 1919, the Police Act which was quickly passed by Parliament made it an offence for any police officer to belong to a Trade Union, but realising that the lower ranks must have some method of representing to higher authority any grievance they may have, the Act provided for the establishment of a Police Federation to which all officers of the rank of Constable, Sergeant and Inspector automatically belong. Through the years, and particularly since 1945, the Federation has become a powerful voice- – some think too powerful – in the world of police politics. Though I have always been a strong supporter of the work of the Federation, I have not, of course, always agreed with their point of view, and I am on record as being critical of their organisation. In my written evidence to the Royal Commission I said:

> 'In my view it is quite wrong that officers of the rank of Inspector should be members of the Police Federation. We do not have in the Police Service, as they have in the Armed Forces of the Crown, a clear distinction between commissioned officers and non-commissioned officers, but if there is to be a line drawn between those who are similar to commissioned officers and those who are not, the line would be drawn between those holding the rank of Sergeant and those holding the rank of Inspector.
>
> Those who hold the rank of Inspector and above are not only police officers but also Officers of the Police Service. Inspectors are, to a great extent, the eyes and ears of the Chief Constable, and with the Super-intendents, help him to formulate the policy of the Force. When the policy has been determined, they explain the policy to the men and ensure on behalf of the Chief Constable that it is carried out.
>
> It is, to my mind, wrong that the occasion should ever occur that there should be a Joint Branch Board resolution to the Chief Constable or to the Police Authority, for if the Inspectors are doing their job properly, they should have brought to the notice of the Chief Constable any matter which in their view requires remedying or altering to further the efficiency or welfare of the Force, before it has reached the stage of

being discussed by the Constables and Sergeants and any resolutions passed.

If the matter has, to their knowledge, been considered by the Chief Constable and rejected by him, they should not join with the Sergeants and the Constables in making any further representations on the matter, though of course, it would be open to them as Inspectors to make separate representations if they wished the matter to be reconsidered by the Chief Constable.

My own view is that there should continue to be three separate bodies to make representations when necessary to the Home Office or to the Police Authority on police matters. These should be:
(i) The Association of Chief Police Officers.
(ii) An Officers' Association.
(iii) The Police Federation.

The Association of Chief Police Officers should remain as it is, while the Officers Association should consist of all Officers of the rank of Chief Superintendent, Superintendent, Chief Inspector and Inspector. The Police Federation would then consist of officers of the rank of Sergeant and Constable.'

However, these views were not accepted either by the Commission nor for that matter by my colleagues, and one must accept the position as it is.

While a Chief Constable, therefore, I encouraged the best men in the lower ranks to take an active part in the work of the Federation, which would have been more difficult to handle if the local committees consisted solely or mainly of any rebellious hotheads one had in the Force. Actually, in all three forces that I have commanded I had a committee of sensible, intelligent and reasonable men to deal with, and most Chief Constables would say the same.

At the Headquarters of the Police Federation in Surbiton are to be found good men, either serving police officers specially seconded for the work, or men who have retired from the Police Service to undertake this work. While I was at the Home Office, the Federation and the Police Service had the good fortune to have as Secretary of the Federation Sergeant Dick Pamplin, a man who was strong minded, intelligent, articulate and an able negotiator. As in Trade Unions, the Secretary in many ways is more important than the Chairmen, for the latter come and go, while the Secretary remains. I like to feel that while at the Home Office I had a close relationship with Dick Pamplin, for he was a man whom I greatly liked and much respected, and it was a sad day for the Police Service, but not a surprise, when he left for wider fields on a higher level.

Another man who behind the scenes was and I believe, still is of considerable influence in Police Federation policies, is Tony

The Home Office

Judge, the Editor of the Police Federation Journal, *Police*. He was at one time a constable in the Blackpool Police and a thorn in the side of his local Chief Constable though I suspect that Judge was usually right. He then left the Police Service to work as a fulltime employee for the Federation. He has been an unsuccessful Labour candidate for Parliament and until May 1977 when the Conservatives regained control of the greater London council, was a hardworking Chairman of the Housing Committee. He started *Police* and through articles he has written he greatly influenced the thinking of policemen throughout the country on matters relating to their conditions of service. While I don't like the way in which he sometimes expresses his view, I nevertheless like the man: I respect him and I find myself usually in agreement with the stand he takes.

Generally, I sympathised with the aims of the Police Federation and on many matters of detail supported their claims for improvements in conditions of service, though I am glad to say that I was never involved with arguments over pay for that is a matter for the Police Council of which I was never a member. The Police Council consists on the one hand of representatives of the Home Office and representatives of local authorities for they represent the employers or paying authorities, and on the other hand are representatives of the Chiefs of Police, the Superintendents and the Police Federation. It has never been, in my view, a satisfactory piece of negotiating machinery and I was not surprised when in 1976, the Police Federation withdrew.

This is, of course, one disadvantage of having an organisation where responsibility is shared between central and local government. It would be much better if the police in negotiating their pay claims had to deal with one or the other but not both at the same time. I am quite sure that on the employers' side, each section is unwilling to accede the police claims because of the effect it will have on its relations with the other half: 'Don't give way to the Police', say central government 'because it will affect our negotiations with the Prison Officers next week.' 'Don't give way to the Police,' say local government representatives, 'because it will affect our negotiations with the dustmen next week.'

Again there are separate negotiations for the pay of the lower ranks, for Superintendents, and for Chiefs of Police, and this all takes time and leads to frustrations, while Local Authority representatives when considering the pay of Chief Constables have regard to the pay they give to chief local government officers.

Once every so often it is announced that there is to be an increase in pay for everyone in the Armed Services from Admirals, Generals and Air Chief Marshals at the top, down to the lowest ranks in each

Service. How much better it would be if it could be the same for the Police Service. Here is another argument for a National Police Service.

On one matter only do I feel that the Police Federation has been consistently wrong through the years, for in their resistance to the idea of accelerated promotion for young men of potential, they have done a disservice to the Police.

Ever since Lord Trenchard introduced the idea of direct entrants to the rank of Inspector, the Police Federation have resolutely opposed any special inducements to men of good education and wider backgrounds to join the Police. In the nineteen thirties the attitude of the lower ranks and indeed of many Chief Constables too, was that promotion should only come to men who have proved themselves by long years on the beat, or in one of the specialised departments, to be trustworthy and experienced. It was generally accepted that a man would reach the age of thirty five or forty before gaining his first promotion though there were, occasionally, a very few exceptions.

Slowly but surely, more progressive administrators have persuaded the Federation members to realise that they must move with the times, especially now that so many more have the advantage of a University education. If we are to produce all our own leaders in the future we must encourage men of good education to join the police and ambitious men will not do so unless they can see themselves in a position of some authority and earning good money within a comparatively short space of time.

When I went to the Home Office in 1967, a man still had to serve for five years as a Constable before being eligible for promotion to the rank of Sergeant. One of the many good things that Roy Jenkins did as Home Secretary was, in 1968, to persuade the Police Federation to agree to reduce the minimum period to two years, though it is rare even today to find a man promoted to Sergeant under five or six years, and most have to wait much longer. One must learn the art of man-management at an early age before one becomes set in one's ways.

We also persuaded the Police Federation to agree to the introduction of a scheme allowing University undergraduates carefully selected on a national basis to join the Police with an undertaking that, if they received favourable reports on their proficiency and passed the necessary examinations, they would be sent to the Police College at an early date. In the first year of the scheme ninety eight graduates and undergraduates in their final year applied. Of the fourteen selected, eight wanted to join the Metropolitan Police and the remaining six applied to join different forces in the provinces.

The selection procedure was in three stages: the applicants were first offered an interview with the Chief Constable of the Force they wished to join: the forty seven survivors were then put through three days of further interviews and tests by a board of Chief Constables and outside experts in personnel selection and the Board then made recommendations to a final Selection Board chaired by myself and including representatives of the Police Federation and the Superintendents' Association. All this was undoubtedly an encouragement and a major reform in the Police Service, though so far the results have not been as good as hoped.

Industry is becoming much more interested in recruiting men who have served in the Army for three years on a short Service Commission, and I tried unsuccessfully to persuade the Police Federation to agree to the University Scheme to be extended to include men with this valuable experience.

A man who has held a short service commission has learnt self-discipline, is physically fit, has learnt to command men and has almost certainly served abroad, thus broadening his outlook on life. All these are attributes which could be put to good use in the police, and none of these qualities are taught to University graduates, for University life moulds a person in quite a different way. But the Federation would have none of it, and without their support I knew that it was hopeless to put forward such a scheme formally.

The strength of the Federation lies not only in their members but in the fact that through their organisation they speak with one voice, while ever since Chuter Ede's day they have increasingly had the ear of successive Home Secretaries, and Home Office officials have tended to be more influenced by them than by Chief Officers of Police. It is somewhat ironical that the only Home Secretary ever strongly to stand up to the Federation was their own one-time Police Adviser, Jim Callaghan.

The Chief Officers have their own organisation, the Association of Chief Police Officers, but their President is an annual appointment, and whereas the Chairman and Secretary of the Federation are quick to give their views to the media and to appear on television, Chief Constables have not in the same way been able to speak with a united voice, for they tend to be individualistic and, because of their more responsible position, have been more reluctant to state their views in public.

Thus the views of the Federation have in the public opinion become the views of the Service, though this has to some extent been counteracted in recent years by the expressed views of Sir Robert Mark. One of the great contributions he has made to the Police Service is that he has never been afraid to speak openly and fearlessly on matters about which he feels strongly, but he has spoken as an individual, and not as the chosen voice of the Chief Officers.

One matter in which I interested myself as soon as I arrived at the Home Office, was the question of honours for members of the Police Service. Whatever one may think of the value of the Honours List, I had felt for a long time that the police as a whole has not had their fair share of recognition though all the time I was in Lancashire I was continually recommending men and women for inclusion, and some ten officers did receive honours of one degree or another in the seventeen years I was there.

The position at the Home Office is that the Police Service automatically, on the recommendation of the Home Secretary, receives in each Honours List a certain number of Queen's Police Medals for Distinguished Service. In addition, we could recommend for the consideration of the Honours Selection Committee a few officers for Orders in the British Empire List.

Immediately after the publication of one list the Inspectors of Constabulary meet to consider whom they should recommend for inclusion in the next list, for it takes some four months for lists to percolate upwards through the various filters in the machine.

I had a survey made of the Honours received by the Police and by the Royal Navy in each of the three years, 1964, 1965 and 1966, and I submitted a memorandum pointing out that whereas the Police Service in England and Wales was now numerically larger than the Royal Navy, the Police had an average of 22 names in each list, including Queen's Police Medals, while the Royal Navy had an average of 85. I pointed out, furthermore, that whereas the Police were lucky to get one knighthood every two years, the Navy had four or five in each list, and moreover that whereas the senior Naval awards were in the various Orders of Chivalry, the Police were almost always only single knighthoods.

In due course I received the inevitable civil servant's reply. Yes, it was agreed that the Navy had in the past got more awards than the Police. In due course they would get a smaller number of awards. This was not, of course, at all what I wanted and I discussed the matter with Philip Allen where I found a sympathetic ear, though he warned me that he would not have an easy passage in the appropriate Committee.

There were two further matters that I felt needed putting right. The Chief Constables of most of the larger forces had been awarded the CBE, but of the Inspectorate only one other colleague beside myself had received that honour. I pointed out that had they remained Chief Constables some of them would have had their CBE's long ago, but because they had become civil servants – as HMI's are classed – they came on the Home Office List and had to take their chance and their turn with all civil servants in the Home Office. They had to inspect forces, talk to Chairmen of Police Authorities and give advice to Chief Constables who were higher up the pecking order in the Honours world, and this could cause embarrassment and criticism.

The third problem affecting Honours that I persuaded the Home Office to deal with, was the right of any officer holding the Queen's Police Medal to put the initials, QPM, after his name. This is technically known as wearing 'post-nominals.'

I found that there was an old file on this matter in the Home Office archives and that the matter had been first raised in the days of the Indian Police. Questions had been asked by MPs in the House from time to time, but for reasons that were not at all clear the Home Office and the Colonial Office had steadfastly refused to agree, so I asked Philip to take this matter up again.

Philip Allen saw the point of my arguments and promised to help. He was as good as his word for the number of awards to the Police in each list was increased to over thirty – still, in my view, not enough, but better than it was. All the HMIs received a CBE, though this took longer than I would have wished, while the use of post-nominals has been allowed since 1968.

Lastly, a matter that was in our own hands. I ensured that every Chief Constable who did not have a QPM when I went to the Home Office was awarded one within the next two years. On recommendations for awards for gallantry for police officers, the Chief Inspector is always consulted, and I studied the files with care and usually was able to support the recommendations made.

In the middle of 1967 the economic situation in the country took a turn for the worse and in November of that year the pound had to be devalued. Jim Callaghan felt that he could no longer remain Chancellor of the Exchequer and in December Roy Jenkins went to the Treasury and Jim Callaghan took his place at the Home Office.

On the surface these changes made no difference to me for I doubt whether I had seen the Home Secretary more than ten times since I arrived in Whitehall, but I was sorry to see Roy Jenkins go, for I knew him to be a staunch supporter and that if necessity required I could at any time have gone to him for help and wise advice. At the same time I knew and respected Jim Callaghan and felt that with his background knowledge of the Police he could be of great assistance to us. In fact only a few months before the changeover I had been with him at a small private dinner party given by the Chairman of the Police Federation, when we had discussed a number of police organisational problems and although he must at the time have been seriously preoccupied with the nation's financial difficulties, he gave us wise and sensible advice.

Soon after he arrived at the Home Office I had several meetings with him, but I found myself for some unaccountable reason ill at ease and I came away from each meeting with a slight feeling that I did not have his confidence, though I could not put my finger on on the trouble.

In March, 1968, Joe Simpson, the Commissioner died suddenly, and immediately after his impressive funeral in Westminster Abbey, the Home Secretary sent for me to discuss whom he should appoint as his successor. I mentioned the names of two provincial Chief Constables, and we discussed their merits. We also discussed the claims of Jack Waldron, the Deputy Commissioner, who was a great friend of mine and formerly my Assistant in Lancashire. I knew Jack had considerable private means, that he had a sick wife, and he had told me he intended to resign in the following year when Joe Simpson, had he lived, would have done so. I told the Home Secretary of this, and summonsed up the courage to say, 'But I hope you will send me there'. When he inquired why he should do that I replied that I knew there was a big job to be done there, particularly in re-organising the CID, and in improving relations with the Press, and although Joe Simpson was a man I much admired and that he had been very popular, he had been there too long and was over-tired, while the situation needed correcting before it was too late. I said I felt I could tackle these problems successfully and I much wanted to do so, adding that it was a bigger job than I now had. The Home Secretary replied that I now had a big job, and that it was up to me to make it even more important. 'No', he said, somewhat abruptly, 'I'm not going to send you there. Let us talk about the others.' I decided that it was unwise to tell him of Roy Jenkins's statement to me before I started work at the Home Office, and when the discussion ended I left his office with a heavy heart and with leaden feet.

Within a few days the announcement was made that Jack Waldron had been appointed Commissioner and Bob Mark was to be his Deputy.

I had, of course, known Bob Mark for some time. He was a Sergeant in Manchester in the year when I became Chief Constable of Lancashire, but I did not meet him until he became Chief Constable of Leicester in 1957. Three years later he first hit the headlines for the way in which he had organised his traffic wardens to assist rather than to prosecute the motorists, and he wrote two articles for *The Guardian*, in which he first started to ride his hobby horse that too many guilty people were being acquitted of charges of crime because of the processes of law. These articles impressed Roy Jenkins and in 1967 he was appointed an Assistant Commissioner of the Metropolitan Police. This was resented by most of the senior officers, though I have a letter from Joe Simpson in which he said that he would give Bob Mark every opportunity to prove his worth.

Besides Jack Waldron at New Scotland Yard there was also Peter Brodie, Assistant Commissioner, (Crime), who had joined the Metropolitan Police as a constable before being selected for the Hendon Police College, where he and I were fellow students. Since 1949 he had been a very successful Chief Constable of Stirlingshire and Clackmannanshire and later of Warwickshire before becoming an Inspector of Constabulary in 1963. Three years later he returned to the Metropolitan Police. The three of us had grown up together in the Police Service and as I knew them both so well, although the Chief Inspector of Constabulary had no responsibility for the Metropolitan Police, I looked forward to a close and happy association with them. But alas, it was not to be. Peter greatly resented the appointment of Bob Mark to Deputy over his head and Bob I know had a most difficult three years when he was to a great extent ostracised by the hierarchy at Scotland Yard. I was entirely sympathetic to him and said so: so I too was out of favour.

The real rift, however, came over the allegation of corruption in the CID in the Metropolitan Police. Even before I left Lancashire, my senior detectives told me how unhappy they were with certain of the senior London detectives, but it was all supposition and there was no evidence. I had to be careful what I said when I was at the Home Office, partly because I had no responsibility in the matter and partly because it could be said that it was a case of sour grapes on the grounds that I had not been made Commissioner. I did tackle Jack Waldron on the subject but he took the view that even if there was any corruption it was of a minor nature and anyway in a Force the size of the Metropolitan Police there was bound to be some, while Peter Brodie more or less refused to discuss the matter with me.

Things came to a head in 1969 when *The Times* published a story that two of their reporters had evidence of corruption in the Metropolitan Police, and the Commissioner undertook to have the matter investigated. I recommended that some senior provincial detectives should be put in charge, but the Commissioner would not agree and the Home Secretary supported him. Then without consulting me – as I feel he should have done – Jim Callaghan sent for Frank Williamson, one of my staff, and told him that he wanted him to monitor the investigation. This was clearly unsatisfactory for Frank

Williamson had responsibility but no power, and with hindsight I now realise I should have asked to see the Home Secretary and tried to persuade him either to put Frank in direct charge of the investigation, or that he should be allowed to withdraw. But as the Home Secretary had not sent for me in the first place, I felt he had lost confidence in me and I did not think that any intervention on my part would have helped.

The investigations dragged on, with no satisfactory ending while I was as the Home Office, and in December 1971 Frank Williamson resigned, mainly because of the way the matter was dealt with.

In any case at the time that the Home Secretary saw Frank Williamson I was having my own personal troubles and this, I am sure, clouded my judgement.

While we were in Lancashire, life was a very busy one with many evening engagements as well as full days in the office, in addition to which very frequent visits to London as well as visits abroad occupied so much time that my home life was sadly neglected. As a result of all this my wife and I grew further and further apart.

I had so hoped that when we moved to London and there would be very few engagements outside office hours, we should be able to make a fresh start. However it was not to be, and when in 1969 our youngest child, Harriet, was old enough to stand on her own feet, we separated. I was divorced and subsequently re-married. This was, in the event, a catastrophic error.

I consulted two members of the House of Lords – both Privy Councillors – and though they thought it unnecessary in this day and age, I offered my resignation to the Home Secretary and to the governing body of every organisation with which I was associated. None of them accepted it, and all asked me to continue my membership, though, later when there was a change in the Head of the Order, I was asked to resign my seat on the Chapter General of the Order of St. John. This was something I much regretted for I had for many years taken a very active interest in the work of the St. John Ambulance Association, of which I had for sixteen years been the Chairman in Lancashire and I was, and still am, a Knight of Justice in the Order. I had hoped that I would be able for a long time to give service to the Order which does so much for so many sick and injured throughout the world.

At that time a Government Committee under the Chairmanship of Lord Fulton had just issued a report recommending that professionals, like myself, attached to Government departments, should retire at the age of 60, as civil servants had to do. The Home Secretary in refusing my resignation at the time when I offered it, nevertheless said that he thought I ought to retire when I reached the age of 60 in two years' time. This I had always intended to do for I wanted to retire early enough to be able to find something else constructive to do outside the police field and which would occupy me until old age.

In any case, having been refused the Commissionership of the Metropolitan Police that I had so much wanted, I knew that there was nothing more for me in the Police Service at home, and I was becoming, as my friends had predicted, very disenchanted with my present job, where I felt that I was not much more than a fifth wheel to the coach.

At that time the problems of Northern Ireland were beginning to occupy much of the time of the Home Secretary, and while the policing of that unhappy province was in no way my responsibility, I was concerned on the periphery.

In 1968, I had been invited by Sir Albert Kennedy, the Inspector General, as he was then called, of the Royal Ulster Constabulary, to take a Passing Out Parade of recruits at the Training School at Inniskillen in County Fermanagh. I spent four or five days having a cursory look at the Force but not inspecting it formally and while I did not notice much wrong with it, there were some aspects which did not impress me favourably. In particular, I did not think that the Deputy was good enough to take over from Sir Albert who was due for retirement shortly. While I was there Sir Albert told me that he feared that there was shortly to be a resurgence of IRA activity but he felt fairly confident that the Royal Ulster Constabulary would be able to contain it.

Shortly afterwards, in January, 1969, I flew up with the Home Secretary to Durham for the opening of the new County Police Headquarters and on the flight I told him of my misgivings about the situation in Northern Ireland, and expressed the opinion that the Deputy, if appointed, was not good enough to compete with the problems that were likely to arise. He asked me that we should do and I suggested he should ask John McKay, one of my colleagues, to go there but I warned him that he was a Roman Catholic and that he would have to consider the political implications of such an appointment. He replied that he thought it might be beneficial and with that I agreed.

Soon afterwards when troubles did break out, as I had predicted, the police were not able to cope with it satisfactorily and the Home Secretary asked Lord Hunt, with three Chief Constables, to visit Northern Ireland to assess the situation. In October, 1969, with the consent of the Corporation of London, Arthur Young, the City Police Commissioner, was sent to take charge.

In the meantime, plans were going ahead for the Investiture of Prince Charles as Prince of Wales. This was to take place at Caernarvon Castle on the 1st of July 1970, and in 1969 a committee under the Chairmanship of the Duke of Norfolk, the Hereditary Earl Marshal, was set up, the members representing every aspect of Welsh life. In addition, representatives of the Central Government, the Royal Household, and the Armed Forces were included and I was appointed to represent the Police as a whole, together with Bill Williams, the Chief Constable of Gwynedd[1], since the ceremony would take place within his jurisdiction.

The Committee held its meetings at St. James's Palace, and on the first occasion the representative of the Welsh Language Society insisted on addressing us all at length in Welsh, his speech being translated for us by Cledwyn Hughes, the Minister of State for Wales – the irony of the situation, I was told by Bill Williams, being that the gentleman concerned had been born in England. In any case, having made his point, he never attended another meeting of the Committee.

Before the first Committee meeting I went up to Caernarvon to discuss the preliminary police planning with Bill Williams. He was a man I knew and liked but he was a strong individualist, and he made it clear that he did not like the idea that I was concerned in the arrangements. He had a very poor Headquarters and at our first meeting he took the whole affair very flippantly. He had dealt with Royal visits before, and though this one might be a little larger than others, he was sure he would be able to cope. I returned to London much concerned and once again felt how impotent was the position of the Chief HMI. After the first meeting of the Committee, however, Bill Williams' attitude changed, and on my next visit to Caernarvon I found the whole Headquarters a hive of activity with a special department working hard to produce plans which on the day worked excellently.

Caernarvon is a small town and this made accommodation and the circulation of traffic much more difficult than it would have been in a more spacious and less ancient environment.

The number of Police had to be greatly increased and they had to be brought in, accommodated, and fed. A comprehensive communications network had to be set up, space had to be found for television vehicles and crews while arrangements for school children to line the route, and strict security arrangements had to be made, even bomb disposal units allocated and trained. Major royal functions usually took place in London, where the Metropolitan

---

[1] later Sir William J. Williams KCVO, OBE, QPM, DL.

Police with its vast resources and experience could cope with ease, but for a small rural force the problems were immense. Bill Williams and his men coped magnificently, and we were all delighted when, after the ceremony, he was awarded the KCVO.

Although I had to satisfy the Home Secretary that from a police point of view all would be well at Caernarvon on the day, I was not concerned with the planning details, but my responsibilities were more widespread for the Investiture celebrations were to cover the whole of Wales and the whole of the week, so that other Chief Constables and other forces had their own planning to do and I had to ensure that they were adequate. The programme was that the Investiture would take place on the Tuesday, the whole of the Royal Family arriving at Caernarvon in HMS *Britannia*. After the ceremony the Queen and the rest of the Royal Family would return to London by train while the Prince, using the Royal Yacht as a base to which to return each evening, would for the following three days make a Royal Progress through Wales from Holyhead to Cardiff.

For some months before the Investiture Welsh extremists had been making a nuisance of themselves and there were threats that the Investiture and the Royal Progress would be interrupted and even that the life of the Prince was in danger.

This had to be taken seriously, and to deal with the problem, I established a team of Special Branch officers drawn from all Welsh Forces and augmented by some Metropolitan Police specialists under the overall command of Mr J. H. Parkman, of the Glamorgan Constabulary, who was at that time in charge of the Welsh Regional Crime Squad.

The team worked in secret from offices we set up in Shrewsbury, and a comprehensive list of everyone known to be associated in any way with Welsh extremism was compiled. Detailed enquiries were made about everyone on the list, and throughout June and during the week of the Investiture each suspect was under constant surveillance.

In April, such was the concern at top level, that I was asked to go to Buckingham Palace where I was closely interrogated on the matter by the Duke of Norfolk and Sir Robert Adeane, the Queen's Private Secretary. The implication was that unless I could assure them that the security arrangements were satisfactory, serious consideration would have to be given to a postponement or cancellation of the whole programme. I told them what we had done and were doing and with natural apprehension, I advised that the ceremony could go ahead, and in the event all was well.

On the Sunday before the Investiture, the Home Secretary, who had an important part to play in the ceremony, and a number of others who were also involved, went to Portmerion some 25 miles from Caernarvon, and I too stayed in the same hotel. It was a picturesque and unique place in which to stay with its profusion of buildings scattered unmethodically around the landscape, all looking like Hansel-and-Gretel houses built by some artistic chef in icing sugar. Here we were received and well looked after by the elderly owner, Clough Williams Ellis, a most unusual and imaginative architect, who was later knighted and who has since died.

As the ceremony was to take place in the open air in the centre of the Castle, we were somewhat apprehensive about the weather; but on the morning of the Investiture it was fine and clear, and the official car park near the Castle was a brave sight as we picnicked before we took our seats, with all the women in their best clothes, the civilian men in morning dress and the high ranking officers of the Armed Services and in our full dress uniforms and wearing our Orders and decorations.

The Gwynedd Police did an excellent job and all went well at the ceremony, with no untoward incidents and I returned to Portmerion at the end of the day well satisfied that all the police arrangements had proved successful. I changed into informal clothes; my driver, who always valeted me when I was away, packed for me and we drove south that evening to stay with my sister at her holiday home at St. Davids. I took no part in Wednesday's tour in the North, and the Prince arrived at Fishguard that night in HMS *Britannia*.

Thursday's programme was to start with a service in St. David's cathedral and for this I had been allocated a seat in the front pew next to the Lord Lieutenant of the County.

I rose early: my driver laid out my boots, spurs, sword, decorations and tunic, and then came to me with a worried expression to ask what I had done with my overalls. We searched the house from top to bottom but they were nowhere to be found. They had been left at Portmerion. As a consequence I sat and had breakfast in my pants while my driver went to the cathedral to present my compliments to the Lord Lieutenant and to inform him that Her Majesty's Chief Inspector of Constabulary had unfortunately been detained and would not be able to be present. While it was disappointing, I was not really annoyed and the most regrettable aspect of the affair was that there was an empty seat in a cathedral that was much too small to hold all those that the Dean and Chapter wished to invite to the service.

In the Spring of 1970 I started seriously to consider what I should do when the time came for me to retire in the following

January, for quite apart from the financial implications of living on a pension, I felt I had plenty of steam left in me and that there were pastures new to be conquered.

Remembering that in 1966 when I was in Australia, Sir Arthur Rylah, CMG, the Chief Secretary of the Government of Victoria had asked me to go out to inspect the Force as soon as I retired, I wrote to John Dillon, the senior civil servant in Rylah's department, to inquire whether the invitation was still open and almost by return of post I had a reply saying not only was I wanted to advise on the organisation of the Force, but that because of serious allegations of corruption in the Police they wanted me as soon as possible, and to this end he had written to Philip Allen to ask for my immediate release.

Unfortunately, Jim Callaghan was not prepared to let me go so quickly, but while the matter was being discussed, Harold Wilson called a General Election, and luckily for me, the Conservatives won and the new Prime Minister, Ted Heath, had appointed as Home Secretary, Reggie Maudling whom I had known slightly in the 1930s and whom I had met again in recent years when we were both guests at the same shooting parties given by Lord Nelson of Stafford.

In July I made an official visit to the Devon and Cornwall Constabulary which I had arranged to coincide with the start of the Tall Ships' Race from Plymouth to Teneriffe. The race was to be started from HMS *Britannia* by HRH Prince Philip, and as Deputy Chairman of the Sail Training Association which had organised the Race, I was due to be on the Royal Yacht at 10.30 am. As we waited on the quayside for the launch which was to take us out to the Yacht anchored off shore, a police car arrived and I was told that Philip Allen wanted to speak to me immediately. While the launch waited, I spoke to Philip who told me that he had just had another telephone call from John Dillon pressing for a decision as the Victoria Government were being chased by the opposition and that it was important that they should make an announcement forthwith. Philip told me that Reggie Maudling had agreed that I could go as soon as convenient, and they wanted an immediate decision from me. I was delighted and said that if the Home Secretary agreed, Philip could tell them I would be there on the 1st October and that I would leave him to arrange the best financial arrangements he could for me. I did stipulate, however, that I would like to take a British police staff officer with me and that I would want one of their men as well. I ran back to the quay and just caught the launch. It was a great privilege to spend a day in the Royal Yacht and it was a wonderful sight to see the world's remaining great sailing ships sail past us, but my thoughts were mostly far away.

When I got back to London I found that all the conditions had been provisionally accepted subject to final negotiations and written confirmation of the terms of the agreement.

As my position as HM Chief Inspector of Constabulary was a personal appointment of the Queen, protocol demanded that she must be consulted about my retirement, before any information could be given to the Press. As the Court was at Balmoral this entailed some slight delay so that by the time the announcement was made I too was in Scotland fishing on the Ness.

I returned to London and there followed four hectic weeks not only winding up outstanding matters at the Home Office, but choosing a staff officer to go with me, deciding what books and documents I would require in Australia, and writing letters of thanks to Service and other organisations with which I was associated.

I flew up to Lancashire to say farewell to friends at Police Headquarters and to attend a reception given by the Officers of the 33rd (Lancashire and Cheshire) Signal Regiment TAVR of which I was Honorary Colonel.

On my last day I went to the Police College at Bramshill where the Annual Conference of the Association of Chief Police Officers was taking place. There were photographs and presentations culminating with a dinner attended by the Home Secretary, Reggie Maudling. I can think of no better may of ending a police career than dining by candlelight in the beautiful dining hall, with the table set with the College silver and police friends all around me. Sandy Willison, the Chief Constable of West Mercia, later Sir John Willison, CBE, QPM, DL, as President, made a speech of welcome to the Home Secretary and then referred to the fact that it was my last night in the Police Service. 'Eric', he said, 'has throughout his career inspired us, aggravated us, charmed us, and infuriated us. He has inspired and stimulated us because he has the most fertile brain in the Police Service in the past two decades: aggravated us because he has introduced new ideas several years before the rest of us, and generally ideas of which we at first disapproved: charmed us because that is his nature so to do: and infuriated us because almost always he has been found to be right in the end.'

If that is to be my epitaph, then I am content.

EPILOGUE

All this ended over seven years ago and much has happened since.

On the day after the Police College dinner I flew to Australia. At the time I hoped that it would be a journey to a new and permanent life, but it was to be only a very happy and interesting interlude for, after several months, I had to return to England for family reasons.

Then followed five years working in London with delightful and intelligent colleagues in a completely new environment, when I had to consider many aspects of the organisation of the industrial and commercial life of this country and I had the good fortune to meet and talk with most captains of industry, many senior trade unionists, leading figures in the City and many leading politicians of both left and right.

Now I am living in a 17th-century house that I have modernised – for over two hundred years it was a small inn – in a very pretty Cotswold village, surrounded by pictures and books collected in the past forty years, and at weekends usually with friends to stay.

For friendship is, to my mind, the very stuff of life and I thrive on it. To sit, listening to men and women with intelligent trained minds and interesting careers and experiences on which to draw, discussing and arguing the economic, social and political problems of the day, especially if one has a glass of claret in one's hand, is to me pure joy. *Paté de foie gras* to the sound of trumpets' was Sydney Smith's recipe for paradise. I don't aspire quite as high.

Or to be travelling overseas is almost as much bliss. Since I left the police, apart from three visits to Australia, four to the West Indies and as many to the United States, I have sailed off the Greek and Turkish Islands as well as along the French coast while I've also been to the Middle East, Bangkok, Japan and Mexico. On only very few occasions have I stayed in hotels for throughout the world

Epilogue

I have friends whom I love to see and who I like to feel, are glad to see me and to put me up.

Added to which I still have a number of business interests which take me to London regularly, while I am still actively concerned with two charitable organisations and also play my part in local village affairs.

So, with my friends and my house and my garden, and with shooting in the winter and with sailing and with cricket to watch at Lords and in the local villages in the summer, life has much to offer and it's all great fun. Above all one is busy 'keeping one's friendships in good repair' as Dr Johnson wisely said.

As an old age pensioner one ought, I suppose at the age of 67, be talking about the evening of one's life. Not a bit of it: I like to think that it is still only the early afternoon and that there is still much to be done, many fascinating places to visit, a whole host of new friendships to be made, and many more young people to be helped and advised, before one reaches even the six o'clock gin, while the eleven o'clock night cap is still far over the horizon.

Whenever I lectured to young men joining the police service and especially when I bade farewell to older men leaving it, I always used to urge them to live a full life. If they keep themselves at full stretch mentally and physically the odds are that not only will they live a happy and worthwhile life, but they will also live long and enjoy their pension. I used to remind them that their pension is paid by the Police Authority and added, 'Aim to be a bad investment to the Authority.'

I now practise what I then preached!

INDEX

Personal details about Sir Eric appear under his name together with a list of the highlights of his career which serves to lead the reader to a specific aspect of his work. Subentries throughout are in sequential order, not alphabetical. The letter 'n' denotes a footnote and the letter-by-letter system of alphabetisation has been followed. Titular abbreviations used are: CC = Chief Constable; Cmr of P = Commissioner of Police; C of P = Chief of Police; DCC = Deputy Chief Constable; IGP = Inspector General of Police. 'St. J' *refers to Sir Eric St. Johnston.*

Abercorn, Duke of, 52
Abu Bakr, 250
Accident, procedure at fatal, 55–6
Accidents, prevention of traffic, 164
   see also Disasters
Accra, 251
Adams, Kenneth, 184
Adeane, Sir Michael, 216, 293
Adelaide, 257
Aintree, *see* Grand National
Albert, Duke of York, 25–7
   after 1936, *see* George VI, King
Alderson, John, 275
Alexandra, Princess (of Kent), 221, 222
Alexandra House, Lichfield, 222
Alington, The Very Rev. Dr Cyril, 121, 122–3, 205
Alington, Hester, 121
Alington, Giles, 121
Allen, Sir Philip, 158, 200–1, 270, 272, 287, 288, 296
Allen, Sir Ronald, 28
Amery, Julian, 163
Aston Cantlow, holiday cottage at, 22

Arbuthnot, Capt. E. K., 69–70
Army:
   St. J joins (1929), 27, 40
   joins 68th (Warwickshire) Brigade, R.A., 27
   with 90th (City of London) Brigade, R.A., 40
   war-time role, start of St. J's, 97
   then see COSSAC: SHAEF
   police assistance from, 133–6
Armitage, Sir Robert, 241–2, 243
ARP work, 56
Association of Chief Police Officers, *see* Chief Constables' Association
Attlee, Lord (Clement), 125, 126–7, 240, 253
Australia, 254, 256–8, 295–6, 297
Avon, Lord (Sir Anthony Eden), 60

Baddeley, Hermione, 47
Balchin, Nigel, 28–9
Banbury, Oxon, raid on 'factory' at, 80
Banks, Maj-Gen. Sir Donald, 41–2, 154

299

Index

Banwell, Capt. G. E., 62, 104 & n
Bar:
    St. J decides to read for, 30–2
    works for finals, 40–1
Baring, Sir Evelyn, 247
'Barlow', Superintendent, 183
Barnard, Lord, 105, 124–5, 139–40
Barristers, influence of, 30
Barrow family, 1
Bayly, Adm. Sir Patrick, 251
BBC, co-operation with, and public relations, 182–5
Beacom, Tom, 233
Beat work and hours, 47–51
Beaufort, Duchess of, 204
Bebbington, Nick, 265
'Bellemere', 22
Benfold, Alderman Thomas, 105, 119
Ben Gurion, Amos, 240
Berkeley, California, 236, 253
Bermuda, 240
Bevan, Aneurin, 126–7, 232, 240
Bevin, Ernest, 126
Bicester, Lord and Lady, 67, 81
Binney Award, 196
Birmingham:
    St. J born in, 15
    family circumstances in, 17
Blackpool:
    illuminations, 178–9
    Royal Variety Show at, 210
Bladon, Oxon, 80
Blenheim Palace, 79, 204
'Blind eye', police technique of, 50
Blunt, Sqn Leader Christopher, 216
Blyth, Anne, 237
Bonshaw Tower, Kirtleside, 16
Borneo, 254–5
Botswana, Police mission in, 176
'Bottle parties', illicit, 49–50
Boys' Club, St. J's interest in, 24
Bradford, Sir Thomas, 141 & n
Brady, Ian, 191
Bramshill, Police College at, 273–6, 284–5, 296
Brayley, Canon Evelyn, 118–19, 123
Britannia, HMS, 292, 294, 295–6

Brize Norton, German air raid on, 75
Brodie, Peter, 289
Bromsgrove School, 23–4
Brook, Sir Frank, 91, 93, 103, 111, 139, 154, 166, 265
Brooke, Lord (Henry), of Cumnor, 199
Bruce, Robert the, 15–16
Brunner, Elaine, 79
Buckingham, Sgt Ralph (*later* DCC), 74
Bullfights, Spanish, St. J sees, 227, 229
Burman, Sir Charles, 173
Burney, Sir Anthony, 28
Busby, Sir Matt., 177–8
Butler, R. A. (*later* Lord, of Saffron Walden), 170–1, 271
Byng of Vimy, Lord, 33, 37

Cadbury, Sir Adrian, 223
Cadiz, 227
Caernarvon, 293–5
Cairns, Professor, 84
California, 234–6, 259
Callaghan, James, 173–4, 285, 287–290, 295
Cambridge University, St. J at, 27, 29–30
Cameron, Donald, 26
Cameron, Hugh (King's Private Detective), 66
Camoys, Lord and Lady, 81
Camp, St. J at Duke of York's (1929), 25–7
Campbell, Sir Harold, 25, 27
Canada, 259
Canberra, 257
Canteens, War-time women-staffed, 79
Canyon, The Grand, 238
Carey, Lionel, 28
Carver, Fd Marshal Lord ('Mike'), 251
Carver, Mr and Mrs, 219–20
Catling, Sir Richard (Cmr of P, Kenya), 246

Index

Cayser, Sir Nicholas, 28
Cenotaph, Armistice service at, 222
Central Link, Waterloo Bridge Road, London, 39–40
Chamberlain, Mr and Mrs Neville, 52
Chamberlain family of Birmingham, 1
Chapman, Sir Robert and Lady, 205
Charles, Prince of Wales, Investiture of, 292–4
Charlton, Bobby, 180
Chelsea, St. J stationed at, 59; and organises the LDV there, 59–60
Chicago, 233, 253–4, 258
Chief Constable:
  annual conferences of, 270–1
  a week in life of, 210–21
  constitutional position of, 153–4
  description of dress uniform of, 205
  disciplinary powers of, 280
  method of appointing, 276–7
  St. J's views as to maximum tenure in office of, 197
Chief Constables' Association, 9, 162, 171–2, 196, 199, 273, 283, 285
  report of, on Police College, 274
Chief Constableships, J's: *see* Oxfordshire; Durham; Lancashire
Chief Inspector of Constabulary:
  creation of post, 199, 261, 164
  St. J third holder of post, 200–1, 264
  thereafter see Home Office, St. J's work in; *see also* Inspector of Constabulary
Chivers, Mr (Royal chauffeur), 216
Churchill, Sir Winston L. S., 42, 71, 81, 95, 108, 163
Chuter Ede, J., *see* Ede, J. Chuter
Circumnavigation of world, St. J's, 254
Citrine, Lord (Walter) and Lady, 212
City of London Police, 262, 266
Cole, Major F. W., 77

Coles, A. M. Sir William, 252
Colonial Service, St. J considers, 30, 32
Columbus, Ohio, 232
Commission, St. J granted Army, 27
Commissioners of Police of the Metropolis:
  see Byng of Vimy, Lord; Game, Sir Philip; Mark, Sir Robert; Nott-Bower, Sir John; Simpson, Sir Joseph; Trenchard, Lord; Waldron, Sir John; *see also* Howgrave-Graham, H. M., *one time Secretary to*
Communism in South Africa, 248–249
Confession, convictions arising from, St. J's views on, 191–4
Contingency plans for disasters, 194–5
Cormorant as lost property, 51
Coronation (1937), 48
Corpus Christi College, Cambridge, St. J accepted at, 27; and attends, 29–30
Corruption, 33, 290
COSSAC, St. J's work with, 93–7:
  work at Norfolk House, 94
  organisational structure, 94
  manual of instructions for re-occupation personnel after war, 95–6
  foreign political intricacies, 95–6
  commuting to Oxfordshire Police as able, 96–7
  learns Normandy invasion details, 97
  now see SHAEF
Coulson, Sir John, 28
Courtesy Cop Scheme, 150, 163
Cowan, Francis, 87
Coward, Noel, 180
Cows, business end of, explained to King George, 208
Crawford, Vice-Adm. Sir William, 245 & n
Crazy Gang, The, 210

301

Index

Cricket, St. J's interest in, 23
Crime Prevention Committee of Industrialists, 269
Criminal jurisprudence, St. J's penchant for, 33-4, 44
Cripps, Sir Stafford, 126
Critchley, Tom, 172
Crossman, Richard, 126
Crowe, Sir Colin, 252
Custody, interrogation of suspects when in Police, 191-4
Cyprus, 241-3

Daley, Mr (Mayor of Chicago), 253-4
Dallas, Texas, 238
Dalton, Hugh, 126
Danube, St. J's canoe trip on (1931), 226
Darbyshire, Albert, 192
Death, duty of passing on news of, 55-6
Defence, Imperial College of, *see under* Imperial
de Gaulle, Gen. Charles, 95, 101, 108
Degree courses at University (for police), 161
de Mello, Señor, 227
de Palma, Joe, 55
Derby, Earl of (Lord Lieutenant of Lancashire), 174-5, 187, 188, 206, 209, 210, 212-19
Derby, Lady, 187-8, 209, 217
de Vitre, Barbara M. Denis, 280
Devon Loch (race-horse), 210, 218-20
Dietrich, Marlene, 180
Dilke, Sir Charles, 200
Dillon, John, 257, 295
Disasters, 133-5, 135-6, 177-8, 194, 221
  contingency plans for, 194-5
Discipline code, 58, 281
Dishforth (Yorks.), Police Recruit Training Centre at, 276
Divorce and remarriage, St. J's, 290
Dixon, Sir Arthur, 171

Dixon of Dock Green (TV series), 181
Dodd, Sir Edward, 47, 199-200, 263-4
Dodd, Lady, 47, 200
Dogs, police, 213, 253
Donnison, F. S. V., 110
DORA, reg., 18b, 84
Douglas, J. W. H. T., 23
Douglas-Hamilton, Lord Malcolm, 26
Douglas-Home, Sir Alec (*now* Lord Home of Hirsel), 121-2
Downey, Leslie Ann, 191
Drug squads, 268
Duff, Sir James, 123, 140
Dunglass, Alec and Elizabeth (*now* Lord and Lady Home of Hirsel), 121-2
Durham cathedral, 112, 121-3
Durham County Constabulary:
  mentioned, 8
  St. J told to apply as CC, 103
  attends interview, 104-5
  varieties of interest in county, 112-13
  antiquated Police HQ, 113
  first tour of inspection, 115
  problems of Geordie lingo, 116
  strength of Force (1945), 116-17
  St. J calls for essays about what needed to be done, 117
  housing problem, 117-18
  returning members from war service, 118-19
  moves HQ to Aycliffe, 119
  regional training centre, start of, 119-20
  introduction of women police, 120
  set a woman to catch a thief, 120-1
  cathedral setting, 120-3
  Police Authority, members of, 124-5
  Members of Parliament and Government Ministers, 125-7
  assizes, 128-9
  posters inviting information from public, 130

Index

criminal investigations, examples of how persistence pays, 129–33
London to Edinburgh express, crash of, 133–5
West Hartlepool Timber Yard fire, 135–6
welfare of force, problems over, 136–8
eyes turn towards Lancashire, 139–42
Durham Miners' Gala, 126

Ede, J. Chuter, 126, 134–5, 136, 140
Edgbaston, family move to, 22
Edinburgh, Prince Philip, Duke of, 204–5, 208, 210, 295
Education, St. J's:
preparatory school (1919), 23
Bromsgrove (1924–29), 23–4
CCC Cambridge (1929–32), 27, 29–30, 32
school contemporaries, names of, 28
Eisenhower, Gen. (*later* President) Dwight D., 97–8, 239
Elizabeth II, Queen, 201, 296:
visits by:
as princess, 204
as Duke of Lancaster, 208
to Grand National, 1956, 217–220
at Cenotaph Services, 222
Elizabeth, Queen (*sometimes known as* Queen Mother), 67, 204, 217–220
Ellis, Sir Clough Williams, 294
Elmes, Frank, 11–12
El Morocco Club, police raid on, 50
Elphinstone, Andrew, 26
Equipment, experimenting with new, 162
see also Radar; Radio
ESB (race-horse), 218–20
Establishments, determining correct Police, 171
Evans, Edward, 191
Eve, Keith, 165

Executive Club, Chicago, 233, 253
Extradition problem, 187

Family crest, 16
Family history, 7–18.
FBI, St. J visits US, 232
'Feast of St Cyril', 122
Fenwick, Robert, 267
Ferguson, Major Sir John, 44
FIDO, 42
Fielden, Major (Chairman of Oxfordshire SJC), 63, 65, 68, 90
Fielden, Gen. Sir Randle, 68
Fiji, 258
Finland, St. J's pre-war trip to, 227
Finlay, Inspector Sybil, 120
Fisher v Oldham Corporation, McCardie J's dictum during, 153
Florey, Mr and Mrs James, 72
Foot, Michael, 126
Force Orders, Weekly, 154–5
Forensic Science, 56, 132
Foster, Alderman J. W., 105
Foster, Paul, 188
Foster, Sir Peter (J), 28
Fox, Charles (CC of Oxford City Police), 67–8, 86, 88
Fraser, Ian, 162
Frewin, Adm. Sir John, 251
Frogmen, police, 162
Fulbright Scholarships, 230–1
Fulham, St. J's policing of, 53–9
Fulton Report (1968–9), 291
Furse, Ralph, 32

Gaitskell, Hugh, 126, 174
Galbraith, Neil, 265
Gallantry medals, 287
Gambling, 173, 239
Game, A-VM Sir Philip, 45
Gandhi, Indira, 257–8
Gargoyle Club, 47
Garrison, Homer (C of P, Texas Rangers), 238
Gee, Superintendent Frank, 165, 167
George V, King, 29
funeral of, 45–6

303

Index

George VI, King:
  before 1936, see Albert, Duke of York
  inspects RAF in Oxfordshire, 66–7
  mentioned, 204
  tours Oxfordshire, 207–8
  learns about cows, 208
Ghana, 251
Gilliat, Sir Martin, 217, 219
Glynn, Sir Ralph, 78
Goddard, Baron (Rayner) (LCJ), 129
Golden, Lt-Col Harold, 104 & n
Goodhart, Arthur (St. J's tutor), 29, 173
Goodman, Lord, 176
Gormley, Joe, 127–8
Gort, Fd Marshal The Viscount Lord, 41
'Gospel according to St Johnston', 154–5
Gough, Gen. Lord, 61
Grand Canyon, The, 238
Grand National (Aintree), 176–7, 210–20
Grandy, Sir John, 252
Grasett, Lt-Gen. Sir Edward, 95, 96, 105–6
Green, Sir Hugh Carleton, 184
Green, Norman, 189
Grenada, Alhambra at, 229
Gretna Green, 16
Gromyko, Andrei, 217

Halland, Col. G. H. R., 43, 61–2, 107
Harcourt, Viscountess, 79
Harding, Fd Marshal Lord, of Petherton, 243
Harewood, Earl and Countess of, 218
  see also Mary, Princess Royal
Harperley Hall, Co. Durham, 120
Harrington, Gen. Sir Charles, 251–2
Hartley, A. C. H. Sir Christopher, 252
Hay, Sir Philip, 222
Haydon, Adrian (St. J's cousin), 20–1

Haydon-Jones, Anne (St. J's cousin once removed), 21
Headlam, Bp Arthur, 122
Healey, Denis, 245
Heath, Edward R. G., 239, 295
Hendon Police College, 8, 36, 42, 43–4, 200, 289
  St. J at, 44–5
  receives Baton of Honour, 45
  contemporaries later joining St. J in Lancashire Co. Constabulary, 147–8
Henn, Col Tom, 95, 96
Henn, Col W., 95
Henson, Dr Herbert Hensley, 123–4
Hertfordshire Co. Constabulary, 103, 104, 105
Hetherington, Alistair, 173, 174
Hill, K. M., 280
Hindley, Myra, 191
Hitler, Adolf, 83–4
Hoare, Sir Samuel, 43
Hobart, Tasmania, 257
Hobbs, Sir Jack, 23
Hogg, W. E. (DCC Durham), 117 & n
Holden, Inspector J., 155
Holden, William, 237
Hollywood, St. J in, 237–8
Holme Mead, Penwortham, Lancs., 151
Holmes, Julius, 231
Holt, Henry, 256
Home, Lord (Alec) of Hirsel, 121–2
Home Guard (LDV), 59, 60, 61, 78
Home Office, St. J's work in, 261–96:
  Inspectors of Constabulary, creation of post and duties of, 261–3
  St. J's predecessors, 263
  Police Journal comments on St. J's appointment, 264
  St. J starts work (1967), 264–5
  his staff, 265
  duties, 265
  names of the six Inspectors of Constabulary, 265

304

constabulary inspections and reports, 266, 276
appointments of HMIs for Crime and Traffic, 267–8
drug squads, 269
Civil Service liaison, 269–70
is the realm of the Home Office responsibility too big?, 271
reduction in number of Police Forces, 271–2
Police College, 273–6
Marks and Spencer Ltd's overseas tours fund, 276
theme of St. J's lectures, 277–79
confidential reports on serving officers, system of, 278–79
St. J's views on working and dealing with subordinates, 279–80
Women Police Officers, 280–1
work on Police Federation, 281–283, 284–6
pay matters, 283–4
promotions, St. J's views on, 284
Universities and Army as sources of Police intakes from, 285
Honours and Awards, 286–7
death of Sir Joseph Simpson, effects and repercussions of, 288–89
corruption scandal exposed by *The Times*, 289–90
St. J's domestic problems, 290
thinks about retirement, 290–1
problems of Northern Ireland, 291
Investiture of Charles, Prince of Wales, 292–4
leaves for Melbourne, Australia, 295–6
Home Secretaries, *see*:
Butler, R. A.; Callaghan, James; Ede, J. Chuter; Jenkins, Roy; Maudling, Reginald; Morrison, Herbert
Hong Kong, 254, 256
Honolulu, 258
Honours and awards, public, for police, 286

Hood, Stuart, 183
Hope, Kenneth, 105
Hordern, Capt. Sir A. F. (*later* Sir Archibald), 45, 139, 144–5, 150–151, 165
Houston, Texas, 238–9
Howe, Sir Ronald, 37–8, 161
Howgrave-Graham, H. M., 34, 35, 37
Hudleston, Air Ch. Marshal, Sir Edmund, 245 & n
Hughes, Cledwyn, 292
Hylton, Jack, 210

Imperial Defence College (1957), 244–52:
St. J election, 244–5
objectives of course, 245
week-ends spent as CC Lancs., 245–6
St. J tours Africa, 246–51
notable class-mates, 251–2
Ince, murder case at, 188–9
Industry:
beckons to St. J, 197–9
current interests, St. J's, 298
Inns of Court, *see* Middle Temple
Inspectors of Constabulary:
creation of office, 11, 261
St. J demands additional posts for Crime and Traffic, 201; and makes these appointments, 267
Woman Assistant Inspector, appointment of, 280
International Date Line, St. J crosses, 258
Interpol, 38, 186, 187
Interrogation, St. J's views on police, 193–4
IRA, 291
Ironside, Fd Marshal, the Lord, 71
Irving, Capt. Sir James, 16
Israel, 240–1

Jackson, Derek, 85
Jackson, Pamela (née Mitford), 85
Jacobs, Sir Wilfred, 18
Jarrow Marchers, 113

Index

Jeeves, Marjorie, 242
Jenkins, Roy, 9, 200, 239, 264, 268, 269, 271, 284, 287, 289
Johns, Stratford (the actor), 183–4
Johnson, Celia (actress), 79
Johnson, Sir William, 183, 199, 263
Johnston, Dr Alexander, 18
Johnston, Alfred (novelist), 18
Johnston, Dr Charles, 17–18
Johnston, Dr George, 18
Johnston, Thomas:
  born 1745, 15
  born 1785, 15
  born 1815, 19
  born 1851, 19
  St. J's grandfather, 19–20
  after 1900 see St. Johnston
Joliet State Penitentiary, 233–4
Jones, Elwyn (script writer), 184, 185
Joseph, Helen, treason trial of, 248
Judge, Tony, 283–4
Judges' Rules, 1965, 193

Kano, 250–1
Kendal, Sir Norman, 37–8
Kennedy, Sir Albert (IGP, Northern Ireland), 291
Kenya, 246–7
Kenyatta, Mzee Jomo, 246–7
Kilbride, John, 190, 191
Kilyen, Imre, 186
Kirby New Town:
  special problem of, 167–9
  'Z' cars at, 182–5
Knighthood, St. J accepts, 201
Knighthoods, police awards of, 287
Knowsley Hall, Prescot:
  incident at, 187–8
  mentioned, 209, 217
Kuching, 255
Kyrenia, Cyprus, 242

Labour Party, St. J's sympathies with, 55
Lancashire County Constabulary:
  mentioned, 8
  St. J first visits, 45
  his predecessor dies, 139
  is selected as CC, 140
  geography of task, 143–4
  history of force, 144
  sports and social club, 148
  St. J senses resentment, 148–9
  Borough Forces problem, 149
  Preston HQ, 150
  Courtesy Cops and accent on traffic problems, 150, 163
  CC's private house, 151
  personality differences with Chairman of Police Authority, 151–154
  Weekly Orders, introduction of, 154–5
  strength and establishment, 155
  Force Standing Orders reviewed and revised, 155
  housing problems, 155–6
  transfers and happiness of men's wives need careful thought, 156
  good housekeeping campaign in offices, 156–7
  programme for new police stations, 157
  training school needs, 157–8
  Mounted Branch, 160
  promotion boards established, 159–60
  staff officers, need and value of, 161
  secondments to universities, 161
  National Police affairs, 162
  experiments with equipment, 162
  underwater teams, 162
  overhaul of Traffic Dept, 163, 164, 169–70
  visits to in USA, 164, 169
  see United States of America
  radio developments, 164–7
  Panda cars, 167–70
  Prime Minister's visits, 175–6
  Grand National, 176–7
  see also Grand National
  Munich Air Disaster, 177–8

holidaying public, coping with, 178
visit to Hollywood, 179–80
criminal and other incidents, 181–203
  'Z' Cars, *see* 'Z' Cars
  serious crime, 185–93
  Interpol called in, 186–7

  Knowsley Hall incident, 187–8
  Ince murder, 188–9
  missing persons, 189–90
  Moors Murder inquiries, 190–1
  interrogation of suspects in custody, 191–3
    St. J's personal views on, 193–4
  air crash 27th Feb. 1958, 195
  Press Council, St. J's complaint to, 195–6
  1961 proves break-even point in re-organisation programme, 196
  industry tries to recruit St. J, 197–199
  Chief Inspector of Constabulary's office becomes vacant, 199–200
  St. J accepts knighthood, 201
Lancashire Police Forces (County and Borough) double re-organisation of, 273
Lancaster, Duchy of, 207–8
Lancaster Castle, 157–9, 207
LANCON, 167
Lang, Archbishop Cosmo Gordon, 124
Last Two to Hang, The (Elwyn Jones), 185
Law, Jessie, 281
Lawrence, Sydney, 182, 265
Lawson, Jack (*later* Lord), 126, 127
Lawther, Will, 127
Lawton, Fred (*later* Lord Justice), 28
LDV, *see* Home Guard
Leave, St. J takes official absence from Lancashire Constabulary: *see* Imperial Defence College;

Royal Occasions; United States of America
Lee, Sir Desmond, 28
Lee, Jennie (Mrs Aneurin Bevan, *later* Dame), 30
Leigh, Vivien, 213
Levée at Court of St James, St. J attends, 29
Lewis, Ted 'Kid', 50
Leyland Motors, Ltd, 197–9
Lindsay, Capt. Lionel, 116
Lisbon, St. J lectures in, 227–8
Lobster for Marlene, 180
Londonderry, Lord and Lady, 51–2, 128
Longridge, St. J resides at, 151
Los Angeles, 237–8, 258
Luizet, Mons., 102, 107
Lumley, Maj-Gen. Sir Roger, 94 & n, 104
Lynskey, Mr Justice, 174

Macclesfield, Lord, 68, 90, 91
MacLoughlin, Inspector, 247
Macmillan, Harold, 164, 246
MacNeil, Hector, 126–7
McCarthy, Senator Joseph, 241
McCartney, Robert, 186–7
McKay, Sir John, 265, 291
McLeod, Gen. Sir Roderick, 245 & n, 246
McNeese-Foster, Air Commodore, 66
McSherry, Brig.-Gen. Frank (US Army), 95, 111
Madrid, 229
Malaysia, 254–5
Malenkov, Mr Georgi (Premier of USSR), 212, 215, 217–18
Malik, Mr (USSR Ambassador to Britain), 212, 217
Manchester United Football Club, 177–8
Manekshaw, Fd Marshal Sam (Indian Army), 252
Manila, 256
Mansfield, Jayne, 179
Manuel, Joseph, 265, 267, 269

Index

Margaret, Princess, 207–8, 217–20
Marie Louise, Princess, 204–5
Marina, Princess, Duchess of Kent, 221
Mark, Sir Robert, 148, 285–89
Marks and Spencer, Ltd, 276
Marlborough, Duchess of, 79, 80, 204
Marlborough, Duke of, 79, 80, 81
Marriage and early married life, St. J's, 46–7
Marriott, Richard, 41, 226
Martell, Adm. Sir Hugh, 251
Martin, Sir Charles, 57
Mary, Queen, 124, 204
Mary, Princess Royal (Countess of Harewood), 215, 217, 219
Mathematics, St. J's keen interest in, 23, 28
Maudling, Reginald, 295, 296
Mau Mau Revolt, Kenya, 246, 247
Maxwell, Sir Alexander, 90–1
Medals for police officers, 286–7
Melbourne, 257, 295–6
Metropolitan Police Act, 1933 (re: Hendon Police College), 43
Metropolitan Police Force:
  corruption allegations in, 289–90
  not responsible to HMIs, 262, 265, 267
  St. J's time in:
    joins, 34
    starts service with, 35–6
    Trenchard's reforms, 36–7
    work in C2 Branch, 37–8
    lodgings, 39
    work with down and outs, 39–40
    Middle Temple, 41
    at Hendon College, 42–3
    on the beat at Vine St, 46–51
    work in Licensed Clubs Office, 49
    moves to Walham Green Police Station, 53–7
    ARP work, 56
    outbreak of war, 56
    reports a superior officer's conduct, 58–9
    moves to Chelsea Divisional Office, 59–60
    appointed CC Oxfordshire, 61–63
  see also Commissioners of Police of the Metropolis
Mettger, Philip, 232, 238
MI5 Registry and Staff, 79, 80, 81, 87
Middle Temple, St. J enters, 8, 30–2, 41
Minnesota, 259
Missing Persons, 189–90
Mitchell, John, 259–60
Mitford, Diana, *see* Mosley, Lady Diana
Mitford, Tom, 84
Mitford, Unity and Nancy, 83–4
Moors Murder inquiries, 190–1
Mordue, Eva, murder case of, 130–1
Morgan, Lt-Gen. Sir Frederick, 93, 97
Moriarty (Policeman's 'Bible'), 68
Morley, Sir George, 113–14, 116
Morris Motors, Ltd, 86
Morris, William (murder victim), 192
Morris, William, *see* Nuffield, Lord
Morrison, Herbert (*later* Lord, of Lambeth), 90, 126
Morrison, Stevie (C of P, Houston), 239
Mortuary, St. J meets pathologist, 56
Moseley Rugby Football Club, 22, 32–3
Mosley, Lady Diana (née Mitford), 85
Mosley, Sir Oswald, 53–4, 82, 84–85
Mounsey, J. (ACC Staffs), 191
Mounted Branch, 159
Murat Scouts in the Jungle, 255–6
Murder, 129–33, 185–9, 191–3
Munich Air Disaster, 177–8
Murphy, Patrick, 88

Index

Murrow, Ed, 100
Mynors, Sir Humphrey, 28, 121
Mynors, Roger and Lavinia, 121

Nairobi, Kenya, 246–7
Nandi Beach, 258
National Police Force, projected, 29, 172, 262, 272, 284
New Orleans, 239
Newsam, Sir Frank, 213, 242, 244
New Scotland Yard, 35
'New Town Police', see 'Z' Cars
New York, 231
New Zealand, 258
Nicholson, Douglas, 128–9
Nicholson, Sir Frank, 105
Nicholson, Muriel (St. J's secretary), 141
Nicosia, 241–2
Nigeria, 250
90th (City of London) Brigade, 40
Nixon, Albert (a murderer), 132
Nkrumah, Kwame, 251
Norfolk, Bernard, 16th Duke of, 52, 293, 294
Norfolk House, London, 94
Northern Ireland, 292
Nott-Bower, Sir John, 58
Nuffield, Lord (William Morris), 86

Obscenity, St. J's views on, 39
Ocean racing, St. J's love of, 224
Official Secrets Acts, 12
Olivier, Sir Laurence, 213
Orme, Daniel, 46
Osmond, Sir Douglas, 267
Overlord, St. J learns decoded secrets of operation, 96–7
Overseas Tours:
  arrangements for officers with potential to make, 276
  by St. J when in office, 226–43:
    as a youth in Europe, 226
    Finland, pre-war, 227
    Spain and Portugal (1949), 227–30
    Algiers (1952), 227–8

USA (1953), 231–40
  see also United States of America
Greece, Cyprus and Israel (1955), 240–3
with Imperial Defence College party to Africa (1957), 246–251
USA (1961), 253–4
Australia and New Zealand (1966), 254–8:
  Far East, 254–6
  Australia, 256–8
  Fiji and Honolulu, 258
  home via USA, 258
tour of American Universities (1969), 259–60
by St. J in retirement, 297
see also SHAEF
Oxfordshire County Constabulary:
mentioned, 8
St. J selected as CC (1940), 61–3
starts work as CC at age 29, 64
City of Oxford Police Force, not a part of, 64
staff members, 64
organisational structure, 64–5
primitive conditions, 65
Royal Visit (George VI), 66–7
recruiting system, 68–9
paucity of divisional stations, 70–1
German spy scare, 71–3
the subordinate who was ill, 73–4
re-organisation set in hand, 74
defence duties and plans, 74–5
enemy agent encounter, 75–6
refugee problem, 76
population almost doubles, 76–7
Special Constabulary, 77
women civilian staff, 78–9
MI5 Registry, 79
enemy bombs, 79–80
Churchill, meetings with, 81
social and private life in wartime, 81–2
disaffection rumours, 82–5
invasion internees' list, 82–3
the naked Irishman, 87–8

Index

Oxfordshire County
Constabulary—*cont.*
  seeds of police amalgamations, 88–9
  force re-organisation completed, 80
  see also COSSAC

Palfrey, W. J. H., 98–9, 102, 147, 177, 181, 185, 211, 216
Pamplin, Sgt Dick, 282
Panda patrols, 167–70
Pandit, Mrs, 257
Parker, Bill (C of P, Los Angeles), 237–8
Parkman, J. H., 293
Pastimes, St. J's pleasurable, 224
Paterson, Capt. J. G., 25–6, 39–40
Pay matters, police, 283
Peck, Stanley, 265
Peel, Earl, 174
Peel, Capt. Sir Jonathan, 140
Peel House, London, 92
Pension, St. J has a problem over, 197, 198–9
Personal radios, 166–7
Perth, W. Australia, 257
Philip, Duke of Edinburgh, Prince, *see* Edinburgh
Philippines, 254, 256
Pickthorn, Sir Kenneth, 28
Players Theatre, 47
PLUTO, 42
Police matters:
  annual confidential reports on all ranks, 279–80
  Authority, difficulties and differences with, 151–4
  College, *see* Bramshill (after 1960); Hendon; Ryton-on-Dunsmore (up to 1960)
  College Advisory Committee, 266
  constitutional position of an officer, 153–4
  Council (on pay), 283
  custody, persons detained in, 191–4

districts, boundaries of, 171
Federation, 9, 172, 173, 274, 281–283, 284–6
Forces, reducing the numbers of autonomous, 271–2
image, *see* 'Z' Cars
Mutual Assurance Society, 222
19th cent. development of, 261
Research Dept, Home Office, 265
Reservists, War-time, 57
secondment of, to Cyprus, 243
women, *see* Women's Auxiliary Police Corps; Women Police Officers
see also Colonial; Forces by their individual names; Interpol; National Police Force; Regional Crime Squads; Special Constabulary; Women Police Officers; Women's Auxiliary Police Corps; Royal Commission on Police
Police (Journal of Police Federation), 283
Police Journal, 264
Police Review, 103, 110, 141
Politics, St. J's, 30
Pornography, Police Library of, 38–9
Portal, Air Chief Marshal Sir Peter (*later* Viscount), 66
Powell, Sir Richard, 244
Pratt, Richard, 172
Prefect, St. J made school, 23
President, St. J visits, of USA, 239–40
Press, occasional deplorable behaviour of, 195–6
Press Liaison Officers, 195
Pretoria, 248
Prisoners, treatment of Police, 191–4
Promotion, selection methods for, 159–61, 285
Prostitutes, 49, 129–33, 239
Provincial Police Award, 196
Public, assistance to police by, 196

Index

Public Relations exercise, *see* 'Z' Cars

QPM, right to use letters, after name, 287
Queen Mary, RMS, 16
Queen's Police Medals, 286–7

Racialism in South Afica, 249
Racing in Australia, 256–7
Radar traps, 164
Rademayer, Gen., 248–9
Radio, police communications using, 164–7
Radio programmes, *see* 'Z' Cars
Raphael, Marley, 79
Ramsey, Archbishop Lord (Michael), 122
Redesdale, Lord, 83–4
Regional, Crime Squads, 184, 211, 267–8
Renison, Sir Patrick, 28, 41
Rennel of Rodd, Lord, 93
Republic of South Africa, 248–50
Retirement, St. J's:
crosses his mind, 290–1
due at end of 1970, 295
leaves post as Ch. HMI, 296
visits Australia (1970), 297
retirement home, 297
and is still a busy man, 297–8
Rhodes, Lord, 191
Rhodesia, 248, 250
Richards, Bp Kenneth (of Lincoln), 28
Richardson, Geoffrey, 38
Roberts, Bp Edward (of Ely), 28
Roberts, Chief Superintendent W., 181
Robertson, Sir James, 250
Robins, George (Cmr of P, Cyprus), 241–2, 243
Rosier, A. C. M., Sir Fred, 252
Roskill, Eustace (*later* Lord Justice), 31
Rosolio, Insp. Saul (*later* IGP, Israel), 242
Routh, R. G., 23–4

Royal Commission on Police, 9, 29, 171–3, 196, 199
St. J's memorandum to, 172–3, 262–3, 272
amalgamation of forces proposals, 271
on Police Federation, 281–2
Royal Occasions, 204–25:
Princess Elizabeth, 204
Princess Maria Louise, 205
programmes and dummy runs for, 206
police escorts, 206
1951, George VI, Queen Elizabeth and Princess Margaret, 207–8
1952, Funeral of George VI, 208
1954, Elizabeth II, 208–9
1955, Elizabeth II, 208
1956, Elizabeth II, Queen Elizabeth and Princess Margaret, 217–20
Princess Alexandra, 221, 222
Princess Marina, 221–2
Edward, Duke of Kent, 221
reception at Buckingham Palace, 222–3
see also names of individual royalty, *esp.* Charles, Prince of Wales; *Britannia*, HMS
Royal Train, 209, 216, 220, 223n
Royal Ulster Constabulary, 291
Rugby, St. J's interest in sport of, 22, 32, 39
Russell, Adm. Sir Guy, 245
Russell Cooke, Mel., 78
Ruxton, Dr (a murderer), 159
Rylah, Sir Arthur, 257, 295
Ryley, Ethel, St. J's mother, 21
Ryley, J. A. (St. J's maternal grandfather), 21
Ryton-on-Dunsmore Police College, 135, 274

Sachs, Leonard, 47
Sahar, Moses (IGP, Israel), 241
Saint, how family incorporated the name, 19

Index

St. John, St. J's membership of the Order of, 290
St. Johnston, Caroline (St. J's daughter), 79, 122, 140
St. Johnston, Daisy (St. J's aunt), 20
St. Johnston, Sir Eric:
  birth, 1911, 21
  childhood, 22
  Birmingham forebears, 19–22
  aunts and uncles, 20
  Scottish ancestry, 15–16
  allowance at university, 29
  PC 640C (Metropolitan Police) and later Sgt, then JSI, 46–53
  birth of daughter, 79
  birth of son, 80
  awarded Croix de Guerre, Legion d'Honneur, and OBE, 111
  his health, 44, 57–8
  retirement, mentioned, 11
    see also Retirement
  high-lights of career, see
    Education
    Army
    Bar finals
    Metropolitan Police
    Hendon Police College
    Marriage
    Oxfordshire
    War Office
    COSSAC
    SHAEF
    Durham County Constabulary
    Lancashire County Constabulary
    Knighthood
    Royal Occasions
    Overseas
    Imperial Defence College
    Home Office
    Divorce and remarriage
    Retirement
St. Johnston, Ethel (née Ryley) (St. J's mother), 21, 22–3
St. Johnston, Joanna (St. J's first wife):
  marriage, 46
  foil in club raid, 50
  presented at Court, 52
  problems with husband's stripes, 53
  war-time canteen work, 79
  birth of daughter, 79
  birth of son, 80
  British Restaurant, Woodstock, 80
  discusses move to Durham, 104–5
  friend of the Alingtons, 121–2
  letters to Bp Henson, 123
  discusses move to Lancashire, 139
  considers St. J's offer of work in industry, 199
  with Princess Marie Louise, 205
  drinks with Sir Laurence Olivier, 213
  reception at Buckingham Palace, 223
    accompanies St. J to Portugal and Spain, 227–9, and to Chicago, 253
  separates and divorces, 290
  death mentioned (1974), 84
St. Johnston, Harriet, 290
St. Johnston, Mary (St. J's sister), 21, 22
St. Johnston, Sir Reginald (Governor of Leeward Islands), 18–19, 30
St. Johnston, Thomas Andrew (St. J's son), 80, 122, 140
St. Johnston, Thomas Gerald (St. J's father), 19, 21–3, 200
For ancestors pre-1900, see Johnston
Salidor, Susy, 180
San Francisco, 235–6
Scarborough, Earl of, see Lumley, Sir Roger
Scarman, Leslie (*later* Lord), 31
School, St. J is made head boy at, 24
Schools, St. J's, see Education
Scott, Sir George, 140
Scott, Gerald, 66
Scroggie, Alan, 266
'Seaport Division', see 'Z' Cars
Senanayake, Sir Dudley, 28, 31
Seville, Spain, 227

SHAEF:
  mentioned, 94, 95, 97
  establishment of (1944), 97
  HQ at Bushey Park, 98
  Eastbourne briefing, 98
  Cherbourg operation, 99
  St. J goes to France, 99–100
  enters Paris and experiences being under fire, 101–3
  at Granville, Normandy, 103
  called to go to Durham, 104–5
  returns to France and Versailles, 106
  works on occupation plans for Germany, 106–7
  concentration camps, plans for opening up, 107–8
  Brussels and differences of opinion with Monty's 21st Army Group, 109–10
  non-fraternisation policy, 110
  Nuremburg Trial, 110–11
  returns home with three medals, 111
Shaw, Joe, 126
Shawcross, Sir Hartley, 126
Shinwell, Emmanuel (*later* Lord)
Short Service Recruit Scheme, 42
Shuckburgh, Sir Evelyn, 245 & n
Sibu, 255
Sieff, Sir Marcus, 28, 240, 277
Simon, Jack (*later* Lord), 31
Simon, Sir John, 45
Simpson, Sir Joseph, 172, 197, 264, 267, 289
  untimely death of, 288
Simpson, Sir Keith, 56
Singapore, 254
Skittery, John, 62, 140
Smith, Ashley, 39
Smith, David (witness in Moors murder), 191
Smith, Inspector Douglas, 162
Smith, PC Rae, 141
Smith-Mundt Programme, 231
'Softly-Softly', derivation of name, 185
Special Branch work, 81

Special Constabulary, 77, 115, 211
Spicer, Col R. G. B., 62
Spurrier, Sir Henry, 197–9, 257
Staff Officers, value of posts of, 161
Stallybrass, W. T. S., 24, 87
Stallard, Sir Peter, 250
Stallard, Walter, 187
Standing Orders, overhauling Force, 155
Stanley, Clifford R., 12
Stanwyck, Barbara, 237
Stephens, Wilson, 48
Steward, Douglas, 187
Stewart, Col J. D., 140
Stokes, Lord (Donald), 198–9
Stonor, Jeanne (Lady Camoys), 79, 81
Strutt, The Hon. Lavinia (*later* Duchess of Norfolk), 52
Studdy, Sir Henry, 103, 114
Student unrest, problem of, 259–60
Subordinates, St. J's views on dealing with and handling, 278–80
Sullivan, William, 187
Summerskill, Baroness (Edith), 55
'Sunrise', 99
Superintendents' Association, 273
Sutcliffe, Herbert, 23
Suttling, Detective Inspector Harold, 92
Swinbrook Church, Oxfordshire, 84
Sydney, Australia, 256

Taverne, Dick, 200
Teeth, the bishop's false, 122–3
Tennant, David, 47
Texas Rangers, 238
Thailand, 254
Thirty-third (Lancashire and Cheshire) Signal Regt, TAVR, 297
Thomas, Lady, 78
Thomas, Sir Miles (*later* Lord), 78
Thornton, Walter (DCC Lancs.), 146, 148
Topham, Mrs Mirabelle, 176–7, 211–12, 214–16

Index

TORCH, operation, 87, 90
Trade Union, membership by police not allowed, 281
 but see Federation *under* Police matters
Treason Trial, Pretoria (1957), 248
Tree, Ronnie and Nancy, 81
Trenchard, Marshal of the Royal Air Force, the Lord, 33–4, 36–7, 42, 43, 164
Trenchard Boys, 8, 33
 see also Hendon Police College
Trubshaw, Wilfred, 144, 157

Uganda, 246
Underwater teams, 162
United States of America, St. J's visits to, 164, 169, 231–41, 253–4, 258, 259–60
Universities:
 graduate intake from, to police, 285–6
 police secondments to, 161
 St. J at, 27–8, 29–30
Ustinov, Peter, 47

Victoria Falls, 250

Waddell, Sir James, 269–70
Waddington, A. E., 146–7, 159, 177, 213, 216
Waldron, Sir John (Jack) (ACC Lancs. and later Cmd of P of the Metropolis), 147–8, 288
Wales, extremism in, 293–4
 see also Charles, Prince of
War, declaration of, 1939, 56
 for a description of war-time life in England see under Oxfordshire
War Office, St. J's work in, 91–3:
 begins work on population control of liberated Europe (1943), 92
 training of re-occupation forces, 92–3
 from Aug. 1943 see COSSAC
Warner, Bill, 232

Washington, DC, 239–40, 258, 259
Watson, Sam and Jenny, 125–6, 140
Webb, Professor Geoffrey, 101, 102
Weekly Orders, Force, 154–5
Welensky, Sir Roy, 248
Welfare problems of men under command, 136–8
West Hartlepool, disastrous fire at, 135–6
West House, Durham, 105, 121
Wharton, Joanna, *see* St. Johnston, Joanna
White, Geoffrey, 243
White, Major Robert, 40
Whiteley, William, 126
Wigg, Lord, 176
Wilder, Mrs (WAPC), 78
Wilkinson, Ellen, 125
Wilkinson, George, 227
Williams, Bp Alwyn, 123
Williams, Sir William J., 292
Williamson, Frank, 267–9, 289–290
Williamson, John, 267
Williamson Mr (of *The Times*), 40
Willink, Sir Henry, 173
Willis, Commander W. J. A., 104 & n
Willison, Sir John (Sandy), 296
Wilson, Sir J. Harold, 7–9, 121, 175–6, 200, 201, 250
Wilson, O. W. (of Berkeley, Cal.), 94, 235, 253–4
Wimbledon, Civil Affairs Staff College at, 91, 92
Windsor, Frank (actor), 184
Winged Spur, Family arms contains, 16
Winstanley, Harold, 187–8
Wireless, *see* Radio
Women Police Officers, 280–1
Women's Auxiliary Police Corps, 78
Wood, Sir Kingsley, 32
Woods, Sir Colin, 276

Woodstock, St. J's house at, 79
Woolley, Frank, 23
Wormwood Scrubs Prison, 79
Wright, John (DCC Durham), 105, 115

York, Camp of the Duke of, 25–7

Young, Col Sir Arthur, 62, 92, 103, 104, 291
Younger, Sir Kenneth, 101

'Z' Cars (TV series), 8, 181–4
Zephyr Express, US trans-continental train, 234